Honey *and* Salt

Honey *and* Salt

SELECTED SPIRITUAL WRITINGS OF

Saint Bernard of Clairvaux

EDITED BY

John F. Thornton and *Susan B. Varenne*

PREFACE BY

Thomas Merton

VINTAGE SPIRITUAL CLASSICS

VINTAGE BOOKS

A DIVISION OF RANDOM HOUSE, INC.

NEW YORK

A VINTAGE SPIRITUAL CLASSICS ORIGINAL, APRIL 2007
FIRST EDITION

Grateful acknowledgment is made for permission to reprint the following:

"The Man and the Saint" and "Saint Bernard's Writings" from
The Last of the Fathers, copyright 1954 and renewed 1982 by
The Trustees of the Merton Legacy
Trust, reprinted by permission of Harcourt, Inc.

＊

Sermon nos. 1, 2, 3, 4, 11, 12, 15, 17, 20, 31, 32, 34, 36, 49, 50, 56, 64, 69, 74, 75, 84, 85,
and 86 from *On the Song of Songs.* Four vols. Vol. 1: trans. by Kilian Walsh, OCSO;
Vol. 2: trans. by Kilian Walsh, OCSO; Vol. 3: trans. by Kilian Walsh, OCSO,
and Irene M. Edmonds; Vol. 4: trans. by Irene Edmonds.

"On Conversion: A Sermon to Clerics," from *Sermons on Conversion.*
Trans. by Marie-Bernard Saïd, OSB.

Homily III from *Magnificat: Sermons in Praise of the Blessed Virgin Mary.*
Trans. by Marie-Bernard Saïd and Grace Perigo.

Reprinted by permission of Cistercian Publications, Kalamazoo, Michigan.
All rights reserved.

＊

"Fourth Sermon for Advent," "Sixth Sermon for Advent," "Seventh Sermon for
Advent," "Fifth Sermon for Christmas Eve," and "Second Sermon for Christmas
Day," from *St. Bernard's Sermons on the Nativity,* Copyright Mount Melleray Abbey
Trust, 1985; reprinted with permission.

Cataloging-in-Publication Data is on file at the Library of Congress.

ISBN: 978-0-375-72565-4

www.vintagebooks.com

Book design by Fritz Metsch

JESU DULCIS MEMORIA

St. Bernard of Clairvaux (trans. E. Caswall)

Jesu, the very thought of Thee
  With sweetness fills the breast;
But sweeter far Thy Face to see,
  And in Thy Presence rest.

No voice can sing, no heart can frame,
  Nor can the memory find
A sweeter sound than Jesu's Name,
  The Savior of mankind.

O Hope of every contrite heart,
  O Joy of all the meek,
To those who ask how kind Thou art,
  How good to those who seek!

But what to those who find? Ah! this
  Nor tongue nor pen can show;
The love of Jesu, what it is
  None but His loved ones know.

Jesu, our only Joy be Thou,
  As Thou our Prize wilt be:
In Thee be all our glory now,
  And through eternity.

CONTENTS

PART III SELECTED LETTERS

ABOUT THE
VINTAGE SPIRITUAL CLASSICS

by John E. Thornton and Susan B. Varenne, General Editors

A turn or shift of sorts is becoming evident in the reflections of men and women today on their life experiences. Not quite as adamantly secular and, perhaps, a little less insistent on material satisfactions, the reading public has recently developed a certain attraction to testimonies that human life is leavened by a Presence that blesses and sanctifies. Recovery, whether from addictions or personal traumas, illness, or even painful misalignments in human affairs, is evolving from the standard therapeutic goal of enhanced self-esteem. Many now seek a deeper healing that embraces the whole person, including the soul. Contemporary books provide accounts of the invisible assistance of angels. The laying on of hands in prayer has made an appearance at the hospital bedside. Guides for the spiritually perplexed have risen to the tops of best-seller lists. The darkest shadows of skepticism and unbelief, which have eclipsed the presence of the Divine in our materialistic age, are beginning to lighten and part.

If the power and presence of God are real and effective, what do they mean for human experience? What does He offer to men and women, and what does He ask in return? How do we recognize Him? Know Him? Respond to Him? God has a reputation for being both benevolent and wrathful. Which will He be for me and when? Can these aspects of the Divine somehow be reconciled? Where is

God when I suffer? Can I lose Him? Is God truthful, and are His promises to be trusted?

Are we really as precious to God as we are to ourselves and our loved ones? Do His providence and amazing grace guide our faltering steps toward Him, even in spite of ourselves? Will God abandon us if the sin is serious enough, or if we have episodes of resistance and forgetfulness? These are fundamental questions any person might address to God during a lifetime. They are pressing and difficult, often becoming wounds in the soul of the person who yearns for the power and courage of hope, especially in stressful times.

The Vintage Spiritual Classics present the testimony of writers across the centuries who have considered all these difficulties and who have pondered the mysterious ways, unfathomable mercies, and deep consolations afforded by God to those who call upon Him from out of the depths of their lives. These writers, then, are our companions, even our champions, in a common effort to discern the meaning of God in personal experience. For God is personal to us. To whom does He speak if not to us, provided we have the desire to hear Him deep within our hearts?

Each volume opens with an essay by a well-known contemporary writer that offers the reader an appreciation of its intrinsic value. A chronology of the general historical context of each author and his work is provided, as are suggestions for further reading.

We offer a final word about the act of reading these spiritual classics. From the very earliest accounts of monastic practice—dating back to the fourth century—it is evident that a form of reading called *lectio divina* ("divine" or "spiritual reading") was essential to any deliberate spiritual life. This kind of reading is quite different from that of scanning a text for useful facts and bits of information, or advancing along an exciting plot line to a climax in the action. It is, rather, a meditative approach by which the reader seeks to savor and taste the beauty and truth of every phrase and passage. This process of contemplative reading has the effect of enkindling in the reader compunction for past behavior that has been less than beautiful and true. At the same time, it increases the desire to seek a realm where all that is lovely and unspoiled may be found. There are four steps in *lectio divina*: first, to read, next to meditate, then to rest in the sense of God's nearness, and, ultimately, to resolve to govern one's actions in the light of new understanding. This kind of reading is itself an act of prayer. And, indeed, it is in prayer that God manifests His Presence to us.

Thomas Merton

I

THE MAN AND THE SAINT

The enigma of sanctity is the temptation and often the ruin of historians. This is all the truer of a saint like Bernard of Clairvaux who dominated the whole history of his time. Sanctity is born of conflict—of contradictories resolved into union. The historian is tempted to see in Bernard only the struggle between social and cultural forces which found in him their incarnation: for Bernard contained the whole twelfth century in himself. That is to say that he embodied and united in himself two other great ages, and lived the transition between them. His life, his career, religious and political, were the working out in himself, but for his contemporaries as well as for himself, of all their common problems. I do not say he achieved their solution, for no age, no generation, no one man, sees the solution of all their problems. There were many things in which Saint Bernard failed. His failures were as great and as significant and ultimately as constructive as his successes. Almost everything that he did had tremendous effect in shaping the course of history.

It is not enough to see in Bernard the union of Romanesque and Gothic, the transition from Saint Gregory VII to Saint Francis of Assisi—from the tenth century to the thirteenth. A brilliant but insufficient explanation of the tremendous work done by Saint Bernard attributes his genius and his energy and his sanctity to a dialectical tension between these two great spiritual forces which confronted one another in his soul. This theory will not serve. Yet the forces were there, and we must take them into account.

On one hand, Bernard was a Burgundian nobleman, a warrior born for knighthood or for prelacy. The walls and towers of the monastic basilica of Cluny were rising massively into the sky when he was born in 1090 in a castle not far from Dijon. Cluny was a living expression of the great, unified, and reformed ecclesiastical structure that had been left by Pope Gregory VII, at his death five years before. Cluny meant power, authority, centralization, law. Its grandeur, the lavishness of its liturgy, the vastness of its monastic empire were the outward expression of the rule of Christ the King in His Church, of the penetration of His Kingship into every department of human life and culture. The Cluny of Saint Hugh and the Rome of Saint Gregory VII belonged to a world that believed Peter had two swords: one his temporal, the other his spiritual power. No one was surprised that he wielded both.

At the same time a new generation was being born. Feudalism was ready to fall apart, and the time of the communes and the guilds and the cathedrals and the univer-sities was at hand. The young Bernard of Fontaines, who might have won himself a high place in the Church, or fame in her schools, refused to be famous or great, renounced his inheritance and his opportunities, and headed for a solitude which the towers of Cluny could only disdain. He feared to serve in the court of the great King because he felt that he was called to something much greater than power. He believed in the Christ *Pantocrator,* but felt that this great Lord would reveal Himself far differently in the forest of Citeaux. The One he sought in poverty, silence, and solitude was the *Verbum Sponsus,* the God who manifests Himself not only to the whole world as its King and Judge, but to the humble and solitary soul as its Bridegroom, in the secrecy of prayer.

Hence there was in Bernard a stronger attraction, a more powerful current which carried him away from the liturgical splendors of Cluny as well as from the subtleties of the schools. It was the current of mysticism, asceticism, liberty, spirituality, personalism which was already beginning to branch out in so many directions: one branch leading to a Francis of Assisi, another to the heresy of Albi.

Saint Bernard seems to have thought it possible to renounce everything of the first element in his soul, and live entirely by the second. Things were not to be so simple. His very reputation as a mystic, an ascetic, a miracle worker, a saint made it impossible for him to avoid becoming a great churchman, a defender of authority, of law, of the papacy, a man of God in politics, a preacher of Crusades. More than that: his spirit could never be one of mere individualistic piety. It was because he was at once so much a person, and so much a mystic, that Bernard was also essentially a man of the Church—*Vir Ecclesiae.*

We shall glance presently at some details of his tremendously active life. Although the tension between these two apparently conflicting powers does not account for that life, or for its achievements, or for its sanctity, it was most certainly a factor in his sanctification, because, as we have said, all sanctity is born of conflict.

To explain the sanctity of Bernard by enumerating the works and struggles and problems he had to confront is like explaining the sanctity of Thérèse of Lisieux by saying that one of her Sisters splashed dirty water on her in the laundry and another distracted her with a noisy rosary during mental prayer. There are in all the saints two other opposed elements to be reconciled and united: the human and the divine. This conflict counters the other, cuts across it at right angles, and even lifts it upward bodily into a new dimension. But here everything takes place in mystery. We cannot see what happens, because no man can see into another man's soul. He can barely see a little into his own!

When talking of Saint Bernard, we must necessarily talk more about what we know than about what we cannot know. But in pointing out the visible accidents and effects on the surface of a deep, invisible life of sanctity, let us always remember that what is not seen is the essential. Everything that falls outside the periphery of the central mystery, everything that can be seen clearly in the life of a saint is actually of little consequence unless it somehow be a sign of his inward sanctity. More precisely, the thoughts and acts and virtues of a saint are not wonderful in themselves, but they are meant to be deeply significant flashes sent forth from the dark bosom of the mystery of God. For the saint does not represent himself, or his time, or his nation: he is a sign of God for his own generation and for all generations to come.

Furthermore, sanctity is supernatural life. The saints not only have life, but they give it. Their sanctity is best known to those who have received life from them. The men of Bernard's time had no doubt of what they were getting from him. He cast fire on the earth wherever he went. The power of Bernard was more than the influence of genius or the persuasive efficacy of heroic virtue: it was charismatic. God worked in him, and worked such wonders that men knew it was God they had seen at work, not man. The grace of the God who had possession of this frail man burst into flame in the hearts of all who heard him speak.

It is for us to understand Saint Bernard's sanctity not merely by studying his history, but by perceiving something of its life-giving effect. It is precisely the aim of a papal encyclical to help us to do this. That is why *Doctor Mellifluus*[1] treats Saint Bernard above all as a *Doctor* and a "*Father*" of the Church, rather than as a great figure in the history of his own time.

The liturgy of Saint Bernard's feast in the Cistercian missal and breviary show how firmly the Church believes in the life-giving power still exercised, in the Communion of Saints, by those whom she reveres as Fathers and Doctors. Like Bernard himself, she teaches that Christ communicates Himself to men through the ministerial action of His saints not only in their own lifetime but also after their death.[2] So the monks chant in one of their responsories, addressing Saint Bernard: "Thou hast entered into the powers of the Lord and now made more powerful as intercessor, obtain for us a share in the light and sweetness which you now enjoy!" (*Introisti in potentias Domini, et jam potentior ad impetrandum, fac nos ejus qua frueris lucis suavitatisque participes.*)[3]

It would therefore be useless for us to attempt, in a short space, to list even a few of Saint Bernard's great achievements, to trace even a broad outline of his travels in the service of

[1] The encyclical of Pope Pius XII (1953) "On Bernard of Clairvaux, the Last of the Fathers." See Appendix, p. 399.
[2] See the article "Bernard, Saint," by Dom Anselme le Bail, OCSO, in *Dictionnaire de Spiritualité,* vol. 1, col. 1491.
[3] *Cistercian Breviary,* Matins of the Feast of Bernard, 9th Responsory.

God, to describe his monastic reforms, his new foundations, his interventions in the affairs of kings, bishops, and popes. But we must give some idea of his life and character. The easiest way of doing so is to look at him at three decisive points in his career. We shall open the book of his life at three places only: first, in 1115, when he is a young abbot of twenty-five; second in 1124, a little beyond the halfway mark in his life, at the turning point of his career; and finally in 1145 when Bernard is, practically speaking, pope.

Saint Bernard had saved the life of a new monastery, Citeaux, by entering it with thirty companions in 1112. The foundation, which had seemed ready to expire in 1111, was strong enough to found three other monasteries in 1114 and 1115. In June of 1115, shortly after the foundation of Morimond, Bernard was sent out by Stephen Harding to start a monastery in a sunny valley in the Langres plateau, on the borders of Burgundy and Champagne. The place was to become famous as Clairvaux, the "Valley of Light"; famous because of Bernard its abbot, because of the saints who lived there, because of the life they lived, because of the God whom they had found. Clairvaux and Bernard both meant one thing above all: the great twelfth-century revival of mysticism, a spiritual renaissance which had its effects in all the other renaissances of the time. For Bernard was to influence everything from politics to the *roman courtois* and the whole humanistic trend to "courtly love." He left his mark on schools of spirituality, on Gregorian chant, on the clerical life, and on the whole development of Gothic architecture and art. One of the signs of a spiritual revival that is really spiritual is that it affects every kind of life and activity around it, inspires new kinds of art, awakens a new poetry and a new music, even makes lovers speak to one another in a new language and think about one another with a new kind of respect.

But in 1115, Clairvaux is not yet famous. Bernard lives there with his twelve companions, in little wooden shacks under the trees of the forest. Bernard has just been ordained priest and blessed as abbot by the Bishop of Châlons-sur-Marne—the philosopher William of Champeaux. And William will presently get himself delegated by the General Chapter, at Citeaux, to watch over the health of Saint Bernard. The young abbot is already cracking up under the burden of a life in which Cistercian austerity is intensified twentyfold by indigence, lack of food, and by his own implacable asceticism. For the first few years of the new foundation Bernard is forced to live apart from the community in a little hut by himself, which serves as an infirmary. He falls into the hands of a neighborhood quack and nearly dies. But meanwhile postulants and friends begin to come to Clairvaux, and he is sharing with them his meditations on the deep mysteries of the Canticle which he will one day comment on in the chapter hall of a great stone abbey which his monks will soon begin to build. Nothing gives him any reason to believe that his life will be anything but a life of contemplation—disturbed only by the unavoidable cares of his abbatial charge and bearing fruit quietly in the formation and direction of his own monks.

In 1124, nine years later, Clairvaux is still not the great and well-established monastery that one naturally connects with Bernard's name. It is still anxious for security, and the foundations of its future development are being solidly laid by Bernard's two brothers, the cellarers Gerard and Guy. They have built the donations of pastures and forest land into a system of granges, or monastic farms kept up by lay brothers. Clairvaux can, at least, support herself, and now with the help of a great neighboring prince, Thibaut of Champagne, the monastery will soon become more prosperous.

Clairvaux has not immediately begun to make numerous foundations. Of the seventy new monasteries actually to be founded by Saint Bernard, only three have been established in his first ten years at Clairvaux. Trois Fontaines came into existence in October 1118. One year later, in the fall of 1119, Fontenay was founded. Foigny, where Saint Bernard "excommunicated" the flies, came two years after Fontenay in 1121. It seems as if Saint Bernard hesitates at this time to make many foundations. He certainly resists the spread of the Order into Spain, refuses to make a foundation in the Holy Land about this time, holds off from making any more in France until 1128 when he will see that it is useless to row against the strong current. He will found Igny in March and Reigny in September of that year. In the early thirties he will extend his foundations into Germany and England (Rievaulx, 1132) and will be the first to send a Cistercian colony to Spain (Moruela, 1132) in spite of his earlier opposition.

All this has not yet begun to happen in 1124. But Bernard is nearing the end of the providential "formation" that has prepared him for his great work in the Church of God. If we say that ten years of ill health and insecurity and suffering and prayer are coming to an end, we do not mean that his health will become good or that his sufferings will not increase or that his life of prayer will not deepen, but he will become strong enough to travel and enter into public life.

Part of his "formation" has been his training in the knowledge of human nature. First, he has had to learn that man is not an angel, that monks still have bodies, and that although he himself has tried not only to mortify his desires, but even to put to death the senses themselves, it is better to remember that man is human and that his human nature is supposed to be divinized by grace, not destroyed by it. Then, too, the saint who has always been too pure and too spiritual to feel anything of the temptations of the flesh has learned not to be surprised that all men are not exactly like himself. In his own terms, he has learned the value of what he calls the "flight from justice to mercy." He knows that self-denial is incomplete unless it leads to a sympathetic understanding of others, to mercy, to charity; that the "ointment" of fraternal compassion is necessary to show his monks how good and how pleasant it is for brethren to live together in unity.[4]

Now, finally, he is being tested by the sight of great defections from the Order that embodies all his monastic ideals. His young cousin Robert, who had followed him to Citeaux and had been sent with the small colony that established Clairvaux, "apostatized" in 1119 and fled to the relatively easy and opulent life of Cluny. The first in Saint Bernard's collection of letters, and one of the longest, is one to Robert, pleading with him to return to the austerity of Citeaux:

> If warm and comfortable furs, if fine and precious cloth, if long sleeves and ample hoods, if dainty coverlets and soft woolen shirts make a saint, why do I delay and not follow you at once? But these things are comforts for the weak, not the arms of fighting men. They who wear soft raiment are in kings' houses. Wine and white bread, honey-wine and pittances, benefit the body, not the soul. The soul is not fattened out of frying pans. Many monks in Egypt served God a long time without fish. Pepper, ginger, cumin, sage, and all the thousand other spices may please the palate, but they inflame lust. And would you make my safety depend on such things? Will you spend your youth safely

[4] Ps. 132:1.

among them? Salt with hunger is seasoning enough for a man living soberly and wisely.[5]

The accents are characteristic of Bernard, especially in the early years at Clairvaux.

But 1125 sees a far more dangerous defection from the Cistercians than the passage of one monk from Citeaux to Cluny. One of the companions of Bernard when he entered Citeaux was Arnold, the first Abbot of Morimond. The two young Cistercians started their abbatial career in the same year, 1115, and had to face the same trials, difficulties, and disappointments. Now, suddenly, news comes that the Abbot of Morimond has vanished from his monastery, taking a few monks with him, and has gone off to settle in the Holy Land without asking any permission. Actually the fugitives will never reach Palestine. Arnold will die in Belgium after ignoring Bernard's letter to him, and the Abbot of Clairvaux will be left with the task of gathering the other monks together and bringing them home. The event is an important one in the life of Saint Bernard and of the Order. Morimond is one cornerstone of the new structure, and there is every reason to fear that with the fall of Arnold the whole Order might collapse. Bernard loses his prior, Gaucher, in the shuffle to set things straight after Arnold's apostasy. Gaucher is sent to replace the departed abbot. But in a short time Clairvaux is to get one of her greatest priors in exchange for this loss. Godfrey de la Roche will return from Fontenay, where he has been abbot, and will assume this office. He will be one of Saint Bernard's most valuable helpers and supporters in the years of activity soon to come.

[5]*The Letters of Saint Bernard of Clairvaux,* transl. Bruno Scott James (Chicago, 1953), p. 8.

These years also find Saint Bernard busy with other Orders. First of all, he has many Benedictine friends. The most intimate of these is William, Abbot of the Black Monks at Saint Thierry, outside Rheims. William has been visiting Clairvaux for some years, and lately he has been insisting that he wants to become a Cistercian. But we must not imagine that Bernard wants all Benedictines to become Cistercians. He is not at all in favor of the change, in this case, and he writes to William:

> If I am to say what I think (about your plan), I must tell you that, unless I am mistaken, it is something I could not advise you to attempt and that you could not carry out. Indeed I wish for you what it has for long been no secret to me that you wish for yourself. But putting aside what both of us wish, as it is right we should, is safer for me and more advantageous for you if I advise you as I think God wishes. Therefore I say hold on to what you have, remain where you are, and try to benefit those over whom you rule. Do not try to escape the responsibility of office while you are still able to discharge it for the benefit of your subjects. Woe to you if you rule them and do not benefit them because you shirk the burden of ruling them.[6]

Another close friend of Saint Bernard is the founder of the Premonstratensian Order, Saint Norbert, the future Bishop of Magdeburg. Since his priestly ordination in the same year as Bernard's, Norbert has won himself a great reputation as a preacher and an ascetic. In 1120 he formed a

[6]Ibid., p. 128.

religious community in the diocese of Laon, not too far from Clairvaux. The Bishop of Laon, who presented Norbert with the domain of Premontré, also gave Bernard land on which to found the monastery of Foigny. In 1124, Saint Bernard is present at the installation of the Premonstratensians in the monastery of Saint Martin of Laon, and in this same year Norbert tells the Abbot of Clairvaux that there will soon be a great crisis in the Church. He is prophesying the schism of Anacletus II which will break out in 1130 and which will draw Bernard forth from his cloister into the turmoil of the world.

[The year] 1124 is probably also the date of Saint Bernard's voyage to Grenoble and the Grande Chartreuse. His friendship with Guigo, or Guy, the legislator and organizer of the Carthusian Order is to be extraordinarily fruitful in both of them. Two remarkable literary works will remain as a witness to its fruitfulness: the austere and deep *Meditations* of Guigo, and Saint Bernard's own *On Loving God* (*De Diligendo Deo*)—one of the most succinct expressions of the central theme of his mystical theology: union with God by pure love.

Finally, the conversion of Saint Bernard's rather worldly sister, Humbeline, and her entrance into the Benedictine convent of Julley-les-Nonnains also belongs to this period of his life (1122).

If the ideas for his *De Diligendo Deo* are now maturing in his mind, two other major works of the *Doctor Mellifluus* have already been completed. They are the sermons on the Virgin Mother (or Homilies on the Gospel "*Missus est*") and the treatise on the Degrees of Humility. The sermons on the Blessed Virgin are without doubt among the most beautiful pages to come from Bernard's pen. They constitute a small but complete treatise in Mariology, one of the first of its kind. This is one of the only books Saint Bernard writes not on request or under obedience, but merely because he feels like writing it.

In short, at the end of the first quarter of the twelfth century we find that Saint Bernard and the century are fully prepared to meet one another. He is already known to be a saint, a worker of miracles, and a theologian whose wisdom is more than a matter of learning. He is already so much of an authority that a cardinal will urge him to write his book on the love of God and the Bishop of Sens will ask him for a treatise on the spiritual life for bishops. "Who are we," exclaims Saint Bernard, "that we should write for bishops!" Yet he adds, "Who are we that we should not obey our bishops?" He does not hesitate to obey.

Two more lines and we shall fill in the background of this sketch and pass on. Saint Bernard is perhaps not thinking much about the Albigensian heresy, but already there is much trouble in the south of France. In the heart of Languedoc, where some of the great Romanesque basilicas of the age are still bright gold in their unweathered stone, the heresiarch Peter de Bruys puts on a surprising and unhappy demonstration. It is Good Friday, and the scene is at Saint-Gilles-du-Gard. Peter gathers a crowd in the public square, heaps up a huge pile of crucifixes, and sets them alight. While the fire is blazing, he starts roasting some meat in the fire, offering it to the crowd. A riot breaks out with fighting on all sides. Peter is himself seized and thrown into the flames, but escapes to continue his work and prepare the way for his successor, Henry, whom Bernard will confront in 1145.

The year 1145 is when Eugene III ascends the throne of Peter, to become the first Cistercian pope. Eugene followed Bernard home from Italy on one of the saint's triumphant journeys, in the early thirties. He lived there for ten years as an obscure and silent monk. Bernard sent him back to Italy in 1140 to be Abbot of Clairvaux's thirty-fourth foundation: the Abbey of Tre Fontane outside Rome. The death of Lucius II, wounded in the Roman civil war, leaves Eugene and Bernard to settle the struggles of a whole world: Mohammedans in the East, revolutionaries in Italy, heretics in southern France, trouble everywhere. It seems amusing to us that Bernard has written, in 1143, to his friend Peter the Venerable, Abbot of Cluny:

> I have decided to stay in my monastery and not go out, except once a year for the general chapter of Abbots at Citeaux. Here, supported by your prayers and consoled by your good will, I shall remain for the few days that are left to me in which to fight until the time comes for me to be relieved at my post.[7]

Bernard also writes to his spiritual son who has now become his spiritual father, Pope Eugene III, and tells him rather bluntly that much work can be spared both of them if the Abbot of Clairvaux can only be allowed to rest in peace in the cloister. "If anyone suggests that more might be put on me, know that as it is I am not equal to supporting what I carry. Inasmuch as you spare me you will spare yourself."[8]

As a matter of fact 1145 finds Bernard and Eugene on the eve of their greatest and most tragic effort: the Second Crusade.

The Crusade is Bernard's work. The singular intensity of his religious idealism appears here in all its strength and all its weakness: for Bernard preaches the Crusade with a sublime

[7]Ibid., p. 375.
[8]Ibid., p. 396.

disregard for political circumstance. He has so completely committed himself to the principles he believes in that he sees nothing but the principles. The whole practical logic of his argument depends on the assumption that each Crusader will take up the Cross with a faith as pure and ardent as Bernard's own. He simply took it for granted that everyone would embrace his religious principles as he did himself, and put them into practice in a manner worthy of saints.

What was this Second Crusade? Fifty years before, in Bernard's childhood, when Citeaux was being founded, the first Crusade had established a strange feudal kingdom of Frankish barons in the Holy Land. Here, in not too well garrisoned castles, and surrounded by hostile and uncomprehending natives, the Franks are not united among themselves. Nor are they on very good terms with the nearest great Christian power: the Empire of Byzantium. Facing them is a powerful Moslem coalition, and in 1144 the Mohammedans, under Ibn al Athir, storm and take the Christian outpost of Edessa. It is an important victory, a religious as well as a political triumph for Islam.

The Franks appeal to Byzantium, without result. In 1145 they are asking for help in Rome. The news arrives in France, and the young King Louis VII, seeing a chance of glory, proposes a Crusade. His proposal is not accepted with any enthusiasm. He turns to Bernard of Clairvaux, asking him to preach a Crusade. Bernard will have nothing to do with it. He formally refuses, adding that he will only undertake the task if commanded by the pope. So Louis VII turns to Rome, and in 1146 Bernard raises the standard of the Cross at the Burgundian shrine of Vezelay.

It is here that we see Bernard, the saint, as a most provoking enigma, as a temptation, perhaps even as a scandal. Here the sleeping power of Bernard's warlike atavism wakes and fights its way to the front of his life like some smiling Romanesque monster pushing through the leafage of a pillar's capital in the cloisters of Cluny. This power, too, is part of his sanctity. Indeed, although it is the fashion (especially among monks) to say that the Bernard of the Crusade was not the true Bernard, I am not sure whether Bernard was not more himself, after all, at Vezelay than he was at Clairvaux. With his whole heart undividedly set upon one magnificent religious principle—the principle of order, of divine authority communicated to men so that the peace of eternity might begin to be reflected even in the changing surface of the seas of time—Bernard seems to have paid little attention to temporal detail.

In any case, we cannot see the "true" Bernard by dividing him against himself, and the truth is that the Bernard of Vezelay is the very same man who is prepared, within a short time, to preach the magnificent last sermons on "The Canticle of Canticles," sermons which have nothing to do with war but with the sublime peace of mystical marriage. The apparent contradiction between Vezelay and the eighty-fifth sermon *In Cantica* is beyond comprehension if we imagine that for Saint Bernard the interior life is purely a matter of personal, subjective, individual union of the soul with God. The interior life is the life of the whole Church, of the Mystical Body of Christ, shared by all who are members of that Body. But the invisible and interior peace of the members among themselves and with their God is not separable, in the mind of Bernard, from an exterior and visible order which reflects the purposes of God in the world, and which guarantees the effect of His salvific action upon souls. If Saint Bernard thought that the way to divine union could only be a way of individual withdrawal from the world, of personal asceticism and recollection, of esoteric techniques, he would hardly urge thousands of Frenchmen and English-men and Germans to take up arms and fight Islam, to guarantee the security of Christian Europe and free access to the Holy Places in Palestine. Needless to say, although his conception of the Crusade is essentially mystical, he certainly does not confuse military action with contemplative prayer. But he believes that the Church can call upon the armies of Christian nations to defend the order established by God. This is a principle which every Catholic will accept. The difficulty comes, of course, in determining just what political setup, if any, represents the order established by God. Bernard's handling of the Crusade surprises us by its apparent neglect of this most important issue. He seems not to have bothered with the political details of the problem.

It is easy enough to say that Saint Bernard had a drastically oversimplified idea of the implications of the Crusade. We may perhaps be inclined to think that he ought to have read the translation of the Koran which Peter the Venerable sent him, from Cluny, to study and to refute. Bernard seems to have felt no need to know or to understand anything about Islam: as if knowing the Mohammedans to be "pagans" were to know quite enough. But let us remember that Bernard belongs to the twelfth century, not to the twentieth.

The two ages are poles apart. The one can barely understand the other. Our time is completely pragmatic, totally immersed in practical contingency, and rarely argues from anything but circumstance. Bernard did not feel himself obliged to do anything but act in accordance with his one big principle. If God sees fit to call upon the arms of the Franks to defend His Kingdom, and if the pope tells Bernard to preach a Crusade, then the Abbot of Clairvaux has a divine mission to preach a Crusade. He will confine himself to the strict limits of his mission. He will show men the meaning of the Holy War as he himself sees it, and will try to communicate to them something of his own terrific faith. It is someone else's job to see that the right alliances are made among Christian kings or to foresee that they will be either not made or not kept. As for the Crusaders themselves, it is their part to make the war a Holy War, one which is as much a pilgrimage as a war, one in which they will assure themselves of the promised remission of the punishment due to their sins by living without sin.

What actually happened was that Bernard alone did his job well. The others all failed. The murderers and adventurers who joined themselves to the well-intentioned Crusaders remained, alas, murderers and adventurers. The French continued to be enemies of the Germans and fought them all the way across Europe. The French king did not find it possible to accept an alliance with Roger of Sicily, which would have insured transport by sea and perhaps would have made the presence of so many Westerners in the Near East less alarming for the emperor at Byzantium. As it was, the armies of the Cross converged on Constantinople and gave the impression that the capital on the Bosporus was the real objective of their Crusade. Manuel Commenius, the Basileus, did what he could to make sure that there would not be a victorious army of Crusaders returning through the city. That meant, in fact, that he made sure there would be no victorious army. To have been a Holy War, as Saint Bernard conceived it, the Crusade ought at least to have manifested some show of unity among Christians. There was none. The whole history of the campaign is one of treachery and murder. "The promises of God," Bernard was to exclaim, "cannot stand in the way of the rights of His justice."[9]

---

[9]*De Consideratione,* bk. 2, chap. 1; Migne, *Patrologia Latina,* 182:745.

It is remarkable that Saint Bernard did not give up with the failure of this Crusade. He was ready to start a new one, and had indeed been named to lead it himself: which he would have done. It is said that the Cistercians intervened, and saw to it that he did not. His energy was irrepressible, miraculous to the end. He seems to have excelled in triumphing over sickness in order to do impossible things. Even in the spring of 1153, when Bernard was on his deathbed, he got up and took to the road because he heard there was a war at Metz. But that was to be his last exploit. He died in his monastery on August 20, 1153, lamented by the whole world of his time. He was canonized by Alexander III in 1174.

//

SAINT BERNARD'S WRITINGS

It seems that one of the things Saint Bernard wanted to get away from, when he entered Citeaux, was literary ambition. Profoundly affected by the humanistic renaissance of the twelfth century, his works still bear witness, by their quotations from Ovid, Persius, Horace, Terence, and other classical authors, to the influences he met with when he studied the liberal arts with the canons of Saint Vorles at Chatillon-sur-Seine. He seems to have become afraid of poetry and rhetoric, and to have run away from them. One of the greatest Latin authors of the Middle Ages, he has left a fairly large body of writings, all of which are in a sense "occasional." He was not one who wrote because he had to. His treatises were usually composed at the request of some fellow monk, some abbot, some other churchman, to answer a question or to meet some particular need. Most of his written works are sermons. Best known, perhaps, are his letters. Finally, not least in quality though they occupy comparatively little space, come his formal treatises. Only one of these, the *De Consideratione,* exceeds the length of a long article in a serious magazine. Most of these short tracts have not been translated into English, except for the treatises, *On Loving God, On Conversion,* and *On the Degrees of Humility.* These have been not only translated but edited with notes and introductions which are not always as helpful as they seem to be. A new translation of "The Canticle of Canticles" is promised us shortly in London, and the letters have been excellently done into English, by Father Bruno James, in the edition already referred to.

Taking a broad, general view of all Saint Bernard's writings, we find that they give us a definite and coherent doctrine, a theology, embracing not merely one department of Christian life but the whole of that life. In other words, Saint Bernard is not merely to be classified as "a spiritual writer," as if his doctrine could be limited to a certain non-dogmatic region of affective intimacy with God. He is spiritual indeed, and a great mystic. But he is a speculative mystic; his mysticism is expressed as a theology. It not only describes his own personal religious experiences but it penetrates into the heart of the "Mystery of God, that is Christ."[10] It contemplates and expounds the providential economy of man's redemption and sanctification. It is at once a mystical theology and a soteriology. It not only explains what it means to be united to God in Christ, but shows the meaning of the whole economy of our redemption in Christ. It tells us how to recognize the "visits" of the Word to the soul; how to respond to the action of the Holy Spirit Who is the "Law" of

[10]Col 2:2.

the inner life of God, when He comes to bring our faculties under the sway of His divine charity.

In teaching us all this, Saint Bernard does not hesitate to turn aside from contemplation in the strict sense to settle certain difficult questions of theological debate. We know that Bernard was esteemed as one of the most authoritative theologians of his time, and that his action led to the refutation of such important errors as those of Abelard and Gilbert de la Porrée.

Saint Bernard's theology of grace presupposes his Neoplatonic conception of the soul created in God's image and destined by God for a perfect union of likeness with Himself. The conception is more than Neoplatonism. The desire of the soul for God, which is in Bernard's eyes inseparable from the very freedom of the soul itself, must be elevated by grace above the level of a mere frustrated velleity. Human freedom, aided by the power of the Holy Spirit, can aspire to far more than a mere intellectual contemplation of eternal ideas: that, in Saint Bernard's mind, would be little better than frustration. God does not remain cold and distant, attracting the soul but never yielding Himself to it. He Himself both begins and finishes the work of the soul's transformation, and this whole work is an *ordinatio caritatis,* that is to say the elevation, disciplining, and redirection of all the soul's capacity for love by the actual motion of the divine Spirit. At the center of this work is Christ, in Whom and by Whom it is all effected. Bernard's devotion to the humanity of the Savior must not be regarded merely as a pious discovery intended to aid monastic meditation. It is simply a rediscovery of the Christ of the Fathers and of Saint Paul. Saint Bernard's intense love for Jesus found expression, it is true, in lyrical terms which were singularly effective in making God's mercy real to those who read his pages. But in its substance his Christology is simply the fruit of his ability "to comprehend with all the saints, what is the breadth and length and height and depth: to know also the charity of Christ which surpasseth all knowledge that you may be filled unto the fullness of God."[11] The basic ideas of Saint Bernard's theology are treated in the encyclical and in our commentary on it. It is sufficient here to name the saint's chief works and to give some idea of their contents. Setting aside the letters, let us consider first his treatises and then his sermons.

On the Degrees of Humility (*De Gradibus Humilitatis*) is one of Saint Bernard's earliest works (1119). It summarizes the commentary of the Abbot of Clairvaux on the central doctrine of Benedictine asceticism—the seventh chapter of the rule, on monastic humility. The tract is made up of two parts, of vastly different importance. The second makes easier reading and is a lively piece of light literature that shows Bernard to be a true Frenchman and a compatriot of La Bruyère. He takes Saint Benedict's degrees of humility, turns them upside down into degrees of pride, and gives us mordant descriptions of monks on each one of the downward steps from "curiosity" to impenitent mortal sin. But the first part of the treatise is the one that matters. It is a formal declaration that the Cistercians, or at least Saint Bernard, interpreted the Rule of Saint Benedict as a preparation for the mystical life, for, says Saint Bernard, when the monk has ascended the twelve degrees of humility, he passes through the degrees of truth, the last of which is contemplation, or the transient experience of God in the *raptus* of divine love. The fact that Saint Bernard talks of degrees of truth does not mean that this is a tract on epistemology. He is talking about a contact with truth that only begins where

[11] Eph 3:18–19.

epistemology leaves off: for the philosophical justification of our conceptual knowledge of truth or of God has little to say about the experiential grasp of divine things by charity which is the subject of Bernard's *De Gradibus*.

The treatise *On Loving God* (*De Diligendo Deo*) again shows the unity of Saint Bernard's great conception of man in his relations with God. The love of God is not merely something that can somehow profitably be fitted into man's life. It is man's whole reason for existing, and until he loves God man does not really begin to live. Hence Saint Bernard examines the question of our universal obligation to love God, the reasons why we should love Him ("because He is God"), and the measure of our love ("to love Him without measure"). The four degrees of love which are the heart of the treatise show that it is man's very nature to love. By reason of the fall, he who should love unselfishly now loves himself first of all. But divine grace re-educates man's natural love, reinstates it in its natural purity, extends it to all men, then purifies it and raises it to God. We begin by loving ourselves, pass on to the love of other men and of God for our own sakes, then begin to love God for His own sake. But the fourth degree of love is that in which we love ourselves for God's sake. This is the high point of Bernard's Christian humanism. It shows that the fulfillment of our destiny is not merely to be lost in God, as the traditional figures of speech would have it, like "a drop of water in a barrel of wine or like iron in the fire," but *found* in God in all our individual and personal reality, tasting our eternal happiness not only in the fact that we have attained to the possession of His infinite goodness, but above all in the fact that we see His will is done in us. Ultimately this perfection demands the resurrection of the bodies of all the saints, for the consummation Saint Bernard looks forward to is no mere philosophical union with the Absolute. It is the term proposed to us by Christian revelation itself: the resurrection, the general judgment, the summing up of all in Christ so that "God will be all in all." Written about the same time as the *De Diligendo Deo* (1126 or 1127), Saint Bernard's tract *On Free Will and Grace* is fundamental to his whole theology. This is one of the main sources for his doctrine on man's soul as the image of God. Liberty constitutes man in God's image. This is only another way of saying what we have already seen: man is made in order that he may love God. In order to love God with disinterested charity he must first be free. His whole ascent to divine union is a progress in liberty. Our basic freedom, *liberum arbitrium* or freedom of choice, is only the beginning of the ascent. The capacity to choose between good and evil is only the shadow of true liberty. Genuine freedom is the work of grace. Grace finds the soul of fallen man in a state of captivity to sin. Our freedom spontaneously turns to evil rather than to good, until it is set in order by grace. Then it becomes capable of consistently avoiding evil choices. Finally by glory the soul achieves its ultimate and perfect liberty: the freedom to choose always what is good and to rejoice always in what is best, without ever being turned aside from the good by any inclination to what is less good or formally evil. We are only perfectly free in heaven, according to this doctrine of Saint Bernard.

The *Apologia,* written in 1127, is seldom translated in its entirety. But it is often quoted in part. The parts quoted are the "purple passages" in which Saint Bernard scathingly criticizes the comforts of Benedictine life at Cluny and the overwhelming splendor of the great Benedictine churches of his time. The book was written at the request of the Benedictine abbot, William of Saint Thierry, as a reply to Peter the Venerable, Abbot of Cluny. Peter had reproved the Cistercians for taking a pharisaical attitude toward their Benedictine brethren. The *Apologia* was intended to be a defense not of Cistercian poverty but of monastic charity. Saint Bernard begins by praising the qualities of different forms of monastic observance saying that this variety is necessary in the Church. This is not merely a diplomatic opening to a Cistercian manifesto. Bernard is not propagandizing his own Order, but defending the unity of the Church: and her unity demands variety. To compel all monks to follow the same observance would be un-Catholic. Therefore Saint Bernard devotes several pages to severe reprehension of those Cistercians who had, in fact, given the Cluniacs just cause for complaint.

> There are some in our Order [he says] who are said to criticize other Orders, contrary to the words of the Apostle who said: "Do not judge before the time, until the Lord come, who both will bring to light the hidden things of darkness and will make manifest the counsels of hearts" (1 Cor 4:5). Desiring to set up a justice of their own they withdraw themselves from subjection to the justice of God. Such men, if such there be, I would say belonged neither to our order nor to any "order." For although they live by the rule of an order, by speaking proudly they make themselves to be citizens of Babylon, that is, of confusion. Indeed they make themselves sons of darkness, sons of hell itself wherein there is no order, but wherein everlasting horror dwells.[12]

If after this Bernard himself goes on to say some rather severe things about Cluniac observance, it is in the interests of the monastic order and of the Church as a whole that he does so. His just criticisms were taken to heart by the Benedictines

---

[12]*Apologia ad Gullielmum,* n. 10; *Patres Latini,* 182:904.

themselves, although his austere views on art were not accepted by them. In any case he always remained on very good terms with Cluny as his correspondence with Peter the Venerable and other Benedictines can prove. The same esteem for all the different interpretations of Saint Benedict's rule can be found in the tract *On Precept and Dispensation* (*De Precepto et Dispensatione*), written in answer to several questions proposed to him by the Benedictines of Saint Peter of Chartres in 1143. This treatise is technically monastic, and is very interesting for its discussion of the value of monastic vows, the obligation to obey the Rule of Saint Benedict, obedience to monastic superiors, silence, stability, and the question of changing from one monastery to another.

Of more universal interest will be the sermon to the university students of Paris, *De Conversione*.[13] It is interesting that the full title of the tract reads: "Sermon Addressed to Clerics, on Conversion." What he was telling the clerics was not how to convert others but how to convert themselves. Anyone who has read the history of medieval schools and universities will recognize that Saint Bernard's remarks were probably not misplaced. The tract concerns itself first of all with the notion of the Christian conscience, on the action of divine grace in the soul through the instrumentality of the word of God, either preached or read in Scripture. Then Saint Bernard talks of the psychology of unbalanced extraversion that infallibly leads to sin, and the necessary ascetical processes of meditation, recollection, self-knowledge, self-denial, which aid the work of grace. Here he is both vivid and practical, and his observations are not without a characteristic note of satire. The second part of the treatise deals with the *ordinatio caritatis,* the positive and

[13]*On Conversion,* trans. Watkin Williams, London, 1938.

constructive work of virtue and purification by trial which build up the interior life of the soul in Christ.

Even before this sermon, preached in 1140, Saint Bernard had written a spiritual directory for the newly formed military order of the Knights Templar. He had also had a share in the composition of their rule.

The "directory" for the Templars is called *The Praises of the New Knighthood* (*De Laude Novae Militiae*) because in the opening chapters he makes a pointed contrast between the new militia and the old "malice" (*malitia*). The only fruit of secular warfare, says Bernard, is that both the killer and the killed end in hell.[14] The Knight Templar who devotes his strength and his arms to the service of God can become a saint by being a good soldier. To fight in a Holy War is to become an instrument of divine justice, reestablishing the order violated by sin. Nor should the force of arms be used to restore order until all other means have failed. But in making this qualification, Bernard takes it for granted that there is no other way with the "pagans" than the way of war.

The third chapter of this interesting treatise shows the basic assumptions behind Bernard's preaching of the Second Crusade, and they bear a striking resemblance to the arguments that also drove the armies of Islam into battle. However, the directory was not written for a crusade, but for a religious army of occupation—men whose vocation it was to patrol and defend the Holy Land and keep peace there. The major part of the little book is devoted to showing the Templars how they can make their residence in Palestine the occasion of a particularly deep life of prayer

---

[14]*"Quis igitur finis fructusve saecularis hujus, non dico militiae sed malitiae, si et occisor letaliter peccat et occisus aeternaliter perit?" De Laude Novae Militiae,* n. 5; *Patrologia Latina,* 182:923.

and meditation. It does not seem that they fully appreciated Saint Bernard's program.

Saint Bernard's tract "Against the Errors of Peter Abelard" (1140) is important in the history of Catholic theology, most of all because in it Bernard defends the strict, literal, and objective value of Christ's redemptive death for man. For Abelard, the death of Christ on the Cross did not, strictly speaking, redeem man: it only offered him an example of supreme humility, charity, and self-sacrifice. Bernard asserts, against Abelard, that Christ became man precisely in order to redeem mankind from sin, deliver man from the power of the devil, and to become, instead of fallen Adam, the new head of a redeemed and sanctified human race. Jesus, says Saint Bernard, not only taught us justice but gave us justice. He not only showed us His love by dying for us on the Cross, but by the effects of His death He really and objectively causes His charity to exist and act in our hearts.[15] In doing so, He actually destroys sin in our souls and communicates to us a new life which is totally supernatural and divine. The effect of our redemption is therefore a complete and literal regeneration of those souls to whom its fruits are applied. Without this dogmatic basis the whole mystical theology of Saint Bernard would be completely incomprehensible. The purpose of all his mystical and ascetic teaching is to show us how to cooperate with the action of divine grace so that our redemption and regeneration may not remain a dead letter but may actually influence all our conduct and find expression in every part of our lives until we arrive at that divine union by which the Christ-life is perfected in our souls. It was in order to bring us to this perfect union that Jesus died on the Cross.

[15]*Contra Errores Abaelardi*, n. 17; *Patrologia Latina,* 182:1067.

Less important than the tract against Abelard is the short treatise *On Baptism* (*De Baptismo*), which Bernard wrote, at the request of Hugh of Saint Victor, to answer several technical arguments that had been raised on the subject.

Finally, not the least charming and readable of Saint Bernard's short works is his biography of Saint Malachy of Armagh. The saintly primate of Ireland died at Clairvaux in 1148, and Bernard wrote his life to console the Cistercians of Malachy's native land. It is amusing to notice that many of the concise and vivid expressions with which Bernard described the qualities of his holy friend have found their way into antiphons of Saint Bernard's own feast. The Church uses them to celebrate the virtues of the biographer himself.

We need only make a passing mention of Saint Bernard's work on Gregorian chant, which was not actually composed by him. The work was done under his guidance by a commission of abbots appointed to supervise the revision of the Cistercian choir books. He also composed a liturgical office for the martyr Saint Victor.

We have on earlier pages seen something of the *De Consideratione* (*Tract on Meditation*), the last and perhaps the most celebrated of Saint Bernard's formal treatises. The five books of this concise and powerful spiritual directory were composed during the last ten years of Bernard's life. He wrote the book for Pope Eugene III, and, as a modern writer has observed, in addressing Pope Eugene, Bernard was really writing for all who would ascend to the papacy. "Valuable for all prelates," says the same writer,[16] "and for all men, the *De Consideratione* is at the same time a valuable document on Bernard himself. . . . To all clerics, in the person of the highest

[16]Dom Jean Leclercq, OSB, *Saint Bernard Mystique,* pp. 197, 198.

among them, Bernard proposes a program inspired by the monastic tradition by which he himself lives."

The importance of the *De Consideratione* lies in its stress on the interior life and on the essential primacy of contemplation over action. The pope must remember, says Bernard, that the interior life ought, by rights, to be preferred to exterior action.[17] Action is a necessity, and we are in fact prevented from remaining always in silence, contemplation, study, and prayer. But action is only valid if it is nourished by a deep interior life. It should not absorb so much of our time and energy that meditation, prayer, and silent reflection become impossible.

Saint Bernard begins then by insisting on the need for prayer above all in the life of those who have the highest and most responsible positions in the Church. He warns the pope against a false zeal that might allow him to be carried away in the strong current of great and important affairs. The fact that our works are done in the service of God is not enough, by itself, to prevent us from losing our interior life if we let them devour all our time and all our strength. Work is good and necessary, but too much of it renders the soul insensitive to spiritual values, hardens the heart against prayer and divine things. It requires a serious effort and courageous sacrifice to resist this hardening of heart. Therefore Saint Bernard warns Pope Eugene against the danger that confronts him if he lets himself be carried away by affairs of state, and keeps no time for himself, for prayer and for the things of God.

In giving this advice, Bernard was not thinking only of the pope's own soul but of the whole Church. His vision

---

[17]Nam si liceret quod deceret, *absolute per omnia et in omnibus praeferendam* ... quae ad omnia valet, id est pietatem irrefragibilis ratio monstrat. Quid sit pietas, quaeris? Vacare considerationi. *De Consideratione,* bk. 1, chap. 7, 8; *Patrologia Latina,* 182:736.

always extended to horizons broad enough to encompass the world and the whole Mystery of Christ. All his spiritual direction was orientated toward this Mystery. Whether he guided a pope, a bishop, a king, or a simple monk, Bernard always thought of that soul's interests in relation to its place in the Church. His direction, therefore, always centered on duties of state and on one's place in the providential plan of God. The practical advice he gives to Pope Eugene on the administration of the Roman Curia does not make this book a tract on papal policies, as is sometimes thought. Bernard soon returns to the theme of contemplation, and the whole fifth book is a profound and succinct handbook on meditation and mental prayer.

Turning to Saint Bernard's sermons, we find ourselves in fertile country. There exist about a hundred and thirty sermons of Saint Bernard preached on the various feasts of the liturgical calendar—whether the feasts of the seasons or of the saints. Then we have about a hundred and twenty more sermons, *On Diverse Subjects* (*De Diversis*), which cover practically the whole field of Bernard's theological interests and are too little studied even by monks, who would profit much from the meditation of them.

The most important of all Bernard's collections of discourses is the group of eighty-six sermons on "The Canticle of Canticles" (*Sermones in Cantica*), which forms his greatest and most important single work. The commentary is incomplete. Saint Bernard died when he was about to begin explaining the third chapter, and the work was continued by an English Cistercian abbot, Gilbert of Hoyland, who was also unable to finish the work. The peculiar importance of all the sermons is in fact due to the way Saint Bernard uses them to penetrate and manifest this central fact of Christianity: the mystery of God's love revealed to men in the incarnation of His Son and in their redemption. It is the "great mystery (or sacrament) of Godliness" (*magnum pietatis sacramentum*) that occupies him before all else. What is that mystery? Not an idea, not a doctrine, but a Person: God Himself, revealed in the Man, Christ. How is this doctrine understood? When the Person is known. How is He known? When loved. How loved? When He lives in us and is Himself our love for His Father. Loving the Father in us, He makes us one with the Father as He Himself is. Therefore Saint Bernard can logically say, "Truly I must love Him perfectly, in whom I have my being, my life and my knowledge. . . . Clearly, Lord Jesus, that man is worthy of death who refuses to live for thee: indeed he is already dead. And he who does not know thee by love [*sapit*] knows nothing. And he who cares to be for anything else but thee, is destined for nothingness, and is become nothing."[18]

I think it would be well to define the whole issue Saint Bernard's sermons raise, by two quotations from Gerard Manley Hopkins which will help the modern reader to understand something of what Saint Bernard meant by the mystery of Christ. First, writing to Robert Bridges, the poet remarks on the meaning of the mystery of Christ to a non-Catholic and to a Catholic. To a non-Catholic, the mystery of Christ is a puzzle. To a Catholic it is a Person.

> To you [says Hopkins to Bridges] it comes to: Christ is in some sense God and in some sense He is not God— and your interest is in the uncertainty; to the Catholic it is: Christ is in every sense God and in every sense man, and the interest is in the locked and inseparable

[18] *In Cantica,* Sermon 20, n. 1; *Patrologia Latina,* 183:867.

combination, or rather it is in the *Person* in whom the combination has its place.

These were exactly Saint Bernard's sentiments toward Abelard's treatment of the dogma of redemption.[19]

The second quotation from Hopkins illustrates Saint Bernard's idea that we fulfill the end for which we were created when, by conformity to Christ, we fully realize our own identity by becoming perfectly free and therefore by loving God without limit. Hopkins says: "This [conformity to Christ] brings out the nature of the man himself as the lettering on a sail or the device upon a flag are best seen when it fills."

All Saint Bernard's sermons more or less fit into the scope defined by these two statements. The scope is, of course, practically limitless. But these are his two great themes: the mystery of Christ in Himself and in those who are conformed to Him in the Holy Spirit. In other words: Christ and the Church.

The finest and most characteristic pages of Saint Bernard on this doctrine are probably to be found in his Advent and Christmas sermons, his sermons on the Virgin Mother (*Homiliae super Missus est*) and on some of her great feasts, as well as in some of the more important sermons on the Canticle.

Advent and Christmas seem to have exercised a more powerful attraction over Saint Bernard and the early Cistercians than any other phases of the liturgical cycle. Here the emphasis is on the Incarnation—on the redemption as it is seen from the viewpoint of the Incarnation rather than from that of the Passion. The "Sacrament of Advent," as Saint Bernard calls it,

[19]*Contra Errores Abaelardi*, n. 17; *Patrologia Latina*, 182:1067.

is the mystery of Christ's presence in the world. It is an important concept, for the Incarnation is not a mere matter of history but a present reality, and the most important reality of all. For it is the one reality that gives significance to everything else that has ever happened. Without it, nothing in history has any ultimate meaning.

If Christ is present, if His Kingdom is "in the midst of us," it is because of the infinite mercy of God. Only a divine decree could decide His coming, His descent into the darkness of a world which, without Him, would be doomed to everlasting despair. Bernard, in his characteristic emphasis on freedom and charity, sees this mystery of divine mercy above all as a supremely free and gratuitous act of God: but it is not a purely arbitrary act, since it depends on the "law" of goodness which rules all God's acts.

In the contemplation of this mystery, Bernard is never abstract. He is always talking about the great concrete facts revealed to us in the Bible, and his sermons are alive with images and figures out of the Scriptures. Color, music, movement, fire, contrasts of light and darkness, impassioned dialogue between the poverty of man and the greatness of God, between the mercy of God and His justice, flights of allegory, realistic examples sketched from life in the cloister—all these elements make Bernard's sermons extraordinarily alive. Indeed the very wealth of them sometimes oppresses the reader who has lost his sense of symbolism, or never had one. All the opulence that Bernard criticized in the plastic arts here runs riot in his prose, but without the exaggeration, the caricature, the grotesque, the crudeness that he reproved. At the heart of all this is the beautiful simplicity of his doctrine itself, in which there is nothing difficult, nothing esoteric, nothing complicated: only the depth and the lucidity of the Gospel. "It does not behoove thee, O man," says the saint, "to cross the seas, to penetrate the clouds, or to climb the Alps [in search of God]. No great journey is necessary for thee. Seek no further than thy own soul: there wilt thou find thy God!" *Usque ad temetipsum occurre Deo tuo.*[20]

The practical details of the interior life and of this search for God are elaborated with greater finesse in a series like the Lenten sermons on Psalm 90, preached to the monks of Clairvaux in the year 1139. But the greatest richness and variety of all are found in the sermons on the Canticle. Saint Bernard was more than explaining the text of this Song of Songs. He lived it, and blended the traditional mystical interpretation of the Canticle with the experience of his own union with God. As we see in *Doctor Mellifluus,* it is in these sermons that Saint Bernard's mystical doctrine reaches its most perfect elaboration. But there is also much in them besides mysticism. There is the lament for the death of his brother, Gerard (Sermon 26). There are attacks on the Manichaean heresy (Sermons 64–66) and on the trinitarian errors of Gilbert de la Porrée (Sermon 80). There are remarks on monastic observance, on the chanting of the divine office in choir, on the relations of the active and contemplative lives, as well as on all the Christian virtues.

Above all, the sermons on the Canticle are a magnificent treatise on the union of Christ and His Church. The mystical union of the Word with the individual soul is simply an expression of the union of the Incarnate Word with His Church. And this, as the encyclical demonstrates, brings us to the real inner unity that binds everything together in the life and work of Bernard of Clairvaux. In all that he writes, in all that he says, in all that he does, Bernard has only

[20]Sermon 1, Advent, nn. 10–11.

one end in view: the integration of nations, dioceses, monasteries, and individuals into the life and order of the Church.

Bernard is a builder, a man at once of liberty and of order, a man who builds individual liberties into a universal order, that all may be more perfectly free. In other words, Bernard is a man of the Church, *Vir Ecclesiae*. This fact, and this alone, explains the miraculous resources which enabled him to become the greatest man of his time.

CHRONOLOGY OF THE LIFE OF SAINT BERNARD OF CLAIRVAUX

1090–1153 A.D.

1090 Bernard is born into a rich family of minor nobility in Fontaines-les-Dijon in Burgundy. His father is a knight named Tescelin Sorrel, Lord of Fontaines, who will perish on a crusade. His pious mother, Aleth, is of the noble house of Montbard. He is the third of seven children, six sons and one daughter.

1099 Bernard attends the famous school of St. Vorles in Chatillon-sur-Seine where he learns Latin, studies literature, and writes poetry in imitation of Cicero, Virgil, Ovid, and Horace. He gives evidence of both great intellect and a genuine piety marked by his devotion to the Blessed Virgin Mary and the fervor with which he studies Scripture.

1107 His mother's death causes Bernard to plunge into depression for a time. Her piety had had a great influence on him, and the occasion of her death causes him to ponder deeply what to do with his life. His biographers tell us that he is a little taller than average, blond with a rusty beard, a fair complexion, and blue eyes. Should he marry, become a soldier, or follow his spiritual attractions, which filled him with a love of God, along with a love of the intellectual life of ideas and science? He hesitates between choosing the career of a monk or that of a professor.

While trained in the ways of soldiering like his brothers and experienced in hunting and competing in tournaments, he is unfit by health for a military career. He does, however, have abundant physical energy combined with personal charm and must fight against the strong physical temptations normal to any youth. He begins to seriously consider giving up a life in the world for one of solitude and prayer.

1109 Bernard's education at school is complete and he returns home. One day while on a solitary excursion, he stops in a church along the way to ask God for guidance about his future. While praying, his mind is cleared of doubt, and he realizes that he wants the life of a strict Cistercian monk.

Cistercian (an order of reformed Benedictine monks) monastic life includes common prayer, manual labor, reading Scripture, meditation, and personal prayer. The day is divided into periods of private prayer, communal prayer, work, meals, and rest. The monastery is called to be a school for charity. The abbot, elected to this position by his brother monks, is a guide for the community. It is he who gives spiritual instruction, organizes both the prayer life and the material works of the abbey, and facilitates the community life of the monks.

Cistercian spirituality is rooted in the words of the Bible: "God created man in his image. In the image of God He created him. Male and female He created them" (Gn 1:27). By sin man has lost this resemblance to God, but he is not abandoned by God. Through His Son, Jesus Christ, Himself the perfect image of the Father, incarnated as man, God seeks to restore man to his divine image. Union with God is a union of love, of reposing in God, full of peace and joy. By His humanity, Jesus has given us the means to follow Him and conform our will to His so that we become one in spirit with Him. One's entire being should, therefore, be consecrated to God: sensibility, imagination, intelligence, and heart, all the forces that mark our lives. It is this monastic structure and spiritual focus that attracts Bernard to the monastery of Citeaux.

1111 Now twenty-one, Bernard decides to enter Citeaux, only a few miles from the château where he was born. He expresses his ardent desire with great enthusiasm to his family and succeeds also in persuading his uncle, his brothers, and a group of young Burgundian noble friends, a party of thirty in all, to join him. This was an age of faith and chivalry. A knight would practice self-sacrificing love for his chosen maiden. In the Cistercian monastery, this capacity for love would now be converted into love for Christ, the Bridegroom of the soul.

Citeaux had been founded in 1098 by St. Robert, abbot of Molesmes, with the idea of restoring the Rule of St. Benedict to its original simplicity and rigor.

1112 Bernard and his group of brothers and friends arrive at Citeaux around Easter and are greeted warmly by the abbot Stephen Harding, an English monk who had come to Citeaux to reform Benedictine monastic life. Stephen has been abbot since 1108, but there have been no new novices for several years. At the end of the year Bernard and the postulants he brought with him make their profession as monks. Bernard puts on the white robe and brown scapular of Citeaux, a habit that more closely resembles that of the first companions of St. Benedict than the black habit of the more contemporary Cluny monastery, then the most famous and wealthy monastic network in Europe.

1115 Stephen sends Bernard as head of a group of twelve monks, including his own brothers, to found a new monastery at Vallée d'Absinth (Valley of Bitterness), in the diocese of Langres in Champagne. The site had once been a haven for bandits. On June 25, Bernard names the new foundation Claire Vallée of Clairvaux. Bernard is blessed as abbot by William of Champeaux, bishop of Châlons-sur-Marne. The bishop, a professor of theology at Notre Dame in Paris, sees Bernard as a man predestined by God to be His servant in extraordinary ways.

In the beginning life is extremely harsh for the new foundation as a result of poor land and the extremes of discipline exercised by Bernard. The monks fall into a state of discouragement, which causes Bernard to take stock of his demands on them. He repents of his severity and sees to it that they are better fed, though the food remains rough and simple. His reputation for holiness spreads, and soon there are 130 monks in the community.

1118 Bernard becomes gravely ill with stomach trouble. Near his place in the choir he keeps a basin to use when he needs to vomit. William of Champeaux gains the authority from the Cistercian chapter held in Citeaux to govern Bernard as his superior for a year. He succeeds in securing rest and quiet for the sick abbot and places him under a physician's care. Bernard's condition improves, and he eventually returns to regular monastic life, though he will be plagued all his life by digestive problems (no doubt made worse by self-imposed extremes of fasting and self-denial).

His father and the youngest son, Nivard, now join Bernard at Clairvaux. They receive their habits from his hands.

Crowded conditions at Clairvaux make it necessary to found new monasteries, resulting in the Monastery of the

Three Fountains in the diocese of Châlons; Fontenay in the diocese of Dijon (1119); and Foigny in the diocese of Soissons (1121). Bernard will make 68 more such foundations in the next 35 years, and by his death there will be 360 Cistercian houses extending across Europe comprising tens of thousands of members.

1119 The first general chapter of the Cistercian order is convoked by Stephen of Citeaux. This meeting focuses on the effort to codify the original Benedictine spirit of regularity and fervor as exhorted by Bernard. It results in the "Charter of Charity," which is confirmed by Pope Callixtus II on December 23. Because of Bernard's generally poor physical condition, the chapter relieves him of work in the fields and directs him to devote his time to preaching and writing.

1120 Bernard produces his first formal work, *Treatise on the Degrees of Humility and Pride,* an astute analysis of human character and motivation. Bernard is devoted to the Virgin Mother of Christ, patroness of Citeaux, and shows himself to be her poet in the homilies he composes (collected as *In Praise of the Blessed Virgin Mary*).

The monks of Cluny are chagrined by the preeminence of Citeaux as a model for regularity and fervor. Cluny, a Benedictine abbey founded in 910, had grown famous for the richness of its liturgical offices and the elaborate expression of religious symbolism in its art and architecture. As a criticism of Citeaux, the Cluniac monks charge that the rules of the new order are not practical. In response to the request of William of St. Thierry, Bernard publishes his *Apologia,* in which he satirizes Cluny for material excesses in food, clothing, and sumptuous decoration. Peter the Venerable, abbot of Cluny, eventually legislates reforms as a result. Bernard's influence establishes the standard for Cistercian art and architecture in all its noble, simple intelligence and sanctity. The Cistercian talent for mediation and the conversion of others will now be constantly imitated by the Church at large.

William of St. Thierry (1085–1148) was made abbot of St. Thierry in 1121. In 1135, out of admiration for Bernard, he will resign his authority in order to become a simple Cistercian monk. He enters the abbey of Signy in the diocese of Rheims. He writes in his biography of Bernard, "the invisible life of Christ lives and speaks through him." William is not only Bernard's biographer but his confidant and disciple, a true alter ego.

Suger, abbot of the Cluniac monastery St. Denis and minister to King Louis le Gros, is influenced by Bernard to resign his secular posts, give up worldly luxuries, and reestablish discipline in his own monastery. In Bernard's words, "You may imagine that what belongs to the Church belongs to you, while you officiate there. But you are mistaken; for though it is reasonable that one who serves the altar should live by the altar, yet it must not be to promote either his luxury or his pride."

1123 In the fall, Bernard is so sick he thinks he is going to die. He is suffering so intensely that the pain causes him to beg the two monks attending him to pray for him. The monks go to the church to pray before the altar. The Blessed Virgin appears to Bernard in his cell, along with St. Lawrence and St. Benedict. They extend their hands and heal him.

1127 Bernard writes his treatise *On Loving God* for Cardinal Haimeric, deacon of the Church of Rome. It is a detailed explanation of twelfth-century monastic love of God: "You asked me why we should love God and how much we should love Him. I reply that we should love God because He is God, and that the measure of our love should be to love Him without measure."

1128 The archbishop of Sens, Henri le Sanglier, soon after he himself is converted from a life of luxury and ambition, asks Bernard for a tract on how bishops should conduct themselves. Bernard writes *On the Conduct and Duties of Bishops,* in which he speaks out clearly to condemn current abuses of power and privilege by prelates. His evident concern for the virtue of church leaders helps to ensure the favorable reception of the work, which will be copied and circulated again and again after its appearance.

The Council of Troyes is held to spell out regulations for the Knights Templar, a religious institute founded in Jerusalem by Hugh of Payns, Bernard's cousin. The role of the Knights is to protect Christians in the Holy Land from attacks by enemies of the faith in these contentious times. Bernard writes *Book in Praise of the New Militia,* in which he provides guidelines for how they are to conduct themselves even if violence must be used to the point of inflicting death when pilgrims are threatened. He urges them to be cognizant that Jerusalem is holy ground, and he provides meditations for the Knights on the great events of Christian salvation that took place in the Holy City, Bethlehem, Nazareth, and on Calvary.

1130 Pope Honorius II dies on February 14. A schism breaks out in the Church with the election of a successor, Innocent II, when a rival, Anacletus II, also establishes a claim. Anacletus is influential and has powerful friends to back his ambitions. Innocent II is forced to take refuge in France, where King Louis le Gros convenes the French bishops in a council at Étampes. Bernard is called upon to establish the identity of the legitimate pope, and he decides in favor of Innocent II. For the next eight years Bernard will travel with the pope, intervene in his favor, and work unremittingly to achieve church unity. In his years of traveling as spokesman for Innocent II, Bernard is able to garner support from King Henry of England and Holy Roman Emperor Lothaire II. Bernard becomes known all over Europe as he travels, preaches, and works to convert people to a holy way of life. Throughout he longs to return to his brother monks at Clairvaux, where he can resume a life of contemplation.

1131 Returning briefly to Clairvaux from Italy, where he had preached on Innocent II's behalf, Bernard brings a number of Italians for admission to the monastery. Among them is a young canon from Pisa, Peter Bernard, who will later become Pope Eugenius III.

In August, Innocent II arrives in Clairvaux for a visit. In October he holds a council of bishops in Rheims, at which King Louis presents himself. His eldest son has died in a fall from a horse. He demands that the pope consecrate his second son, Louis, to be heir presumptive of the throne. Bernard remonstrates with the king for his previous persecution of the archbishop of Paris. Bernard demands that the king respect the Church. The next morning the pope consecrates the eleven-year-old prince. This act, Bernard proclaims, manifests the legitimacy of Innocent II as pope.

During this period of travel and preaching on behalf of Innocent II, Bernard writes a treatise, *On Grace and Free Will,* borrowing his title from St. Augustine. He praises "the work accomplished in him [Bernard] by God's grace." He states: "On the one hand, I recognized that grace had placed goodness within my reach; on the other hand, I perceived that it was responsible for my progress; and finally I hoped that it would help me to advance even further." He analyzes chapters 5 to 8 of Paul's Epistle to the Romans, central to the interpretation of Christian salvation experience. He dedicates this work to William of St. Thierry.

1135 Bernard of Portes, a Carthusian friend of Bernard's, urges him to write a commentary on the Song of Songs in the Old Testament. In his treatment of this biblical poem, Bernard describes what is dearest to him in his own spiritual life of intimate relationship with Christ. He comments on the love that is the symbol of God's covenant, first with Israel and later with the Church. And he considers the mission of the Church and the role of the Spirit. He will work on this interpretation for the next eighteen years. At his death his commentary will remain incomplete. Altogether there will be eighty-six sermons, in which Bernard's mysticism is most eloquently and beautifully expressed.

1138 The papal schism ends with the death of Anacletus and by means of Bernard's preaching in Rome, which convinces the contender's followers finally to accept Innocent II as rightful pope. Bernard then hastens to return to Clairvaux and to his own monks. He turns down the offers of five bishoprics to do so.

1139 Bernard's patron, William of St. Thierry, speaks out to condemn the heretical views of the influential "new rationalist," Peter Abelard (1079–1142), a rival to Bernard in both eloquence and fame. Bernard is exhorted to speak with

Abelard, and he meets with him three times. Bernard is steeped in the study of Scripture and the Church Fathers. Abelard represents the new intellectual paradigm, scholasticism, which emphasizes the power of human reason in logic and debate. Bernard is convinced that Abelard uses reason to undermine the faith and its mysteries. At first it seems as if Abelard will withdraw the controversial views he espouses, but in the end he does not. He is then denounced as a heretic by William to the legate of the Holy See.

1140 While passing through Paris, Bernard preaches to student clerics, urging them to abandon their vices and lead holier lives. So persuasive was he that many of them turned to monastic life, following Bernard back to Clairvaux. One of these is Geoffrey of Auxerre, a former disciple of Peter Abelard. He becomes Bernard's secretary, his biographer, and will succeed him as abbot. He will also continue writing the commentary on the Song of Songs after Bernard's death. Bernard gives his Paris sermon the title *On the Conversion of Clerics*. In it he describes how selfishness can come to rule the human heart, whereas true joy may be found by those who decide to live by the Beatitudes found in the Gospels.

1141 Abelard is arraigned for heresy at the Council of Sens. It is Bernard who brings the charges. Abelard is condemned by the bishops on the basis of seventeen heretical propositions in his writings. He is sentenced to silence, effectively ending his career as a teacher. Pope Innocent II confirms the sentence. Bernard writes to the pope that Abelard is "trying to reduce to nothing the merits of the Christian faith, since he seems himself able by human reason to comprehend God altogether." Abelard dies a year later in Cluny, where he has gone to live under the abbot, Peter the Venerable.

1142 The first Cistercian monastery is established in Ireland. Bishop Malachy, having retired from the seat of Armagh, has come to Clairvaux where he is befriended by Bernard. Young Irish monks, bought to France by Malachy and trained at Clairvaux, return to Ireland to make the foundation.

1143 Innocent II dies. Two successors, Celestine II (d. 1144) and Lucius II (d. 1144), rule only briefly.

1144 Bernard of Pisa, abbot of Three Fountains monastery and disciple of Bernard, is elected to the Chair of Peter as Pope Eugenius III.

On Christmas day, the Turks of Seljuk capture Edessa, one of the chief cities established as a Christian principality during the First Crusade. All Christians in Syria are now at risk of attack, as are those in Antioch and Jerusalem, and an appeal goes out for their defense. King Louis VII of France announces that he will lead a new crusade. Pope Eugenius III commissions Bernard to preach the Holy War.

1145 Bernard is asked by Cardinal Alberic, papal legate to France, to travel to Languedoc to try and quell the brush-fires of the Albigensian heresy. Similar to a heresy of the first centuries of Christianity, Manichaeanism, it had resurfaced in the region of Albi and was spreading. Its adherents are also called *cathares* (Greek for "pure ones"). It is based on two principles: the good, which was thought to have created the spiritual world, and evil, creator of everything material. Salvation comes by way of liberating the soul from matter. Christ is believed to have a body only in appearance. Marriage is condemned as evil. A form of sacred suicide is considered the highest act of virtue. Bernard, through preaching and various miracles, restores orthodox Christian teaching for a time. Pope Innocent III will launch a crusade against the Cathars in 1208 that will last for ten years. The Inquisition established by Pope Gregory IX in 1233 is used to vanquish the power of the Albigenses, which had begun to threaten the very existence of the Church in France.

1146 At Vezelay on March 31, the king's herald reads the papal document calling for the start of the Second Crusade, at which King Louis le Jeune and Queen Eleanor of France take up the cross. Bernard preaches, calling followers to renounce sin, turn to God with total generosity, and fight for the faith. His eloquence and fervor call forth an overwhelming response. He writes to the pope the next day: "I have opened my mouth, I have spoken, and immediately the crosses [badges worn as signs of the pledge to serve] are infinitely multiplied. The villages and towns are deserted. You would have difficulty finding a man among seven women. One sees everywhere only widows whose husbands are still living." He then travels across the north of France and Flanders and into the regions of the Rhine in Germany. His fame grows because of the healing miracles he performs wherever he goes. Muslims are attacked in the east by the French and Germans and in the west by the English and Flemish. The Germans fight the pagan Slavs on their coast.

1147 In May, Emperor Conrad III and his nephew, Frederick Barbarossa, take up the cross and set out on crusade. Louis of France follows. Eugenius III comes in person to France to bless and encourage the crusaders.

Bernard hurls himself into controversy with Gilbert de la Porrée, the formidable intellectual bishop of Poitiers who has attracted many eminent followers to himself. Fueled by resentment and jealousy over Bernard's influence with the pope, Gilbert and his disciples call for a debate to be held in Paris and presided over by the pope. For two days the debate goes on regarding the divine persons of the Trinity and their attributes, with Gilbert proposing that the divine persons of the Trinity are only analogous to God, not one Person in God. All of Bernard's passion for the orthodoxy of faith is engaged, and Gilbert is forced to correct his thesis.

1148 The pope, in France for the Council of Rheims, visits Clairvaux and conducts a general chapter, or review, of the order. Eugenius asks Bernard for a treatise on papal spirituality. Bernard writes *Five Books on Consideration.* The work is a manual for the spiritual life of bishops and priests, guiding them to remain centered on God while active in the service of the Church. In his own words: "I should like you to note carefully, Eugenius, since you are the wisest of men that whenever your consideration wanders from these things to lesser and visible things, whether in search of knowledge or something for practical use, or to do your duty in administration or action, you go into exile. You do not do so if your consideration concentrates on these higher things, so that through them it seeks what is above. To consider in this way is to come home" (1.1).

1149 The Second Crusade ends in abject failure. Emperor Conrad's army is destroyed in the mountains of Asia Minor. King Louis' forces are diverted to the East, where they fail in their seige of Damascus. The crusaders themselves are to blame for the ruin of their enterprise by indulging themselves in lawless, rapacious acts along the way fueled by greedy motives. Bernard's enthusiastic preaching of the crusade leads to the blame for failure being cast at his feet. Bernard, once so admired, becomes for a time an object of heavy criticism and abuse. He writes a humble letter of apology to the pope. Bernard accepts his humiliating circumstances, but he does not become depressed, taking the attitude that success and failure, according to God's will, are hard to measure. "How is it," he asks, "that the rashness of mortals dares condemn what they cannot understand?"

Bernard nonetheless starts in to organize a third crusade with the help of Abbot Suger and the approval of Pope Eugenius III. Soon, however, this project is abandoned when Suger dies in 1151.

1150 Bernard writes the *Life of St. Malachy.* The former archbishop of Armagh, Malachy, had died at Clairvaux while traveling in France. Bernard admires Malachy for the monastic reforms he had implemented in Ireland.

1151 Bernard suffers a rupture in his relationship with Peter the Venerable. Peter is a man of insight and goodness who desires to lead his monks in a life more ascetic and rigorous than that currently in vogue at Cluny, but he believes in moving slowly and prudently with the necessary reforms. Bernard's impatience comes to the fore, and he writes a letter to Peter of scatalogical criticism for Cluny's failures, accusing the monks of gorging themselves on sumptuous meals of fish and roasts, wonderful sauces, and many glasses of wine. And how could they, after such feasting, go to the choir to sing the Divine Office of God's praises? Peter lets Bernard's storm of protest pass, and continues to discretely introduce his reforms.

1153 On July 8 news comes from Rome of the death of Pope Eugenius III. Seriously ill himself, Bernard will never again leave his cell in Clairvaux. Lying on a small bed, his body tormented by multiple forms of sickness, his spirit remains free and powerful and active to the end. He continues to dictate his meditations on sacred subjects, prays fervently, and exhorts his brother monks with great zeal. He dies on Thursday, August 20, at about nine in the morning. Drawn by the announcement of the gravity of his illness, princes, lords, prelates, the Cistercian abbots, as well as those of neighboring abbeys, and crowds of ordinary people gather to be present when the end comes to the life of this holy man.

1174 Bernard is canonized a saint by Pope Alexander II on January 18.

1830 St. Bernard of Clairvaux is declared a Doctor of the Church by Pope Pius VIII. Because of his great holiness and mystical teaching, he is called "the last of the Church Fathers."

1953 On the Feast of Pentecost, May 24, Pope Pius XII publishes his encyclical letter *Doctor Mellifluus* (Doctor-flowing-with-honey) on the occasion of the eighth-century anniversary of the death of St. Bernard of Clairvaux. Since the end of the twelfth-century, Bernard had carried the honorific title "Mellifluus," which was given him in appreciation of his skill in explicating Scripture. For this reason, he is known as the patron of beekeepers and candlemakers.

St. Bernard of Clairvaux, seized to the core of his being by the grace of God, wrote that "Jesus is honey in the mouth, melody in the ear, a cry of joy in the heart." His life was wholly dominated by his determination to work out the salvation of his soul. For him, the monastic life embodied the ideal of Christianity. It must be lived as fervently and purely as possible. He despised material luxury in monastic life and once wrote to the monks of Cluny that "Salt with hunger is seasoning enough for a man living soberly and wisely."

In perhaps the most famous of his sermon series, *On the Song of Songs* (Sermon 74:6, 91), Bernard describes the effect of God's presence in his soul:

As soon as He enters in, He awakens my slumbering soul: He stirs and soothes and pierces my heart, for before it was hard as stone, and diseased. So He has begun to pluck it out and destroy, to build up and to plant, to water dry places and illuminate dark ones, to open what was closed and to warm what was cold; to make the crooked straight and the rough places smooth, so that my soul may bless the Lord, and all that is within me may praise His Holy Name.

A NOTE ON THE TEXTS

The literary legacy of Saint Bernard of Clairvaux has come down to us chiefly in the form of sermons, treatises, and letters, and of all three genres he was a master. Steeped as his medieval education and monastic training and thought were in Scripture, it shines forth on these pages in the form of phrases and paraphrases woven into nearly every sentence, or at least every paragraph. So, when reading Bernard, as when reading any Fathers and Doctors of the Church, it is advisable to have a Bible on hand. For the most part, Scripture citations are to the English translation of the Latin Vulgate, the only version of the Bible available to St. Bernard in the eleventh century (although some of Bernard's own versions, put down from memory, also occur).

The texts for this volume have been chosen from both older and more modern translations. For the sources of the modern selections, see the acknowledgments on the copyright page. The treatise *On Loving God* and the Selected Letters are taken from the important Web site Christian Classics Ethereal Library (see Suggestions for Further Reading, p. 419). The editors have done their best to harmonize disparate editorial approaches by imposing American spelling and punctuation. Presentation of the various texts as to design, headings, notes, and so on, are consistent with the rest of the Vintage Spiritual Classics series. If occasional archaisms remain, our intention has been to order these texts for what we hope will be the reader's best interests. The numbering of various "chapters" and subsections of the selections conforms to original sources, but these are by no means consistent for all of Bernard's works, which have been edited and arranged by different hands over the centuries before and after Gutenberg.

THE EDITORS

PART I

On Loving God

Dedication

To the illustrious Lord Haimeric, Cardinal Deacon of the Roman Church, and Chancellor: Bernard, called Abbot of Clairvaux, wishes long life in the Lord and death in the Lord.

Hitherto you have been wont to seek prayers from me, not the solving of problems; although I count myself sufficient for neither. My profession shows that, if not my conversation; and to speak truth, I lack the diligence and the ability that are most essential. Yet I am glad that you turn again for spiritual counsel, instead of busying yourself about carnal matters: I only wish you had gone to someone better equipped than I am. Still, learned and simple give the same excuse and one can hardly tell whether it comes from modesty or from ignorance, unless obedience to the task assigned shall reveal. So, take from my poverty what I can give you, lest I should seem to play the philosopher, by reason of my silence. Only, I do not promise to answer other questions you may raise. This one, as to loving God, I will deal with as He shall teach me; for it is sweetest, it can be handled most safely, and it will be most profitable. Keep the others for wiser men.

Chapter 1

WHY WE SHOULD LOVE GOD
AND THE MEASURE OF THAT LOVE

You want me to tell you why God is to be loved and how much. I answer, the reason for loving God is God Himself; and the measure of love due to Him is immeasurable love. Is this plain? Doubtless, to a thoughtful man; but I am debtor to the unwise also. A word to the wise is sufficient; but

I must consider simple folk too. Therefore I set myself joyfully to explain more in detail what is meant above.

We are to love God for Himself, because of a twofold reason; nothing is more reasonable, nothing more profitable. When one asks, Why should I love God?, he may mean, What is lovely in God? or What shall I gain by loving God? In either case, the same sufficient cause of love exists, namely, God Himself.

And first, of His title to our love. Could any title be greater than this, that He gave Himself for us unworthy wretches? And being God, what better gift could He offer than Himself? Hence, if one seeks for God's claim upon our love here is the chiefest: Because He first loved us.[21]

Ought He not to be loved in return, when we think who loved, whom He loved, and how much He loved? For who is He that loved? The same of whom every spirit testifies: "You are my God: my goods are nothing unto You."[22] And is not His love that wonderful charity which "seeks not her own"?[23] But for whom was such unutterable love made manifest? The apostle tells us: "When we were enemies, we were reconciled to God by the death of His Son."[24] So it was God who loved us, loved us freely, and loved us while yet we were enemies. And how great was this love of His? St. John answers: "God so loved the world that He gave His only-begotten Son, that whosoever believes in Him should not perish, but have everlasting life."[25] St. Paul adds: "He

[21] 1 Jn 4:19.
[22] Ps 16:2, Vulgate.
[23] 1 Cor 13:5.
[24] Rom 5:10.
[25] Jn 3:16.

spared not His own Son, but delivered Him up for us all";
and the Son says of Himself, "Greater love has no man than
this, that a man lay down his life for his friends."[26]

This is the claim which God the holy, the supreme, the
omnipotent, has upon men, defiled and base and weak.
Someone may urge that this is true of mankind, but not of
angels. True, since for angels it was not needful. He who
succored men in their time of need, preserved angels from
such need; and even as His love for sinful men wrought
wondrously in them so that they should not remain sinful,
so that same love which in equal measure He poured out
upon angels kept them altogether free from sin.

Chapter II

ON LOVING GOD. HOW MUCH GOD DESERVES LOVE FROM MAN IN RECOGNITION OF HIS GIFTS, BOTH MATERIAL AND SPIRITUAL, AND HOW THESE GIFTS SHOULD BE CHERISHED WITHOUT NEGLECT OF THE GIVER

Those who admit the truth of what I have said know, I am
sure, why we are bound to love God. But if unbelievers will
not grant it, their ingratitude is at once confounded by His
innumerable benefits, lavished on our race, and plainly
discerned by the senses. Who is it that gives food to all flesh,
light to every eye, air to all that breathe? It would be foolish
to begin a catalog, since I have just called them innumerable: but I name, as notable instances, food, sunlight, and air;
not because they are God's best gifts, but because they are

---

[26]Rom 8:32; Jn 15:13.

essential to bodily life. Man must seek in his own higher nature for the highest gifts; and these are dignity, wisdom, and virtue. By dignity I mean free will, whereby he not only excels all other earthly creatures, but has dominion over them. Wisdom is the power whereby he recognizes this dignity, and perceives also that it is no accomplishment of his own. And virtue impels man to seek eagerly for Him who is man's Source, and to lay fast hold on Him when He has been found.

Now, these three best gifts have each a twofold character. Dignity appears not only as the prerogative of human nature, but also as the cause of that fear and dread of man which is upon every beast of the earth. Wisdom perceives this distinction, but owns that though in us, it is, like all good qualities, not of us. And last, virtue moves us to search eagerly for an Author, and, when we have found Him, teaches us to cling to Him yet more eagerly. Consider too that dignity without wisdom is worth nothing; and wisdom is harmful without virtue, as this argument following shows: There is no glory in having a gift without knowing it. But to know only that you have it, without knowing that it is not of yourself that you have it, means self-glorying, but no true glory in God. And so the apostle says to men in such cases, "What have you that you did not receive? Now, if you did receive it, why do you glory as if you had not received it?"[27] He asks, Why do you glory? but goes on, as if you had not received it, showing that the guilt is not in glorying over a possession, but in glorying as though it had not been received. And rightly such glorying is called vainglory, since it has not the solid foundation of truth. The apostle shows how to discern the true glory from the false, when he says,

[27] 1 Cor 4:7.

"He that glories, let him glory in the Lord, that is, in the Truth, since our Lord is Truth."[28]

We must know, then, what we are, and that it is not of ourselves that we are what we are. Unless we know this thoroughly, either we shall not glory at all, or our glorying will be vain. Finally, it is written, "If you know not, go your way forth by the footsteps of the flock."[29] And this is right. For man, being in honor, if he know not his own honor, may fitly be compared, because of such ignorance, to the beasts that perish. Not knowing himself as the creature that is distinguished from the irrational brutes by the possession of reason, he commences to be confounded with them because, ignorant of his own true glory which is within, he is led captive by his curiosity, and concerns himself with external, sensual things. So he is made to resemble the lower orders by not knowing that he has been more highly endowed than they.

We must be on our guard against this ignorance. We must not rank ourselves too low; and with still greater care we must see that we do not think of ourselves more highly than we ought to think, as happens when we foolishly impute to ourselves whatever good may be in us. But far more than either of these kinds of ignorance, we must hate and shun that presumption which would lead us to glory in goods not our own, knowing that they are not of ourselves but of God, and yet not fearing to rob God of the honor due unto Him. For mere ignorance, as in the first instance, does not glory at all; and mere wisdom, as in the second, while it has a kind of glory, yet does not glory in the Lord. In the third evil case, however, man sins not in ignorance but deliberately,

[28] 1 Cor 1:31; Jn 14:6.
[29] Sg 1:8.

usurping the glory which belongs to God. And this arrogance is a more grievous and deadly fault than the ignorance of the second, since it contemns God, while the other knows Him not. Ignorance is brutal, arrogance is devilish. Pride only, the chief of all iniquities, can make us treat gifts as if they were rightful attributes of our nature, and, while receiving benefits, rob our Benefactor of His due glory.

Wherefore to dignity and wisdom we must add virtue, the proper fruit of them both. Virtue seeks and finds Him who is the Author and Giver of all good, and who must be in all things glorified; otherwise, one who knows what is right yet fails to perform it will be beaten with many stripes.[30] Why? you may ask. Because he has failed to put his knowledge to good effect, but rather has imagined mischief upon his bed;[31] like a wicked servant, he has turned aside to seize the glory which, his own knowledge assured him, belonged only to his good Lord and Master. It is plain, therefore, that dignity without wisdom is useless and that wisdom without virtue is accursed. But when one possesses virtue, then wisdom and dignity are not dangerous but blessed. Such a man calls on God and lauds Him, confessing from a full heart, "Not unto us, O Lord, not unto us, but unto Your name give glory."[32] Which is to say, "O Lord, we claim no knowledge, no distinction for ourselves; all is Yours, since from You all things do come."

But we have digressed too far in the wish to prove that even those who know not Christ are sufficiently admonished by the natural law, and by their own endowments of soul and body, to love God for God's own sake. To sum up:

[30]Lk 12:47.
[31]Ps 36:4.
[32]Ps 115:1.

what infidel does not know that he has received light, air, food—all things necessary for his own body's life—from Him alone who gives food to all flesh, who makes His sun to rise on the evil and on the good, and sends rain on the just and on the unjust.[33] Who is so impious as to attribute the peculiar eminence of humanity to any other except to Him who says, in Genesis, "Let us make man in Our image, after Our likeness"?[34] Who else could be the Bestower of wisdom, but He that teaches man knowledge?[35] Who else could bestow virtue except the Lord of virtue? Therefore even the infidel who knows not Christ but does at least know himself, is bound to love God for God's own sake. He is unpardonable if he does not love the Lord his God with all his heart, and with all his soul, and with all his mind; for his own innate justice and common sense cry out from within that he is bound wholly to love God, from whom he has received all things. But it is hard, nay rather, impossible, for a man by his own strength or in the power of free will to render all things to God from whom they came, without rather turning them aside, each to his own account, even as it is written, "For all seek their own"; and again, "The imagination of man's heart is evil from his youth."[36]

---

[33] Ps 136:5; Mt 5:45.
[34] Gn 1:26.
[35] Ps 94:10.
[36] Phil 2:21; Gn 8:21.

Chapter III

WHAT GREATER INCENTIVES CHRISTIANS HAVE, MORE THAN THE HEATHEN, TO LOVE GOD

The faithful know how much need they have of Jesus and Him crucified; but though they wonder and rejoice at the ineffable love made manifest in Him, they are not daunted at having no more than their own poor souls to give in return for such great and condescending charity. They love all the more, because they know themselves to be loved so exceedingly; but to whom little is given the same loves little.[37] Neither Jew nor pagan feels the pangs of love as doth the Church, which says, "Stay me with flagons, comfort me with apples; for I am sick of love."[38] She beholds King Solomon, with the crown wherewith his mother crowned him in the day of his espousals; she sees the Sole-begotten of the Father bearing the heavy burden of His Cross; she sees the Lord of all power and might bruised and spat upon, the Author of life and glory transfixed with nails, smitten by the lance, overwhelmed with mockery, and at last laying down His precious life for His friends. Contemplating this, the sword of love pierces through her own soul also and she cries aloud, "Stay me with flagons, comfort me with apples; for I am sick of love." The fruits, which the Spouse gathers from the Tree of Life in the midst of the garden of her Beloved, are pomegranates,[39] borrowing their taste from the Bread of heaven, and their color from the Blood of Christ. She sees death dying and its author overthrown: she beholds captivity led captive from hell to earth, from earth to heaven, so "that at

[37]Lk 7:47.   [39]Sg 4:13.
[38]Sg 2:5.

the name of Jesus every knee should bow, of things in heaven and things in earth and things under the earth."[40] The earth under the ancient curse brought forth thorns and thistles; but now the Church beholds it laughing with flowers and restored by the grace of a new benediction. Mindful of the verse, "My heart dances for joy, and in my song will I praise Him," she refreshes herself with the fruits of His Passion which she gathers from the Tree of the Cross, and with the flowers of His Resurrection whose fragrance invites the frequent visits of her Spouse.

Then it is that He exclaims, "Behold you are fair, My beloved, yes pleasant: also our bed is green."[41] She shows her desire for His coming and whence she hopes to obtain it; not because of her own merits but because of the flowers of that field which God has blessed. Christ who willed to be conceived and brought up in Nazareth, that is, the town of branches, delights in such blossoms. Pleased by such heavenly fragrance the Bridegroom rejoices to revisit the heart's chamber when He finds it adorned with fruits and decked with flowers—that is, meditating on the mystery of His Passion or on the glory of His Resurrection.

The tokens of the Passion we recognize as the fruitage of the ages of the past, appearing in the fullness of time during the reign of sin and death.[42] But it is the glory of the Resurrection, in the new springtime of regenerating grace, that the fresh flowers of the later age come forth, whose fruit shall be given without measure at the general resurrection, when time shall be no more. And so it is written, "The winter is past, the rain is over and gone, the flowers appear on the earth"; signifying that summer has come back with

[40]Phil 2:10.
[41]Sg 1:16.

[42]Gal 4:4.

Him who dissolves icy death into the spring of a new life and says, "Behold, I make all things new."[43] His Body sown in the grave has blossomed in the Resurrection;[44] and in like manner our valleys and fields which were barren or frozen, as if dead, glow with reviving life and warmth.

The Father of Christ who makes all things new, is well pleased with the freshness of those flowers and fruits, and the beauty of the field which breathes forth such heavenly fragrance; and He says in benediction "See, the smell of My Son is as the smell of a field which the Lord has blessed"; blessed to overflowing, indeed, since of His fullness have all we received.[45] But the Bride may come when she pleases and gather flowers and fruits therewith to adorn the inmost recesses of her conscience; that the Bridegroom when He comes may find the chamber of her heart redolent with perfume.

So it behooves us, if we would have Christ for a frequent guest, to fill our hearts with faithful meditations on the mercy He showed in dying for us, and on His mighty power in rising again from the dead. To this David testified when he sang, "God spoke once, and twice I have also heard the same; that power belongs unto God; and that You, Lord, are merciful."[46] And surely there is proof enough and to spare in that Christ died for our sins and rose again for our justification, and ascended into heaven that He might protect us from on high, and sent the Holy Spirit for our comfort. Hereafter He will come again for the consummation of our

[43]Sg 2:11ff.; Rv 21:5.
[44]1 Cor 15:42.
[45]Gn 27:27; Jn 1:16.
[46]Ps 62:11ff.

bliss. In His Death He displayed His mercy, in His Resurrection His power; both combine to manifest His glory.

The Bride desires to be stayed with flagons and comforted with apples, because she knows how easily the warmth of love can languish and grow cold; but such helps are only until she has entered into the bride chamber. There she will receive His long-desired caresses even as she sighs, "His left hand is under my head and His right hand embraces me."[47] Then she will perceive how far the embrace of the right hand excels all sweetness, and that the left hand with which He at first caressed her cannot be compared to it. She will understand what she has heard: "It is the spirit that quickens; the flesh profits nothing."[48] She will prove what she has read: "My memorial is sweeter than honey, and mine inheritance than the honeycomb."[49] What is written elsewhere, "The memorial of Your abundant kindness shall be showed," refers doubtless to those of whom the psalmist had said just before: "One generation shall praise Your works unto another and declare Your power."[50] Among us on the earth there is His memory; but in the Kingdom of heaven His very Presence. That Presence is the joy of those who have already attained to beatitude; the memory is the comfort of us who are still wayfarers, journeying toward the Fatherland.

[47] Sg 2:6.
[48] Jn 6:63.
[49] Eccl 24:20.
[50] Ps 145:7, 4.

Chapter IV

OF THOSE WHO FIND COMFORT IN THE REC-OLLECTION OF GOD, OR ARE FITTEST FOR HIS LOVE

But it will be well to note what class of people takes comfort in the thought of God. Surely not that perverse and crooked generation to whom it was said, "Woe unto you that are rich; for you have received your consolation."[51] Rather, those who can say with truth, "My soul refuses comfort."[52] For it is meet that those who are not satisfied by the present should be sustained by the thought of the future, and that the contemplation of eternal happiness should solace those who scorn to drink from the river of transitory joys. That is the generation of them that seek the Lord, even of them that seek, not their own, but the face of the God of Jacob. To them that long for the presence of the living God, the thought of Him is sweetness itself: but there is no satiety, rather an ever-increasing appetite, even as the Scripture bears witness, "they that eat me shall yet be hungry";[53] and if the one so hungered spoke, "When I wake up after Your likeness, I shall be satisfied with it." Yes, blessed even now are they which do hunger and thirst after righteousness, for they, and they only, shall be filled. Woe to you, wicked and perverse generation; woe to you, foolish and abandoned people, who hate Christ's memory, and dread His second Advent! Well may you fear, who will not now seek deliverance from the snare of the hunter; because "they that will be rich fall into temptation and a snare, and into many foolish

[51] Lk 6:24.
[52] Ps 77:2.
[53] Eccl 24:21.

and hurtful lusts."[54] In that day we shall not escape the dreadful sentence of condemnation, "Depart from Me, you cursed, into everlasting fire."[55] O dreadful sentence indeed, O hard saying! How much harder to bear than that other saying which we repeat daily in church, in memory of the Passion: "Whoso eats My flesh and drinks My blood has eternal life."[56] That signifies, whoso honors My death and after My example mortifies his members which are upon the earth shall have eternal life, even as the apostle says, "If we suffer, we shall also reign with Him."[57] And yet many even today recoil from these words and go away, saying by their action if not with their lips, "This is a hard saying; who can hear it?"[58] "A generation that set not their heart aright, and whose spirit cleaves not steadfastly unto God,"[59] but chooses rather to trust in uncertain riches, it is disturbed at the very name of the Cross, and counts the memory of the Passion intolerable. How can such sustain the burden of that fearful sentence, "Depart from Me, you cursed, into everlasting fire, prepared for the devil and his angels"? "On whomsoever that stone shall fall it will grind him to powder"; but "the generation of the faithful shall be blessed," since, like the apostle, they labor that whether present or absent they may be accepted of the Lord.[60] At the last day they too shall hear the Judge pronounce their award, "Come, you blessed of My Father, inherit the kingdom prepared for you from the foundation of the world."[61]

[54] 1 Tm 6:9.
[55] Mt 25:41.
[56] Jn 6:54.
[57] Col 3:5; 1 Tm 2:12.
[58] Jn 6:60.
[59] Ps 78:8.
[60] Lk 20:18; Ps 112:2; 1 Cor 5:9.
[61] Mt 25:34.

On that day those who set not their hearts aright will feel, too late, how easy is Christ's yoke, to which they would not bend their necks and how light His burden, in comparison with the pains they must then endure. O wretched slaves of Mammon, you cannot glory in the Cross of our Lord Jesus Christ while you trust in treasures laid up on earth: you cannot taste and see how gracious the Lord is, while you are hungering for gold. If you have not rejoiced at the thought of His coming, that day will be indeed a day of wrath to you.

But the believing soul longs and faints for God; she rests sweetly in the contemplation of Him. She glories in the reproach of the Cross, until the glory of His face shall be revealed. Like the Bride, the dove of Christ, that is covered with silver wings,[62] white with innocence and purity, she reposes in the thought of Your abundant kindness, Lord Jesus; and above all she longs for that day when in the joyful splendor of Your saints, gleaming with the radiance of the Beatific Vision, her feathers shall be like gold, resplendent with the joy of Your countenance.

Rightly then may she exult, "His left hand is under my head and His right hand embraces me." The left hand signifies the memory of that matchless love, which moved Him to lay down His life for His friends; and the right hand is the Beatific Vision which He has promised to His own, and the delight they have in His presence. The psalmist sings rapturously, "At Your right hand there is pleasure for evermore":[63] so we are warranted in explaining the right hand as that divine and deifying joy of His presence.

Rightly too is that wondrous and ever-memorable love symbolized as His left hand, upon which the Bride rests her

[62]Ps 68:13.
[63]Ps 16:11.

head until iniquity be done away: for He sustains the purpose of her mind, lest it should be turned aside to earthly, carnal desires. For the flesh wars against the spirit: "The corruptible body presses down the soul, and the earthly tabernacle weighs down the mind that muses upon many things."[64] What could result from the contemplation of compassion so marvelous and so undeserved, favor so free and so well attested, kindness so unexpected, clemency so unconquerable, grace so amazing except that the soul should withdraw from all sinful affections, reject all that is inconsistent with God's love, and yield herself wholly to heavenly things? No wonder is it that the Bride, moved by the perfume of these unctions, runs swiftly, all on fire with love, yet reckons herself as loving all too little in return for the Bridegroom's love. And rightly, since it is no great matter that a little dust should be all consumed with love of that Majesty which loved her first and which revealed itself as wholly bent on saving her. For "God so loved the world that He gave His only-begotten Son, that whosoever believes in Him should not perish but have everlasting life."[65] This sets forth the Father's love. But "He has poured out His soul unto death," was written of the Son.[66] And of the Holy Spirit it is said, "The Comforter which is the Holy Ghost whom the Father will send in My name, He shall teach you all things, and bring all things to your remembrance, whatsoever I have said unto you."[67] It is plain, therefore, that God loves us, and loves us with all His heart; for the Holy Trinity altogether loves us, if we may venture so to speak of the infinite and incomprehensible Godhead who is essentially one.

[64] Ws 9:15.
[65] Jn 3:16.
[66] Is 53:12.
[67] Jn 14:26.

Chapter V
OF THE CHRISTIAN'S DEBT OF LOVE, HOW GREAT IT IS

From the contemplation of what has been said, we see plainly that God is to be loved, and that He has a just claim upon our love. But the infidel does not acknowledge the Son of God, and so he can know neither the Father nor the Holy Spirit; for he that honors not the Son, honors not the Father which sent Him, nor the Spirit whom He has sent.[68] He knows less of God than we; no wonder that he loves God less. This much he understands at least—that he owes all he is to his Creator. But how will it be with me? For I know that my God is not merely the bounteous Bestower of my life, the generous Provider for all my needs, the pitying Consoler of all my sorrows, the wise Guide of my course: but that He is far more than all that. He saves me with an abundant deliverance: He is my eternal Preserver, the portion of my inheritance, my glory. Even so it is written, "With Him is plenteous redemption"; and again, "He entered in once into the holy place, having obtained eternal redemption for us."[69] Of His salvation it is written, "He forsakes not His that be godly; but they are preserved forever"; and of His bounty, "Good measure, pressed down and shaken together, and running over, shall men give into your bosom"; and in another place, "Eye has not seen nor ear heard, neither have entered into the heart of man, those things which God has prepared for them that love Him."[70] He will glorify us, even as the apostle bears witness, saying, "We look for the Savior,

[68] Jn 5:23.
[69] Ps 130:7; Heb 9:12.
[70] Ps 37:28; Lk 6:38; 1 Cor 2:9.

the Lord Jesus Christ, who shall change our vile body that it may be fashioned like unto His glorious body"; and again, "I reckon that the sufferings of this present time are not worthy to be compared with the glory which shall be revealed in us"; and once more, "Our light affliction, which is but for a moment, works for us a far more exceeding and eternal weight of glory; while we look not at the things which are seen, but at the things which are not seen."[71]

"What shall I render unto the Lord for all His benefits toward me?"[72] Reason and natural justice alike move me to give up myself wholly to loving Him to whom I owe all that I have and am. But faith shows me that I should love Him far more than I love myself, as I come to realize that He has given me not my own life only, but even Himself. Yet, before the time of full revelation had come, before the Word was made flesh, died on the Cross, came forth from the grave, and returned to His Father; before God had shown us how much He loved us by all this plenitude of grace, the commandment had been uttered, "You shall love the Lord Your God with all Your heart, and with all Your soul and with all Your might,"[73] that is, with all Your being, all Your knowledge, all Your powers. And it was not unjust for God to claim this from His own work and gifts. Why should not the creature love his Creator, who gave him the power to love? Why should he not love Him with all his being, since it is by His gift alone that he can do anything that is good? It was God's creative grace that out of nothingness raised us to the dignity of manhood; and from this appears our duty to love Him, and the justice of His claim to that love. But how

[71]Phil 3:20ff.; Rom 8:18; 1 Cor 4:17ff.
[72]Ps 116:12.
[73]Dt 6:5.

infinitely is the benefit increased when we bethink ourselves of His fulfillment of the promise, "you, Lord, shall save both man and beast: how excellent is your mercy, O Lord!"[74] For we, who "turned our glory into the similitude of a calf that eats hay,"[75] by our evil deeds debased ourselves so that we might be compared unto the beasts that perish. I owe all that I am to Him who made me: but how can I pay my debt to Him who redeemed me, and in such wondrous wise? Creation was not so vast a work as redemption; for it is written of man and of all things that were made, "He spoke the word, and they were made."[76] But to redeem that creation which sprang into being at His word, how much He spoke, what wonders He wrought, what hardships He endured, what shames He suffered! Therefore what reward shall I give unto the Lord for all the benefits which He has done unto me? In the first creation He gave me myself; but in His new creation He gave me Himself, and by that gift restored to me the self that I had lost. Created first and then restored, I owe Him myself twice over in return for myself. But what have I to offer Him for the gift of Himself? Could I multiply myself a thousandfold and then give Him all, what would that be in comparison with God?

[74]Ps 36:6ff.
[75]Ps 106:20.
[76]Ps 148:5.

Chapter VI

A BRIEF SUMMARY

Admit that God deserves to be loved very much, yea, bound-lessly, because He loved us first, He infinite and we nothing, loved us, miserable sinners, with a love so great and so free. This is why I said at the beginning that the measure of our love to God is to love immeasurably. For since our love is toward God, who is infinite and immeasurable, how can we bound or limit the love we owe Him? Besides, our love is not a gift but a debt. And since it is the Godhead who loves us, Himself boundless, eternal, supreme love, of whose greatness there is no end, yes, and His wisdom is infinite, whose peace passes all understand-ing; since it is He who loves us, I say, can we think of repaying Him grudgingly? "I will love You, O Lord, my strength. The Lord is my rock and my fortress and my deliverer, my God, my strength, in whom I will trust."[77] He is all that I need, all that I long for. My God and my help, I will love You for Your great goodness; not so much as I might, surely, but as much as I can. I cannot love You as You deserve to be loved, for I cannot love You more than my own feebleness permits. I will love You more when You deem me worthy to receive greater capacity for loving; yet never so perfectly as You have deserved of me. "Your eyes did see my substance, yet being imperfect; and in Your book all my members were written."[78] Yet You record in that book all who do what they can, even though they cannot do what they ought. Surely I have said enough to show how God should be loved and why. But who has felt, who can know, who express, how much we should love Him.

[77]Ps 18:1ff.
[78]Ps 139:16.

Chapter VII

OF LOVE TOWARD GOD NOT WITHOUT REWARD, AND HOW THE HUNGER OF MAN'S HEART CANNOT BE SATISFIED WITH EARTHLY THINGS

And now let us consider what profit we shall have from loving God. Even though our knowledge of this is imperfect, still that is better than to ignore it altogether. I have already said (when it was a question of wherefore and in what manner God should be loved) that there was a double reason constraining us: His right and our advantage. Having written as best I can, though unworthily, of God's right to be loved, I have still to treat of the recompense which that love brings. For although God would be loved without respect of reward, yet He wills not to leave love unrewarded. True charity cannot be left destitute, even though she is unselfish and seeks not her own.[79] Love is an affection of the soul, not a contract: it cannot rise from a mere agreement, nor is it so to be gained. It is spontaneous in its origin and impulse; and true love is its own satisfaction. It has its reward; but that reward is the object beloved. For whatever you seem to love, if it is on account of something else, what you do really love is that something else, not the apparent object of desire. St. Paul did not preach the Gospel that he might earn his bread; he ate that he might be strengthened for his ministry. What he loved was not bread, but the Gospel. True love does not demand a reward, but it deserves one. Surely no one offers to pay for love; yet some recompense is due to one who loves, and if his love endures he will doubtless receive it.

[79] 1 Cor 13:5.

On a lower plane of action, it is the reluctant, not the eager, whom we urge by promises of reward. Who would think of paying a man to do what he was yearning to do already? For instance, no one would hire a hungry man to eat, or a thirsty man to drink, or a mother to nurse her own child. Who would think of bribing a farmer to dress his own vineyard, or to dig about his orchard, or to rebuild his house? So, all the more, one who loves God truly asks no other recompense than God Himself; for if he should demand anything else it would be the prize that he loved and not God.

It is natural for a man to desire what he reckons better than that which he has already, and be satisfied with nothing which lacks that special quality which he misses. Thus, if it is for her beauty that he loves his wife, he will cast longing eyes after a fairer woman. If he is clad in a rich garment, he will covet a costlier one; and no matter how rich he may be, he will envy a man richer than himself. Do we not see people every day, endowed with vast estates, who keep on joining field to field, dreaming of wider boundaries for their lands? Those who dwell in palaces are ever adding house to house, continually building up and tearing down, remodeling and changing. Men in high places are driven by insatiable ambition to clutch at still greater prizes. And nowhere is there any final satisfaction, because nothing there can be defined as absolutely the best or highest. But it is natural that nothing should content a man's desires but the very best, as he reckons it. Is it not, then, mad folly always to be craving for things which can never quiet our longings, much less satisfy them? No matter how many such things one has, he is always lusting after what he has not; never at peace, he sighs for new possessions. Discontented, he spends himself in fruitless toil, and finds only weariness in the evanescent and unreal pleasures of the world. In his greediness, he counts all that he has clutched as nothing in comparison with what is beyond his grasp, and loses all pleasure in his actual possessions by longing after what he has not, yet covets. No man can ever hope to own all things. Even the little one does possess is got only with toil and is held in fear; since each is certain to lose what he has when God's day, appointed though unrevealed, shall come. But the perverted will struggles toward the ultimate good by devious ways, yearning after satisfaction, yet led astray by vanity and deceived by wickedness. Ah, if you wish to attain to the consummation of all desire, so that nothing unfulfilled will be left, why weary yourself with fruitless efforts, running hither and thither, only to die long before the goal is reached?

It is so that these impious ones wander in a circle, longing after something to gratify their yearnings, yet madly rejecting that which alone can bring them to their desired end, not by exhaustion but by attainment. They wear themselves out in vain travail, without reaching their blessed consummation, because they delight in creatures, not in the Creator. They want to traverse creation, trying all things one by one, rather than think of coming to Him who is Lord of all. And if their utmost longing were realized, so that they should have all the world for their own, yet without possessing Him who is the Author of all being, then the same law of their desires would make them contemn what they had and restlessly seek Him whom they still lacked, that is, God Himself. Rest is in Him alone. Man knows no peace in the world; but he has no disturbance when he is with God. And so the soul says with confidence, "Whom have I in heaven but You; and there is none upon earth that I desire in comparison of You. God is the strength of my heart, and my portion forever. It is good for me to hold me fast by God, to put my trust in the Lord God."[80] Even by this way one would eventually come to God, if only he might have time to test all lesser goods in turn.

But life is too short, strength too feeble, and competitors too many, for that course to be practicable. One could never reach the end, though he were to weary himself with the long effort and fruitless toil of testing everything that might seem desirable. It would be far easier and better to make the assay in imagination rather than in experiment. For the mind is swifter in operation and keener in discrimination than the bodily senses, to this very purpose that it may go before the sensuous affections so that they may cleave to nothing which the mind has found worthless. And so it is written, "Prove all things: hold fast that which is good."[81] Which is to say that right judgment should prepare the way for the heart. Otherwise we may not ascend into the hill of the Lord nor rise up in His holy place.[82] We should have no profit in possessing a rational mind if we were to follow the impulse of the senses, like brute beasts, with no regard at all to reason. Those whom reason does not guide in their course may indeed run, but not in the appointed racetrack, neglecting the apostolic counsel, "So run that ye may obtain." For how could they obtain the prize who put that last of all in their endeavor and run around after everything else first?

But as for the righteous man, it is not so with him. He remembers the condemnation pronounced on the multitude who wander after vanity, who travel the broad way that leads to death; and he chooses the King's highway, turning aside neither to the right hand nor to the left, even as the prophet says, "The way of the just is uprightness."[83]

[80]Ps 73:25ff.
[81]1 Thes 5:21.

[82]Ps 24:3.
[83]Mt 7:13; Num 20:17; Is 26:7.

Warned by wholesome counsel he shuns the perilous road, and heeds the direction that shortens the search, forbidding covetousness and commanding that he sell all that he has and give to the poor.[84] Blessed, truly, are the poor, for theirs is the Kingdom of Heaven.[85] They which run in a race, run all, but distinction is made among the racers. "The Lord knows the way of the righteous: and the way of the ungodly shall perish."[86] "A small thing that the righteous has is better than great riches of the ungodly."[87] Even as the preacher says, and the fool discovers, "He that loves silver shall not be satisfied with silver."[88] But Christ says, "Blessed are they which do hunger and thirst after righteousness, for they shall be filled."[89] Righteousness is the natural and essential food of the soul, which can no more be satisfied by earthly treasures than the hunger of the body can be satisfied by air. If you should see a starving man standing with mouth open to the wind, inhaling draughts of air as if in hope of gratifying his hunger, you would think him lunatic. But it is no less foolish to imagine that the soul can be satisfied with worldly things which only inflate it without feeding it. What have spiritual gifts to do with carnal appetites, or carnal with spiritual? Praise the Lord, O my soul: who satisfies your mouth with good things.[90] He bestows bounty immeasurable; He provokes you to good, He preserves you in goodness; He prevents, He sustains, He fills you. He moves you to longing, and it is He for whom you longest.

[84]Mt 19:21.
[85]Mt 5:3.
[86]Ps 1:6.
[87]Ps 37:16.

[88]Eccl 5:10.
[89]Mt 5:6.
[90]Ps 103:1ff.

I have said already that the motive for loving God is God Himself. And I spoke truly, for He is as well the efficient cause as the final object of our love. He gives the occasion for love, He creates the affection, He brings the desire to good effect. He is such that love to Him is a natural due; and so hope in Him is natural, since our present love would be vain did we not hope to love Him perfectly someday. Our love is prepared and rewarded by His. He loves us first, out of His great tenderness; then we are bound to repay Him with love; and we are permitted to cherish exultant hopes in Him. "He is rich unto all that call upon Him,"[91] yet He has no gift for them better than Himself. He gives Himself as prize and reward: He is the refreshment of holy soul, the ransom of those in captivity. "The Lord is good unto them that wait for Him."[92] What will He be then to those who gain His presence? But here is a paradox, that no one can seek the Lord who has not already found Him. It is your will, O God, to be found that You may be sought, to be sought that You may the more truly be found. But though You can be sought and found, You cannot be forestalled. For if we say, "Early shall my prayer come before You,"[93] yet doubtless all prayer would be lukewarm unless it was animated by Your inspiration.

We have spoken of the consummation of love toward God: now to consider whence such love begins.

[91]Rom 10:12.
[92]Lam 3:25.
[93]Ps 88:13.

Chapter VIII

OF THE FIRST DEGREE OF LOVE, WHEREIN MAN LOVES GOD FOR SELF'S SAKE

Love is one of the four natural affections, which it is needless to name since everyone knows them. And because love is natural, it is only right to love the Author of nature first of all. Hence comes the first and great commandment, "You shall love the Lord your God." But nature is so frail and weak that necessity compels her to love herself first; and this is carnal love, wherewith man loves himself first and selfishly, as it is written, "That was not first which is spiritual but that which is natural; and afterward that which is spiritual."[94] This is not as the precept ordains but as nature directs: "No man ever yet hated his own flesh."[95] But if, as is likely, this same love should grow excessive and, refusing to be contained within the restraining banks of necessity, should overflow into the fields of voluptuousness, then a command checks the flood, as if by a dike: "You shall love your neighbor as yourself." And this is right: for he who shares our nature should share our love, itself the fruit of nature. Wherefore if a man finds it a burden, I will not say only to relieve his brother's needs, but to minister to his brother's pleasures, let him mortify those same affections in himself, lest he become a transgressor. He may cherish himself as tenderly as he chooses, if only he remembers to show the same indulgence to his neighbor. This is the curb of temperance imposed on you, O man, by the law of life and conscience, lest you should follow your own lusts to destruction, or become enslaved by those passions which are

[94] 1 Cor 15:46.
[95] Eph 5:29.

the enemies of your true welfare. Far better divide your enjoyments with your neighbor than with these enemies. And if, after the counsel of the son of Sirach, you go not after your desires but refrain yourself from your appetites; if according to the apostolic precept having food and raiment you are therewith content, then you will find it easy to abstain from fleshly lusts which war against the soul, and to divide with your neighbors what you have refused to your own desires.[96] That is a temperate and righteous love which practices self-denial in order to minister to a brother's necessity. So our selfish love grows truly social, when it includes our neighbors in its circle.

But if you are reduced to want by such benevolence, what then? What indeed, except to pray with all confidence unto Him who gives to all men liberally and upbraids not, who opens His hand and fills all things living with plenteousness.[97] For doubtless He that gives to most men more than they need will not fail you as to the necessaries of life, even as He has promised: "Seek the Kingdom of God, and all those things shall be added unto you."[98] God freely promises all things needful to those who deny themselves for love of their neighbors; and to bear the yoke of modesty and sobriety, rather than to let sin reign in our mortal body,[99] that is indeed to seek the Kingdom of God and to implore His aid against the tyranny of sin. It is surely justice to share our natural gifts with those who share our nature.

But if we are to love our neighbors as we ought, we must have regard to God also: for it is only in God that we can pay that debt of love aright. Now a man cannot love his neighbor in God, except he love God Himself; wherefore

[96]Eccl 18:30; 1 Tm 6:8.   [98]Lk 12:31.
[97]Jas 1:5; Ps 145:16.   [99]Rom 6:12.

we must love God first, in order to love our neighbors in Him. This too, like all good things, is the Lord's doing, that we should love Him, for He has endowed us with the possibility of love. He who created nature sustains it; nature is so constituted that its Maker is its protector forever. Without Him nature could not have begun to be; without Him it could not subsist at all. That we might not be ignorant of this, or vainly attribute to ourselves the beneficence of our Creator, God has determined in the depths of His wise counsel that we should be subject to tribulations. So when man's strength fails and God comes to his aid, it is meet and right that man, rescued by God's hand, should glorify Him, as it is written, "Call upon Me in the time of trouble; so will I hear you, and you shall praise Me."[100] In such wise man, animal and carnal by nature, and loving only himself, begins to love God by reason of that very self-love; since he learns that in God he can accomplish all things that are good, and that without God he can do nothing.

Chapter IX

OF THE SECOND AND THIRD DEGREES OF LOVE

So then in the beginning man loves God, not for God's sake, but for his own. It is something for him to know how little he can do by himself and how much by God's help, and in that knowledge to order himself rightly toward God, his sure support. But when tribulations, recurring again and again, constrain him to turn to God for unfailing help, would not even a heart as hard as iron, as cold as marble, be

[100]Ps 50:15.

softened by the goodness of such a Savior, so that he would love God not altogether selfishly, but because He is God? Let frequent troubles drive us to frequent supplications; and surely, tasting, we must see how gracious the Lord is.[101] Thereupon His goodness once realized draws us to love Him unselfishly, yet more than our own needs impel us to love Him selfishly: even as the Samaritans told the woman who announced that it was Christ who was at the well: "Now we believe, not because of Your saying: for we have heard Him ourselves, and know that this is indeed the Christ, the savior of the world."[102] We likewise bear the same witness to our own fleshly nature, saying, "No longer do we love God because of our necessity, but because we have tasted and seen how gracious the Lord is." Our temporal wants have a speech of their own, proclaiming the benefits they have received from God's favor. Once this is recognized it will not be hard to fulfill the commandment touching love to our neighbors; for whosoever loves God aright loves all God's creatures. Such love is pure, and finds no burden in the precept bidding us purify our souls, in obeying the truth through the Spirit unto unfeigned love of the brethren.[103] Loving as he ought, he counts that command only just. Such love is thankworthy, since it is spontaneous; pure, since it is shown not in word nor tongue, but in deed and truth;[104] just, since it repays what it has received. Whoso loves in this fashion, loves even as he is loved, and seeks no more his own but the things which are Christ's, even as Jesus sought not His own welfare, but ours, or

---

[101] Ps 34:8.
[102] Jn 4:42.
[103] 1 Pt 1:22.
[104] 1 Jn 3:18.

rather ourselves. Such was the psalmist's love when he sang: "O give thanks unto the Lord, for He is gracious."[105] Whosoever praises God for His essential goodness, and not merely because of the benefits He has bestowed, does really love God for God's sake, and not selfishly. The psalmist was not speaking of such love when he said: "So long as You do well to him, he will speak good of You."[106] The third degree of love, we have now seen, is to love God on His own account, solely because He is God.

Chapter X

OF THE FOURTH DEGREE OF LOVE, WHEREIN MAN DOES NOT EVEN LOVE SELF SAVE FOR GOD'S SAKE

How blessed is he who reaches the fourth degree of love, wherein one loves himself only in God! Your righteousness stands like the strong mountains, O God. Such love as this is God's hill, on which it pleases Him to dwell. "Who shall ascend into the hill of the Lord?" "O that I had wings like a dove; for then would I flee away and be at rest." "At Salem is His tabernacle; and His dwelling in Sion." "Woe is me, that I am constrained to dwell with Mesech!"[107] When shall this flesh and blood, this earthen vessel which is my soul's tabernacle, attain thereto? When shall my soul, rapt with divine love and altogether self-forgetting, yes, become like a broken vessel, yearn wholly for God, and, joined unto the

[105]Ps 118:1.
[106]Ps 49:18.
[107]Ps 24:3; 55:6; 76:2; 120:5.

Lord, be one spirit with Him? When she shall exclaim, "My flesh and my heart fails; but God is the strength of my heart and my portion forever."[108] I would count him blessed and holy to whom such rapture has been vouchsafed in this mortal life, for even an instant to lose yourself, as if you were emptied and lost and swallowed up in God, is no human love; it is celestial. But if sometimes a poor mortal feels that heavenly joy for a rapturous moment, then this wretched life envies his happiness, the malice of daily trifles disturbs him, this body of death weighs him down, the needs of the flesh are imperative, the weakness of corruption fails him, and above all brotherly love calls him back to duty. Alas! that voice summons him to re-enter his own round of existence; and he must ever cry out lamentably, "O Lord, I am oppressed: undertake for me"; and again, "O wretched man that I am! who shall deliver me from the body of this death?"[109]

Seeing that the Scripture says, God has made all for His own glory,[110] surely His creatures ought to conform themselves, as much as they can, to His will. In Him should all our affections center, so that in all things we should seek only to do His will, not to please ourselves. And real happiness will come, not in gratifying our desires or in gaining transient pleasures, but in accomplishing God's will for us: even as we pray every day: "Your will be done in earth as it is in heaven."[111] O chaste and holy love! O sweet and gracious affection! O pure and cleansed purpose, thoroughly washed and purged from any admixture of selfishness, and

---

[108] Ps 73:26.
[109] Is 38:14; Rom 7:24.
[110] Is 43:7.
[111] Mt 6:10.

sweetened by contact with the divine will! To reach this state is to become godlike. As a drop of water poured into wine loses itself, and takes the color and savor of wine; or as a bar of iron, heated red hot, becomes like fire itself, forgetting its own nature; or as the air, radiant with sunbeams, seems not so much to be illuminated as to be light itself; so in the saints all human affections melt away by some unspeakable transmutation into the will of God. For how could God be all in all, if anything merely human remained in man? The substance will endure, but in another beauty, a higher power, a greater glory. When will that be? Who will see, who possess it? "When shall I come to appear before the presence of God?"[112] "My heart has talked of You, Seek ye My face: Your face, Lord, will I seek."[113] Lord, think You that I, even I shall see Your holy temple?

In this life, I think, we cannot fully and perfectly obey that precept, "You shall love the Lord Your God with all Your heart, and with all Your soul, and with all Your strength, and with all Your mind."[114] For here the heart must take thought for the body, and the soul must energize the flesh, and the strength must guard itself from impairment. And by God's favor, must seek to increase. It is therefore impossible to offer up all our being to God, to yearn altogether for His face, so long as we must accommodate our purposes and aspirations to these fragile, sickly bodies of ours. Wherefore the soul may hope to possess the fourth degree of love, or rather to be possessed by it, only when it has been clothed upon with that spiritual and immortal body, which will be perfect, peaceful, lovely, and in everything wholly subjected

[112] Ps 42:2.
[113] Ps 27:8.
[114] Lk 10:27.

to the spirit. And to this degree no human effort can attain: it is in God's power to give it to whom He wills. Then the soul will easily reach that highest stage, because no lusts of the flesh will retard its eager entrance into the joy of its Lord, and no troubles will disturb its peace. May we not think that the holy martyrs enjoyed this grace, in some degree at least, before they laid down their victorious bodies? Surely that was immeasurable strength of love which enraptured their souls, enabling them to laugh at fleshly torments and to yield their lives gladly. But even though the frightful pain could not destroy their peace of mind, it must have impaired somewhat its perfection.

Chapter XI

OF THE ATTAINMENT OF THIS PERFECTION OF LOVE ONLY AT THE RESURRECTION

What of the souls already released from their bodies? We believe that they are overwhelmed in that vast sea of eternal light and of luminous eternity. But no one denies that they still hope and desire to receive their bodies again: whence it is plain that they are not yet wholly transformed, and that something of self remains yet unsurrendered. Not until death is swallowed up in victory, and perennial light overflows the uttermost bounds of darkness, not until celestial glory clothes our bodies, can our souls be freed entirely from self and give themselves up to God. For until then souls are bound to bodies, if not by a vital connection of sense, still by natural affection; so that without their bodies they cannot attain to their perfect consummation, nor would they if they could. And although there is no defect in the soul itself before the restoration of its body, since it has already attained to the highest state of which it is by itself capable, yet the spirit would not yearn for reunion with the flesh if without the flesh it could be consummated.

And finally, "Right dear in the sight of the Lord is the death of His saints."[115] But if their death is precious, what must such a life as theirs be! No wonder that the body shall seem to add fresh glory to the spirit; for though it is weak and mortal, it has availed not a little for mutual help. How truly he spoke who said, "All things work together for good to them that love God."[116] The body is a help to the soul that loves God, even when it is ill, even when it is dead, and all the more when it is raised again from the dead: for illness is an aid to penitence; death is the gate of rest; and the resurrection will bring consummation. So, rightly, the soul would not be perfected without the body, since she recognizes that in every condition it has been needful to her good.

The flesh then is a good and faithful comrade for a good soul: since even when it is a burden it assists; when the help ceases, the burden ceases too; and when once more the assistance begins, there is no longer a burden. The first state is toilsome, but fruitful; the second is idle, but not monotonous: the third is glorious. Hear how the Bridegroom in Canticles bids us to this threefold progress: "Eat, O friends; drink, yes, drink abundantly, O beloved."[117] He offers food to those who are laboring with bodily toil; then He calls the resting souls whose bodies are laid aside, to drink; and finally He urges those who have resumed their bodies to drink abundantly. Surely those He styles "beloved" must

[115] Ps 116:15.
[116] Rom 8:28.
[117] Sg 5:1.

overflow with charity; and that is the difference between them and the others, whom He calls not "beloved" but "friends." Those who yet groan in the body are dear to Him, according to the love that they have; those released from the bonds of flesh are dearer because they have become readier and abler to love than hitherto. But beyond either of these classes are those whom He calls "beloved": for they have received the second garment, that is, their glorified bodies, so that now nothing of self remains to hinder or disturb them, and they yield themselves eagerly and entirely to loving God. This cannot be so with the others; for the first have the weight of the body to bear, and the second desires the body again with something of selfish expectation.

At first then the faithful soul eats her bread, but alas! in the sweat of her face. Dwelling in the flesh, she walks as yet by faith, which must work through love. As faith without works is dead, so work itself is food for her; even as our Lord says, "My meat is to do the will of Him that sent Me."[118] When the flesh is laid aside, she eats no more the bread of carefulness, but is allowed to drink deeply of the wine of love, as if after a repast. But the wine is not yet unmingled; even as the Bridegroom says in another place, "I have drunk My wine with My milk."[119] For the soul mixes with the wine of God's love the milk of natural affection, that is, the desire for her body and its glorification. She glows with the wine of holy love which she has drunk; but she is not yet all on fire, for she has tempered the potency of that wine with milk. The unmingled wine would enrapture the soul and make her wholly unconscious of self; but here is no such transport for she is still desirous of her body. When that desire is

[118] Jn 4:34.
[119] Sg 5:1.

appeased, when the one lack is supplied, what should hinder her then from yielding herself utterly to God, losing her own likeness and being made like unto Him? At last she attains to that chalice of the heavenly wisdom, of which it is written, "My cup shall be full." Now indeed she is refreshed with the abundance of the house of God, where all selfish, carking care is done away, and where, forever safe, she drinks the fruit of the vine, new and pure, with Christ in the Kingdom of His Father.[120]

It is Wisdom who spreads this threefold supper where all the repast is love; Wisdom who feeds the toilers, who gives drink to those who rest, who floods with rapture those that reign with Christ. Even as at an earthly banquet custom and nature serve meat first and then wine, so here. Before death, while we are still in mortal flesh, we eat the labors of our hands, we swallow with an effort the food so gained; but after death, we shall begin eagerly to drink in the spiritual life and finally, reunited to our bodies, and rejoicing in fullness of delight, we shall be refreshed with immortality. This is what the Bridegroom means when He says: "Eat, O friends; drink, yes, drink abundantly, O beloved." Eat before death; begin to drink after death; drink abundantly after the resurrection. Rightly are they called beloved who have drunk abundantly of love; rightly do they drink abundantly who are worthy to be brought to the marriage supper of the Lamb, eating and drinking at His table in His Kingdom.[121] At that supper, He shall present to Himself a glorious Church, not having spot, or wrinkle, or any such thing.[122] Then truly shall He refresh His beloved; then He

[120]Mt 26:29.
[121]Rv 19:9; Lk 22:30.
[122]Eph 5:27.

shall give them drink of His pleasures, as out of the river.[123] While the Bridegroom clasps the Bride in tender, pure embrace, then the rivers of the flood thereof shall make glad the city of God.[124] And this refers to the Son of God Himself, who will come forth and serve them, even as He has promised; so that in that day the righteous shall be glad and rejoice before God: they shall also be merry and joyful.[125] Here indeed is appeasement without weariness: here never-quenched thirst for knowledge, without distress; here eternal and infinite desire which knows no want; here, finally, is that sober inebriation which comes not from drinking new wine but from enjoying God.[126] The fourth degree of love is attained forever when we love God only and supremely, when we do not even love ourselves except for God's sake; so that He Himself is the reward of them that love Him, the everlasting reward of an everlasting love.

Chapter XII

OF LOVE: FROM A LETTER TO THE CARTHUSIANS

I remember writing a letter to the holy Carthusian brethren, wherein I discussed these degrees of love, and spoke of charity in other words, although not in another sense, than here. It may be well to repeat a portion of that letter, since it is easier to copy than to dictate anew.

[123] Ps 36:8.
[124] Ps 46:4.
[125] Ps 68:3.
[126] Acts 2:13.

To love our neighbor's welfare as much as our own: that is true and sincere charity out of a pure heart, and of a good conscience, and of faith unfeigned.[127] Whosoever loves his own prosperity only is proved thereby not to love good for its own sake, since he loves it on his own account. And so he cannot sing with the psalmist, "O give thanks unto the Lord, for He is gracious."[128] Such a man would praise God, not because He is goodness, but because He has been good to him: he could take to himself the reproach of the same writer, "So long as You do well to him, he will speak good of You."[129] One praises God because He is mighty, another because He is gracious, yet another solely because He is essential goodness. The first is a slave and fears for himself; the second is greedy, desiring further benefits; but the third is a son who honors his Father. He who fears, he who profits, are both concerned about self-interest. Only in the son is that charity which seeks not her own.[130] Wherefore I take this saying, "The law of the Lord is an undefiled law, converting the soul" to be of charity;[131] because charity alone is able to turn the soul away from love of self and of the world to pure love of God. Neither fear nor self-interest can convert the soul. They may change the appearance, perhaps even the conduct, but never the object of supreme desire. Sometimes a slave may do God's work; but because he does not toil voluntarily, he remains in bondage. So a mercenary may serve God, but because he puts a price on his service, he is enchained by his own greediness. For where there is self-interest there is isolation; and such isolation is like the dark corner of a room where dust and rust befoul. Fear is the

---

[127] 1 Tm 1:5.
[128] Ps 118:1.
[129] Ps 49:18, Vulgate.

[130] 1 Cor 13:5.
[131] Ps 19:7.

motive which constrains the slave; greed binds the selfish man, by which he is tempted when he is drawn away by his own lust and enticed.[132] But neither fear nor self-interest is undefiled, nor can they convert the soul. Only charity can convert the soul, freeing it from unworthy motives.

Next, I call it undefiled because it never keeps back anything of its own for itself. When a man boasts of nothing as his very own, surely all that he has is God's; and what is God's cannot be unclean. The undefiled law of the Lord is that love which bids men seek not their own, but every man another's wealth. It is called the law of the Lord as much because He lives in accordance with it as because no man has it except by gift from Him. Nor is it improper to say that even God lives by law, when that law is the law of love. For what preserves the glorious and ineffable Unity of the blessed Trinity, except love? Charity, the law of the Lord, joins the Three Persons into the unity of the Godhead and unites the holy Trinity in the bond of peace. Do not suppose me to imply that charity exists as an accidental quality of Deity; for whatever could be conceived of as wanting in the divine Nature is not God. No, it is the very substance of the Godhead; and my assertion is neither novel nor extraordinary, since St. John says, "God is love."[133] One may therefore say with truth that love is at once God and the gift of God, essential love imparting the quality of love. Where the word refers to the Giver, it is the name of His very being; where the gift is meant, it is the name of a quality. Love is the eternal law whereby the universe was created and is ruled. Since all things are ordered in measure and number and weight, and nothing is left outside the realm of law, that universal law cannot itself be without a law, which

[132]Jas 1:14.
[133]1 Jn 4:8.

is itself. So love, though it did not create itself, does surely govern itself by its own decree.

Chapter XIII

OF THE LAW OF SELF-WILL AND DESIRE, OF SLAVES AND HIRELINGS

Furthermore, the slave and the hireling have a law, not from the Lord, but of their own contriving; the one does not love God, the other loves something else more than God. They have a law of their own, not of God, I say; yet it is subject to the law of the Lord. For though they can make laws for themselves, they cannot supplant the changeless order of the eternal law. Each man is a law unto himself when he sets up his will against the universal law, perversely striving to rival his Creator, to be wholly independent, making his will his only law. What a heavy and burdensome yoke upon all the sons of Adam, bowing down our necks, so that our life draws nigh unto hell. "O wretched man that I am! Who shall deliver me from the body of this death?"[134] I am weighed down, I am almost overwhelmed, so that "If the Lord had not helped me, it had not failed but my soul had been put to silence."[135] Job was groaning under this load when he lamented: "Why have You set me as a mark against You, so that I am a burden to myself?"[136] He was a burden to himself through the law which was of his own devising: yet he could not escape God's law, for he was set as a mark against God. The eternal law of righteousness ordains that

[134]Rom 7:24.
[135]Ps 94:17.
[136]Jb 7:20.

he who will not submit to God's sweet rule shall suffer the bitter tyranny of self: but he who wears the easy yoke and light burden of love[137] will escape the intolerable weight of his own self-will. Wondrously and justly does that eternal law retain rebels in subjection, so that they are unable to escape. They are subject to God's power, yet deprived of happiness with Him, unable to dwell with God in light and rest and glory everlasting. O Lord my God, "why do You not pardon my transgression and take away my iniquity?"[138] Then freed from the weight of my own will, I can breathe easily under the light burden of love. I shall not be coerced by fear, nor allured by mercenary desires; for I shall be led by the Spirit of God, that free Spirit whereby Your sons are led, which bear witness with my spirit that I am among the children of God.[139] So shall I be under that law which is Yours; and as You are, so shall I be in the world. Whosoever does what the apostle bids, "Owe no man anything, but to love one another,"[140] are doubtless even in this life conformed to God's likeness: they are neither slaves nor hirelings but sons.

Chapter XIV
OF THE LAW OF THE LOVE OF SONS

Now the children have their law, even though it is written, "The law is not made for a righteous man."[141] For it must be remembered that there is one law having to do with the spirit of servitude, given to fear, and another with the spirit of liberty, given in tenderness. The children are not constrained by the first, yet they could not exist without the

[137]Mt 11:30.
[138]Jb 7:21.
[139]Rom 8:16.

[140]Rom 13:8.
[141]1 Tm 1:9.

second: even as St. Paul writes, "You have not received the spirit of bondage again to fear; but you have received the spirit of adoption, whereby we cry, Abba, Father."[142] And again to show that that same righteous man was not under the law, he says: "To them that are under the law, I became as under the law, that I might gain them that are under the law; to them that are without law, as without law (being not without law to God, but under the law to Christ)."[143] So it is rightly said, not that the righteous do not have a law, but, "The law is not made for a righteous man," that is, it is not imposed on rebels but freely given to those willingly obedient, by Him whose goodness established it. Wherefore the Lord says meekly: "Take My yoke upon you," which may be paraphrased thus: "I do not force it on you, if you are reluctant; but if you will you may bear it. Otherwise it will be weariness, not rest, that you shall find for your souls."

Love is a good and pleasant law; it is not only easy to bear, but it makes the laws of slaves and hirelings tolerable; not destroying but completing them; as the Lord says: "I did not come to destroy the law, but to fulfill."[144] It tempers the fear of the slave, it regulates the desires of the hireling, it mitigates the severity of each. Love is never without fear, but it is godly fear. Love is never without desire, but it is lawful desire. So love perfects the law of service by infusing devotion; it perfects the law of wages by restraining covetousness. Devotion mixed with fear does not destroy it, but purges it. Then the burden of fear which was intolerable while it was only servile, becomes tolerable; and the fear itself remains ever pure and filial. For though we read: "Perfect love casts out

[142]Rom 8:15.
[143]1 Cor 9:20ff.
[144]Mt 5:17.

fear,"[145] we understand by that the suffering which is never absent from servile fear, the cause being put for the effect, as often elsewhere. So, too, self-interest is restrained within due bounds when love supervenes; for then it rejects evil things altogether, prefers better things to those merely good, and cares for the good only on account of the better. In like manner, by God's grace, it will come about that man will love his body and all things pertaining to his body, for the sake of his soul. He will love his soul for God's sake; and he will love God for Himself alone.

Chapter XV

OF THE FOUR DEGREES OF LOVE, AND OF THE BLESSED STATE OF THE HEAVENLY FATHERLAND

Nevertheless, since we are carnal and are born of the lust of the flesh, it must be that our desire and our love shall have its beginning in the flesh. But rightly guided by the grace of God through these degrees, it will have its consummation in the spirit: for that was not first which is spiritual but that which is natural; and afterward that which is spiritual.[146] And we must bear the image of the earthly first, before we can bear the image of the heavenly. At first, man loves himself for his own sake. That is the flesh, which can appreciate nothing beyond itself. Next, he perceives that he cannot exist by himself, and so begins by faith to seek after God, and to love Him as something necessary to his own welfare. That is the second degree, to love God, not for

[145] 1 Jn 4:18.
[146] 1 Cor 15:46.

God's sake, but selfishly. But when he has learned to worship God and to seek Him aright, meditating on God, reading God's Word, praying and obeying His commandments, he comes gradually to know what God is, and finds Him altogether lovely. So, having tasted and seen how gracious the Lord is,[147] he advances to the third degree, when he loves God, not merely as his benefactor but as God. Surely he must remain long in this state; and I know not whether it would be possible to make further progress in this life to that fourth degree and perfect condition wherein man loves himself solely for God's sake. Let any who have attained so far bear record; I confess it seems beyond my powers. Doubtless it will be reached when the good and faithful servant shall have entered into the joy of his Lord, and been satisfied with the plenteousness of God's house.[148] For then in wondrous wise he will forget himself and as if delivered from self, he will grow wholly God's. Joined unto the Lord, he will then be one spirit with Him.[149] This was what the prophet meant, I think, when he said: "I will go forth in the strength of the Lord God and will make mention of your righteousness only."[150] Surely he knew that when he should go forth in the spiritual strength of the Lord, he would have been freed from the infirmities of the flesh, and would have nothing carnal to think of, but would be wholly filled in his spirit with the righteousness of the Lord.

In that day the members of Christ can say of themselves what St. Paul testified concerning their Head: Yea, though we have known Christ after the flesh, yet now henceforth know we Him no more.[151] None shall thereafter know himself after the flesh; for "flesh and blood cannot inherit the

[147]Ps 34:8.
[148]Mt 25:21; Ps 36:8.
[149]1 Cor 6:17.

[150]Ps 71:16.
[151]1 Cor 5:16.

Kingdom of God."[152] Not that there will be no true substance of the flesh, but all carnal needs will be taken away,
and the love of the flesh will be swallowed up in the love of
the spirit, so that our weak human affections will be made
divinely strong. Then the net of charity which as it is drawn
through the great and wide sea does not cease to gather
every kind of fish, will be drawn to the shore; and the bad
will be cast away, while only the good will be kept.[153] In this
life the net of all-including love gathers every kind of fish
into its wide folds, becoming all things to all men, sharing
adversity or prosperity, rejoicing with them that do rejoice,
and weeping with them that weep.[154] But when the net is
drawn to shore, whatever causes pain will be rejected, like
the bad fish, while only what is pleasant and joyous will be
kept. Do you not recall how St. Paul said: "Who is weak and
I am not weak? Who is offended and I burn not?" And yet
weakness and offense were far from him. So too he bewailed
many which had sinned already and had not repented,
though he was neither the sinner nor the penitent. But there
is a city made glad by the rivers of the flood of grace,
and whose gates the Lord loves more than all the dwellings
of Jacob.[155] In it is no place for lamentation over those condemned to everlasting fire, prepared for the devil and his
angels.[156] In these earthly dwellings, though men may rejoice, yet they have still other battles to fight, other mortal
perils to undergo. But in the heavenly Fatherland no sorrow
or sadness can enter: as it is written, "The habitation of all

---

[152] 1 Cor 15:50.
[153] Mt 13:48.
[154] Rom 12:15.
[155] Ps 46:4, 87:2.
[156] Mt 25:41.

rejoicing ones is in You"; and again, "Everlasting joy shall be unto them."[157] Nor could they recall things piteous, for then they will make mention of God's righteousness only. Accordingly, there will be no need for the exercise of compassion, for no misery will be there to inspire pity.

[157]Ps 87:7, Vulgate; Is 61:7.

PART II

Selected Sermons

From *On the Song of Songs*

SERMON I
On the Title of the Book

The instructions that I address to you, my brothers, will differ from those I should deliver to people in the world, at least the manner will be different. The preacher who desires to follow St. Paul's method of teaching will give them milk to drink rather than solid food,[158] and will serve a more nourishing diet to those who are spiritually enlightened: "We teach," he said, "not in the way philosophy is taught, but in the way that the Spirit teaches us: we teach spiritual things spiritually."[159] And again: "We have a wisdom to offer those who have reached maturity,"[160] in whose company, I feel assured, you are to be found, unless in vain have you prolonged your study of divine teaching, mortified your senses, and meditated day and night on God's law.[161] Be ready then to feed on bread rather than milk. Solomon has bread to give that is splendid and delicious, the bread of that book called the Song of Songs. Let us bring it forth then if you please, and break it.

2. Now, unless I am mistaken, by the grace of God you have understood quite well from the book of Ecclesiastes

---

[158] 1 Cor 3:1–2; Heb 5:12–14.

[159] 1 Cor 2:13.

[160] 1 Cor 2:6.

[161] Ps 1:2. References to the Psalms are numbered according to the Vulgate version as this was the one familiar to St. Bernard.

how to recognize and have done with the false promise of this world. And then the book of Proverbs—has not your life and your conduct been sufficiently amended and enlightened by the doctrine it inculcates? These are two loaves of which it has been your pleasure to taste, loaves you have welcomed as coming from the cupboard of a friend.[162] Now approach for this third loaf that, if possible, you may always recognize what is best.[163] Since there are two evils that comprise the only, or at least the main, enemies of the soul: a misguided love of the world and an excessive love of self,[164] the two books previously mentioned can provide an antidote to each of these infections. One uproots pernicious habits of mind and body with the hoe of self-control. The other, by the use of enlightened reason, quickly perceives a delusive tinge in all that the world holds glorious, truly distinguishing between it and deeper truth. Moreover, it causes the fear of God and the observance of his commandments to be preferred to all human pursuits and worldly desires.[165] And rightly so, for the former is the beginning of wisdom,[166] the latter its culmination, for there is no true and consummate wisdom other than the avoidance of evil and the doing of good,[167] no one can successfully shun evil without the fear of God, and no work is good without the observance of the commandments.

3. Taking it then that these two evils have been warded off by the reading of those books, we may suitably proceed with this holy and contemplative discourse which, as the fruit of the other two, may be delivered only to well-prepared ears and minds.

[162] Lk 11:5.
[163] Phil 1:10.
[164] 1 Pt 2:11.

[165] Eccl 12:13.
[166] Ps 111:10.
[167] Ps 36:27; Prv 3:7.

II. Before the flesh has been tamed and the spirit set free by zeal for truth, before the world's glamour and entanglements have been firmly repudiated, it is a rash enterprise on any man's part to presume to study spiritual doctrines. Just as a light is flashed in vain on closed or sightless eyes, so "an unspiritual person cannot accept anything of the Spirit of God."[168] For "the Holy Spirit of instruction shuns what is false,"[169] and that is what the life of the intemperate man is. Nor will he ever have a part with the pretensions of the world, since he is the Spirit of Truth.[170] How can there be harmony between the wisdom that comes down from above and the wisdom of the world,[171] which is foolishness to God, or the wisdom of the flesh which is at enmity with God?[172] I am sure that the friend who comes to us on his travels will have no reason to murmur against us after he has shared in this third loaf.

4. But who is going to divide this loaf? The Master of the house is present, it is the Lord you must see in the breaking of the bread.[173] For who else could more fittingly do it? It is a task that I would not dare to arrogate to myself. So look upon me as one from whom you look for nothing. For I myself am one of the seekers, one who begs along with you for the food of my soul, the nourishment of my spirit. Poor and needy, I knock at that door of his which, "when he opens, nobody can close,"[174] that I may find light on the profound mystery to which this discourse leads. Patiently all creatures look to you, O Lord.[175] "Little children go begging

---

[168] 1 Cor 2:14.
[169] Ws 1:5.
[170] Jn 14:17.
[171] Jas 3:17; 1 Cor 3:19.

[172] Rom 8:7.
[173] Lk 24:35.
[174] Rv 3:7.
[175] Ps 144:15.

for bread; no one spares a scrap for them";[176] they await it from your merciful love O God most kind, break your bread for this hungering flock,[177] through my hands indeed if it should please you, but with an efficacy that is all your own.

III. 5. Tell us, I beg you, by whom, about whom and to whom it is said: "Let him kiss me with the kiss of his mouth."[178] How shall I explain so abrupt a beginning, this sudden irruption as from a speech in midcourse? For the words spring upon us as if indicating one speaker to whom another is replying as she demands a kiss—whoever she may be. But if she asks for or demands a kiss from somebody, why does she distinctly and expressly say *with the mouth,* and even with *his own* mouth, as if lovers should kiss by means other than the mouth, or with mouths other than their own? But yet she does not say: "Let him kiss me *with his mouth*"; what she says is still more intimate: "with the kiss of his mouth." How delightful a ploy of speech this,[179] prompted into life by the kiss, with Scripture's own engaging countenance inspiring the reader and enticing him on, that he may find pleasure even in the laborious pursuit of what lies hidden, with a fascinating theme to sweeten the fatigue of research. Surely this mode of beginning that is not a beginning, this novelty of diction in a book so old, cannot but increase the reader's attention. It must follow too that this work was composed, not by any human skill but by the artistry of the Spirit, difficult to understand indeed but yet enticing one to investigate.

IV. 6. So now what shall we do? Shall we bypass the title? No, not even one iota may be omitted, since we are

---

commanded to gather up the tiniest fragments lest they be lost.[180] The title runs: "The beginning of Solomon's Song of Songs." First of all take note of the appropriateness of the name "Peaceful," that is, Solomon, at the head of a book which opens with the token of peace, with a kiss. Take note too that by this kind of opening only men of peaceful minds, men who can achieve mastery over the turmoil of the passions and the distracting burden of daily chores, are invited to the study of this book.

7. Again, the title is not simply the word "Song," but "Song of Songs," a detail not without significance. For though I have read many songs in the Scriptures, I cannot recall any that bear such a name. Israel chanted a song to Yahweh[181] celebrating his escape from the sword and the tyranny of Pharaoh, and the twofold good fortune that simultaneously liberated and avenged him in the Red Sea. Yet even though chanted, this has not been called a "Song of Songs"; Scripture, if my memory serves me right, introduces it with the words: "Israel sang this song in honor of Yahweh."[182] Song poured from the lips of Deborah, of Judith, of the mother of Samuel, of several of the prophets, yet none of these songs is styled a "Song of Songs."[183] You will find that all of them, as far as I can see, were inspired to song because of favors to themselves or to their people, songs for a victory won, for an escape from danger or the gaining of a boon long sought. They would not be found ungrateful for the divine beneficence, so all sang for reasons proper to each, in accord with the psalmist's words: "He gives thanks to you, O God, for blessing him."[184]

[180] Mt 5:18; Jn 6:12.
[181] Ex 15:1–19.
[182] Ex 15:1.
[183] Jgs 5:1, 16:1; 1 Sm 2:1. Cf. Is 5:1–2, 26:1–10.
[184] Ps 43:19.

But King Solomon himself, unique as he was in wisdom, renowned above all men, abounding in wealth, secure in his peace, stood in no need of any particular benefit that would have inspired him to sing those songs. Nor does Scripture in any place attribute such a motive to him.

8. We must conclude then it was a special divine impulse that inspired these songs of his that now celebrate the praises of Christ and his Church, the gift of holy love, the sacrament of endless union with God. Here too are expressed the mounting desires of the soul, its marriage song, an exultation of spirit poured forth in figurative language pregnant with delight. It is no wonder that like Moses he put a veil on his face,[185] equally resplendent as it must have been in this encounter, because in those days few if any could sustain the bright vision of God's glory.[186] Accordingly, because of its excellence, I consider this nuptial song to be well deserving of the title that so remarkably designates it, the Song of Songs, just as he in whose honor it is sung is uniquely proclaimed King of kings and Lord of lords.[187]

V. 9. Furthermore if you look back on your own experience, is it not in that victory by which your faith overcomes the world, in "your exit from the horrible pit and out of the slough of the marsh," that you yourselves sing a new song to the Lord for all the marvels he has performed?[188] Again, when he purposed to "settle your feet on a rock and to direct your steps,"[189] then too, I feel certain, a new song was

---

[185]Ex 34:33; 2 Cor 3:13.
[186]2 Cor 3:18.
[187]1 Tm 6:15.
[188]1 Jn 5:4; Ps 39:3, 97:1.
[189]Ps 39:3–4.

sounding on your lips, a song to our God for his gracious renewal of your life. When you repented, he not only forgave your sins but even promised rewards, so that rejoicing in the hope of benefits to come, you sing of the Lord's ways: how great is the glory of the Lord![190] And when, as happens, texts of Scripture hitherto dark and impenetrable at last become bright with meaning for you, then, in gratitude for this nurturing bread of heaven you must charm the ears of God with a voice of exultation and praise, a festal song.[191] In the daily trials and combats arising from the flesh, the world, and the devil, that are never wanting to those who live devout lives in Christ, you learn by what you experience that man's life on earth is a ceaseless warfare, and are impelled to repeat your songs day after day for every victory won.[192] As often as temptation is overcome, an immoral habit brought under control, an impending danger shunned, the trap of the seducer detected, when a passion long indulged is finally and perfectly allayed, or a virtue persistently desired and repeatedly sought is ultimately obtained by God's gift, so often, in the words of the prophet, let thanksgiving and joy resound.[193] For every benefit conferred, God is to be praised in his gifts. Otherwise when the time of judgment comes, that man will be punished as an ingrate who cannot say to God: "Your statutes were my song in the land of exile."[194]

10. Again I think that your own experience reveals to you the meaning of those psalms, which are called not Songs of

[190]Rom 12:12; Ps 137:5.
[191]Ps 41:5.
[192]2 Tm 3:12; Jb 7:1.
[193]Is 51:3.
[194]Ps 118:54.

Songs but Songs of the Steps, in that each one, at whatever stage of growth he be, in accord with the upward movements of his heart may choose one of these songs to praise and give glory to him who empowers you to advance.[195] I don't know how else these words could be true: "There are shouts of joy and victory in the tents of the just."[196] And still more that beautiful and salutary exhortation of the apostle: "With psalms and hymns and spiritual canticles, singing and chanting to the Lord in your hearts."[197]

VI. 11. But there is that other song which, by its unique dignity and sweetness, excels all those I have mentioned and any others there might be; hence by every right do I acclaim it as the Song of Songs. It stands at a point where all the others culminate. Only the touch of the Spirit can inspire a song like this, and only personal experience can unfold its meaning.[198] Let those who are versed in the mystery revel in it; let all others burn with desire rather to attain to this experience than merely to learn about it. For it is not a melody that resounds abroad but the very music of the heart, not a trilling on the lips but an inward pulsing of delight, a harmony not of voices but of wills. It is a tune you will not hear in the streets, these notes do not sound where crowds assemble;[199] only the singer hears it and the one to whom he sings—the lover and the beloved. It is preeminently a marriage song telling of chaste souls in loving embrace, of their wills in sweet concord, of the mutual exchange of the heart's affections.

12. The novices, the immature, those but recently converted from a worldly life, do not normally sing this song or hear it

[195]Ps 83:6.
[196]Ps 117:15.
[197]Eph 5:19.

[198]Cf. 1 Jn 2:27.
[199]Is 42:2.

sung. Only the mind disciplined by persevering study, only the man whose efforts have borne fruit under God's inspiration, the man whose years, as it were, make him ripe for marriage—years measured out not in time but in merits—only he is truly prepared for nuptial union with the divine partner, a union we shall describe more fully in due course.[200] But the hour has come when both our rule and the poverty of our state demand that we go out to work.[201] Tomorrow,[202] with God's help, we shall continue to speak about the kiss, because today's discourse on the title sets us free to resume where we had begun.

SERMON 2

Various Meanings of the Kiss

During my frequent ponderings on the burning desire with which the patriarchs longed for the incarnation of Christ, I am stung with sorrow and shame. Even now I can scarcely restrain my tears, so filled with shame am I by the lukewarmness, the frigid unconcern of these miserable times. For which of us does the consummation of that event fill

[200] See Sermon 83 |not included in this selection. Eds.|.
[201] *St. Benedict's Rule for Monasteries* (hereafter RB), c. 48. |See *The Rule of St. Benedict in English*, Timothy Fry, OSB, ed., Vintage Spiritual Classics ed. (New York, 1998), p. 47. Eds.|
[202] The early Cistercians gathered daily in chapter after prime to receive instruction from the abbot. See *Consuetudines* of 1152, Part I, *Officia Ecclesiastica,* c. 70 in *Nomasticon Cisterciense,* ed. Séjalon (Solesmes, 1892), p. 147. It is in this context that St. Bernard places his sermons. See J. Leclercq. introduction, *Works of Bernard of Clairvaux,* vol. 3 (Cistercian Fathers Series 7).

with as much joy as the mere promise of it inflamed the desires of the holy men of pre-Christian times? Very soon now there will be great rejoicing as we celebrate the feast of Christ's birth.[203] But how I wish it were inspired by his birth! All the more therefore do I pray that the intense longing of those men of old, their heartfelt expectation, may be enkindled in me by these words: "Let him kiss me with the kiss of his mouth."[204] Many an upright man in those far-off times sensed within himself how profuse the graciousness that would be poured upon those lips.[205] And intense desire springing from that perception[206] impelled him to utter: "Let him kiss me with the kiss of his mouth," hoping with every fiber of his being that he might not be deprived of a share in a pleasure so great.

2. The conscientious man of those days might repeat to himself: "Of what use to me the wordy effusions of the prophets? Rather let him who is the most handsome of the sons of men,[207] let him kiss me with the kiss of his mouth. No longer am I satisfied to listen to Moses, for he is a slow speaker and not able to speak well.[208] Isaiah is 'a man of unclean lips,'[209] Jeremiah does not know how to speak, he is a child;[210] not one of the prophets makes an impact on me with his words. But he, the one whom they proclaim, let him speak to me, 'let him kiss me with the kiss of his mouth.' I have no desire that he should approach me in their person, or

---

[203]Bernard places this sermon in the context of Advent, whose liturgy has undoubtedly influenced its thought.
[204]Sg 1:1.
[205]Ps 44:3.
[206]Is 26:8.
[207]Ps 44:3.
[208]Ex 4:10.
[209]Is 6:5.
[210]Jn 1:6.

address me with their words, for they are 'a watery darkness, a dense cloud'; rather in his own person 'let him kiss me with the kiss of his mouth'; let him whose presence is full of love, from whom exquisite doctrines flow in streams, let him become 'a spring inside me, welling up to eternal life.'[211] Shall I not receive a richer infusion of grace from him whom the Father has anointed with the oil of gladness above all his rivals,[212] provided that he will bestow on me the kiss of his mouth? For his living, active word is to me a kiss,[213] not indeed an adhering of the lips that can sometimes belie a union of hearts, but an unreserved infusion of joys, a revealing of mysteries, a marvelous and indistinguishable mingling of the divine light with the enlightened mind, which, joined in truth to God, is one spirit with him.[214] With good reason then I avoid trucking with visions and dreams; I want no part with parables and figures of speech; even the very beauty of the angels can only leave me wearied. For my Jesus utterly surpasses these in his majesty and splendor.[215] Therefore I ask of him what I ask of neither man nor angel: that he kiss me with the kiss of his mouth.

II. "Note how I do not presume that it is with his mouth I shall be kissed, for that constitutes the unique felicity and singular privilege of the human nature he assumed. No, in the consciousness of my lowliness I ask to be kissed with the kiss of his mouth, an experience shared by all who are in a position to say: 'Indeed from his fullness we have, all of us, received.'"[216]

3. I must ask you to try to give your whole attention here. The mouth that kisses signifies the Word who assumes

---

[211] Ps 17:12; Jn 4:14.
[212] Ps 44:8.
[213] Heb 4:12.

[214] 1 Cor 6:17.
[215] Ps 44:5.
[216] Jn 1:16.

human nature; the nature assumed receives the kiss; the kiss however, that takes its being both from the giver and the receiver, is a person that is formed by both, none other than "the one mediator between God and mankind, himself a man, Christ Jesus."[217] It is for this reason that none of the saints dared say: "let him kiss me with his mouth," but rather, "with the kiss of his mouth." In this way they paid tribute to that prerogative of Christ, on whom uniquely and in one sole instance the mouth of the Word was pressed, that moment when the fullness of the divinity yielded itself to him as the life of his body.[218] A fertile kiss therefore, a marvel of stupendous self-abasement that is not a mere pressing of mouth upon mouth; it is the uniting of God with man. Normally the touch of lip on lip is the sign of the loving embrace of hearts, but this conjoining of natures brings together the human and divine, shows God reconciling "to himself all things, whether on earth or in heaven."[219] "For he is the peace between us, and has made the two into one."[220] This was the kiss for which just men yearned under the old dispensation, foreseeing as they did that in him they would "find happiness and a crown of rejoicing,"[221] because in him were hidden "all the jewels of wisdom and knowledge."[222] Hence their longing to taste that fullness of his.[223]

4. You seem to be in agreement with this explanation, but I should like you to listen to another.

III. Even the holy men who lived before the coming of Christ understood that God had in mind plans of peace for the human race.[224] "Surely the Lord God does nothing without revealing his secret to his servants, the prophets."[225]

---

[217] 1 Tm 2:5.
[218] Col 2:9.
[219] Col 1:20.

[220] Eph 2:14.
[221] Sir 15:6.
[222] Col 2:3.

[223] Jn 1:16.
[224] Jer 29:11.
[225] Am 3:7.

What he did reveal however was obscure to many.[226] For in those days faith was a rare thing on the earth, and hope but a faint impulse in the heart even of many of those who looked forward to the deliverance of Israel.[227] Those indeed who foreknew also proclaimed that Christ would come as man, and with him, peace. One of them actually said: "He himself will be peace in our land when he comes."[228] Enlightened from above they confidently spread abroad the message that through him men would be restored to the favor of God. John, the forerunner of the Lord, recognizing the fulfillment of that prophecy in his own time, declared: "Grace and truth have come through Jesus Christ."[229] In our time every Christian can discover by experience that this is true.

5. In those far-off days, however, while the prophets continued to foretell the covenant, and its author continued to delay his coming,[230] the faith of the people never ceased to waver because there was no one who could redeem or save.[231] Hence men grumbled at the postponements of the coming of this Prince of Peace so often proclaimed by the mouth of his holy prophets from ancient times.[232] As doubts about the fulfillment of the prophecies began to recur, all the more eagerly did they make demands for the kiss, the sign of the promised reconcilement. It was as if a voice from among the people would challenge the prophets of peace: "How much longer are you going to keep us in suspense?[233] You

---

[226] Lk 18:34.
[227] Lk 2:38.
[228] Mi 5:5. St. Bernard's text may be a free rendering or taken from a lost ms.
[229] Jn 1:17.
[230] Mt 25:5.
[231] Ps 7:3.
[232] Is 9:6; Lk 1:70.
[233] Jn 10:24.

are always foretelling a peace that is never realized; you promise a world of good but trouble on trouble comes.[234] At various times in the past and in various different ways this same hope was fostered by angels among our ancestors, who in turn have passed the tidings on to us.[235] 'Peace! Peace!' they say, 'but there is no peace.'[236] If God desires to convince me of that benevolent will of his, so often vouched for by the prophets but not yet revealed by the event, then let him kiss me with the kiss of his mouth, and so by this token of peace make my peace secure. For how shall I any longer put my trust in mere words? It is necessary now that words be vindicated by action. If those men are God's envoys, let him prove the truth of their words by his own advent, so often the keynote of their predictions, because unless he comes, they can do nothing.[237] He sent his servant bearing a staff, but neither voice nor life is forthcoming.[238] I do not rise up, I am not awakened, I am not shaken out of the dust,[239] nor do I breathe in hope, if the Prophet himself does not come down and kiss me with the kiss of his mouth."

6. Here we must add that he who professes to be our mediator with God is God's own Son, and he is God. But what is man that he should take notice of him, the son of man that he should be concerned about him?[240] Where shall such as I am find the confidence, the daring, to entrust myself to him who is so majestic? How shall I, mere dust and ashes, presume that God takes an interest in me?[241] He is entirely taken up with loving his Father; he has no need of me nor of what I possess.[242] How then shall I find assurance that if he is my mediator he will never fail me? If it be really

---

[234]Jer 14:19.
[235]Heb 1:1; Ps 43:2.
[236]Jer 6:14.

[237]Jn 15:5.
[238]2 Kgs 4:26–31.
[239]Is 52:2.

[240]Ps 143:3.
[241]Sir 10:9.
[242]Ps 15:2.

true, as you prophets have said, that God has determined to show mercy, to reveal himself in a more favorable light, let him establish a covenant of peace, an everlasting covenant with me by the kiss of his mouth.[243] If he will not revoke his given word, let him empty himself, let him humble himself, let him bend to me and kiss me with the kiss of his mouth.[244] If the mediator is to be acceptable to both parties, equally dependable in the eyes of both, then let him who is God's Son become man, let him become the Son of Man, and fill me with assurance by this kiss of his mouth. When I come to recognize that he is truly mine, then I shall feel secure in welcoming the Son of God as mediator. Not even a shadow of mistrust can then exist, for after all he is my brother, and my own flesh.[245] It is impossible that I should be spurned by him who is bone from my bones, and flesh from my flesh.[246]

7. We should by now have come to understand how the discontent of our ancestors displayed a need for this sacrosanct kiss, that is, the mystery of the incarnate Word, for faith, hard-pressed throughout the ages with trouble upon trouble, was ever on the point of failing, and a fickle people, yielding to discouragement, murmured against the promises of God. Is this a mere improvisation on my part? I suggest that you will find it to be the teaching of the Scriptures: for instance, consider the burden of complaint and murmuring in those words: "Order on order, order on order, rule on rule, rule on rule, a little here, a little there."[247] Or those prayerful exclamations, troubled yet loyal: "Give those who wait for you their reward, and let your prophets be proved worthy of belief."[248] Again: "Bring about what

---

[243]Ps 76:8; Sir 45:30; Is 61:8.
[244]Ps 88:35; Phil 2:7.
[245]Gn 37:27.

[246]Gn 2:23.
[247]Is 28:10.
[248]Sir 36:18.

has been prophesied in your name."[249] There too you will find those soothing promises, full of consolation: "Behold the Lord will appear and he will not lie. If he seems slow, wait for him, for he will surely come and he will not delay."[250] Likewise: "His time is close at hand when he will come and his days will not be prolonged."[251] Speaking in the name of him who is promised the prophet announces: "Behold I am coming toward you like a river of peace, and like a stream in spate with the glory of the nations."[252] In all these statements there is evidence both of the urgency of the preachers and of the distrust of those who listened to them. The people murmured, their faith wavered, and in the words of Isaiah: "the ambassadors of peace weep bitterly."[253] Therefore because Christ was late in coming,[254] and the whole human race in danger of being lost in despair, so convinced was it that human weakness was an object of contempt with no hope of the reconciliation with God through a grace so frequently promised, those good men whose faith remained strong eagerly longed for the more powerful assurance that only his human presence could convey. They prayed intensely for a sign that the covenant was about to be restored for the sake of a spiritless, faithless people.

8. Oh root of Jesse, that stands as a signal to the peoples,[255] how many prophets and kings wanted to see what you see, and never saw it![256]

IV. Happy above them all is Simeon, by God's mercy still bearing fruit in old age![257] He rejoiced to think that he would see the long-desired sign. He saw it and was glad;[258] and having received the kiss of peace he is allowed to go in

[249]Sir 36:17.
[250]Heb 2:3.
[251]Is 14:1.
[252]Is 66:12.

[253]Is 33:7.
[254]Mt 25:5.
[255]Is 11:10.

[256]Lk 10:24.
[257]Ps 91:14.
[258]Jn 8:56.

peace, but not before he had told his audience that Jesus was born to be a sign that would be rejected.[259] Time proved how true this was. No sooner had the sign of peace arisen than it was opposed, by those, that is, who hated peace, for his peace is with men of goodwill, but for the evil-minded he is "a stone to stumble over, a rock to bring men down."[260] Herod accordingly was perturbed, and so was the whole of Jerusalem.[261] Christ "came to his own domain, and his own people did not accept him."[262] Those shepherds, however, who kept watch over their flocks by night,[263] were fortunate for they were gladdened by a vision of this sign. Even in those early days he was hiding these things from the learned and the clever, and revealing them to mere children.[264] Herod, as you know, desired to see him,[265] but because his motive was not genuine he did not succeed. The sign of peace was given only to men of goodwill, hence to Herod and others like him was given the sign of the prophet Jonah.[266] The angel said to the shepherds: "Here is a sign for you," you who are humble, obedient, not given to haughtiness, faithful to prayer and meditating day and night on God's law.[267] "This is a sign for you," he said. What sign? The sign promised by the angels, sought after by the people, foretold by the prophets; this is the sign that the Lord Jesus has now brought into existence and revealed to you, a sign by which the incredulous are made believers, the dispirited are made hopeful and the fervent achieve security. This therefore is the sign for you. But as a sign what does it signify? It reveals mercy, grace, peace, the peace that has no

[259] Lk 2:25–34.
[260] Ps 119:7; Lk 2:14; 1 Pt 2:8.
[261] Mt 2:3.
[262] Jn 1:11.
[263] Lk 2:8–20.
[264] Mt 11:25; Lk 10:21.
[265] Lk 23:8.
[266] Mt 12:19.
[267] Lk 2:12; Rom 12:16; Ps 1:2.

end.[268] And finally, the sign is this: "You will find a baby, wrapped in swaddling clothes and lying in a manger."[269] God himself, however, is in this baby, reconciling the world to himself.[270] He will be put to death for your sins and raised to life to justify you, so that made righteous by faith you may be at peace with God.[271] This was the sign of peace that the Prophet once urged King Achez to ask of the Lord his God, "either from the depths of Sheol or from the heights above."[272] But the ungodly king refused. His wretched state blinded him to the belief that in this sign the highest things above would be joined to the lowest things below in peace. This was achieved when Christ, descending into Sheol, saluted its dwellers with a holy kiss,[273] the pledge of peace, and then going up to heaven, enabled the spirits there to share in the same pledge in joy without end.

9. I must end this sermon. But let me sum up briefly the points we have raised. It would seem that this holy kiss was of necessity bestowed on the world for two reasons. Without it the faith of those who wavered would not have been strengthened, nor the desires of the fervent appeased. Moreover, this kiss is no other than the Mediator between God and man, himself a man, Christ Jesus,[274] who with the Father and Holy Spirit lives and reigns as God forever and ever. Amen.

[268] Is 9:7.
[269] Lk 2:12.
[270] 2 Cor 5:19.
[271] Rom 4:25, 5:1.
[272] Is 7:11.
[273] 1 Cor 16:20.
[274] 1 Tm 2:5.

SERMON 3

The Kiss of the Lord's Feet, Hands, and Mouth

Today the text we are to study is the book of our own experience. You must therefore turn your attention inward, each one must take note of his own particular awareness of the things I am about to discuss. I am attempting to discover if any of you has been privileged to say from his heart: "Let him kiss me with the kiss of his mouth."[275] Those to whom it is given to utter these words sincerely are comparatively few, but anyone who has received this mystical kiss from the mouth of Christ at least once, seeks again that intimate experience, and eagerly looks for its frequent renewal. I think that nobody can grasp what it is except the one who receives it. For it is "a hidden manna," and only he who eats it still hungers for more.[276] It is "a sealed fountain" to which no stranger has access; only he who drinks still thirsts for more.[277] Listen to one who has had the experience, how urgently he demands: "Be my savior again, renew my joy."[278] But a soul like mine, burdened with sins, still subject to carnal passions,[279] devoid of any knowledge of spiritual delights, may not presume to make such a request, almost totally unacquainted as it is with the joys of the supernatural life.

2. I should like however to point out to persons like this that there is an appropriate place for them on the way of salvation. They may not rashly aspire to the lips of a most benign Bridegroom, but let them prostrate with me in fear at the feet of a most severe Lord. Like the publican full of misgiving,[280]

---

[275] Sg 1:1.
[276] Rv 2:17; Sir 24:29.
[277] Sg 4:12; Sir 24:29.
[278] Ps 50:14.
[279] 2 Tm 3:6.
[280] Lk 18:13.

they must turn their eyes to the earth rather than up to heaven. Eyes that are accustomed only to darkness will be dazzled by the brightness of the spiritual world,[281] over-powered by its splendor, repulsed by its peerless radiance and whelmed again in a gloom more dense than before. All you who are conscious of sin, do not regard as unworthy and despicable that position where the holy sinner laid down her sins, and put on the garment of holiness. There the Ethiopian changed her skin,[282] and, cleansed to a new brightness, could confidently and legitimately respond to those who insulted her:[283] "I am black but lovely, daughters of Jerusalem."[284] You may ask what skill enabled her to accomplish this change, or on what grounds did she merit it? I can tell you in a few words. She wept bitterly,[285] she sighed deeply from her heart, she sobbed with a repentance that shook her very being, till the evil that inflamed her passions was cleansed away. The heavenly physician came with speed to her aid, because "his word runs swiftly."[286] Perhaps you think the Word of God is not a medicine? Surely it is, a medicine strong and pungent, testing the mind and the heart.[287] "The Word of God is something alive and active. It cuts like any double-edged sword but more finely. It can slip through the place where the soul is divided from the spirit, or the joints from the marrow: it can judge the secret thoughts."[288] It is up to you, wretched sinner, to humble yourself as this happy penitent did so that you may be rid of your wretchedness.[289] Prostrate yourself on the ground, take hold of his feet, soothe them with kisses, sprinkle them with your tears and so wash not them but yourself. Thus you will become one of the

[281] Prv 25:27.
[282] Jer 13:23.
[283] Ps 118:42.
[284] Sg 1:4.
[285] Lk 22:62.
[286] Ps 147:15.
[287] Ps 7:10.
[288] Heb 4:12.
[289] Lk 7:37ff.

"flock of shorn ewes as they come up from the washing."[290] But even then you may not dare to lift up a face suffused with shame and grief, until you hear the sentence: "Your sins are forgiven,"[291] to be followed by the summons: "Awake, awake, captive daughter of Sion, awake, shake off the dust."[292]

II. 3. Though you have made a beginning by kissing the feet, you may not presume to rise at once by impulse to the kiss of the mouth; there is a step to be surmounted in between, an intervening kiss on the hand for which I offer the following explanation. If Jesus says to me: "Your sins are forgiven," what will it profit me if I do not cease from sinning? I have taken off my tunic, am I to put it on again?[293] And if I do, what have I gained? If I soil my feet again after washing them, is the washing of any benefit? Long did I lie in the slough of the marsh,[294] filthy with all kinds of vices; if I return to it again I shall be worse than when I first wallowed in it. On top of that I recall that he who healed me said to me as he exercised his mercy: "Now you are well again, be sure not to sin any more, or something worse may happen to you."[295] He, however, who gave me the grace to repent, must also give me the power to persevere, lest by repeating my sins I should end up by being worse than I was before.[296] Woe to me then, repentant though I be, if he without whom I can do nothing should suddenly withdraw his supporting hand.[297] I really mean nothing; of myself I can achieve neither repentance nor perseverance, and for that reason I pay heed to the Wise Man's advice: "Do not repeat yourself at your prayers."[298] The

[290] Sg 4:2.
[291] Lk 7:48.
[292] Is 52:1–2.
[292] Is 52:1–2.

[293] Sg 5:3.
[294] Ps 39:3.
[295] Jn 5:14.

[296] Lk 11:26.
[297] Jn 15:5.
[298] Sir 7:15.

Judge's threat to the tree that did not yield good fruit is another thing that makes me fearful.[299] For these various reasons I must confess that I am not entirely satisfied with the first grace by which I am enabled to repent of my sins; I must have the second as well, and so bear fruits that befit repentance, that I may not return like the dog to its vomit.[300]

4. I am now able to see what I must seek for and receive before I may hope to attain to a higher and holier state.[301] I do not wish to be suddenly on the heights, my desire is to advance by degrees. The impudence of the sinner displeases God as much as the modesty of the penitent gives him pleasure. You will please him more readily if you live within the limits proper to you, and do not set your sights at things beyond you.[302] It is a long and formidable leap from the foot to the mouth, a manner of approach that is not commendable. Consider for a moment: still tarnished as you are with the dust of sin, would you dare touch those sacred lips? Yesterday you were lifted from the mud, today you wish to encounter the glory of his face? No, his hand must be your guide to that end. First it must cleanse your stains, then it must raise you up. How raise you? By giving you the grace to dare to aspire. You wonder what this may be. I see it as the grace of the beauty of temperance and the fruits that befit repentance,[303] the works of the religious man. These are the instruments that will lift you from the dunghill and cause your hopes to soar.[304] On receiving such a grace then, you must kiss his hand, that is, you must give glory to his name, not to yourself.[305] First of all you must glorify him because he has forgiven your sins, secondly because he has adorned you with virtues. Otherwise

[299]Mt 3:10.
[300]Lk 3:8; Prv 26:11.
[301]Mt 7:8.
[302]Sir 3:22.
[303]Lk 3:8.
[304]Ps 112:7.
[305]Ps 113:9.

you will need a bold front to face reproaches such as these: "What do you have that was not given to you? And if it was given, how can you boast as though it were not?"[306]

III. 5. Once you have had this twofold experience of God's benevolence in these two kisses, you need no longer feel abashed in aspiring to a holier intimacy. Growth in grace brings expansion of confidence. You will love with greater ardor, and knock on the door with greater assurance, in order to gain what you perceive to be still wanting to you. "The one who knocks will always have the door opened to him."[307] It is my belief that to a person so disposed, God will not refuse that most intimate kiss of all, a mystery of supreme generosity and ineffable sweetness. You have seen the way that we must follow, the order of procedure: first, we cast ourselves at his feet, we weep before the Lord who made us,[308] deploring the evil we have done. Then we reach out for the hand that will lift us up, that will steady our trembling knees.[309] And finally, when we shall have obtained these favors through many prayers and tears, we humbly dare to raise our eyes to his mouth, so divinely beautiful, not merely to gaze upon it, but—I say it with fear and trembling—to receive its kiss. "Christ the Lord is a Spirit before our face,"[310] and he who is joined to him in a holy kiss becomes through his good pleasure, one spirit with him.[311]

6. To you, Lord Jesus, how truly my heart has said: "My face looks to you. Lord, I do seek your face."[312] In the dawn you brought me proof of your love,[313] in my first approach to

---

[306] 1 Cor 4:7.
[307] Lk 11:10.
[308] Ps 94:6.
[309] Is 35:3.
[310] Lam 4:20. St. Bernard's Latin version seems close to the Greek Septuagint version. It may be from the Itala or some ms. no longer available.
[311] 1 Cor 16:20; 1 Cor 6:17.
[312] Ps 26:8.
[313] Ps 142:8.

kiss your revered feet you forgave my evil ways as I lay in the dust. With the advancement of the day you gave your servant reason to rejoice when, in the kiss of the hand, you imparted the grace to live rightly.[314] And now what remains, O good Jesus, except that suffused as I am with the fullness of your light, and while my spirit is fervent, you would graciously bestow on me the kiss of your mouth, and give me unbounded joy in your presence.[315] Serenely lovable above all others, tell me where will you lead your flock to graze, where will you rest it at noon?[316] Dear brothers, surely it is wonderful for us to be here,[317] but the burden of the day calls us elsewhere. These guests, whose arrival has just now been announced to us, compel me to break off rather than to conclude a talk that I enjoy so much. So I go to meet the guests, to make sure that the duty of charity, of which we have been speaking, may not suffer neglect, that we may not hear it said of us: "They do not practice what they preach."[318] Do you pray in the meantime that God may accept the homage of my lips for your spiritual welfare, and for the praise and glory of his name.[319]

SERMON 4

The Kiss of the Lord's Feet, Hands, and Mouth (continued)

Yesterday our talk dealt with three stages of the soul's progress under the figure of the three kisses. You still remember this, I hope, for today I intend to continue that same discussion, according as God in his goodness may provide for one so needy.[320] We said, as you remember, that

[314]Ps 85:4.
[315]Ps 15:11.
[316]Sg 1:6.

[317]Lk 9:33.
[318]Mt 23:3.
[319]Ps 118:108; 1 Pt 1:7.

[320]Ps 67:11.

these kisses were given to the feet, the hand, and the mouth, in that order. The first is the sign of a genuine conversion of life, the second is accorded to those making progress, the third is the experience of only a few of the more perfect. The book of Scripture that we have undertaken to expound begins with this last kiss, but I have added the other two in the hope that you will attain a better understanding of the last. I leave it to you to judge whether this was necessary, but I do really think that the very nature of the discourse clearly suggests that they be included. And I should be surprised if you did not see that she who said: "Let him kiss me with the kiss of his mouth,"[321] wished to make a distinction between the kiss of the mouth and another or several other kisses. It might have been enough for her to have said simply: "Let him kiss me." Why then should she distinctly and pointedly add: "with the kiss of his mouth," a usage that is certainly not customary? Is it not that she wished to indicate that this kiss at the summit of love's intimacy is not the sole one? People normally say, do they not: "Kiss me," or "Give me a kiss"? Nobody adds the words: "with your mouth," or, "with the kiss of your mouth." When we wish to kiss somebody, we do not have to state explicitly what we want when we offer our lips to each other. For example, St. John's story of Christ's reception of the traitor's kiss simply says: "He kissed him,"[322] without adding "with his mouth or with the kiss of his mouth." This is normal procedure then both in speech and in writing. We have here three stages of the soul's growth in love, three stages of its advance toward perfection that are sufficiently known and intelligible to those who have experienced them. There is first the forgiveness of

[321] Sg 1:1.
[322] Mk 14:45.

sins, then the grace that follows on good deeds, and finally that contemplative gift by which a kind and beneficent Lord shows himself to the soul with as much clarity as bodily frailty can endure.

2. Perhaps I should here attempt a better explanation of my reason for calling the first two favors kisses. We all know that the kiss is a sign of peace. If what Scripture says is true: "Our iniquities have made a gulf between us and God,"[323] then peace can be attained only when the intervening gulf is bridged. When therefore we make satisfaction and become reconciled by the rejoining of the cleavage caused by sin, in what better way can I describe the favor we receive than as a kiss of peace? Nor is there a more becoming place for this kiss than at the feet; the amends we make for the pride of our transgressions ought to be humble and diffident.

II. 3. But when God endows us with the more ample grace of a sweet friendship with him, in order to enable us to live with a virtue that is worthy of such a relationship, we tend to raise our heads from the dust with a greater confidence for the purpose of kissing, as is the custom, the hand of our benefactor. It is essential however that we should not make this favor the occasion of self-glorification, we must give the glory to him from whom it comes. For if you glory in yourself rather than in the Lord,[324] it is your own hand that you kiss, not his, which, according to the words of Job, is the greatest evil and a denial of God.[325] If therefore, as Scripture suggests, the seeking of one's own glory is like kissing one's own hand, then he who gives glory to God is

---

[323] Is 59:2.
[324] 1 Cor 1:31.
[325] Jb 31:28. See the note on this verse in the Jerusalem Bible (hereafter JB) (Garden City, N.Y.: Doubleday, 1966), note f. p. 763.

quite properly said to be kissing God's hand.[326] We see this to be the case among men. Slaves beg pardon of their offended masters by kissing their feet, and the poor kiss their benefactor's hand when they receive an alms.

III. 4. This poses a problem for you? God is spirit,[327] his simple substance cannot be considered to have bodily members, so then, you say, show us what you mean by the hands and feet of God; explain to us the kiss of these hands and feet. But if I in turn put a question to my critic about the mouth of God—for, after all, Scripture does speak of the kiss of the mouth—will he tell me that this of course does refer to God? Surely if we attribute a mouth to God we may also attribute hands and feet, for, if he lacks these latter he must lack the former too.

But God has a mouth by which "he teaches men knowledge," he has a hand with which "he provides for all living creatures," and he has feet for which the earth is a footstool.[328] When the sinners of the earth are converted from their ways, it is in abasement before these feet that they make satisfaction. I allow of course that God does not have these members by his nature, they represent certain modes of our encounter with him. The heartfelt desire to admit one's guilt brings a man down in lowliness before God, as it were to his feet; the heartfelt devotion of a worshipper finds in God renewal and refreshment, the touch, as it were, of his hand; and the delights of contemplation lead on to that ecstatic repose that is the fruit of the kiss of his mouth. Because his providence rules over all, he is all things to all, yet, to speak with accuracy, he is in no way what these things are. If we consider him in himself, his home

---

[326]Jn 7:18; 9:24.
[327]Jn 4:24.
[328]Ps 93:10, 135:25; Is 66:1.

is in inaccessible light, his peace is so much greater than we can understand, his wisdom has no bounds.[329] No one can measure his greatness, no man can see him and live.[330] Yet he who by his very nature is the principle through whom all creatures spring into being, cannot be far from any of us, since without him all are nothing.[331] More wonderful still, though no one can be more intimately present to us than he, no one is more incomprehensible. For what is more intimate to anything than its own being? And yet, what is more incomprehensible to any of us than the being of all things? Of course when I say that God is the being of all things, I do not wish it to be understood in the sense that he and they are identical, but rather in the sense of the words of Scripture: "All that exists comes from him, all is by him and in him."[332] He is the creator, the efficient cause, not the material, of every creature. Such is the way the God whose majesty is so great has decided to be present to his creatures: as the being of all things that are, as the life of all things that live; a light to all those who think, virtue to all who think rightly, and glory to those who prevail in life's battle.

5. In this work of creation, of government, of administration, of imparting motion, of steering toward particular ends, of renewal and strengthening, he has no need of bodily instruments. By his word alone he had made all things, both corporeal and spiritual. Souls have a need for bodies, and bodies in turn a need for senses, if they are to know and influence each other. Not so the omnipotent God, who by the immediate act of his will, and that alone, both creates and governs at his good pleasure. His influence touches whom he wills, as much as he wills, without calling on the aid or service of bodily powers.

[329] 1 Tm 6:16; Phil 4:7; Ps 146:5.
[330] Ps 144:3; Ex 33:20.
[331] Acts 17:27; Jn 1:3.
[332] Rom 11:36.

What possible help could he receive from bodily senses when he decides to take cognizance of the things he brought into being? Nothing has the remotest chance of hiding from him, or of escaping that light of his that penetrates everywhere; sense awareness can never be the medium of his knowledge. Not merely does he know all things without a body's intervention, he also makes himself known to the pure in heart without the need for recourse to it.[333] I have spoken extensively on this point in order to make it more plain for you, but now pressure of time demands that I come to an end, so we must postpone further discussion till tomorrow.

SERMON II

Thanksgiving for Christ's Saving Work

I said at the end of my last sermon, and I have no hesitation in repeating it, that I long to see you all sharing in that holy anointing, that religious attitude in which the benefits of God are recalled with gladness and thanksgiving. This involves a twofold grace: it lightens the burdens of the present life, makes them more supportable for those who can give themselves with joy to the work of praising God;[334] and nothing more appropriately represents on earth the state of life in the heavenly fatherland than spontaneity in this outpouring of praise. Scripture implies as much when it says: "Happy those who live in your house and can praise you all day long."[335] It was with a special reference to this anointing

[333]Mt 5:8.
[334]Zep 3:17.
[335]Ps 83:5.

that the Prophet exclaimed: "How good, how delightful it is for all to live together like brothers; fine as oil on the head."[336] These words do not seem applicable to the first anointing. Though that is good in itself, it is not by any means pleasant, because the recollection of one's sins begets bitterness rather than pleasure. Nor do those involved in it live together, since each one bewails and mourns over his own particular sins. Those, however, who are employed in the work of thanksgiving are contemplating and thinking about God alone, and so they cannot help but dwell in unity. That which they do is good because they offer to God the glory that is most rightly his; and it is also pleasant, since of its very nature it gives delight.

2. And for that reason my advice to you, my friends, is to turn aside occasionally from troubled and anxious pondering on the paths you may be treading, and to travel on smoother ways where the gifts of God are serenely savored, so that the thought of him may give breathing space to you whose consciences are perplexed. I should like you to experience for yourselves the truth of the holy Prophet's words: "Make the Lord your joy and he will give you what your heart desires."[337] Sorrow for sin is indeed necessary, but it should not be an endless preoccupation. You must dwell also on the glad remembrance of God's loving-kindness, otherwise sadness will harden the heart and lead it more deeply into despair. Let us mix honey with our absinthe, it is more easily drunk when sweetened, and what bitterness it may still retain will be wholesome. You must fix your attention on the ways of God, see how he mitigates the bitterness of the heart that is crushed, how he wins back the pusillanimous

---

[336]Ps 132:1–2.
[337]Ps 36:4.

soul from the abyss of despair, how he consoles the grief-stricken and strengthens the wavering with the sweet caress of his faithful promise. By the mouth of the Prophet he declares: "For my praise I will bridle you, lest you should perish."[338] By this he seems to say: "Lest you should be cast down by excessive sadness at the sight of your sins, and rush despairingly to perdition like an unbridled horse over a precipice, I shall rein you in, I shall curb you with my mercy and set you on your feet with my praises. Then you will breathe freely again in the enjoyment of my benefits, over-whelmed though you be by evils of your own making, because you will find that my kindness is greater than your culpability." If Cain had been curbed by this kind of bridle he would never have uttered that despairing cry: "My iniquity is greater than that I may deserve pardon."[339] God forbid! God forbid! His loving mercy is greater than all iniquity. Hence the just man is not always accusing himself, he does so only in the opening words of his intercourse with God;[340] he will normally conclude that intercourse with the divine praises. You can see therefore that the order of the just man's progress is expressed in the words: "After reflecting on my behavior, I turn my feet to your decrees,"[341] that is, he who has endured grief and unhappiness in following his own ways can finally say: "In the way of your decrees lies my joy, a joy beyond all wealth."[342] Therefore, if you are to follow the just man's example, if you are to form a humble

---

[338] Is 48:9, Vulgate. St. Bernard's version is slightly different.

[339] Gn 4:13, Vulgate.

[340] Prv 18:17. St. Bernard's rendering is not found in the Vulgate. It is a Latin version of the Greek Septuagint text also to be found in writings of the early Fathers. Cf. St. Ambrose, *De Offic. Ministrorum*, bk. 1, chap. 25; and St. Cyril, *In Joan*, bk. 2, chap. 14.

[341] Ps 118:59.

[342] Ps 118:14.

opinion of yourselves, you must think of the Lord with goodness. So you are told in the Book of Wisdom: "Think of the Lord with goodness, seek him in simplicity of heart."[343] You will all the more easily achieve this if you let your minds dwell frequently, even continually, on the memory of God's bountifulness. Otherwise, how will you fulfill St. Paul's advice: "In all things give thanks to God,"[344] if your hearts will have lost sight of those things for which thanks are due? I would not have you bear the reproach flung at the Jews of old, who, according to Scripture, "had forgotten his achievements, the marvels he had shown them."[345]

II. 3. We must admit though that it is impossible for any man to remember and recount all the benefits that the Lord, so merciful and tenderhearted,[346] ceaselessly bestows on mortal men, for who can recount the Lord's triumphs, who can praise him enough?[347] Yet one at least of his benefits, the work by which he redeemed us, his chief and greatest achievement, should by no means be allowed to slip from the memory of the redeemed. Concerning this work I wish to suggest for your consideration two important points that now occur to me, which I shall state as briefly as possible in accord with the wise man's saying: "Give the wise man an opportunity, he grows wiser still."[348] The two are these: manner and fruit. The manner involved the self-emptying of God, the fruit was that we should be filled with him. Meditation on the former is the seedbed of holy hope, meditation on the latter an incentive to the highest love. Both of them are essential for our progress, because hope without love is the lot of the timeserver, and love without reward grows cold.

---

[343]Ws 1:1.
[344]Thes 5:18.
[345]Ps 77:11.
[346]Ps 110:4.
[347]Ps 105:2.
[348]Prv 9:9.

4. I shall add, too, that the fruit we must expect as our love's fulfillment should be worthy of the promise of him whom we love: "A full measure, pressed down, shaken together and running over, will be poured into your lap."[349] And that measure, as I have heard, will be without measure.[350]

III. But what I should like to know, however, is the nature of that which is to be measured out, what that immense reward is which has been promised. "The eye has not seen, O God, besides you, what things you have prepared for them that love you."[351] Tell us then, since you do the preparing, tell us what it is you prepare. We believe, we are confident, that in accordance with your promise, "we shall be filled with the good things of your house."[352] But—I persist in asking—what are these good things, what are they like? Would it be with corn and wine and oil,[353] with gold and silver or precious stones? But these are things that we have known and seen, that we have grown weary of seeing. We seek for the things that no eye has seen and no ear has heard, things beyond the mind of man.[354] To search after these things, whatever they may be, is a source of pleasure and relish and delight. "They will all be taught by God," says Scripture, and he will be all in all.[355] As I see it, the fullness that we hope for from God will be only something of God himself.

5. Who indeed can comprehend what an abundance of goodness is contained in that brief expression: "God will be all in all"?[356] Not to speak of the body, I discern in the soul three faculties, the reason, the will, the memory, and these three

---

[349] Lk 6:38.
[350] Jn 3:34.
[351] Is 64:4. Vulgate has "wait for you."
[352] Ps 64:5.

[353] Ps 4:8.
[354] 1 Cor 2:9.
[355] Jn 6:45; 1 Cor 15:28.
[356] Ps 30:20; 1 Cor 15:28.

may be said to be identified with the soul itself.[357] Everyone who is "guided by the Spirit"[358] realizes how greatly in the present life these three are lacking in integrity and perfection. And what reason can there be for this, except that God is not yet "all in all"? Hence it comes about that the reason very often falters in its judgments, the will is agitated by a fourfold perturbation and the memory confused by its endless forgetfulness.[359] Man, noble though he be, was unwillingly subjected to this triple form of futility, but hope nonetheless was left to him.[360] For he who satisfies with good the desire of the soul[361] will one day himself be for the reason fullness of light, for the will, the fullness of peace, for the memory, eternity's uninterrupted flow. O truth! O love! O eternity! Oh blessed and beatifying Trinity! To you the wretched trinity that I bear within me sends up its doleful yearnings because of the unhappiness of its exile. Departing from you, in what errors, what pains, what fears it has involved itself! Unhappy me! What a trinity we have won in exchange for you! "My heart is throbbing," and hence my pain; "my strength is deserting me" and hence my fear; "the light of my eyes itself has left me,"[362] and hence my error. O trinity of my soul, how utterly different the Trinity you have offended in your exile.

---

[357] St. Bernard here seems to hold that there is no distinction between the soul and its faculties. This doctrine, also accepted by St. Bonaventura, was taught by Avicenna, who died in 1037, over fifty years before Bernard was born. The debate still goes on. The school of Jung, including some Catholics, maintain the identity of soul and faculties; followers of St. Thomas Aquinas hold for a real distinction between them. See H. Grenier, *Cursus Philosophiae,* vol. 1, p. 350; J. Donceel, *Philosophical Psychology* (New York: Sheed and Ward, 1961), pp. 2ff.

[358] Gal 5:16, 25.

[359] He refers here to the four passions, love, joy, fear, and sadness, which he treats of in Sermon 50 of the Occasional Sermons, Cistercian Fathers Series 49.

[360] Rom 8:20.

[361] Ps 102:5.

[362] Ps 37:11.

6. And still, why so downcast, my soul, why do you sigh within me? Put your hope in God. I shall praise him yet,[363] when error will have gone from the reason, pain from the will, and every trace of fear from the memory. Then will come that state for which we hope, with its admirable serenity, its fullness of delight, its endless security. The God who is truth is the source of the first of these gifts; the God who is love, of the second; the God who is all-powerful, of the third. And so it will come to pass that God will be all in all,[364] for the reason will receive unquenchable light, the will imperturbable peace, the memory an unfailing fountain from which it will draw eternally. I wonder if it seems right to you that we should assign that first operation to the Son, the second to the Holy Spirit, the last to the Father. In doing so, however, we must beware of excluding either the Father or the Son or the Holy Spirit from any one of these communications, lest the distinction of Persons should diminish the divine fullness proper to each of them, or their perfection be so understood as to annul the personal properties. Consider too that the children of this world experience a corresponding threefold temptation from the allurements of the flesh,[365] the glitter of life in the world, the self-fulfillment patterned on Satan. These three include all the artifices by which the present life deceives its unhappy lovers, even as St. John proclaimed: "All that is in the world is the lust of the flesh and the lust of the eyes and the pride of life."[366] So much for the fruit of the redemption.

7. Now with regard to the manner, which if you remember, we defined as God's self-emptying,[367] I venture to offer three important points for your consideration. For that emptying

[363] Ps 41:6.
[364] 1 Cor 15:28.
[365] Lk 16:8; 20:34.
[366] 1 Jn 2:16.
[367] Sermon 9:3.

was neither a simple gesture nor a limited one; but he emptied himself even to the assuming of human nature, even to accepting death, death on a cross.[368] Who is there that can adequately gauge the greatness of the humility, gentleness, self-surrender, revealed by the Lord of majesty in assuming human nature, in accepting the punishment of death, the shame of the cross? But somebody will say: "Surely the Creator could have restored his original plan without all that hardship?" Yes, he could, but he chose the way of personal suffering so that man would never again have a reason to display that worst and most hateful of all vices, ingratitude. If his decision did involve painful weariness for himself, it was meant also to involve man in a debt that only great love can pay. Where the ease with which man was created sapped his spirit of devotion, the hardship with which he was redeemed should urge him on to gratitude. For how did man the ingrate regard his creation? "I was created freely indeed but with no trouble or labor on my Creator's part; for at his command I was made,[369] just like every other thing. What is big about that gift if not the great facility of the Word that made it?" Thus does human impiety belittle the boon of creation, and turn that which of its nature is a source of love into an occasion for ingratitude. Those who live by these sentiments share the godlessness of evildoers.[370] But these lying mouths are silenced.[371] For, more obvious than the light of day is the immense sacrifice he has made for you, O man; he who was Lord became a slave, he who was rich became a pauper, the Word was made flesh, and the Son of God did not disdain to become the son of man. So may it please you to remember that, even if made out of nothing, you have not

[368] Phil 2:7ff.
[369] Ps 148:5.
[370] Ps 140:4.
[371] Ps 62:12.

been redeemed out of nothing. In six days he created all things, and among them, you. On the other hand, for a period of thirty whole years he worked your salvation in the midst of the earth.[372] What endurance was his in those labors! To his bodily needs and the molestations of his enemies did he not add the mightier burden of the ignominy of the cross, and crown it all with the horror of his death? And this was indeed necessary. Man and beast you save, O Lord. How you have multiplied your mercy, O God.[373]

8. Meditate on these things, turn them over continually in your minds. Refresh those hearts of yours with perfumes such as these, hearts writhing so long under the repugnant odor of your sins. May you abound with these ointments, as sweet as they are salutary. But yet, you must beware of thinking that you now possess those superior ones that are commended to us in the breasts of the bride. The necessity of bringing this sermon to an end does not allow me to begin discussing them now. But all that has been said about the others you must retain in your memory and reveal in your way of life; and do please help me with your prayers that I may worthily portray with appropriate sentiments those superior delights of the bride, that I may fill your own souls with the love of the Bridegroom, Jesus Christ our Lord.

SERMON 12

The Grace of Loving-kindness

As I recall, I have been discussing two ointments with you:[374] one of contrition, that takes account of numerous

---

[372]Ps 73:12.
[373]Ps 35:7ff.

[374]Cf. Sermon 10:4.

sins, the other of devotion, that embodies numerous benefits. Both are wholesome experiences but not both pleasant. The first one is known to carry a sting, because the bitter remembrance of sins incites compunction and causes pain, whereas the second is soothing, it brings consolation through a knowledge of God's goodness and so assuages pain. But there is another ointment, far excelling these two, to which I give the name loving-kindness, because the elements that go to its making are the needs of the poor, the anxieties of the oppressed, the worries of those who are sad, the sins of wrongdoers, and finally, the manifold misfortunes of people of all classes who endure affliction, even if they are our enemies. These elements may seem rather depressing, but the ointment made from them is more fragrant than all other spices.[375] It bears the power to heal, for "Happy the merciful; they shall have mercy shown them."[376] A collection therefore of manifold miseries on which the eye rests with loving-kindness, represents the ingredients from which the best ointments are made, ointments that are worthy of the breasts of the bride and capable of winning the Bridegroom's attention. Happy the mind that has been wise enough to enrich and adorn itself with an assortment of spices such as these, pouring upon them the oil of mercy and warming them with the fire of charity! Who, in your opinion, is the good man who takes pity and lends,[377] who is disposed to compassionate, quick to render assistance, who believes that there is more happiness in giving than in receiving,[378] who easily forgives but is not easily angered, who will never seek to be avenged, and will in all things take

[375] Sg 4:10.
[376] Mt 5:7.
[377] Ps 111:5.
[378] Acts 20:35.

thought for his neighbor's needs as if they were his own? Whoever you may be, if your soul is thus disposed, if you are saturated with the dew of mercy, overflowing with affectionate kindness, making yourself all things to all men[379] yet pricing your deeds like something discarded[380] in order to be ever and everywhere ready to supply to others what they need, in a word, so dead to yourself that you live only for others—if this be you, then you obviously and happily possess the third and best of all ointments and your hands have dripped with liquid myrrh that is utterly enchanting.[381] It will not run dry in times of stress nor evaporate in the heat of persecution; but God will perpetually "remember all your oblations and find your holocaust acceptable."[382]

2. There are men of riches in the city of the Lord of hosts.[383] I wonder if some among them possess these ointments.

II. As invariably happens, the first to spring to my mind is that chosen vessel,[384] St. Paul, truly a vessel of myrrh and frankincense and every perfume the merchant knows.[385] He was Christ's incense to God in every place.[386] His heart was a fountain of sweet fragrance that radiated far and wide, seized as he was with an anxiety for all the churches.[387] See what those ingredients were, those spices that he had accumulated for himself: "I face death every day," he said, "for your glory."[388] And again: "Who was weak, and I was not weak with him? Who was scandalized, and I did not burn?"[389] Many similar passages, well known to all of you, show how prolific this rich man was in compounding the best of ointments. It was so fitting that the breasts which fed the members of Christ should be redolent of the finest and purest

[379] 1 Cor 9:22.
[380] Ps 30:13.
[381] Sg 5:5.
[382] Ps 19:4.

[383] Ps 47:9.
[384] Acts 9:15.
[385] Sg 3:6.
[386] 2 Cor 2:15.

[387] 2 Cor 11:28.
[388] 1 Cor 15:31.
[389] 2 Cor 11:29.

of spices; they were members to whom Paul was truly a mother, giving birth to them all over and over again, until Christ was formed in them,[390] that the members might be renewed in the likeness of their head.

3. Another man, too, rich in the possession of these choice materials from which he prepared ointments of superior quality, said: "No stranger ever had to sleep outside, my door was always open to the travelers";[391] and again: "I was eyes for the blind, and feet for the lame. Who but I was father of the poor? I used to break the fangs of wicked men, and snatch their prey from between their jaws.[392] Have I been insensible to poor men's needs, or let a widow's eyes grow dim? Or taken my share of bread alone, not giving a share to the orphan?[393] Have I ever seen a wretch in need of clothing, or a beggar going naked, without his having cause to bless me from his heart, as he felt the warmth of the fleece from my lambs?"[394] What a sweet perfume that man must have radiated throughout the earth by works such as these? Every action bore its own aroma. Even his own conscience was filled with accumulating perfumes, so that pleasant odors from within tempered the stench of his rotting flesh.

4. Joseph, after he had drawn all the Egyptians to run after him to the odor of his ointments,[395] ultimately proffered the same perfumed favor to the very men who had sold him. He began indeed by angrily reproaching them, but could not for long restrain the tears that burst forth from the fullness of his heart, tears that effaced the signs of anger and betrayed his love.[396] Samuel mourned for Saul, the man who was intent on killing him; his heart grew warm with the fire

---

[390]Gal 4:19.
[391]Jb 31:32.
[392]Jb 29:15ff.
[393]Jb 31:16ff.
[394]Jb 31:19ff.
[395]Sg 1:3.
[396]Gn 42:7; 43:30.

of charity, his spirit melted within him, and love made him weep.[397] And because his reputation was diffused abroad like a perfume, Scripture tells of him that "all Israel from Dan to Beersheba came to know that Samuel was accredited as a prophet of the Lord."[398] What shall I say of Moses? With what a rich feast did he not fill his heart?[399] Not even that rebellious house in which for a time he sojourned,[400] could destroy by its rude anger the spiritual grace bestowed on him at the beginning of his career. His gentleness remained unshaken despite unremitting discords and conflicts day after day. Well did he deserve that testimony of the Holy Spirit that he was the humblest man on earth.[401] For with them that hated peace he was peaceable,[402] since he not only curbed his anger in face of an ungrateful and rebellious people, but even appeased by his intervention the anger of God, as Scripture says: "He talked of putting an end to them and would have done, if Moses his chosen had not stood in the reach, confronting him, deflecting his destructive anger."[403] He even went so far as to say: "If it please you to forgive, forgive. But if not, then blot me out from the book that you have written."[404] Surely a man truly filled with the grace of mercy! Clearly he speaks as a mother would for whom there is no delight or happiness that is not shared by her children. For instance, if a wealthy man should say to a poverty-stricken woman: "Come and join me at dinner, but better leave outside the child in your arms, his crying will only disturb us," do you think she would do it? Would she not rather choose to fast than to put away the child so dear to

[397]1 Sm 15:35.
[398]1 Sm 3:20.
[399]Ps 62:6.
[400]Ezk 2:5.

[401]Nm 12:3.
[402]Ps 119:7.
[403]Ps 105:23. Cf. Ex 32:11ff.
[404]Ex 32:31ff.

her and dine alone with the rich man? Hence Moses was resolved not to go alone to join in his Master's happiness,[405] while those people to whom he clung as a mother, with all a mother's affection despite their restlessness and ingratitude, remained outside. Inwardly he suffered, but he judged that suffering to be more tolerable than separation from them.

5. Who was more gentle than David who bewailed the death of the man who had ever thirsted for his own?[406] What greater evidence of kindness could there be than his unhappiness at the demise of him into whose place he stepped as king? How hard it was to console him when his parricidal son was killed![407] Affection such as this certainly witnessed to an abundance of the best ointment. Therefore there is an assured ring in the words of that prayer: "O Lord, remember David and all his meekness."[408] All these persons possessed the best ointments and even today diffuse their perfumes through all the churches. A similar influence is achieved by those too who, in the course of this life have been indulgent and charitable, who have made an effort to show kindness to their fellow men, not vindicating to themselves alone any grace they were gifted with, but exercising it for the common good in the consciousness that they owe a duty to enemies no less than friends, to the wise just as much

---

[405]Mt 25:21.

[406]2 Sm 1:11ff.

[407]2 Sm 19:4.

[408]Ps 131:1. According to the tradition based on 2 Chron 6:14ff., this psalm was sung by Solomon at the dedication of the temple. Some modern authors tend to disagree with this and say it was more probably composed when the house of David was overthrown in spite of Nathan's prophecy of its permanence (Cf. 2 Sm 7:5–16). It may date from the reign of Joachim, released from a Babylonian prison in 561. B.C. Cf. P. Boylan, *The Psalms,* vol. 2 (Dublin: Gill & Son Ltd., 1948); E. J. Kissane, *The Book of Psalms,* vol. 2 (Dublin: Browne & Nolan, 1954).

as to the unwise.[409] Since their purpose was to be of help to everybody they evinced a great humility before all in all that they did, they were beloved by God and men,[410] their good odor a perfume in the memory. Men like these, whatever their number, permeated their own times and today, too, with the best of ointments.[411]

III. And you too, if you will permit us your companions to share in the gift you have received from above, if you are at all times courteous, friendly, agreeable, gentle, and humble, you will find men everywhere bearing witness to the perfumed influence you radiate. Everyone among you who not only patiently endures the bodily and mental weaknesses of his neighbors, but, if permissible and possible, even plies them with attentions, inspires them with encouragement, helps them with advice, or, where the rules do not so permit, at least does not cease to assist them by fervent prayers— everyone, I repeat, who performs such deeds among you, gives forth a good odor among the brethren like a rare and delicate perfume. As balsam in the mouth so is such a man in the community; people will point him out and say: "This is a man who loves his brothers and the people of Israel; this is a man who prays much for the people and for the holy city."[412]

IV. 6. But let us turn to the Gospels to see if they contain any reference to these perfumes. "Mary of Magdala, Mary the mother of James, and Salome, bought spices with which to go and anoint Jesus."[413] What were these ointments, so precious that they were bought and prepared for the body of Christ, so abundant that they sufficed to anoint every part of it? For nowhere do we find that the other two ointments were either

---

[409]Rom 1:14.
[410]Sir 45:1.
[411]Sg 1:2.

[412]2 Mc 15:14.
[413]Mk 16:1.

bought or specially prepared for use on the body of Christ, or that they were spread over every part of it. There is a moment when we are suddenly brought face-to-face with a woman who in one place kisses Christ's feet and covers them with a perfume,[414] and in another either she or a different woman brings in an alabaster box of ointment and pours it on his head.[415] But in this instance we are told: "They bought spices with which to go and anoint Jesus."[416] They buy spices, not ointments; the ointment for his body was not bought readymade, a totally new one was prepared; and not for application merely to a part of his body such as the feet or the head, but—as is indicated in the words: "to anoint Jesus"— to cover his whole body, not any particular part.

7. You too, if you are to become deeply compassionate,[417] must behave generously and kindly not only to parents and relatives, or those from whom you have received or hope to receive a good turn—after all non-Christians do as much— but, following Paul's advice, you must make the effort to do good to all.[418] Inspired by this God-oriented purpose, you will never refuse to do an act of charity, whether spiritual or corporal, to an enemy, or withdraw it once offered. It will thus be clear that you abound with the best ointments, that you have undertaken to care not only for the head or feet of the Lord, but, as far as in you lies, for his whole body which is

---

[414]Lk 7:37ff.

[415]Mt 26:7ff.; Mk 14:3ff. Bernard's doubts about the identity of these women have still not been satisfactorily solved. The JB holds that the sinful woman of Lk 7:37ff. is most probably not Mary of Magdala, mentioned in Lk 8:2, nor Mary the sister of Martha, Lk 10:39. McKenzie (*Dictionary of the Bible,* p. 552) also denies that the sinful woman of Lk 7:37 and Mary of Magdala are the same. Nor does he think that Mary of Bethany may be identified with Mary of Magdala.

[416]Mk 16:1.

[417]Col 3:12.

[418]Mt 5:47; Gal 6:10.

the Church.[419] It was perhaps for this reason the Lord Jesus would not allow the mixture of spices to be used on his dead body; he wished to reserve it for his living body. For that Church which eats the living bread which has come down from heaven is alive:[420] she is the more precious Body of Christ that was not to taste death's bitterness, whereas every Christian knows that his other body did suffer death.[421] His will is that she be anointed, that she be cared for, that her sick members be restored to health with remedies that are the fruit of diligence. It was for her that he withheld these precious ointments, when, anticipating the hour and hastening the glory of his resurrection, he eluded the women's devout purpose only to give it new direction. Mercy and not contempt was the reason for this refusal; the service was not spurned but postponed that others might benefit. And the benefit I refer to is not the fruit of this material thing, this anointing of the body; it is a spiritual benefit symbolized by it. On this occasion he who is the teacher of religious devotion refused these choice ointments that are symbols of devotion, because it was his absolute wish that they be used for the spiritual and corporal welfare of his needy members. A short time previously, when valuable ointment was poured on his head and even on his feet, did he try to prevent it? Did he not rather oppose those who objected to it?[422] Simon, indignant that he should allow a sinful woman to touch him, received a stern rebuke in the course of a long parable, while others who grumbled at the waste of the ointment were silenced with the question: "Why are you upsetting the woman?"[423]

V. 8. There have been times, if I may digress a little, when as I sat down sadly at the feet of Jesus,[424] offering up my distressed

---

[419]Col 1:24.
[420]Jn 6:51.
[421]Heb 2:9.

[422]Lk 7:39ff.
[423]Mt 26:10.
[424]Ezr 9:3.

spirit in sacrifice, recalling my sins,[425] or again, at the rare moments when I stood by his head, filled with happiness at the memory of his favors, I could hear people saying: "Why this waste?"[426] They complained that I thought only of myself when, in their view, I could be working for the welfare of others. In effect they said: "This could have been sold at a high price and the money given to the poor."[427] But what a poor transaction for me, to forfeit my own life and procure my own destruction, even if I should gain the whole world![428] Hence I compared such talk to the scriptural mention of dead flies that spoil the perfumed oil,[429] and remembered the words of God: "O my people, those who praise you lead you into error."[430] But let those who accuse me of indolence listen to the Lord who takes my part with the query: "Why are you upsetting this woman?"[431] By this he means: "You are looking at the surface of things and therefore you judge superficially.[432] This is not a man, as you think, who can handle great enterprises, but a woman.[433] Why then try to impose on him a burden that to my mind he cannot endure?[434] The work that he performs for me is good,[435] let him be satisfied with this good until he finds strength to do better. If he eventually emerges from womanhood to manhood, to mature manhood,[436] then let him engage in a work of corresponding dignity."

VI. 9. My brothers, let us give due honor to bishops but have a wholesome fear of their jobs, for if we comprehend the nature of their jobs, we shall not hanker after the honor. Let us admit that our powers are unequal to the task, that our soft effeminate shoulders cannot be happy in supporting burdens made for men. It is not for us to pry into their

---

[425]Ps 50:19.
[426]Mt 26:8.
[427]Mt 26:9.
[428]Mt 16:26.

[429]Eccl 10:1.
[430]Is 3:12.
[431]Mt 26:10.
[432]Mk 12:14.

[433]Prv 31:19.
[434]Acts 15:10.
[435]Mk 14:6.
[436]Eph 4:13.

business but to pay them due respect. For it is surely churlish to censure their doings if you shun their responsibilities; you are no better than the woman at home spinning, who foolishly reprimands her husband returning from the battle. And I add: if a monk happens to notice that a prelate working in his diocese lives with less constraint than he, and with less circumspection; that he speaks more freely, eats as he pleases, sleeps when he will, laughs spontaneously, gives rein to anger, passes judgment readily, let him not rush precipitately to wrong conclusions, but rather call to mind the Scripture: "Better is the wickedness of a man than a woman who does good."[437] For you do well in keeping a vigilant eye on your own behavior, but the man who helps many acts with more virile purpose fulfilling a higher duty. And if in the performance of this duty he is guilty of some imperfection, if his life and behavior are less than regular, remember that love covers a multitude of sins.[438] I want this to be a warning against that twofold temptation with which the devil assails men in religious life: to covet the fame of a bishop's status, and to pass rash judgment on his excesses.

VII. 10. But let us get back to the ointments of the bride. Do you not see how that ointment of merciful love, the only one that may not be wasted, is to be preferred to the others? The fact that not even the gift of a cup of cold water goes unrewarded shows that nothing actually is wasted.[439] The ointment of contrition of course is good, made up as it is from the recollection of past sins and poured on the Lord's feet, because "You will not scorn, O God, this crushed and broken heart."[440] But better by far is the ointment of devotion,

---

[437]Sir 42:14.
[438]1 Pt 4:8.

[439]Mt 10:42.
[440]Ps 50:19.

distilled from the memory of God's beneficence, and worthy of being poured on Christ's head. Concerning it we have God's own witness: "Whoever makes thanksgiving his sacrifice honors me."[441] The function of merciful love, however, is superior to both; it works for the welfare of the afflicted and is diffused through the whole Body of Christ. By this I do not mean the body which was crucified, but the one that he acquired by his passion. An ointment that by its excellence blinds him to the worth of the other two is beyond question the best, for he said: "What I want is mercy, not sacrifice."[442] This, more than all the other virtues, is diffused like a perfume from the breasts of the bride, who desires to conform in all things to the will of her Bridegroom. Was it not the fragrance of mercy that enveloped the deathbed of Tabitha.[443] And like a life-giving perfume, it hastened her resurgence from death.

11. Finally a few brief words to end this present subject. The man whose speech intoxicates and whose good deeds radiate may take as addressed to himself the words: "Your breasts are better than wine, redolent of the best ointments."[444] Now who is worthy of such a commendation? Which of us can live uprightly and perfectly even for one hour, an hour free from fruitless talk and careless work? Yet there is one who truthfully and unhesitatingly can glory in this praise. She is the Church, whose fullness is a never-ceasing fount of intoxicating joy, perpetually fragrant. For what she lacks in one member she possesses in another according to the measure of Christ's gift and the plan of the Spirit who distributes to each one just as he chooses.[445] The Church's

[441] Ps 49:23.
[442] Mt 9:13.
[443] Acts 9:36ff.
[444] Sg 1:1ff.
[445] Eph 4:7; 1 Cor 12:11.

fragrance is radiated by those who use their money, tainted though it be, to win themselves friends;[446] she intoxicates by the words of her preachers, who drench the earth and make it drunk with the wine of spiritual gladness, and yield a harvest through their perseverance.[447] With the bold assurance of one confident that her breasts are better than wine and redolent of the choicest perfumes,[448] she lays claim to the title of bride. And although none of us will dare arrogate for his own soul the title of bride of the Lord, nevertheless we are members of the Church which rightly boasts of this title and of the reality that it signifies, and hence may justifiably assume a share in this honor. For what all of us simultaneously possess in a full and perfect manner, that each single one of us undoubtedly possesses by participation. Thank you, Lord Jesus, for your kindness in uniting us to the Church you so dearly love, not merely that we may be endowed with the gift of faith, but that like brides we may be one with you in an embrace that is sweet, chaste, and eternal, beholding with unveiled faces that glory which is yours in union with the Father and the Holy Spirit forever and ever.[449] Amen.

SERMON 15

The Name of Jesus

Wisdom is a kindly spirit,[450] and easy of access to those who call upon him. Quite often he anticipates their request and says: "Here I am."[451] Listen now to what, because of your

---

[446]Lk 16:9.
[447]Ps 64:10; Lk 8:15.
[448]Sg 1:1ff.

[449]2 Cor 3:18.
[450]Ws 1:6.
[451]Is 58:9; 65:24.

prayers, he has revealed to me about the subject we post-poned yesterday; be ready to gather the ripe fruit of your intercession. I put before you a name that is rightly compared to oil, how rightly I shall explain. You encounter many names for the Bridegroom scattered through the pages of Scripture, but all these I sum up for you in two. I think you will find none that does not express either the gift of his love or the power of his majesty. The Holy Spirit tells us this through the mouth of one of his friends: "Two things I have heard: it is for God to be strong, for you, Lord, to be merci-ful."[452] With reference to his majesty we read: "Holy and ter-rible is his name";[453] with reference to his love: "Of all the names in the world given to men, this is the only one by which we can be saved."[454] Further examples make it clearer still. Jeremiah says: "This is the name by which he will be called: 'the Lord our righteous one' "[455]—a name suggesting power; but when Isaiah says: "His name will be called Emmanuel,"[456] he indicates his love. He himself said: "You call me Master and Lord."[457] The first title implies love, the second majesty. Love's business is to educate the mind as well as to provide the body's food. Isaiah also said: "His name shall be called Wonderful, Counselor, God, the Mighty One, Ever-lasting Father, Prince of Peace."[458] The first, third, and fourth signify majesty, the others love. Which of these therefore is poured out? In some mysterious way the name of majesty and power is transfused into that of love and mercy, an amalgam that is abundantly poured out in the person of our Savior Jesus Christ.[459] The name "God" liquefies and dis-solves into the title "God with us," that is, into "Emmanuel." He who is "Wonderful" becomes "Counselor"; "God" and "the

[452]Ps 61:12ff. [455]Jer 23:6. [458]Is 9:6.
[453]Ps 110:9. [456]Is 7:14. [459]Ti 3:6.
[454]Acts 4:12. [457]Jn 13:13.

Mighty One" become the "Everlasting Father" and the "Prince of Peace." "The Lord our righteous one" becomes the "gracious and merciful Lord."[460] This process is not new: in ancient times "Abram" became "Abraham" and "Sarai" became "Sara";[461] and we are reminded that in these events the mystery of the communication of salvation was prefigured and celebrated.

2. So I ask where now is that warning cry: "I am the Lord, I am the Lord,"[462] that resounded with recurring terror in the ears of the people of old? The prayer with which I am familiar, that begins with the sweet name of Father,[463] gives me confidence of obtaining the petitions with which it continues. Servants are called friends in this new way,[464] and the resurrection is proclaimed not to mere disciples but to brothers.[465]

II. Nor am I surprised if, when the time has fully come,[466] there is an outpouring of Jesus's name as God fulfills what he had promised through Joel,[467] an outpouring of his Spirit on all mankind, since I read that a similar event took place among the Hebrews in former times.[468] But I feel that your thoughts fly ahead of my words, that you already guess what I intend to say. How is it, I ask, that God's first answer to Moses's question was: "I Am Who I Am," and "I Am has sent me to you"?[469] I doubt if even Moses himself would have grasped its import if it had not been poured out. But it was poured and he understood it; and not only poured but poured out, for an inward pouring had already occurred: the citizens of heaven already possessed it, the angels knew it. Now it is sent abroad, and what was infused into the angels as an intimate secret was poured out upon men, so that

[460]Ps 110:4.
[461]Gn 17:5; 17:15.
[462]Ex 20:2, 5.
[463]Mt 6:9.
[464]Jn 15:14.
[465]Mt 28:10.
[466]Gal 4:4.
[467]Jl 2:28.
[468]Nm 11:26.
[469]Ex 3:14.

henceforth they could justly proclaim from the earth: "Your name is oil poured out,"[470] if the obstinacy of a thankless people did not prevent it. For he had said: "I am the God of Abraham, the God of Isaac and the God of Jacob."[471]

3. Run then, O pagans, salvation is at hand, that name is poured out which saves all who invoke it.[472] The God of the angels calls himself the God of men. He poured out oil on Jacob and it fell on Israel.[473] Say to your brothers: "Give us some of your oil."[474] If they refuse, ask the Lord of the oil to give it to you. Say to him: "Take away our reproach."[475]

See that no envious tongue insults your beloved, whom it has pleased you to call from the ends of the earth with a compassion all the greater for her unworthiness. Is it fitting, I ask, that a wicked servant should shut out the invited guests of the master of the house? You have said: "I am the God of Abraham, the God of Isaac, and the God of Jacob."[476] Of no more than these? Pour out, continue to pour; open your hand still wider and satisfy the desire of everything that lives.[477]

Let them come from the east and the west and take their places with Abraham and Isaac and Jacob in the kingdom of heaven.[478] Let them come, let the tribes come up, the tribes of the Lord, to praise his name according to his command to Israel.[479] Let them come and take their place, let them feast and be filled with gladness,[480] let the banqueters sing as one man the resounding song of exultation and praise:[481] "Your name is oil poured out."[482] One thing I know: if we find that the porters are Andrew and Philip,[483] we shall not

[470]Sg 1:2.
[471]Ex 3:6.
[472]Acts 2:21.
[473]Is 9:8.
[474]Mt 25:8.

[475]Is 4:1.
[476]Ex 3:6.
[477]Ps 144:16.
[478]Mt 8:11.
[479]Ps 121:4.

[480]Ps 67:4.
[481]Ps 41:5.
[482]Sg 1:2.
[483]Jn 12:20ff.

be repulsed when we ask for oil, when we desire to see Jesus.[484] Philip will at once tell Andrew, and Andrew and Philip will tell Jesus. And what will Jesus say? Precisely because he is Jesus he will tell them: "Unless a wheat-grain falls into the ground and dies, it remains only a single grain; but if it dies, it yields a rich harvest."[485] Let the grain die therefore, and let the harvest of the pagans spring to fruition. It is necessary for Christ to suffer and to rise from the dead, and that penance and forgiveness of sin should be preached in his name,[486] not alone in Judaea but even among all nations, because from the sole name of Christ thousands upon thousands of believers are called Christians, whose hearts all re-echo: "Your name is oil poured out."

4. I recognize now the name hinted at by Isaiah: "My servants are to be given a new name. Whoever is blessed on earth in that name will be blessed by the Lord, Amen."[487] O blessed name, oil poured out without limit! From heaven it pours down on Judaea and from there over all the earth, so that round the whole world the Church proclaims: "Your name is oil poured out." And what an outpouring! It not only bathes the heavens and the earth, it even bedews the underworld, so that all beings in the heavens, on earth, and in the underworld should bend the knee in the name of Jesus, and that every tongue should acclaim:[488] "Your name is oil poured out." Take the name Christ, take the name Jesus; both were infused into the angels, both were poured out upon men, even upon men who rotted like animals in their own dung.[489] Thus you became a savior both of men and beasts, so countless are your mercies, O God.[490] How

---

[484] Jn 12:21ff.
[485] Jn 12:24.
[486] Lk 24:46ff.

[487] Is 65:15ff.
[488] Phil 2:10f.
[489] Jl 1:17.

[490] Ps 35:8.

precious your name, and yet how cheap! Cheap, but the instrument of salvation. If it were not cheap it would not have been poured out for me; if it lacked saving power it would not have won me. Made a sharer in the name, I share too in its inheritance. For I am a Christian, Christ's own brother. If I am what I say, I am the heir of God, coheir with Christ.[491] And what wonder if the name of the Bridegroom is poured out, since he himself is poured out? For he emptied himself to assume the condition of a slave.[492] Did he not even say: "I am poured out like water"?[493] The fullness of the divine life was poured out and lived on earth in bodily form,[494] that all of us who live in this body doomed to death may receive from that fullness,[495] and being filled with its life-giving odor say: "Your name is oil poured out." Such is what is meant by the outpouring of the name, such its manner, such its extent.

III. 5. But why the symbol of oil? I have yet to explain this. In the previous sermons I had begun to do so when another matter that seemed to demand mention suddenly presented itself,[496] though I may have dallied with it longer than I intended. In this I resembled the valiant woman, Wisdom, who put her hand to the distaff, her fingers to the spindle.[497] Skillfully she produced from her scanty stock of wool or flax a long spool of thread, out of which she wove the material that made warm clothes for the members of her household. The likeness between oil and the name of the Bridegroom is beyond doubt; the Holy Spirit's comparison of the two is no arbitrary gesture. Unless you can persuade me otherwise, I hold that the likeness is to be found in the threefold property

---

[491]Rom 8:17.
[492]Phil 2:7.
[493]Ps 21:15.
[494]Col 2:9.

[495]Rom 7:24; Jn 1:16.
[496]Sermon 14:8.
[497]Prv 31:10–21.

of oil: it gives light, it nourishes, it anoints. It feeds the flame, it nourishes the body, it relieves pain: it is light, food, medicine. And is not this true too of the Bridegroom's name? When preached it gives light, when meditated it nourishes, when invoked it relieves and soothes. Let us consider each point.

6. How shall we explain the worldwide light of faith, swift and flaming in its progress, except by the preaching of Jesus's name? Is it not by the light of this name that God has called us into his wonderful light,[498] that irradiates our darkness and empowers us to see the light?[499] To such as we Paul says: "You were darkness once, but now you are light in the Lord."[500] This is the name that Paul was commanded to present before kings and pagans and the people of Israel;[501] a name that illumined his native land as he carried it with him like a torch, preaching on all his journeys that the night is almost over, it will be daylight soon—let us give up all the things we prefer to do under cover of the dark; let us arm ourselves and appear in the light. Let us live decently as people do in the daytime.[502] To every eye he was a lamp on its lamp-stand;[503] to every place he brought the good news of Jesus, and him crucified.[504] What a splendor radiated from that light, dazzling the eyes of the crowd, when Peter uttered the name that strengthened the feet and ankles of the cripple, and gave light to many eyes that were spiritually blind![505] Did not the words shoot like a flame when he said: "In the name of Jesus Christ of Nazareth, arise and walk"?[506] But the name of Jesus is more than light, it is also food. Do you not

---

[498] 1 Pt 2:9.
[499] Ps 35:10.
[500] Eph 5:8.
[501] Acts 9:15.
[502] Rom 13:12ff.

[503] Mt 5:15.
[504] 1 Cor 2:2.
[505] Acts 3:6ff.
[506] Acts 3:6.

feel increase of strength as often as you remember it? What other name can so enrich the man who meditates? What can equal its power to refresh the harassed senses, to buttress the virtues, to add vigor to good and upright habits, to foster chaste affections? Every food of the mind is dry if it is not dipped in that oil; it is tasteless if not seasoned by that salt. Write what you will, I shall not relish it unless it tells of Jesus. Talk or argue about what you will, I shall not relish it if you exclude the name of Jesus. Jesus to me is honey in the mouth, music in the ear, a song in the heart.

IV. Again, it is a medicine. Does one of us feel sad?[507] Let the name of Jesus come into his heart, from there let it spring to his mouth, so that shining like the dawn it may dispel all darkness and make a cloudless sky. Does someone fall into sin? Does his despair even urge him to suicide? Let him but invoke this life-giving name and his will to live will be at once renewed. The hardness of heart that is our common experience, the apathy bred of indolence, bitterness of mind, repugnance for the things of the spirit—have they ever failed to yield in presence of that saving name? The tears dammed up by the barrier of our pride—how have they not burst forth again with sweeter abundance at the thought of Jesus's name? And where is the man, who, terrified and trembling before impending peril, has not been suddenly filled with courage and rid of fear by calling on the strength of that name? Where is the man who, tossed on the rolling seas of doubt, did not quickly find certitude by recourse to the clarity of Jesus's name? Was ever a man so discouraged, so beaten down by afflictions, to whom the sound of this name did not bring new resolve? In short, for all the ills and disorders to which flesh is heir, this name is medicine. For

[507] Jas 5:13.

proof we have no less than his own promise: "Call upon me in the day of trouble; I will deliver you, and you shall glorify me."[508] Nothing so curbs the onset of anger, so allays the upsurge of pride. It cures the wound of envy, controls unbridled extravagance and quenches the flame of lust; it cools the thirst of covetousness and banishes the itch of unclean desire. For when I name Jesus I set before me a man who is meek and humble of heart,[509] kind, prudent, chaste, merciful,[510] flawlessly upright and holy in the eyes of all; and this same man is the all-powerful God whose way of life heals me, whose support is my strength. All these re-echo for me at the hearing of Jesus's name. Because he is man I strive to imitate him; because of his divine power I lean upon him. The examples of his human life I gather like medicinal herbs; with the aid of his power I blend them, and the result is a compound like no pharmacist can produce.

7. Hidden as in a vase, in this name of Jesus, you, my soul, possess a salutary remedy against which no spiritual illness will be proof. Carry it always close to your heart, always in your hand, and so ensure that all your affections, all your actions, are directed to Jesus. You are even invited to do this: "Set me as a seal," he says, "upon your heart, as a seal upon your arm."[511] Here is a theme we shall treat of again. For the moment you have this ready medicine for heart and hand. The name of Jesus furnishes the power to correct your evil actions, to supply what is wanting to imperfect ones; in this name your affections find a guard against corruption, or if corrupted, a power that will make them whole again.

[508]Ps 49:15.
[509]Mt 11:29.
[510]Ti 1:8.
[511]Sg 8:6.

V. 8. Judaea too has had her Jesus—Messiahs in whose empty names she glories. For they give neither light nor food nor medicine. Hence the Synagogue is in the darkness still,[512] enduring the pangs of hunger and disease, and she will neither be healed nor have her fill until she discovers that my Jesus rules over Jacob to the ends of the earth, until she comes back in the evening, hungering like a dog and prowling about the city.[513] True, they were sent on in advance, like the staff preceding the Prophet to where the child lay dead,[514] but they could not see a meaning in their own names because no meaning was there. The staff was laid upon the corpse but produced neither voice nor movement since it was a mere staff. Then he who sent the staff came down and quickly saved his people from their sins,[515] proving that men spoke truly of him when they said: "Who is this man that he even forgives sins?"[516] He is no other than the one who says: "I am the salvation of my people."[517] Now the Word is heard, now it is experienced, and it is clear that, unlike the others, he bears no empty name. As men feel the infusion of spiritual health they refuse to conceal their good fortune. The inward experience finds outward expression. Stricken with remorse I speak out his praise, and praise is a sign of life: "For from the dead, as from one who does not exist, praise has ceased."[518] But see! I am conscious, I am alive! I am perfectly restored, my resurrection is complete. What else is the death of the body than to be deprived of life and feeling? Sin, which is the death of the soul, took from me the feeling of compunction, hushed my prayers of praise;

[512] 1 Jn 2:9.
[513] Ps 58:14ff.
[514] The prophet here is Elisha; 2 Kgs 4:29–31.
[515] Mt 1:21.
[516] Lk 7:49.
[517] Ps 34:3.
[518] Sir 17:26.

I was dead. Then he who forgives sin came down,[519] restored my senses again, and said: "I am your deliverer."[520] Why wonder that death should yield when he who is life comes down? "For a man believes with his heart and so is justified, and he confesses with his lips and so is saved."[521] The child who was dead is now yawning,[522] he yawns seven times as if to say: "Seven times daily I praise you, Lord."[523] Take note of this number seven. It is not a meaningless number, it bears a sacred significance. But because you are by now sated, we should do well to hold this theme over for another sermon, and come with whetted appetites to a table newly laden, to which we are invited by the Church's Spouse, our Lord, Jesus Christ, who is God over all, blessed forever. Amen.[524]

SERMON 17
On the Ways of the Holy Spirit and the Envy of the Devil

Do you think we have advanced far enough into a sphere that is holy to God, in unraveling this wonderful mystery, or should we dare follow the Holy Spirit into still more secret places to search for meanings that may yet be attained? For the Holy Spirit searches not only the minds and hearts of men but even the depths of God;[525] so whether it be into our own hearts or into the divine mysteries, I shall be secure in following him wherever he goes.[526] He must keep watch over our hearts and our minds,[527] lest we think him present when he is not, and follow the erratic light of our own

---

[519] Lk 7:49.
[520] Ps 34:3.
[521] Rom 10:10.

[522] 2 Kgs 4:35.
[523] Ps 118:164.
[524] Rom 9:5.

[525] Ps 7:10; 1 Cor 2:10.
[526] Rv 14:4.
[527] Phil 4:7.

feelings instead. He comes and goes as he wills, and no man can easily discover whence he comes and whither he goes.[528] Ignorance of this will not lessen our hopes of salvation; but to be ignorant of when he comes and when he goes would certainly involve risk. Unless we use the utmost vigilance in attending to these gift-laden visits of the Holy Spirit, we shall neither desire him when he seems absent nor respond to him when present. If he withdraws from us to stimulate us to a more eager search for him, how shall we seek for him if we do not perceive his absence? Or when he comes to animate us, how shall we give him the welcome due his majesty if his visit passes unnoticed? The man who is indifferent to his absence will be led astray by other influences; the man who is blind to his coming cannot offer thanks for the visit.

2. When Elisha perceived that his master was about to be taken away from him, he asked for a favor.[529] He obtained it, as you know, only on the condition that he would see him as he was being taken. This is an allegory recorded for our instruction.[530] This story of the prophets carries both a lesson and a warning, to make us vigilant and careful about the work of salvation ceaselessly performed in our inmost being with all the skill and sweetness of the Holy Spirit's artistry. If we do not wish to be deprived of a twofold gift, let us make sure that this heaven-sent Director, who can teach us all things,[531] is never taken away from us without our knowledge. Let him never find us unprepared when he comes, but always with faces uplifted and hearts expanded to receive the copious blessing of the Lord. Let him find us like men who are waiting for their master to come home from the marriage feast,[532] for he never comes empty-handed from

[528]Jn 3:8.
[529]2 Kgs 2:9ff.
[530]1 Cor 10:11.
[531]1 Jn 2:27.
[532]Lk 12:36.

heaven's richly laden table. Therefore we must watch, even hour by hour, for we do not know at what hour he will come and depart again.[533] The Holy Spirit comes and goes, and if a man can stand firmly only with his support, it follows that he must fall when abandoned by him;[534] fall, yes, but never fatally, since the Lord supports him by the hand.[535] Persons who are spiritual or whom the Holy Spirit purposes to make spiritual, never cease to experience these alternations; he visits them every morning and tests them at any moment.[536] For a righteous man falls seven times and rises again,[537] provided that he falls in the daytime and so is able to see his fall, to know that he has fallen, to make up his mind to rise and look for a helping hand, and say: "Your favor, Lord, stood me on a peak impregnable; but then you hid your face and I was terrified."[538]

II. 3. It is scarcely possible to avoid doubts about the truth when we lack the light of the Holy Spirit; but it is another thing to hanker after erroneous opinions which a man might easily guard against if he would acknowledge his ignorance, as Job did when he said: "And even if it be true that I have erred, my error remains with myself."[539] Ignorance, an evil mother, has borne two evil daughters, falsehood and doubt, the first is the more reprobate, the other more an object of compassion; the first more pernicious, the other more troubled. When the Holy Spirit speaks, both of these yield, for he speaks not merely the truth but the certain truth. He is the Spirit of truth[540] with whom falsehood cannot be reconciled; and the spirit of wisdom, who will not accept opinions that are equivocal or obscure, since he is a reflection of eternal life, so

---

[533] Mt 24:42; Lk 12:40.
[534] 1 Cor 10:12.
[535] Ps 36:24.
[536] Jb 7:18.
[537] Prv 24:16.
[538] Ps 29:8.
[539] Jb 19:4.
[540] Jn 15:26.

pure that he pervades and permeates all things.[541] When this Spirit is silent we must be alert and hold falsehood in abhorrence, even if bound in the clutches of perplexing incertitude. Doubting the truth of an opinion is vastly different from rashly proposing something of which we know nothing. Either let the Holy Spirit always speak, a procedure that no influence of ours can procure; or let him at least warn us when he withdraws into silence, that his very silence may then be our guide; otherwise, mistakenly thinking he is still leading us on, we shall pursue with disastrous assurance an erroneous course of our own. Even if he does keep us in suspense, may he never abandon us to what is false. A man may tentatively express what is false without incurring the guilt of a lie, while another man may lie in asserting a truth of which he has no knowledge. Because the first man, far from maintaining non-facts to be facts, rather states he believes what he does believe, he speaks in truth, even though what he believes is not true; but the second man, who says he is certain when he is not, does not speak in truth, even though what he asserts is true.

4. I have said these things for the sake of those who are unaware of such pitfalls, and now I shall follow what I trust to be the guidance of the Spirit who lights my way, taking account as far as I can of the warnings I have issued. I will try to be faithful to my own teaching lest someone say in turn to me: "You who teach others, will you not teach yourself?"[542] We must observe the distinction between what is clear and what is doubtful, not casting doubt on the one nor rashly upholding the other. This is where we must hope for direction from the Spirit, for even assiduous efforts on our part may be altogether insufficient.

---

[541] Ws 7:26.
[542] Rom 2:21.

III. What man knows whether the judgment of God over men, that we discussed in a previous sermon,[543] was not preceded by a judgment pronounced in heaven?

5. Is it possible that Lucifer, son of the morning,[544] yielding precipitately to the impulse of pride, began to envy the outpouring of oil on our human race before he was cast out into the darkness? In the rage that possessed him did he murmur and say to himself: "Why this waste?"[545] I do not hold that the Holy Spirit has made this known, nor do I hold the contrary; I simply do not know. But even though some may think it incredible, it could have happened that because of his lofty endowments of wisdom and grace,[546] he could have foreseen that members of the human race would one day be raised to be his equals in glory. And if he did foresee this it was because it was revealed to him in the Word of God. Then, stung by a wild impulse of envy, he plotted to maintain as subjects those whom he scorned as companions. To him they were by nature both lower and weaker, unworthy to be fellow citizens, to share an equal glory. Was this impious scheming of his the consequence of his presumptuous self-exaltation, of his pretensions to a seat of power? For he said: I will climb up to the heavens; I will sit in the recesses of the north.[547] He would assume the very likeness of the most high God; for just as God, from his throne above the cherubim,[548] governs the whole angelic host, so Lucifer, from his usurped position, would control the race of men. God forbid. He plotted mischief in his bed,[549] let him be trapped in his own plot,[550] for we refuse to acknowledge any overlord but our Creator. Not the devil but the Lord will be

[543]See Sermon 14:1.   [546]Ez 28:12.   [549]Ps 35:5.
[544]Is 14:12.   [547]Is 14:13.   [550]Ps 26:12.
[545]Mt 26:8.   [548]1 Sm 4:4.

judge of the world;[551] he who is our God forever and ever will be our ruler forever and ever.[552]

6. In heaven then, the devil conceived a bitter resentment that in the garden of Paradise came forth as iniquity,[553] the offspring of malice, the mother of death and of every other misery; all these evils have pride as their first parent. For although it was through the devil's envy that death entered into the world,[554] every sin has its origin in pride.[555] But what has he gained from it? For you, Lord, are still in our midst, we are called by your name;[556] and the people you have chosen,[557] the Church of the redeemed, cries out: "Your name is oil poured out."[558] And when I in turn am cast forth, this oil comes pouring after me and upon me, because despite your anger you remember to be merciful.[559] Satan however has gained a hold over all who yield themselves to pride.[560] He has made his realm of this world's darkness,[561] yet his proud assaults serve but to increase the realm of the humble. While that realm remains his, temporal as it is, he establishes multitudes of the humble on high and eternal thrones. What a happy outcome that this tyrant who would hammer the humble into subjection should unwittingly be fashioning their eternal crowns for them. Attacking along every front, he is everywhere forced to yield. For always and everywhere it is God who will judge his people, it is he who will save the children of the needy and crush their oppressors.[562] Always and everywhere he will defend his own, he will drive off their persecutors, take away the scepter that the wicked wield over the virtuous, lest the virtuous in turn

[551]Ps 9:9.
[552]Ps 47:15.
[553]Ps 7:15.
[554]Ws 2:24.
[555]Sir 10:15.

[556]Jer 14:9.
[557]1 Pt 2:9.
[558]Sg 1:2.
[559]Hb 3:2.

[560]Jb 41:25.
[561]Eph 6:12.
[562]Ps 71:4.

should take to evil.[563] A time is coming when he will break the bow completely, shatter the spear, and burn the shields with fire.[564] As for you, unhappy one, you set up your seat in the north, a region of cloud and cold;[565] and see! the poor are being raised up from the dust and the needy from the dunghill, that they may be placed among the princes and attain a seat of honor.[566] To your utter frustration you will see that the poor and needy have cause to praise God's name.[567]

7. We thank you, Father of orphans and Vindicator of abandoned children,[568] because a mountain fat and fertile has shed its warmth upon us.[569] The heavens have poured down rain at the presence of the God of Sinai.[570] The oil is poured out. There is universal glorification of the Name which Satan envied because it was ours, and we live in its shadow. It is acclaimed, I repeat, in the hearts and words of children; even in the mouths of infants and babes at the breast praise is assured.[571] The wicked one will see this and be filled with fury;[572] an unrelenting fury that will feed the unquenchable fire prepared for him and his ministers.[573] "The zeal of the Lord of hosts will do this."[574]

IV. How wonderful your love for me, my God, my love! How wonderful your love for me, everywhere mindful of me, everywhere eager for the welfare of one who is needy and poor, protecting him both from the arrogance of men and from the might of evil spirits. Both in heaven and on earth, O Lord, you accuse my accusers, you attack my attackers;[575] everywhere you bring help, always you are close

---

[563]Ps 124:4.
[564]Ps 45:10.
[565]Is 14:13.
[566]1 Sm 2:8; Ps 112:7.
[567]Ps 73:21.

[568]Ps 67:6.
[569]Ps 67:16.
[570]Ps 67:9.
[571]Mt 21:16.

[572]Ps 111:10.
[573]Mk 9:44.
[574]Is 9:7.
[575]Ps 34:1.

to my right hand lest I be disturbed.[576] "I will sing to the Lord as long as I live, I will sing praise to my God while I have being."[577] How great are his powers, what wonders has he not done![578] The first and greatest of his achievements is that revealed to me by one initiated to his mysteries, the Virgin Mary: "He has pulled down princes from their thrones and exalted the lowly. The hungry he has filled with good things, the rich sent away empty."[579] The second you have heard of too, it is like the first: "That those without sight may see, and those with sight turn blind."[580] These two judgments are the poor man's consolation, they enable him to say: "Remembering your rulings in the past, Lord, I take comfort."[581]

8. Let us return now to ourselves, let us examine our paths;[582] and in order to accomplish this in truth, let us invoke the Spirit of truth,[583] let us call to him from the deep into which he has led us, because he leads us on the way by which we discover ourselves, and without him we can do nothing.[584] Nor should we be afraid that he will disdain to come down to us, for the contrary is true: he is displeased if we attempt even the least thing without him. For he is not one "who passes and does not return,"[585] he leads us on from brightness to brightness because he is the Spirit of the Lord.[586] Sometimes he fills us with rapture by communication of his light, sometimes he adapts himself to our weakness and sends beams of light into the dark about us.[587] But whether we are raised above ourselves or left with ourselves, let us stay always in the light, always walk as

[576]Ps 15:8.
[577]Ps 103:33; Ps 145:2.
[578]Ps 77:4.
[579]Lk 1:52–53.
[580]Mt 22:39; Jn 9:39.
[581]Ps 118:52.
[582]Lam 3:40.
[583]Jn 14:17.
[584]Jn 15:5.
[585]Ps 77:39.
[586]2 Cor 3:18.
[587]Ps 17:29.

children of the light.[588] And now that we have passed through the shadow-land of allegories, it is time to explore the great plains of moral truths.[589] Our faith has been strengthened, let our lives reveal its influence; our intellects have been enlightened, let them prescribe the right behavior. For they have sound sense who do this,[590] if they direct their actions and understanding toward the praise and glory of our Lord Jesus Christ,[591] who is blessed forever.[592]

SERMON 20
Three Qualities of Love

I would like to begin with a word from St. Paul: "If anyone does not love the Lord Jesus, let him be anathema."[593] Truly, I ought to love the one through whom I have my being, my life, my understanding. If I am ungrateful, I am unworthy too. Lord Jesus, whoever refuses to live for you is clearly worthy of death, and is in fact dead already. Whoever does not know you is a fool. And whoever wants to become something without you, without doubt that man is considered nothing and is just that. For what is man, unless you take notice of him?[594] You have made all things for yourself, O God, and whoever wants to live for himself and not for you, in all that he does, is nothing. "Fear God, and keep his commandments," it is said, "for this is the whole duty of man."[595] So if this is all, without

---

[588] Eph 5:8.
[589] See Sermon 16:1.
[590] Ps 110:10.
[591] Phil 1:11.
[592] Rom 1:25.

[593] 1 Cor 16:22. Sermon 20 was translated by one of the editors, Edward John Mullaney, ocso.
[594] Ps 143:3.
[595] Eccl 12:13.

this, man is nothing. Turn toward yourself, O God, this little that you have granted me to be; take from this miserable life, I beg you, the years that remain.[596] In place of all that I lost in my evil way of living, O God, do not refuse a humble and penitent heart.[597] My days have lengthened like a shadow and passed without fruit.[598] I cannot bring them back, but let it please you at least if I offer them to you in the bitterness of my soul.[599] As for wisdom—my every desire and intention is before you[600]—if there were any in me, I would keep it for you. But, God, you know my stupidity,[601] unless perhaps it is wisdom for me to recognize it, and even this is your gift. Grant me more; not that I am ungrateful for this small gift, but that I am eager for what is lacking. For all these things, and as much as I am able, I love you.

2. But there is something else that moves me, arouses and enflames me even more. Good Jesus, the chalice you drank, the price of our redemption, makes me love you more than all the rest. This alone would be enough to claim our love. This, I say, is what wins our love so sweetly, justly demands it, firmly binds it, deeply affects it. Our Savior had to toil so hard in this, in fact in making the whole world the Creator did not labor so much. Then he spoke and they were made; he commanded and they were created.[602] But in saving us he had to endure men who contradicted his words, criticized his actions, ridiculed his sufferings, and mocked his death. See how much he loved us. Add to this the fact that he was not returning love but freely offering it. For who had given him anything first, that it should be returned to him? As St. John said: "Not that we had loved him, but that he first

[596] Is 38:10.
[597] Ps 50:19.
[598] Ps 101:12.
[599] Is 38:15.
[600] Ps 37:10.
[601] Ps 68:5.
[602] Ps 32:9; 148:5.

loved us."[603] He loved us even before we existed, and in addition he loved us when we resisted him. According to the witness of St. Paul: "Even when we were still his enemies we were reconciled to God through the blood of his Son."[604] If he had not loved his enemies, he could not have had any friends, just as he would have had no one to love if he had not loved those who were not.

II. 3. His love was sweet, and wise, and strong. I call it sweet because he took on a human body, wise because he avoided sin, strong because he endured death. Even though he took a body, his love was never sensual, but always in the wisdom of the Spirit. "A Spirit before our face is Christ the Lord,"[605] jealous of us but with the jealousy of God,[606] not man, and certainly not like that of the first man, Adam, for Eve. So those whom he sought after in a body, he loved in the spirit and redeemed in power. How sweet it is to see as man the Creator of humanity. While he carefully protected nature from sin, he forcefully drove death from that nature also. In taking a body he stooped to me, in avoiding sin he took counsel with himself, in accepting death he satisfied the Father. A dear friend, a wise counselor, a strong helper. Should I not willingly entrust myself to the one who had the goodwill, the wisdom, the strength to save me? He sought me out, he called me through grace; will he refuse me as I come to him?[607] I fear neither force nor fraud which can snatch me from his hand.[608] He is the one who conquered all things, even death, and tricked the serpent, the seducer of the world, with a holy deception. He was more prudent than the one, more powerful than the other. He took to himself a

---

[603] 1 Jn 4:10.
[604] Rom 5:10.
[605] Lam 4:20.

[606] 2 Cor 11:2.
[607] Rom 8:30; Jn 6:37.
[608] Jb 10:7.

true body but only the likeness of sin,[609] giving a sweet consolation to weak men in the one and in the other hiding a trap to deceive the devil. To reconcile us to the Father he bravely suffered death and conquered it, pouring out his blood as the price of our redemption.[610] His divine majesty would not have sought me in chains unless he had loved me so tenderly, but he added wisdom to his affection by which he deceived the serpent. Then he added patience with which to appease his divine Father who had been offended.

III. These are the qualities of love of which I promised to tell you. But I have shown them to you first in Christ, to make them so much more acceptable to you.

4. Christian, learn from Christ how you ought to love Christ. Learn a love that is tender, wise, strong; love with tenderness, not passion, wisdom, not foolishness, and strength, lest you become weary and turn away from the love of the Lord. Do not let the glory of the world or the pleasure of the flesh lead you astray; the wisdom of Christ should become sweeter to you than these. The light of Christ should shine so much for you that the spirit of lies and deceit will not seduce you. Finally, Christ as the strength of God should support you so that you may not be worn down by difficulties.[611] Let love enkindle your zeal, let knowledge inform it, let constancy strengthen it. Keep it fervent, discreet, courageous. See it is not tepid, or temerarious, or timid. See for yourself if those three commands are not prescribed in the law when God says: "You shall love the Lord your God with your whole heart, your whole soul and your whole strength."[612] It seems to me, if no more suitable meaning for this triple distinction comes to mind, that the love of the heart relates to

---

[609] Rom 8:3.
[610] Ps 48:9.

[611] 1 Cor 1:24.
[612] Dt 6:5.

a certain warmth of affection, the love of the soul to energy or judgment of reason, and the love of strength can refer to constancy and vigor of spirit. So love the Lord your God with the full and deep affection of your heart, love him with your mind wholly awake and discreet, love him with all your strength, so much so that you would not even fear to die for love of him. As it is written: "For love is strong as death, jealousy is bitter as hell."[613] Your affection for your Lord Jesus should be both tender and intimate, to oppose the sweet enticements of sensual life. Sweetness conquers sweetness as one nail drives out another. No less than this keep him as a strong light for your mind and a guide for your intellect, not only to avoid the deceits of heresy and to preserve the purity of your faith from their seductions, but also that you might carefully avoid an indiscreet and excessive vehemence in your conversation. Let your love be strong and constant, neither yielding to fear nor cowering at hard work. Let us love affectionately, discreetly, intensely. We know that the love of the heart, which we have said is affectionate, is sweet indeed, but liable to be led astray if it lacks the love of the soul. And the love of the soul is wise indeed, but fragile without that love which is called the love of strength.

IV. 5. See how many examples support what we say. When the disciples were sad at the departure of their Master just before his ascension, after they had heard him talk about this subject, they heard him say: "If you loved me you would rejoice because I am going to the Father."[614] How can he say this? Didn't they love him when his departure made them so sad? In a way they loved him, and in another way they did

---

[613]Sg 8:6.
[614]Jn 14:28.

not. Their love was more tender than prudent, it was sensual but not reasonable; they loved with the whole heart but not with the whole soul. What they loved was not for their own welfare, and so he said to them: "It is good for you that I am going,"[615] correcting not their feelings but their foresight. When he was speaking in the same way about his approaching death, Peter who loved him so dearly, tried to stand in the way.[616] When, as you remember, he rebuked him, what was it but his imprudence that he was correcting? Finally what did he mean in saying: "You do not mind the things of God,"[617] except: you do not love wisely, you are following your human feeling in opposition to the divine plan. He even called him Satan because although it was in ignorance, he was impeding salvation in trying to prevent the Savior's death. Peter, who had been corrected, later when the sad prophecy was repeated, no longer objected to death but promised he would die with him.[618] But he could not fulfill this promise because he had not yet reached that third degree where he would love with all his strength. Taught to love with his whole soul, Peter was still weak. He was well instructed but not well prepared, aware of the mystery but afraid of bearing witness to it. Obviously that love was not as strong as death which still yielded before it.[619] Later, robed with strength from on high according to the promise of Jesus Christ,[620] Peter began to love with such strength that when forbidden by the Council to proclaim the holy Name, he boldly answered those who gave the order: "We must obey God rather than men."[621] Then finally he attained the

[615] Jn 16:7.
[616] Mk 8:31–32.
[617] Mk 8:33.
[618] Mk 14:31.

[619] Sg 8:6.
[620] Lk 24:49.
[621] Acts 5:29.

fullness of love, when for love's sake he would not spare even his own life. Truly "greater love than this no man has, than that he lay down his life for his friends."[622] Even if Peter did not actually surrender his life then, he did offer it.

V. So then, to love with your whole heart, your whole soul, and your whole strength means not being led astray by allurements, or seduced by lies, or broken by injuries.

6. Notice that the love of the heart is, in a certain sense, carnal, because our hearts are attracted most toward the humanity of Christ and the things he did or commanded while in the flesh. The heart that is filled with this love is quickly touched by every word on this subject. Nothing else is as pleasant to listen to, or is read with as much interest, nothing is as frequently in remembrance or as sweet in reflection. The soul prepares the holocausts of its prayers with this love as if they were the fattened offerings of bullocks. The soul at prayer should have before it a sacred image of the God-man, in his birth or infancy or as he was teaching, or dying, or rising, or ascending. Whatever form it takes this image must bind the soul with the love of virtue and expel carnal vices, eliminate temptations and quiet desires. I think this is the principal reason why the invisible God willed to be seen in the flesh and to converse with men as a man. He wanted to recapture the affections of carnal men who were unable to love in any other way, by first drawing them to the salutary love of his own humanity, and then gradually to raise them to a spiritual love. Were they not at just this level when they said: "See, we have left everything and have followed you"[623] It was only by the love of his physical presence that they had left everything. They could

[622] Jn 15:13.
[623] Mt 19:27.

not even bear to hear a word of his approaching passion and death, although this was to be their salvation. Even after it had all happened they could not gaze upon the glory of his ascension without deep sorrow. This is why Christ said to them: "Because I have said this to you sadness has filled your hearts."[624] So it was only by his physical presence that their hearts were detached from carnal loves.

7. Afterward he showed them a higher degree of love when he said, "It is the Spirit who gives life, the flesh profits nothing."[625] I think Paul had reached this level when he said: "Even if we once knew Christ in the body, we know him thus no longer."[626] Perhaps this was also true of the prophet who said: "A Spirit before our face is Christ the Lord."[627] When he adds: "Under his shadow we will live among the heathens,"[628] he seems to me to speak on behalf of the beginners, in order that they may at least rest in the shade since they know they are not strong enough to bear the heat of the sun. They may be nourished by the sweetness of his humanity since they are not yet able to perceive the things which are of the Spirit of God.[629] The shade of Christ, I suggest, is his flesh which overshadowed Mary and tempered for her the bright splendor of the Spirit.[630] Therefore in this human devotion there is in the meantime consolation for whomever does not as yet have the Spirit which gives life, at least who do not have him in the same way as those who say: "A Spirit before our face is Christ the Lord,"[631] and again: "If we once knew Christ in the flesh we know him thus no longer."[632] For there is no love of Christ at all without the Holy Spirit, even if this love is in the flesh, and

---

[624]Jn 16:6.
[625]Jn 6:64.
[626]2 Cor 5:16.

[627]Lam 4:20.
[628]Ibid.
[629]1 Cor 2:14.

[630]Lk 1:35.
[631]Lam 4:20.
[632]2 Cor 5:16.

without its fullness. The measure of such love is this: its sweetness seizes the whole heart, and draws it completely from the love of all flesh and every sensual pleasure. Really this is what it means to love with the whole heart. If I prefer to the humanity of my Lord someone joined to me by ties of blood, or some sensual pleasure, this would obviously prove that I do not love with my whole heart since it is divided between its own interests and the love of the one who taught me as a man, both by his words and examples. Would I not seem to give my love partly to him and partly to my own? As he once said: "Whoever loves father or mother more than me is not worthy of me, and whoever loves son or daughter more than me is not worthy of me."[633] To put it briefly, to love with the whole heart means to put the love of his sacred humanity before everything that tempts us, from within or without. Among these temptations we must also count the glory of the world, because its glory is that of the flesh, and those who delight in it without a doubt are men of the flesh.

8. Of course this devotion to the humanity of Christ is a gift, a great gift of the Spirit. I have called it carnal with comparison to that other love which does not know the Word as flesh so much as the Word as wisdom, as justice, truth, holiness, loyalty, strength, and whatever else could be said in this manner. Christ is truly all these things. "He became for us the wisdom of God, and justice, and sanctification and redemption."[634] Take as an example two men: one of them feels a share in Christ's sufferings, is affected and easily moved at the thought of all that he suffered; he is nourished and strengthened by the sweetness of this devotion to good and

[633]Mt 10:37.
[634]1 Cor 1:30.

honest and worthy actions. But the other is always aflame with zeal for justice, eager for the truth and for wisdom. His life, his habits are saintly, ashamed of boasting, avoiding criticism, never knowing envy, hating pride. He not only flees all human glory but shrinks from it and avoids it, every stain of impurity both in body and soul he loathes and eradicates; finally he spurns every evil as if naturally, and embraces what is good. If you would compare the feelings of these two men would it not appear how the latter was superior in respect to the former, whose love was somehow more carnal?

9. But that carnal love is worthwhile since through it sensual love is excluded, and the world is condemned and conquered. It becomes better when it is rational, and becomes perfect when it is spiritual. Actually it is rational when the reason is so strong in faith that in all things concerning Christ it strays in not even the slightest degree because of any false likeness of truth, nor by any heretical or diabolical deceit does it wander from the integrity of the sense of the Church. In the same way when speaking on its own it exercises such caution as never to exceed the proper limits of discretion by superstition or frivolity or the vehemence of a too eager spirit. This is loving God with the whole soul, as we said before.[635] If, with the help of the Spirit, the soul attains such strength that it remains steadfast no matter what the effort or difficulty, if the fear of death itself cannot make it act unjustly, but even then it loves with the whole strength, this then is spiritual love. I think the name is very fitting for this special love because of the special fullness of the Spirit in which it excels. This is enough for those words of the bride: "Therefore the young maidens

[635]Dt 6:5.

love you so much."[636] In those things that are to follow may he open to us the treasure of his mercy, the one who guards them, Jesus Christ, our Lord, who lives and reigns in the unity of the Holy Spirit, God, forever and ever. Amen.

SERMON 31

The Various Ways of Seeing God

"Tell me, you whom my soul loves, where you pasture your flock, where you make it lie down at noon?"[637] The Word, who is the Bridegroom, often makes himself known under more than one form to those who are fervent. Why so? Doubtless because he cannot be seen yet as he is.[638] That vision is unchanging, because the form in which he will then be seen is unchanging; for he is, and can suffer no change determined by present, past, or future. Eliminate past and future, and where then is alteration or any shadow of a change?[639] For whatever evolves out of the past and does not cease to move toward future development passes through the instant that is the present, but one cannot say: it is. How can one say: it is, when it never remains in the same state?[640] That alone truly is, which is neither altered from its past mode of being nor blotted out by a future mode, but "is" alone is predicated of it impregnably and unchangeably, and it remains what it is. No reference to the past can deny that it is from all eternity, nor any reference to the future that it is for all eternity. In this way it proves that it truly is, that is, it

[636]Sg 1:2.
[637]Sg 1:6.
[638]1 Jn 3:2.

[639]Jas 1:17.
[640]Jb 14:2.

is uncreated, interminable, immutable. When he therefore who exists in this manner—who, furthermore, cannot be one moment in this form, another in that—is seen just as he is, that vision endures, as I have said, since no alteration interrupts it. This is the moment when that one denarius mentioned in the Gospel is given in the one vision that is offered to everyone who sees.[641] For as he who is seen is immutable in himself, he is present immutably to all who contemplate him; to these there is nothing more desirable that they wish to see, nothing more enticing that they could see. Can their eager appetite, then, ever grow weary, or that sweetness ebb away, or that truth prove deceptive, or that eternity come to a close? And if both the ability and will to contemplate are prolonged eternally, what is lacking to total happiness? Those who contemplate him without ceasing are short of nothing, those whose wills are fixed on him have nothing more to desire.

2. But this vision is not for the present life; it is reserved for the next, at least for those who can say: "We know that when he appears we shall be like him, for we shall see him as he is."[642] Even now he appears to whom he pleases, but as he pleases, not as he is. Neither sage nor saint nor prophet can or could ever see him as he is, while still in this mortal body; but whoever is found worthy will be able to do so when the body becomes immortal. Hence, though he is seen here below, it is in the form that seems good to him, not as he is. For example, take that mighty source of light, I speak of that sun which you see day after day; yet you do not see it as it is, but according as it lights up the air, or a mountain, or a wall. Nor could you see even to this extent if the light of your body, the eye,[643]

---

[641]Mt 20:9–10.
[642]1 Jn 3:2.

[643]Mt 6:22.

because of its natural steadiness and clearness, did not bear some degree of likeness to that light in the heavens. Since all the other members of the body lack this likeness, they are incapable of seeing the light. Even the eye itself, when troubled, cannot approach the light, because it has lost that likeness. Just as the troubled eye, then, cannot gaze on the peaceful sun because of its unlikeness, so the peaceful eye can behold it with some efficacy because of a certain likeness. If indeed it were wholly equal to it in purity, with a completely clear vision it would see it as it is, because of the complete likeness. And so when you are enlightened you can see even now the Sun of Justice that "enlightens every man who comes into this world,"[644] according to the degree of the light he gives, by which you are made somehow like him; but see him as he is you cannot, because you are not yet perfectly like him. That is why the psalmist says: "Come to him and be enlightened, and your faces shall never be ashamed."[645] That is very true, provided we are enlightened as much as we need, so that "with our unveiled faces contemplating the glory of God, all grow brighter and brighter as we are turned into the same image, as by the spirit of the Lord."[646]

3. Note that we must approach gently, not intrude ourselves upon him, lest the irreverent searcher of majesty be overwhelmed by glory.[647] This approach is not a movement from place to place but from brightness to brightness, not in the body but in the spirit, as by the Spirit of the Lord; evidently by the spirit of the Lord, not by ours, although in ours. The brighter one becomes, the nearer is the end; and to be absolutely bright is to have arrived. For those thus arrived in his presence, to see him as he is means to be as he is, and

[644]Mal 4:2; Jn 1:9.
[645]Ps 33:6.

[646]2 Cor 3:18.
[647]Prv 25:27.

not to be put to shame by any form of unlikeness. But, as I have said, this is for the next life.

II. In the meantime this immense variety of forms, these countless species of creatures, what are they but rays emanating from the Godhead, showing that he from whom they come truly is, but not fully explaining what he is. Hence what you see is what emanates from him, not himself. Nevertheless, though not seeing himself but what comes from him, you are made aware beyond all doubt that he exists, and that you must seek him. Grace will not be wanting to the seeker, nor ignorance excuse the negligent. All have access to this kind of vision. According to the Apostle Paul, it is common to everyone who has the use of reason: "The invisible attributes of God have been clearly perceived in the things that have been made."[648]

4. Another kind of vision is that by which in former times the Fathers were often graciously admitted to sweet communion with God, who became present to them, though they did not see him as he is but only in the form he thought fitting to assume. Nor does he appear to all in a similar manner, but as the apostle says: "in many and various ways," still remaining one in himself, in accord with his word to Israel: "The Lord your God is one God."[649] This manifestation, though not apparent to everybody, took place exteriorly, and consisted of images or the spoken word. But there is another form of divine contemplation, very different from the former because it takes place in the interior, when God himself is pleased to visit the soul that seeks him,[650] provided it is committed to seeking him with all its desire and love. We are told what the sign of such a visit is by one who

[648]Rom 1:20.   [650]Lam 3:25.
[649]Heb 1:1; Dt 6:4.

experienced it. "Fire goes before him and burns up his adversaries round about."[651] The fire of holy desire ought to precede his advent to every soul whom he will visit, to burn up the rust of bad habits and so prepare a place for the Lord. The soul will know that the Lord is near when it perceives itself to be aflame with that fire,[652] and can say as the prophet did: "He has sent a fire from on high down into my bones, and enlightened me";[653] and again: "My heart became hot within me and in my meditation fire burst forth."[654]

5. When the Beloved who is thus sought for pays a visit in his merciful love to the soul that is filled with longing, that prays often, even without intermission,[655] that humiliates itself in the ardor of its desire, that soul may fittingly say with St. Jeremiah: "You are good, O Lord, to those who hope in you, to the soul that seeks you."[656] And that soul's angel, one of the friends of the Bridegroom,[657] and by him commissioned to be the minister and witness of that secret and mutual exchange—that angel, I say, must be dancing with joy! Does he not participate in their gladness and bliss, and turning to the Lord, say: "I thank you, Lord of majesty, because 'you have granted him his heart's desire, not denied him what his lips entreated'"?[658] He is everywhere the soul's tireless attendant, never ceasing to lure it on and guide it with constant inspirations, as he whispers: "Take delight in the Lord, and he will give you the desire of your heart";[659] and again: "Wait for the Lord and keep his way."[660] Or: "If he seems slow, wait for him; he will surely come, he will not delay."[661] Turning to the Lord, he says: "'As a hart longs for flowing streams, so that soul longs for you, O God.'[662] It has

---

[651]Ps 96:3.
[652]Ps 33:19.
[653]Lam 1:13.
[654]Ps 38:4.

[655]1 Thes 5:17.
[656]Lam 3:25.
[657]Sg 1:6.
[658]Ps 20:3.

[659]Ps 36:4.
[660]Ps 36:34.
[661]Hb 2:3.
[662]Ps 41:2.

yearned for you in the night, and your Spirit within it watched for you from morning onward"[663] And again: "All the day this soul reaches out to you;[664] grant what it wants because it is shouting after you;[665] relent a little and show your mercy.[666] Look down from heaven and see, and visit this desolate spirit."[667] This loyal groomsman, watching without envy over this interchange of love, seeks the Lord's glory rather than his own;[668] he is the go between for the lover and his beloved, making known the desires of one, bearing the gifts of the other. He quickens the soul's affections, he conciliates the Bridegroom. Sometimes too, though rarely, he brings them into each other's presence, either snatching her up to him, or leading him down to her: for he is a member of the household, a familiar figure in the palace, one who has no fear of being rebuffed, who daily sees the face of the Father.[669]

6. Be careful, however, not to conclude that I see something corporeal or perceptible to the senses in this union between the Word and the soul. My opinion is that of the apostle, who said that "he who is united to the Lord becomes one spirit with him."[670] I try to express with the most suitable words I can muster the ecstatic ascent of the purified mind to God, and the loving descent of God into the soul, submitting spiritual truths to spiritual men.[671] Therefore let this union be in the spirit, because "God is a spirit,"[672] who is lovingly drawn by the beauty of that soul whom he perceives to be guided by the Spirit,[673] and devoid of any desire to submit to the ways of the flesh, especially if he sees that it burns with love for himself.

[663] Is 26:9.
[664] Ps 87:10.
[665] Mt 15:23.
[666] Ps 89:13.
[667] Ps 79:15.
[668] Jn 7:18.
[669] Mt 18:10.
[670] 1 Cor 6:17.
[671] 1 Cor 2:13.
[672] Jn 4:24.
[673] Ps 44:12; Gal 5:16.

III. One who is so disposed and so beloved will by no means be content either with that manifestation of the Bridegroom given to the many in the world of creatures,[674] or to the few in visions and dreams. By a special privilege she wants to welcome him down from heaven into her inmost heart, into her deepest love; she wants to have the one she desires present to her not in bodily form but by inward infusion, not by appearing externally but by laying hold of her within. It is beyond question that the vision is all the more delightful the more inward it is, and not external. It is the Word, who penetrates without sound; who is effective though not pronounced, who wins the affections without striking on the ears. His face, though without form, is the source of form, it does not dazzle the eyes of the body but gladdens the watchful heart; its pleasure is in the gift of love and not in the color of the lover.

7. Not yet have I come round to saying that he has appeared as he is although in this inward vision he does not reveal himself as altogether different from what he is. Neither does he make his presence continuously felt, not even to his most ardent lovers, nor in the same way to all. For the various desires of the soul it is essential that the taste of God's presence be varied too, and that the infused flavor of divine delight should titillate in manifold ways the palate of the soul that seeks him. You must already have noticed how often he changes his countenance in the course of this love song, how he delights in transforming himself from one charming guise to another in the beloved's presence: at one moment like a bashful bridegroom maneuvering for the hidden embraces of his holy lover, for the bliss of her kisses; at another coming along like a physician with oil and

---

[674]Rom 1:20.

ointments, because weak and tender souls still need remedies and medicines of this kind, which is why they are rather
daintily described as maidens. Should anybody find fault
with this, let him be told that "it is not the healthy who need
the doctor, but the sick."[675] Sometimes, too, he joins up as a
traveler with the bride and the maidens who accompany her
on the road, and lightens the hardships of the journey for the
whole company by his fascinating conversation, so that
when he has parted from them they ask: "Did not our hearts
burn within us as he talked to us on the road?"[676] A silver-
tongued companion who, by the spell of his words and man-
ners, persuades everyone, as if in a sweet-smelling cloud
arising from the ointments, to follow him. Hence they say:
"We will run after you in the odor of your ointments."[677] At
another time he comes to meet them as a wealthy father of a
family "with bread enough and to spare" in his house;[678] or
again like a magnificent and powerful king, giving courage
to his timid and poverty-stricken bride, stirring up her
desire by showing her the ornaments of his glory, the riches
of his winepresses and storehouse, the produce of his gardens and fields, and finally introducing her into his private
apartments.[679] For "her husband's heart has confidence in
her,"[680] and among all his possessions there is nothing that he
thinks should be hidden from her whom he redeemed from
indigence, whose fidelity he has proved, whose attractive-
ness wins his embraces. And so he never ceases, in one way
or another, to reveal himself to the inward eye of those who
seek him, thus fulfilling the promise that he made: "Be
assured I am with you always, to the end of time."[681]

[675]Mt 9:12.
[676]Lk 24:32.
[677]Sg 1:3.
[678]Lk 15:17.

[679]Sg 1:3.
[680]Prv 31:11.
[681]Mt 28:20.

8. On all these occasions he is kind and gentle, full of merciful love.[682] In his kisses he shows that he is both loving and charming; with the oil and the ointments that he is boundlessly considerate and compassionate and forgiving; on the journey he is gay, courteous, ever gracious and ready to help; in the display of his riches and possessions he reveals a kingly liberality, a munificent generosity in the bestowal of rewards. Through the whole context of this song you will find images of this nature to delineate the Word. Hence I feel that the prophet was thinking on these lines when he said: "Christ the Lord is a spirit before our face; under his shadow we shall live among the nations,"[683] because now we see in a mirror dimly and not yet face-to-face.[684] So it will be while we live among the nations; among the angels it will be otherwise. For then we shall enjoy the very same happiness as they; even we shall see him as he is, in the form of God,[685] no longer in shadow.

IV. Just as we say that our ancestors possessed only shadows and images, whereas the truth itself shines on us by the grace of Christ present in the flesh, so also no one will deny that in relation to the world to come, we still live in the shadow of the truth, unless he wishes to deny what the apostle asserts: "our knowledge is imperfect and our prophecy is imperfect";[686] or when he says: "I do not reckon myself to have got hold of it yet."[687] Why should there not be a distinction between him who walks by faith and him who walks by sight?[688] Hence the just man lives by faith,[689] the blessed rejoices in the vision; the holy person here below lives in the shadow of Christ,[690] the holy angel above is glorified in the splendor of his shining countenance.

---

[682] Ps 85:5.
[683] Lam 4:20.
[684] 1 Cor 13:12.

[685] 1 Jn 3:2; Phil 2:6.
[686] 1 Cor 13:9.
[687] Phil 3:13.

[688] 2 Cor 5:7.
[689] Hb 2:4; Rom 1:17.
[690] Lam 4:20.

9. That the faith is shadowy is a blessing; it tempers the light to the eye's weakness and prepares the eye for the light; for it is written: "He cleansed their hearts by faith."[691] Faith therefore does not quench the light but protects it. Whatever it may be that the angel sees is preserved for me by the shadow of faith, stored up in its trusty breast until it be revealed in due time. If you cannot yet grasp the naked truth is it not worthwhile to possess it wrapped in a veil? Our Lord's Mother herself lived in the shadow of faith, for she was told: "Blessed are you who believed."[692] Even the body of Christ was a shadow for her, as implied in the words: "The power of the Most High will cover you with its shadow."[693] That is no mean shadow which is formed by the power of the Most High. Assuredly there was power in the flesh of Christ that overshadowed the Virgin, since by means of the envelope of his vivifying body she was able to bear his majestic presence, and endure the unapproachable light,[694] a thing impossible to mortal woman. That was power indeed by which every opposing might was overcome. Both the power and the shadow put the demons to flight and became a shelter for men: an invigorating power surely, a shadow radiating coolness.

10. We therefore who walk by faith[695] live in the shadow of Christ; we are fed with his flesh as the source of our life. For Christ's flesh is real food.[696] And perhaps for that reason he is now described here as appearing in the guise of a shepherd, when the bride addresses him as though one of the shepherds: "Tell me where you pasture your flock, where you make it lie down at noon."[697] The Good Shepherd who

---

[691] Acts 15:9.
[692] Lk 1:45.
[693] Lk 1:35.

[694] 1 Tm 6:16.
[695] 2 Cor 5:7.
[696] Jn 6:56.

[697] Sg 1:7.

lays down his life for his sheep![698] He gives them his life, he gives them his flesh; his life their ransom, his flesh their food. How wonderful! He is their shepherd, their food, their redemption. But this sermon is getting too long, the subject is extensive and contains great truths that cannot be explained in a few words. This necessitates that we break off rather than finish off. Since the matter is merely suspended we must keep it alive in our memories, so as to resume soon again where we have left off, and continue it with the aid of our Lord Jesus Christ, the Church's Bridegroom, who is God blessed forever. Amen.[699]

SERMON 32

How Christ Adapts His Graces to Personal Needs

"Tell me where you pasture your flock, where you make it lie down at noon."[700] This is where we are, from here we proceed. But before I begin to treat of these words and the vision they imply, I think we should summarize briefly the other visions that preceded it, and see how they can be applied spiritually to us according to each one's desires and merits. If we receive the grace to understand these, we shall more easily find light on the matter we are about to discuss. For we are faced with a difficult task. The words that describe these visions or images seem to refer to bodies or bodily substances, yet they are means of conveying spiritual truths to us, and hence there must be a spiritual character to

[698] Jn 10:11.
[699] Rom 1:25.
[700] Sg 1:6.

our inquiry into their causes and meaning. And who is qualified to investigate and comprehend those countless affective movements of the soul caused by the presence of the Bridegroom dispensing his multiform graces?[701] Yet if we turn our gaze to our interior, and if the Holy Spirit will be pleased to give us his light to see the fruits that by his action he constantly produces within us, I think we shall not remain entirely devoid of understanding about these mysteries. For I trust that "we have not received the spirit of the world but the Spirit which is from God, that we might understand the gifts bestowed on us by God."[702]

2. If then, any of us, like the holy prophet, finds that it is good to cling close to God,[703] and—that I may make my meaning more clear—if any of us is so filled with desire that he wants to depart and to be with Christ,[704] with a desire that is intense, a thirst ever burning, an application that never flags, he will certainly meet the Word in the guise of a Bridegroom on whatever day he comes.[705] At such an hour he will find himself locked in the arms of Wisdom; he will experience how sweet divine love is as it flows into his heart. His heart's desire will be given to him,[706] even while still a pilgrim on earth, though not in its fullness and only for a time, a short time.[707] For when after vigils and prayers and a great shower of tears he who was sought presents himself, suddenly he is gone again, just when we think we hold him fast. But he will present himself anew to the soul that pursues him with tears, he will allow himself to be taken hold of but not detained, for suddenly a second time he flees from between our hands. And if the fervent soul persists with prayers and tears, he will

---

[701] 1 Pt 4:10.
[702] 1 Cor 2:12.
[703] Ps 72:28.
[704] Dn 9:23; Phil 1:23.

[705] 1 Pt 5:6.
[706] Ps 20:3.
[707] 2 Cor 5:6.

return each time and not defraud him of his express desire,[708] but only to disappear soon again and not to return unless he is sought for with all one's heart. And so, even in this body we can often enjoy the happiness of the Bridegroom's presence, but it is a happiness that is never complete because the joy of the visit is followed by the pain at his departure. The beloved has no choice but to endure this state until the hour when she lays down the body's weary weight, and raised aloft on the wings of desire, freely traverses the meadows of contemplation, and in spirit follows the One she loves without restraint wherever he goes.[709]

3. Nevertheless, he will not reveal himself in this way to every person, even momentarily, but only to the one who is proved to be a worthy bride by intense devotion, vehement desire, and the sweetest affection. And the Word who comes to visit will be clothed in beauty,[710] in every aspect a Bridegroom.

II. But the person who has not yet been raised to this state, who smarts at the remembrance of past deeds and says to God in bitterness of soul:[711] "Do not condemn me,"[712] or who may still be caught up in the snare of his own evil propensities, still perilously tempted,[713] this person needs a physician, not a bridegroom; hence kisses and embraces are not for him, but only oil and ointments, remedies for his wounds. Is not this how we too often feel? Is not this our experience at prayer, we who are tempted daily by our passions and filled with remorse for our past sins? O good Jesus, from what great bitterness have you not freed me by your coming, time after time? When distress has made me weep, when untold sobs and groans have shaken me, have you not anointed my wounded

[708] Ps 20:3.
[709] Rv 14:4.
[710] Ps 92:1.

[711] Jb 10:1.
[712] Jb 10:2.
[713] Jas 1:14.

conscience with the ointment of your mercy and poured in the oil of gladness?[714] How often has not prayer raised me from the brink of despair and made me feel happy in the hope of pardon? All who have had these experiences know well that the Lord Jesus is a physician indeed, "who heals the broken-hearted and binds up their wounds."[715] And those who cannot lay claim to experience must for that very reason put their trust in him when he says: "The Spirit of the Lord has anointed me, he has sent me to bring good news to the humble, to bind up the brokenhearted."[716] And if they should still be in doubt, let them draw near and put it to the test and so learn by inward experience what this means: "I desire mercy and not sacrifice."[717] But let us pursue the subject.

4. When men grow weary of studying spiritual doctrine and become lukewarm when their spiritual energies are drained away, then they walk in sadness along the ways of the Lord.[718] They fulfill the tasks enjoined on them with hearts that are tired and arid, they grumble without ceasing, they complain of the long days and the long nights in words like those of Job: "When I lie down I say: 'When shall I arise?' And then I shall be waiting for evening."[719] If when we are subject to these moods, the compassionate Lord draws near to us on the way we are traveling,[720] and being from heaven begins to talk to us about heavenly truths,[721] sings our favorite air from among the songs of Sion,[722] discourses on the city of God, on the peace of that city, on the eternity of that peace and on the life that is eternal, I assure you that this happy discourse will bear along as in a carriage the man who has grown tired and listless; it drives all trace

[714]Ps 44:8.
[715]Ps 146:3.
[716]Is 61:1.

[717]Mt 9:13.
[718]Lk 24:17.
[719]Jb 7:4.

[720]Lk 24:17.
[721]Jn 3:31.
[722]Ps 136:3.

of aversion from the hearer's mind and weariness from his body. Does it not seem that this is what was felt, this is what was asked for by the man who said: "My soul has slumbered through weariness, strengthen me according to your word"?[723] And when he obtains his request will he not cry out: "O how I love your law! It is my study all day long"?[724] For our meditations on the Word who is the Bridegroom, on his glory, his elegance, power and majesty, become in a sense his way of speaking to us. And not only that, but when with eager minds we examine his rulings, the decrees from his own mouth;[725] when we meditate on his law day and night,[726] let us be assured that the Bridegroom is present, and that he speaks his message of happiness to us lest our trials should prove more than we can bear.

5. When you find yourself caught up in this kind of thinking, beware of seeing the thoughts as your own; you must rather acknowledge that he is present who said to the prophet: "It is I, announcing righteousness."[727]

III. Our own thoughts bear a very close resemblance to the words Truth speaks within us; no one can easily differentiate between what springs from the heart and what he hears from without unless he attends carefully to what the Lord says in the Gospel: "Out of the heart come evil thoughts";[728] or that question: "Why do you think evil in your hearts?"[729] And again: "When he [the devil] lies, he speaks according to his own nature."[730] The apostle says: "Not that we are sufficient of ourselves to think of anything as coming from us," meaning here anything good, "but our sufficiency is from God."[731]

[723]Ps 118:28.   [726]Ps 1:2.   [729]Mt 9:4.
[724]Ps 118:97.   [727]Is 63:1.   [730]Jn 8:44.
[725]Ps 118:13.   [728]Mt 15:19.   [731]2 Cor 3:5.

So when we yield our hearts to wicked thoughts, the thoughts are our own; if we think on good things, it is God's word. Our hearts produce the evil thoughts, they listen for those that are good. "Let me hear," the heart says, "what God the Lord will speak, for he will speak peace to his people."[732] God accordingly utters words of peace, of goodness, of righteousness within us; we do not think these things of ourselves, we hear them in our interior. On the other hand, murders, adulteries, robberies, blasphemies, and similar evils come forth from the heart;[733] we do not hear them, we produce them. For "the fool says in his heart: 'there is no God.' "[734] And hence, "The wicked has provoked God, for he has said in his heart: 'He will not call to account.' "[735] But there is still another kind of thought that is perceived indeed in the heart but not uttered by it. It does not come forth from the heart as our thought does, nor is it that word which we have said is directed to the heart, namely, the word of the Word, because it is evil. It is produced within us by hostile powers, like the images that come to us from bad angels,[736] such as we read the devil put into the heart of Judas, son of Simon the Iscariot, to betray the Lord.[737]

6. For who can keep watch over his inward thoughts so closely and so assiduously, whether they merely occur to him or whether he is their author, as to be able to decide clearly which of the heart's illicit desires are the fruit of his own frailty, which an insinuation of the devil? I believe this is more than mortals can achieve, unless by the light of the Holy Spirit they receive that special gift which the apostle lists with the other charisms under the name of discernment

---

[732]Ps 84:9.
[733]Mt 15:19.
[734]Ps 13:1.

[735]Ps 9:34.
[736]Ps 77:49.
[737]Jn 13:2.

of spirits.[738] According to Solomon, no matter how vigilantly a man may guard his heart and watch with the closest scrutiny every movement of his inward being,[739] he will not be able to diagnose or judge exactly between the evil that is inborn and the evil implanted from without, even after prolonged study and frequent experience of these matters. For "who can understand sins?"[740] It is of little consequence to us to know the source of the evil within us, provided we know it is there; no matter what its source we must watch and pray that we may not consent to it.[741] The prophet prays against both these evils: "Cleanse me from my secret sins, O Lord, and spare your servant from those others."[742] As for me, I cannot hand on to you what I have not received.[743] And I certainly have not received the power to distinguish with certitude between what springs from the heart and what is sown there by the enemy. Both are evil, both have an evil source; both are in the heart, though both do not originate there. I am fully certain that I bear them within, but by no means certain which to attribute to the heart, which to the enemy. But this problem, as I have said, entails no danger.

7. But where the error is dangerous, even fatal, there we are provided with a rule that is certain: not to attribute to ourselves what comes from God within us, thinking that the visit of the Word is no more than a thought of our own. The distance of good from evil is the distance between these two things: for just as evil cannot proceed from the Word, neither can good proceed from the heart unless it has been previously inspired by the Word, because "a sound tree cannot bear evil fruit, nor can a bad tree bear good fruit."[744] But I think

---

[738] 1 Cor 12:10.
[739] Prv 4:23.
[740] Ps 18:13.
[741] Mt 26:41.

[742] Ps 18:13.
[743] 1 Cor 15:3.
[744] Mt 7:18.

enough has been said to clarify which movements of the heart are from God and which from ourselves. And this, I feel, had to be done in order that the enemies of grace[745] may know that without grace man's heart is incapable of thinking good thoughts, that its capacity to do so comes from God:[746] the good thought is God's inspiration, not the heart's offspring. You therefore, if you hear his voice, will no longer be ignorant of whence it comes or whither it goes,[747] because you will know it proceeds from God and goes to the heart. But make sure that the word which goes forth from the mouth of God does not return to him empty, see that it prospers and accomplishes all those things for which he sent it,[748] so that you too will be able to say: "The grace of God in me has not been fruitless."[749] Happy the man who has the Word for an inseparable companion who is always accessible, whose delightful conversation is an unceasing pleasure that frees him at all times from the flesh's bothersome vices, and enables him to use his time profitably in a wicked age.[750] He shall be neither wearied nor troubled, since, according to Scripture, no matter what happens to the righteous man, it will not make him sad.[751]

IV. 8. It seems to me that he appears in the guise of a mighty Father of a family or sovereign ruler to those whose hearts are high as they approach him,[752] who, filled with

---

[745]An allusion to Abelard and his followers whom Bernard compares to Pelagius in his letter "On the Errors of Abelard." Ep. 9:23ff; trans. Bruno S. James, *Letters* (Burns Oates: London, 1953), Letter 240.
[746]2 Cor 3:5.
[747]Jn 3:8.
[748]Is 55:11.
[749]1 Cor 15:10.
[750]Eph 5:16.
[751]Prv 12:21.
[752]Ps 63:7.

magnanimous courage because of greater liberty of spirit and purity of conscience, love to dare what is above the common measure. These are restless men, eager to penetrate the deeper mysteries, to grasp sublimer truths, to strive for what is more perfect, not so much in the physical as in the spiritual order. Because of the grandeur of their faith these are considered worthy of experiencing all fullness; in all the treasure-houses of wisdom there is nothing from which the Lord, the God who knows all things,[753] would think of turning these men away; avid for truth as they are, and their motives free of vanity. Moses was such a man, and he dared to say to God: "If I have found favor in your sight show me yourself."[754] Such was Philip, who begged that the Father be shown to him and his fellow disciples.[755] Thomas, too, was such a man, for he refused to believe unless he touched with his hand the spear wound in Christ's side.[756] This meant indeed a lack of faith, but it was a superb consequence of his greatness of soul. Again there was David, who said to God: "My heart has said to you: 'I have been searching for you'; Lord, I do seek your face."[757] Men of this kind undertake great deeds because they are themselves great; and what they undertake they achieve, in accord with the promise which runs: "Every place on which the sole of your foot treads shall be yours."[758] Great faith deserves great rewards; and if you step out with trust where the good things of the Lord are to be found, you will possess them.

9. God spoke to Moses face-to-face;[759] not by riddles and images was he privileged to see the Lord, but openly; whereas the Lord points out that he appears to other prophets only in

[753] 1 Sm 2:3.
[754] Ex 33:13.
[755] Jn 14:8.
[756] Jn 20:25.

[757] Ps 26:8.
[758] Dt 11:24.
[759] Nm 12:8.

vision, and speaks to them in dreams. Philip too received his heart's desire[760] when shown the Father in the Son, in that immediate reply of Christ: "Philip, he who has seen me, has seen the Father";[761] and, "I am in the Father and the Father is in me."[762] Thomas, according to his heart's desire and the protestation he had made, was permitted to touch him.[763] And what of David? Does he not show that he has not been entirely deprived of his wish when he says that he will not give sleep to his eyes nor slumber to his eyelids until he finds a place for the Lord?[764] To great men like these the Bridegroom will come in his greatness; he will perform mighty deeds with them,[765] sending out his light and his truth,[766] leading them on and directing them to his holy mountain and the tent where he dwells. Any one of these men can say: "He who is mighty has done great things for me."[767] His eyes will see the king in his beauty going before him into the beautiful places of the desert,[768] to the flowering roses and the lilies of the valley,[769] to gardens where delights abound and streams run from the fountains, where storerooms are filled with delightful things and the odors of perfume, till last of all he makes his way to the privacy of the bedchamber.

10. There you have the treasures of wisdom and knowledge hidden where the Bridegroom dwells,[770] and there the pastures of life, prepared for the nourishment of men seeking holiness. "Blessed is the man who has fulfilled his desire from them."[771] But let him be given at least this warning: not to wish to possess for himself alone goods that can suffice for the many. And perhaps for this reason after all these things the Bridegroom is described as appearing in a shepherd's guise,

[760]Ps 36:4.
[761]Jn 14:9.
[762]Jn 14:10.
[763]Ps 20:3; Jn 20:27.

[764]Ps 131:4–5.
[765]Ps 125:2.
[766]Ps 42:3.
[767]Lk 1:49.

[768]Is 33:17.
[769]Sg 2:1.
[770]Col 2:3.
[771]Ps 126:5.

to provide a guideline to the man who has received the task of feeding a flock that contains so many of the ordinary people who are unable to understand those truths by their own efforts, just as sheep will not attempt to go out to the fields unless led by a shepherd. The bride thoughtfully takes note of this, and asks to be shown where he eats, where he rests in the midday heat,[772] being ready, as may be gathered from her remark, both to be fed and to give food, as his helper and under his direction. She does not think it safe for the flock to wander far from their chief Shepherd because of wolves on the prowl, especially those who come to us in the clothing of sheep;[773] and hence her endeavor to eat in the same pastures with him and rest in the same shady places. And she gives the reason: "Lest I begin to wander after the flocks of your companions."[774] These are they who want to appear to be friends of the Bridegroom, but are not; and though their concern is to feed their own flocks rather than his, they cunningly spread the rumor: "Look, here is the Christ, look, he is there,"[775] and so seduce many people whom they lead away from the flocks of Christ and join to their own. So far I have been dealing with the obvious meaning of the words. But for the spiritual meaning that lies hidden beneath, you must await a new sermon. This will depend on whatever our Lord Jesus Christ, the Church's Bridegroom, will be pleased to impart to me in his mercy and through your prayers. He is God, blessed forever. Amen.[776]

---

[772]Sg 1:6.
[773]Mt 7:15.
[774]Sg 1:6.

[775]Mt 24:5; Mk 13:21.
[776]Rom 1:25.

SERMON 34
True Humility

"If you do not know, O fairest among women, go forth and follow the flocks of your companions and pasture your kids beside the shepherds' tents."[777] Of old, taking advantage of the familiar friendship that had developed between him and God, that holy man Moses so longed for the great favor of seeing him that he said to God: "If I have found favor in your sight, show yourself to me."[778] Instead of that he received a vision of an inferior kind, but one which nevertheless would help him to attain eventually to the one for which he longed. Following the guileless urging of their hearts, the sons of Zebedee also dared to ask for a great favor, but they too were directed back to the way by which they must ascend to higher things.[779] In similar fashion now, when the bride seems to demand a very special concession, she is rebuffed with an answer that, though harsh, is meant to be helpful and trustworthy. Anyone who strives forward toward the spiritual heights must have a lowly opinion of himself; because when he is raised above himself he may lose his grip on himself, unless through true humility, he has a firm hold on himself. It is only when humility warrants it that great graces can be obtained, hence the one to be enriched by them is first humbled by correction that by his humility he may merit them. And so when you perceive that you are being humiliated, look on it as the sign of a sure guarantee that grace is on the way.[780] Just as the heart is puffed up with pride before its destruction, so it is

[777]Sg 1:7.
[778]Ex 33:13.

[779]Mt 20:21.
[780]Ps 85:17.

humiliated before being honored.[781] You read in Scripture of these two modes of acting, how the Lord resists the proud and gives his grace to the humble.[782] Did he not decide to reward his servant Job with generous blessings after the outstanding victory in which his great patience was put to the severest test? He was prepared for blessings by the many searching trials that humbled him.[783]

II. 2. But it matters little if we willingly accept the humiliation which comes from God himself, if we do not maintain a similar attitude when he humiliates us by means of another. And I want you to take note of a wonderful instance of this in St. David, that time when he was cursed by a servant and paid no heed to the repeated insults, so sensitive was he to the influence of grace. He merely said: "What has this to do with me and you, O sons of Zeruiah?"[784] Truly a man after God's own heart,[785] who decided to be angry with the one who would avenge him rather than with the one who reviled him. Hence he could say with an easy conscience: "If I have repaid with evils those who offended me, let me rightly fall helpless before my enemies."[786] He would not allow them to silence this evil-spoken scoundrel; to him the curses were gain. He even added: "The Lord has sent him to curse David."[787] A man altogether after God's own heart, since the judgment he passed was from the heart of God. While the wicked tongue raged against him, his mind was intent on discovering the hidden purpose of God. The voice of the reviler sounded in his ears, but in his heart he disposed himself for blessings. Was God in the mouth of the blasphemer? God forbid! But he made use of it to humil-

[781]Prv 16:18.
[782]Jas 4:6.
[783]Jb 1:8; 2:3.
[784]2 Sm 16:10.
[785]Acts 13:22.
[786]Ps 7:5.
[787]2 Sm 16:10.

iate David. And this was not hidden from the prophet, to whom God had manifested the unpredictable secrets of his wisdom.[788] Hence he says: "It was good for me that you humiliated me, that I might learn your statutes."[789]

3. Do you see that humility makes us righteous? I say humility and not humiliation. How many are humiliated who are not humble! There are some who meet humiliation with rancor, some with patience, some again with cheerfulness. The first kind are culpable, the second are innocent, the last just. Innocence is indeed a part of justice, but only the humble possess it perfectly. He who can say: "It was good for me that you humiliated me," is truly humble. The man who endures it unwillingly cannot say this; still less the man who murmurs. To neither of these do I promise grace on the grounds of being humiliated, although the two are vastly different from each other, since the one possesses his own soul in his patience,[790] while the other perishes in his murmuring. For even if only one of them does merit anger, neither of them merits grace, because it is not to the humiliated but to the humble that God gives grace.[791] But he is humble who turns humiliation into humility, and he is the one who says to God: "It was good for me that you humiliated me." What is merely endured with patience is good for nobody, it is an obvious embarrassment. On the other hand we know that "God loves a cheerful giver."[792] Hence even when we fast we are told to anoint our head with oil and wash our face,[793] that our good work might be seasoned with spiritual joy and our holocaust made fat.[794] For it is the possession of a joyful and genuine humility that alone enables

[788] Ps 50:8.
[789] Ps 118:71.
[790] Lk 21:19.

[791] Jas 4:6.
[792] 2 Cor 9:7.

[793] Mt 6:17.
[794] Ps 19:4.

us to receive grace. But the humility that is due to necessity or constraint, that we find in the patient man who keeps his self-possession,[795] cannot win God's favor because of the accompanying sadness, although it will preserve his life because of patience. Since he does not accept humiliation spontaneously or willingly, one cannot apply to such a person the scriptural commendation that the humble man may glory in his exaltation.[796]

III. 4. If you wish for an example of a humble man glorying with all due propriety, and truly worthy of glory, take Paul when he says that gladly will he glory in his weaknesses that the power of Christ may dwell within him.[797] He does not say that he will bear his weaknesses patiently, but he will even glory in them, and that willingly, thus proving that to him it is good that he is humiliated,[798] and that it is not sufficient that one keep his self-possession by patience when he is humbled; to receive grace one must embrace humiliation willingly. You may take as a general rule that everyone who humbles himself will be exalted.[799] It is significant that not every kind of humility is to be exalted, but that which the will embraces; it must be free of compulsion or sadness.[800] Nor on the contrary must everyone who is exalted be humiliated, but only he who exalts himself, who pursues a course of vain display. Therefore it is not the one who is humiliated who will be exalted, but he who voluntarily humiliates himself; it is merited by this attitude of will. Even suppose that the occasion of humiliation is supplied by another, by means of insults, damages, or sufferings, the victim who determines to accept all these for God's sake with a quiet, joyful conscience, cannot properly be said to be humiliated by anyone but himself.

[795]Lk 21:19.   [797]2 Cor 12:9.   [799]Lk 14:11.
[796]Jas 1:9.   [798]Ps 118:71.   [800]2 Cor 9:7.

5. But where does this take me? I feel that your endurance of this protracted discussion on humility and patience is an exercise in patience; but let us return to the place from which we digressed. All that I have said developed from the answer in which the Bridegroom decided that the bride's aspiration toward lofty experiences should be restrained, not in order to confound her, but to provide an occasion for more solid, more deep humility, by which her capacity and worthiness for the sublimer experiences she desired would be increased. However, we are but at the beginning of this present verse, so with your permission, I shall postpone discussion of it to another sermon, lest the Bridegroom's words be recounted or heard with weariness. May our Lord Jesus Christ, who is blessed forever,[801] avert this from his servants. Amen.

SERMON 36
The Acquiring of Knowledge

Here I am as I promised; here I am, both in compliance with your request and to give to God the service I owe him. Three reasons therefore compel me to speak to you: fidelity to my promise, brotherly love, and the fear of the Lord. If I refuse to speak, my own mouth condemns me.[802] But what if I do speak? Then I dread a similar judgment, that my mouth will condemn me as one who speaks but fails to accomplish. Help me therefore with your prayers that I may always speak as I ought, and act in accord with my words.[803] You are aware that I propose to speak today of ignorance, or

[801] Rom 1:25.
[802] Jb 16:7; 9:20.
[803] 1 Tm 5:13.

rather of different kinds of ignorance. You remember I mentioned two kinds, one with regard to ourselves, the other with regard to God. And I warned that we must beware of these two, because both are reprehensible. It remains for me now to expound this more clearly and at greater length. But first I think we must try to discover if all ignorance is reprehensible. It seems to me that this is not true—nor does all ignorance occasion loss—since there are various and countless things of which one may know nothing without detriment to salvation. If you are ignorant of the craftsman's art, for example that of the carpenter or mason, or any other craft practiced by men for the purposes of the present life, does this prevent your being saved? But while unacquainted with any of the liberal arts—though not denying that they may be learned and practiced for honorable and useful ends—how many people are saved by living well and doing good, those whom the apostle mentions in the Epistle to the Hebrews,[804] men who were dear to God not because of knowledge of literature but because of a good conscience and a sincere faith?[805] They all pleased God in their lives by the merits of their lives, not by their knowledge. Peter and Andrew and the sons of Zebedee, and all the other disciples, were not chosen from a school of rhetoric or philosophy; and yet through them the Savior made his salvation effective throughout the world.[806] Unlike a certain holy man who made this claim for himself,[807] it was not because their wisdom surpassed that of all other living men, but because of their faith and meekness,[808] that he made them his friends, sanctified them, and appointed them teachers. And when they revealed to the world the paths of life,[809] it

[804]Heb 11.
[805]1 Tm 1:5.

[806]Ps 73:12.
[807]Eccl 1:16.

[808]Sir 45:4.
[809]Ps 15:11.

was not with sublime language or the polished words of human wisdom.[810] Rather it pleased God, since the world in its wisdom did not recognize him, that through the foolishness of their preaching believers should be saved.[811]

II. 2. Perhaps you think that I have sullied too much the good name of knowledge, that I have cast aspersions on the learned and proscribed the study of letters. God forbid! I am not unmindful of the benefits its scholars conferred, and still confer, on the Church, both by refuting her opponents and instructing the simple.[812] And I have read the text: "As you have rejected knowledge, so do I reject you from my priesthood":[813] read that the learned will shine as brightly as the vault of heaven, and those who have instructed many in virtue as bright as stars for all eternity.[814] But I recall reading too that knowledge puffs up,[815] and "the more the knowledge, the more the sorrow."[816] There are then different kinds of knowledge, one contributing to self-importance, the other to sadness. Which of the two do you think is more useful or necessary to salvation, the one that makes you vain or the one that makes you weep? I feel sure you would prefer the latter to the former, for vanity but pretends to health whereas pain expresses a need. Anyone who thus demands is on the way to being saved, because the one who asks receives.[817] Furthermore, Paul tells us that he who heals the brokenhearted abhors the proud: "God opposes the proud but gives grace to the humble."[818] Paul also said, "By the grace given to me I bid every one among you not to think more than he ought to think, but to think with sober judgment."[819] He does not

[810] 1 Cor 2:1.
[811] 1 Cor 1:21; Jn 1:10.
[812] Ti 2:8.
[813] Hos 4:6.
[814] Dn 12:3.

[815] 1 Cor 8:1.
[816] Eccl 1:18.
[817] Lk 11:10.
[818] Ps 146:3; Jas 4:6; 1 Pt 5:5.
[819] Rom 12:3.

forbid thinking, but inordinate thinking. And what is meant by thinking with sober judgment? It means taking the utmost care to discover what are the essential and primary truths, for the time is short.[820] All knowledge is good in itself, provided it be founded on the truth; but since because of the brevity of time you are in a hurry to work out your salvation in fear and trembling,[821] take care to learn, principally and primarily, the doctrines on which your salvation is more intimately dependent. Do not doctors of medicine hold that part of the work of healing depends on a right choice in the taking of food, what to take first, what next, and the amount of each kind to be eaten? For although it is clear that all the foods God made are good, if you fail to take the right amount in due order, you obviously take them to the detriment of your health. And what I say about foods I want you to apply to the various kinds of knowledge.

3. I prefer though to let you consult the Master. The doctrine I have preached is not really mine but his; though mine as well insofar as it is the word of him who is Truth. For Paul said: "If anyone imagines that he knows something, he does not yet know as he ought to know."[822] He does not approve of the well-read man who observes no scale of values in the knowledge he possesses. See how the fruit and usefulness of knowledge is determined by the manner in which one knows. And what does that manner imply? It implies the order, the application, and the sense of purpose with which one approaches the object of study. The order implies that we give precedence to all that aids spiritual progress; the application, that we pursue more eagerly all that strengthens love more; and the purpose, that we pursue

[820] 1 Cor 7:29.
[821] Phil 2:12.

[822] 1 Cor 8:2.

it not through vainglory or inquisitiveness or any base motive, but for the welfare of oneself or one's neighbor.

III. For there are some who long to know for the sole purpose of knowing, and that is shameful curiosity; others who long to know in order to become known, and that is shameful vanity. To such as these we may apply the words of the Satirist: "Your knowledge counts for nothing unless your friends know you have it."[823] There are others still who long for knowledge in order to sell its fruits for money or honors, and this is shameful profiteering; others again who long to know in order to be of service, and this is charity. Finally there are those who long to know in order to benefit themselves, and this is prudence.

4. Of all these categories, only the last two avoid the abuse of knowledge, because they desire to know for the purpose of doing good.[824] People with sound judgment act in this way.[825] Let all others heed the warning: he who knows what he ought to do and fails to do it, commits sin;[826] just as food eaten but not digested is injurious to one's health. Food that is badly cooked and indigestible induces physical disorders and damages the body instead of nourishing it. In the same way if a glut of knowledge stuffed in the memory, that stomach of the mind, has not been cooked on the fire of love, and transfused and digested by certain skills of the soul, its habits and actions—since, as life and conduct bear witness, the mind is rendered good through its knowledge of good—will not that knowledge be reckoned sinful,[827] like the food that produces irregular and harmful humors? Is not sin a humor of evil? Are not bad habits humors of evil? Will not a man in this

[823]Persius, *Satires,* 1:27.
[824]Ps 35:4.
[825]Ps 110:10.
[826]Jas 4:17.
[827]Dt 23:21.

condition suffer in his conscience inflammations and torments, since he does not act as he knows he should? And will he not find within himself the threat of death and damnation as often as he calls to mind the saying of God,[828] that the man who knows what his Lord wants, but fails to respond as he should, will receive many strokes of the lash?[829] Perhaps the prophet was lamenting in the guise of such a man when he said: "There is an anguish within me, anguish within!"[830] Or perhaps the repetition of the woes hint at a different meaning that I ought to follow up. It is possible that the prophet spoke these words in his own person when, filled with a knowledge and over-flowing with a love that he longed with all his soul to communicate, he found no one who wanted to listen; the knowledge that he could not impart became a burden on his mind. This holy teacher of the Church therefore bewails both those who scorn to learn how to live, and those who, knowing the truth, yet live evil lives. This could explain the prophet's repetition of those words.

5. Do you not see then, how truly the apostle perceived that knowledge puffs up?[831]

IV. I wish therefore that before everything else a man should know himself, because not only usefulness but right order demand this. Right order, since what we are is our first concern; and usefulness, because this knowledge gives humility rather than self-importance, it provides a basis on which to build. For unless there is a durable foundation of humility,[832] the spiritual edifice has no hope of standing.[833] And there is nothing more effective, more adapted to the acquiring of humility than to find out the truth about

---

[828] 2 Cor 1:9.
[829] Lk 12:47.
[830] Jer 4:19.

[831] 1 Cor 8:1.
[832] 1 Cor 3:12.
[833] Mk 3:25.

oneself. There must be no dissimulation, no attempt at self-deception, but a facing up to one's real self without flinching and turning aside. When a man thus takes stock of himself in the clear light of truth, he will discover that he lives in a region where likeness to God has been forfeited,[834] and groaning from the depths of a misery to which he can no longer remain blind, will he not cry out to the Lord as the prophet did: "In your truth you have humbled me"?[835] How can he escape being genuinely humbled on acquiring this true self-knowledge, on seeing the burden of sin that he carries,[836] the oppressive weight of his mortal body, the complexities of earthly cares, the corrupting influence of sensual desires; on seeing his blindness, his worldliness, his weakness, his embroilment in repeated errors; on seeing himself exposed to a thousand dangers, trembling amid a thousand fears, confused by a thousand difficulties, defenseless before a thousand suspicions, worried by a thousand needs; one to

---

[834]*Regio dissimilitudinis*. This is an expression which is very commonly used by the Cistercian Fathers. See, e.g., William of St. Thierry, *Exposition on the Song of Songs* 65 (CF 6:52); *Meditations* 4:6 (CF 3:113); Aelred of Rievaulx, *Jesus at the Age of Twelve* (CF 2:6) and *Sermons on Isaiah* 8 (*Patrologia Latina,* 195:391); Isaac of Stella, *Second Sermon for the Feast of All Saints* 13 (SCh 130:106); and elsewhere in Bernard, *On Grace and Free Choice* 28 (OB 3:185), 32 (OB 3:188); *Occasional Sermons* 40:4 (OB 6–1:237), 42:2–3 (OB 6–1:256–57); and *Letters* 8:2 (BSJ, Ep 9, p. 39). Originating with Plato and Plotinus the idea of a land or region of unlikeness was adopted by Christian writers such as Eusebius, St. Athanasius, and St. Augustine (e.g., see *Confessions* vii, 10), until it is found to be of almost universal use in the Middle Ages. Most of the Cistercian authors associate the land of unlikeness with that faraway country in Luke 15:13 and thus the emphasis is on the notion of sin; however, sometimes, especially in the case of St. Bernard, it is merely a question of the soul being an alien on earth, an exile in a land that is not its true country. See also, J. M. Déchanet, introduction, CF 3:xlvii; A. Hallier, *The Monastic Theology of Aelred of Rievaulx,* CS 2 (Spencer, 1969), p. 12; and F. Vandenbrouke, *Why Monks?* CS 17 (Washington, 1972), pp. 25–26.
[835]Ps 118:75.
[836]2 Tm 3:6.

whom vice is welcome, virtue repugnant? Can this man afford the haughty eyes, the proud lift of the head?[837] With the thorns of his misery pricking him, will he not rather be changed for the better?[838] Let him be changed and weep, changed to mourning and sighing, changed to acceptance of the Lord, to whom in his lowliness he will say: "Heal me because I have sinned against you."[839] He will certainly find consolation in this turning to the Lord, because he is "the Father of mercies and the God of all comfort."[840]

6. As for me, as long as I look at myself, my eye is filled with bitterness.[841] But if I look up and fix my eyes on the aid of the divine mercy, this happy vision of God soon tempers the bitter vision of myself, and I say to him: "I am disturbed within so I will call you to mind from the land of the Jordan."[842] This vision of God is not a little thing. It reveals him to us as listening compassionately to our prayers, as truly kind and merciful, as one who will not indulge his resentment.[843] His very nature is to be good, to show mercy always, and to spare. By this kind of experience, and in this way, God makes himself known to us for our good. When a man first discovers that he is in difficulties, he will cry out to the Lord who will hear him and say: "I will deliver you and you shall glorify me."[844] In this way your self-knowledge will be a step to the knowledge of God; he will become visible to you according as his image is being renewed within you.[845] And you, gazing confidently on the glory of the Lord with unveiled face, will be transformed into that same image with ever increasing brightness, by the work of the Spirit of the Lord.[846]

[837] Sir 23:5.
[838] Ps 31:4.
[839] Ps 40:5.
[840] 2 Cor 1:3.

[841] Jb 17:2.
[842] Ps 41:7.
[843] Jl 2:13.
[844] Ps 90:15; Ps 49:15.

[845] Col 3:10.
[846] 2 Cor 3:18.

7. You can see now how each of these kinds of knowledge is so necessary for your salvation, that you cannot be saved if you lack either of them. If you lack self-knowledge you will possess neither the fear of God nor humility. And whether you may presume to be saved without the fear of God and humility, is for you to judge. The murmuring that I hear among you shows me quite clearly that this is not your idea of wisdom, or rather not your way of being foolish, so we need not linger over what is obvious. But there are other things to attend to, or should we come to an end for the sake of those who are asleep down there? I thought that with one sermon I should fulfill my promise about the two kinds of ignorance, and I would have, but it is already too long for those who are tired of it. Some, I can see, are yawning, and some are asleep. And no wonder, for last night's vigils were prolonged; that excuses them. But what shall I say to those who were asleep then, and now sleep again? I am not now going to add to their shame, it is enough to have mentioned it. But for the future they must be on the alert, or they will have to endure the sting of further reproach. With this hope in view I pass over the matter for the moment; and though reason demands that I continue the sermon, out of charity for them I shall postpone it to another time, making an end where there is no end. And they, because of the mercy shown them, must give glory along with us to the Church's Bridegroom, our Lord, who is God blessed forever. Amen.[847]

[847]Rom 1:25.

SERMON 49

I. The Wine Cellar: this indicates the early Church, or a Zeal for Righteousness that Burns in the Soul from Contemplating God. II. The Discipline of Love is Discretion. III. Projects that Come up for Decision Must Sometimes be Postponed for the Sake of Orderly Love, and that We Should be All the More Happy Because of the Greater Gain to God.
IV. How We May Attain to the Right Order of Love.

I. 1. "The king led me into the wine cellar, he set love in order in me."[848] The words of the proposed text seem to mean that after the bride had achieved her desire of sweet and intimate conversation with her beloved, she returned, at his departure, to the maidens so refreshed and animated in speech and appearance that she looked drunken. And when they, surprised at this novelty, asked for the reason, she answered that it is not surprising if one who entered the wine cellar should be tipsy with wine. So much for the literal meaning. But she also does not deny that she is drunk in the spirit, but with love, not wine—except that love is wine. "The king led me into the wine cellar." When the bridegroom is present and the bride addresses him, then "bridegroom" is said, or "beloved" or "whom my soul loves"; but when she speaks about him to the maidens she calls him "the king." Why? Because it is appropriate for the bride who loves and is loved to use familiarly, as she pleases, the titles of love, and it is necessary that the maidens, who need discipline, be constrained by the awesome title of majesty.

2. "The king led me into the wine cellar." I omit mentioning what that wine cellar is, because I remember having described

---

[848] Sg 2:3.

it.[849] But if the term is referred to the Church—since the disciples, filled with the Holy Spirit, were thought by the people to be drunk with wine[850]—then Peter, the friend of the bridegroom,[851] standing in their midst said on behalf of the bride: "These men are not drunk as you suppose."[852] Take note that he denies not that they are drunk, but drunk in the manner supposed by the people. For they were drunk, but with the Holy Spirit, not with wine. And as if they would witness to the people that they had really been led into the wine cellar, again Peter says on behalf of all:[853] "But this is what was spoken by the prophet Joel: 'and in the last days it shall be, God declares, that I will pour out my Spirit upon all flesh, and your sons and your daughters shall prophesy, and your young men shall see visions, and your old men shall dream dreams.' "[854] Does it not seem to you that the wine cellar was that house in which the disciples were assembled,[855] when "suddenly a sound came from heaven like the rush of a mighty wind, and it filled all the house where they were sitting,"[856] and fulfilled Joel's prophecy? And as each of them went out intoxicated by the abundance of that house and drunk from a torrent of a pleasure so great,[857] could he not truly say: "the king led me into the wine cellar"?

3. But even you too, if recollected in spirit, if with a mind serious and devoid of cares, you enter the house of prayer[858] alone, and standing in the Lord's presence at one of the altars touch the gate of heaven with the hand of holy desire, if in the presence of the choirs of saints where your devotion penetrates—for "the prayer of the righteous man pierces the

[849]Sermon 23:5; (cf. 7:29).
[850]Acts 2:4–13.
[851]Jn 3:29.
[852]Acts 2:15.
[853]Acts 2:16–17.
[854]Jl 2:28.
[855]Jn 20:19.
[856]Acts 2:2.
[857]Ps 35:9.
[858]Mt 21:13.

heavens"[859]—you bewail pitiably before them the miseries and misfortunes you endure, manifest your neediness, implore their mercy with repeated sighs and groanings too deep for words; if, I say, you do this, I have confidence in him who said: "ask and you shall receive,"[860] that if you continue knocking you will not go empty away.[861] Indeed when you return to us full of grace and love, you will not be able, in the ardor of your spirit,[862] to conceal the gift you have received; you will communicate it without unpopularity,[863] and in the grace that was given to you, you will win the acceptance and even the admiration of everyone. And you can declare with truth: "the king led me into the wine cellar"; only be careful that you glory not in yourself but in the Lord.[864] I would not vouch that every gift, even if spiritual, proceeds from the wine cellar, since the bridegroom has other cellars or repositories in which are hidden varying gifts and charisms, in accord with the riches of his glory.[865] I have discoursed on these cellars quite extensively elsewhere.[866] "Are these not laid up in store with me," he said, "sealed up in my treasuries?"[867] Therefore there is a distribution of graces in accord with the diversity of cellars,[868] and "to each is given the manifestation of the Spirit for the common good." And although one is given wisdom in speech, another the power to instruct, another prophecy, another the grace of healing, another the gift of tongues, another the ability to interpret doctrine,[869] and still others gifts similar to these, yet none of

---

[859] Sir 35:21.
[860] Jn 16:24.
[861] Lk 11:8.
[862] Rom 12:11.
[863] Ws 7:13.
[864] 1 Cor 1:31.

[865] Eph 3:16.
[866] Sermon 23, 5–8 (cf. 7:29–33).
[867] Dt 32:34.
[868] 1 Cor 12:14.
[869] 1 Cor 12:7–10.

them can say in consequence that he was led into the wine cellar. For these are taken from other cellars or treasuries.

4. But if anyone obtains, while praying, the grace of going forth in spirit into the mystery of God,[870] and then returns in a glowing ardor of divine love, overflowing with zeal for righteousness, fervent beyond measure in all spiritual studies and duties, so that he can say: "My heart became hot within me; as I mused the fire burned,"[871] since the abundance of love shows he has clearly begun to live in that state of good and salutary intoxication, he is not unjustly said to have entered the wine cellar. For as holy contemplation has two forms of ecstasy, one in the intellect, the other in the will; one of enlightenment, the other of fervor; one of knowledge, the other of devotion: so a tender affection, a heart glowing with love, the infusion of holy ardor, and the vigor of a spirit filled with zeal, are obviously not acquired from any place other than the wine cellar. And everyone to whom it is granted to rise up from prayer with an abundance of these can truly say: "the king led me into the wine cellar."

II. 5. She continues: "He set love in order in me."[872] Utterly necessary. Zeal without knowledge is insupportable.[873] Therefore where zeal is enthusiastic, there discretion, that moderator of love, is especially necessary. Because zeal without knowledge always lacks efficacy, is wanting in usefulness, and all too often is harmful. And so the more eager the zeal, the more vigorous the spirit, the more generous the love, so also the greater the need for more vigilant knowledge to restrain the zeal, to temper the spirit, to moderate the love. Hence the bride, lest she be feared by the maidens as overbearing and insufferable because of the impetuosity

[870] 2 Cor 5:13.
[871] Ps 38:4.
[872] Sg 2:4.
[873] Rom 10:2.

of spirit that she seems to have brought back from the wine cellar, adds that she too has received the fruit of discretion, a regulating of love. Discretion regulates every virtue, order assigns proportion and beauty, and even permanence. For it is written: "By your ordinance the day goes on,"[874] day meaning virtue. Discretion therefore is not so much a virtue as a moderator and guide of the virtues, a director of the affections, a teacher of right living. Take it away and virtue becomes vice, and natural affection itself a force that disturbs and destroys nature. "He set love in order in me." This took place when he appointed some in the Church to be apostles, some prophets, others evangelists, others pastors and teachers, for the perfecting of the saints.[875] It is essential that the one love should bind and merge all these into the unity of Christ's body, and it is entirely incapable of doing this if it is not itself regulated. For if each one is carried away by his own impulse in accord with the spirit he receives, and applies himself indifferently to everything as he feels suggests rather than as he judges by reason, until no one is content with his assigned duty but all simultaneously undertake to administer everything indiscriminately, there will clearly be no unity but confusion instead.

III. 6. "He set love in order in me." Would that the Lord Jesus would set in order in me the little fund of love he gave me, that while my interest may extend to all his concerns, I may care before everything else for the project or duty he has appointed especially for me. My primary concern for this, however, should be such that I may be drawn all the more to the many things that do not especially pertain to me. For that which demands first care does not always demand

[874] Ps 118:91.
[875] Eph 4:11.

greater love, since often the thing that we worry about most is of no great use, and should not constrain our love. So frequently what is duty's first concern is less esteemed by the judgment, and what truth considers of first importance true love demands must be embraced more ardently. For example, does duty not impose on me the care of all of you? Now if by chance I should prefer to this work something that would prevent me striving with all my strength to execute it worthily and profitably, the principle of order would not approve it, even though I might seem to do it for love's sake. Yet if I apply myself as I ought to this charge before everything else, but fail to rejoice in the greater gains for God that I see another achieving, it is evident that I partially observe the order of love and partially do not. If however I reveal genuine concern for that which is my special charge, and nevertheless a still finer sympathy for a work that is greater, I find that I have fulfilled the order of love in both ways, and there is no reason why even I should not be able to say that "he set love in order in me."

7. Yet if you say it is hard for a person to rejoice more in another's great achievement than in his own small effort, you certainly perceive from this the excellence of the bride's grace, and that not every soul can say: "he set love in order in me." Why have the faces of some of you fallen at this statement? These deep sighs bear witness to a sad mind and dispirited conscience. Measuring ourselves against ourselves,[876] we feel, from the experience of our own imperfection, some of us, how rare a virtue it is not to envy the virtue of another, not to mention rejoicing in it, not to mention that one should be all the more happy with himself the more he considers himself surpassed in virtue. There is yet a

---

[876] 2 Cor 10:12.

little light among us, brothers, as many of us feel this way about ourselves.

IV. Let us walk while we have the light, lest darkness overtake us.[877] To walk is to make progress. The apostle was walking when he said: "I do not consider that I have made it my own"; and added: "but one thing I do, forgetting what lies behind I strain forward to what lies ahead."[878] What is this one thing? One thing, he says, has remained with me, as a remedy, a hope, a consolation. What is it? Evidently "forgetting what lies behind I strain forward to what lies ahead." What sublime confidence. That distinguished "chosen instrument,"[879] denying that he is perfect, declares that he is moving ahead! The danger therefore is that not he who walks but he who takes his ease will be overcome by the darkness of death.[880] And who takes his ease but the man who has no will to advance? Pay heed to this, and if you die early, you will be at rest.[881] You may say to God: "Your eyes beheld my imperfect being." And nevertheless "in your book all shall be written."[882] Who are all? Surely those who possess the desire to advance. The text continues: "days shall be formed, and no one in them";[883] you supply: shall perish. Understand "days" as those who are advancing, who, if they are surprised by death, will be made perfect in that which is lacking in them. They shall be formed, and none among them left imperfect.

8. "And how can I advance," you say, "I, who am jealous of my brother's progress?" If you grieve for your jealousy, you feel it without yielding to it. It is a passion that time will

---

[877]Jn 12:35.
[878]Phil 3:13.
[879]Acts 9:15.
[880]Lk 1:79.

[881]Ws 4:7.
[882]Ps 138:16.
[883]Ibid.

heal, not an action to be condemned. But you must not relax in it, plotting mischief in your bed,[884] how to foster the disease, that is, how to pander to the contagion, how to persecute the innocent by disparaging his fine achievements, by discouraging, misrepresenting, or obstructing his undertakings. Otherwise it does not injure the one who advances and strives for better things,[885] because it is no longer he who does it but the sin that dwells within him.[886] Condemnation therefore is not for him who does not give his body to wickedness,[887] nor his tongue to slander, nor any other part of his body to the infliction of damage or injury; on the contrary he is ashamed of his evil disposition, and strives to expel the deep-seated vice by continued confession, by tears, by prayer. And should he not succeed he is thereby more gentle toward others, more humble in himself. Can a wise man condemn the sensible person who has learned from the Lord to be gentle and humble of heart?[888] It must not be that we should find devoid of salvation one who follows the Savior, the Church's bridegroom, our Lord, who is God blessed forever.[889] Amen.

[884]Ps 35:5.
[885]Phil 3:13
[886]Rom 7:20

[887]Rom 6:19
[888]Mt 11:29.
[889]Rom 1:25.

SERMON 50

I. Concerning Love in the Affections and in Action; the Law of Love; and Why God Commands Impossible Things.
II. The Threefold Love of the Flesh, of Reason, and of Wisdom, and the Transposed Order of Love in Action. III. The Order of Affective Love, that Understands all Things as They Are.

I. 1. Perhaps you expect a discussion of the next verses, thinking that the verse just dealt with is finished. But I am working on something else, for I have still to set before you some leftovers from yesterday's feast that I collected to prevent them spoiling.[890] They will spoil if I give them to nobody: and if I wish to enjoy them alone, I myself shall be spoiled. I am unwilling then to keep them from that gullet of yours which I know so well, especially as they are presented from the tray of love, as sweet as they are delicate, as tasty as they are small. Furthermore it is altogether contrary to love to deprive people of love. So here I am: "he has set love in order in me."[891]

2. Love exists in action and in feeling.[892] And with regard to love in action, I believe that a law, an explicit commandment, has been given to men;[893] yet how can one's feelings correspond to the commandment? The former therefore is commanded in view of merit, the latter is given as a reward. We do not deny that the present life, by divine grace, can also experience its beginning and progress, but we unreservedly maintain that its consummation is in the happiness of the life to come. How then should that be ordered which can in no way be fulfilled? Or if you prefer to hold that

---

[890] Jn 6:12.
[891] Sg 2:4.

[892] *actus; affectus.*
[893] Dt 5:6.

affective love has been commanded, I do not dispute it, provided you agree with me that in this life it can never and will never be able to be fulfilled by any man. For who will dare to arrogate to himself what even Paul confessed he did not comprehend?[894] The Lawgiver was not unaware that the burden of the law exceeded the powers of men, but he judged it useful for this reason to advise men of their own insufficiency, that they might know the proper end toward which they ought to strive according to their powers. Therefore in commanding impossible things he made men humble, not prevaricators, so that every mouth may be stopped and the whole world be made subject to God, because nobody will be justified in his sight by the works of the law.[895] Accepting that command then, and conscious of our deficiency, we shall cry to heaven and God will have mercy on us.[896] And on that day we shall know that God has saved us, not by the righteous works that we ourselves have done, but according to his mercy.[897]

3. This is what I should say if we were agreed that affective [love] were a law commanded. But that seems especially to apply to [love in] action, because when the Lord said: "Love your enemies," he referred right afterward to actions: "Do good to those who hate you."[898] Scripture also says: "If your enemy is hungry, feed him; if he is thirsty, give him drink."[899] Here you have a question of actions, not of feeling. But listen also to the Lord's command about love of himself: "If you love me keep my words."[900] And here too, by enjoining the observance of the commandments, he assigns us to action. It would have been superfluous for him

[894]Phil 3:13.
[895]Rom 3:19–20.
[896]Mc 4:10.
[897]Ti 3:5.

[898]Lk 6:27.
[899]Rom 12:20.
[900]Jn 14:15.

to warn us to act if love were but a matter of feeling. Hence it is necessary that you accept as well that commandment to love your neighbor as yourself,[901] even if it is not expressed as clearly as this. Do you then consider that you do enough to fulfill the command to love of neighbor if you observe perfectly what the natural law prescribes for every man: "What you would not wish done to yourself, avoid doing to another";[902] and also: "Always treat others as you like them to treat you"?[903]

4. I am not saying that we should be without affection, and that with an arid heart we move only our hands to work. Among the many great and grievous evils that the apostle ascribes to men I have read this one is reckoned: to be without affection.[904]

II. But there is an affection which the flesh begets, and one which reason controls, and one which wisdom seasons. The first is that which the apostle says is not subject to the law of God, nor can be;[905] the second, on the contrary, he shows to in agreement with the law of God because it is good[906]—one cannot doubt that the insubordinate and the agreeable differ from each other. The third, however, is far from either of them, because it tastes and experiences that the Lord is sweet;[907] it banishes the first and rewards the second. The first is pleasant, of course, but shameful; the second is emotionless but strong; the last is rich and delightful. Therefore by the second good deeds are done, and in it love reigns: not that of the feelings, which, growing richer with the seasoning of wisdom's salt,[908] fills the mind with a mighty abundance of the sweetness of the Lord,[909] but that rather which is practical, not yet indeed imparting the

---

[901]Mt 22:39.　　　　[904]Rom 1:31; 2 Tm 3:3.　　　[907]Ps 33:9.
[902]Tb 4:16; RB 61.　　[905]Rom 8:7.　　　　　　　[908]Col 4:6.
[903]Mt 7:12.　　　　　[906]Rom 7:16.　　　　　　　[909]Ps 30:20.

delightful refreshment of sweet love, but still vehemently aflame with the love of love itself. "Do not love in word or speech," he said, "but in deed and in truth."[910]

5. Do you see how cautiously he takes a middle path between vitiated and affective love, while distinguishing from both the love that is active and salutary? He neither finds room in this love for the figment of a lying tongue, nor does he yet demand the flavor of loving wisdom. "Let us love in deed and in truth,"[911] he says, because we are moved to do good more by the vigorous urging of truth than by the feeling of relished love. "He set love in order in me."[912] Which of these loves do you think? Both of them, but in reverse order. Now the active prefers what is lowly, the affective what is lofty. For example, there is no doubt that in a mind that loves rightly, the love of God is valued more than love of men, and among men themselves the more perfect [is esteemed] more than the weaker, heaven more than earth, eternity more than the flesh. In well-regulated action, on the other hand, the opposite order frequently or even always prevails. For we are more strongly impelled toward and more often occupied with the welfare of our neighbor; we attend our weaker brothers with more exacting care; by human right and very necessity we concentrate more on peace on earth than on the glory of heaven;[913] by worrying about temporal cares we are not permitted to think of eternal things; in attending almost continually to the ills of our body we lay aside the care of our soul; and finally, in accord with the saying of the apostle, we invest our weaker members with greater honor,[914] so fulfilling in a sense the word of the Lord: "the last shall be first and the first last."[915] Who

[910] 1 Jn 3:18.
[911] 1 Jn 3:18.
[912] Sg 2:4.

[913] Lk 2:14.
[914] 1 Cor 12:23.
[915] Mt 20:16.

will doubt that in prayer a man is speaking with God? But how often, at the call of charity, we are drawn away, torn away, for the sake of those who need to speak to us or be helped! How often does dutiful repose yield dutifully to the uproar of business! How often is a book laid aside in good conscience that we may sweat at manual work! How often for the sake of administering worldly affairs we very rightly omit even the solemn celebration of masses! A preposterous order; but necessity knows no law. Love in action devises its own order, in accord with the command of the householder, beginning with the most recent;[916] it is certainly dutiful and correct, without favoritism,[917] swayed not by worldly values but by human needs.

6. But not so affective love, since it always leads the ordering from the first. It is the wisdom by which all things are experienced as they are; as for example, the higher the nature the more perfect the love it evokes; the lower evokes less, the lowest nothing. The truth of love determines the previous order, but this order the love of truth lays claim to itself. Now true love is found in this, that those whose need is greater receive first;[918] and again loving truth is evident if we maintain in our feelings the order it maintains in the reason.

III. But you, if you love the Lord your God with your whole heart, whole mind, whole strength,[919] and leaping with ardent feeling beyond that love of love with which active love is satisfied and having received the Spirit in fullness, are wholly aflame with that divine love to which the former is a step, then God is indeed experienced, although not as he truly is, a thing impossible for any creature, but rather in relation to your power to enjoy. Then you will experience as well your own true self, since you perceive that

---

[916]Mt 20:8.

[917]Acts 10:34; Jb 32:21.

[918]1 Jn 4:10.

[919]Mk 12:30.

you possess nothing at all for which you love yourself, except insofar as you belong to God: you pour out upon him your whole power of loving. I repeat: you experience yourself as you are, when by that experience of love of yourself and of the feeling that you feel toward him, you discover that you are an altogether unworthy object even of your own love, except for the sake of him without whom you are nothing.

7. As for your neighbor whom you are obliged to love as yourself:[920] if you are to experience him as he is, you will actually experience him only as you do yourself: he is what you are. You who do not love yourself then, except because you love God, consequently love as yourself all those who similarly love him. But you who love God cannot love as yourself a human enemy, for he is nothing in that as he does not love God;[921] yet you will love him so that he may love. But, to love in order that he may love, and to love because he loves, are not the same thing. That you may experience him as he is, therefore, you must experience him not for what he is, because he is nothing, but for what perhaps he will become, which is almost nothing since it still hangs in doubt. But when it becomes clear that he will not return to the love of God, it is essential that you regard him, not as almost nothing but as totally nothing, in that he will be eternally nothing. With this one exception, since not only is he not to be loved, but even to be looked on with hatred, in accord with the text: "Lord, do I not hate those who hate you, and loathe those who defy you?"[922] The love that is open does not permit the refusal of some feeling, however small, to any man, even to one's greatest enemy. Who is wise enough to understand these things?[923]

---

[920]Mt 19:19.
[921]1 Jn 4:20.

[922]Ps 138:21.
[923]Ps 106:43.

8. Give me a man who loves God before all things and with his whole being, self and neighbor in proportion to their love of God, the enemy as one who perhaps someday will love his physical parents very deeply because of the natural bond, but his spiritual guides more generously because of grace. In like manner let him deal with the other things of God too with an ordered love, disregarding the earth, esteeming heaven, using this world as if not using it,[924] and discriminating between the things used and those enjoyed with an intimate savoring in his mind. Let him pay but passing attention to things that pass, as existing need demands. Let him embrace eternal things with an eternal desire. Give me such a man, I repeat, and I shall boldly proclaim him wise, because he appreciates things for what they really are, because he can truthfully and confidently boast and say: "he set love in order in me."[925] But where is he, and when shall these be? In tears I ask.[926] How long shall we smell and not taste, gazing toward the fatherland and not taking possession, sighing for it and saluting from afar? O Truth, fatherland of exiles, end of their exile! I see you, but held fast by the flesh I may not enter. Filthy with sins, I am not fit to be admitted. O Wisdom, reaching mightily from end to end in establishing and controlling things[927] and arranging all things sweetly by enriching the affections and setting them in order! Guide our actions as your eternal truth requires, that each of us may confidently boast in you and say: "he set love in order in me."[928] For you are the strength of God and the Wisdom of God,[929] Christ the Church's bridegroom, our Lord and God who is blessed forever.[930] Amen.

[924] I Cor 7:31.
[925] Sg 2:4.
[926] Phil 3:18.
[927] Ws 8:1.
[928] Sg 2:4.
[929] I Cor 1:24.
[930] Rom 1:25.

SERMON 56

*I. What Is the Wall, What Are the Windows or Chinks
Through Which the Bridegroom Looks? II. How He Is Behind
the Wall for Each of Us; His Presence and His Absence.
III. How Some Erect Many Walls between Themselves and
the Bridegroom, and the Moral of the Lattices and Windows.*

I. 1. "Behold, there he stands behind our wall, gazing in at
the windows, looking through the lattices."[931] As the words
stand, they seem to say that he who was seen coming by leaps
and bounds has arrived at the Bride's dwelling and, standing
behind the wall, peeps inquisitively through the windows
and chinks, because he is too modest to presume to enter.
According to the spiritual meaning, however, he is understood to have drawn near, but in a different way, as it befits
the heavenly Bridegroom to behave and the Holy Spirit to
describe it. A true spiritual understanding will not condone
what ill becomes either the one who acts or the one who
describes the action. He drew near the wall, therefore, when
he joined himself to our flesh. Our flesh is the wall, and the
Bridegroom's approach is the incarnation of the Word. The
windows and lattices through which he is said to gaze can be
understood, I think, as the bodily senses and human feelings
by which he began to experience all our human needs. For
"he has borne our griefs and carried our sorrows."[932] On being
made man, therefore, he has used our bodily feelings and
senses as openings or windows, so that he would know by
experience the miseries of men and might become merciful.[933]

[931]Sg 2:9.
[932]Is 53:4.
[933]Heb 2:17.

These were things he already knew but in a different way. As Lord of the virtues he knew the virtue of obedience, and yet the apostle bears witness that "he learned obedience through what he suffered."[934] By this means he also learned mercy, although the mercy of the Lord is from eternity.[935] This same teacher of the Gentiles teaches this again when he states that He was tempted in all things as we are without sin, in order to become merciful.[936] Do you see him becoming what he [already] was, and learning what he [already] knew, seeking in our midst openings and windows by which to search more attentively into our misfortunes? He found as many openings in our tumbling down and fissured wall as he experienced proofs of our weakness and corruption in his own body.

2. This then is how the Bridegroom stands behind the wall and looks through the windows and lattices. "Stands" is the right word, because he alone who never experienced the sin of the flesh, truly stood in the flesh. This we can duly discern, because he who sank down through the weakness of the flesh stood erect by the power of divinity, as he said himself: "The spirit indeed is willing but the flesh is weak."[937] I think too that this interpretation is supported by what David said of Christ with regard to this mystery; for he prophesied as the Lord's prophet, and though speaking of Moses was contemplating Christ. For [Christ] is the true Moses who came indeed by water, though "not by water only but by water and blood."[938] Hence the fore-mentioned prophet says, referring to God the Father: "He said he would destroy

[934] Heb 5:8.
[935] Ps 102:17.
[936] Heb 4:15.

[937] Mt 26:41.
[938] 1 Jn 5:6.

them, had not Moses his chosen one stood in the breach before his gaze, to turn away his wrath lest He destroy them."[939] How, I ask, did Moses stand in the breach? How, I repeat, could he stand if he were broken down or, if he stood, how could he have been broken down?[940] But I'll let you see, if you wish, who really stood in the breach. I know of no one else who could achieve this except my Lord Jesus, who certainly lived in death, who while broken in body on the cross stood erect with the Father in his divinity: petitioning with us in the one, appeasing the Father in the other. His standing behind the wall then means that his prostrate weakness was revealed in the flesh, while that which stood erect in him was hidden by the flesh: the man revealed and the hidden God are one and the same.[941]

II. 3. And for each one of us who desire his coming he also stands behind the wall as long as this body of ours, which is certainly sinful,[942] hides his face from us and shuts out his presence. For "so long as we are in this body we are exiles from the Lord."[943] Not because we are embodied, but because we are in this body which has a sinful lineage, and is never without sin. So you may know that it is not our bodies but our sins that stand in the way, listen to what Scripture says: "it is our sins that raise a barrier between us and God."[944] How I wish that the body's wall were the only obstacle, that I should suffer only that single barrier of fleshly sin and not the many fences of vice that intervene! I am afraid that through my own weakness I have added a

---

[939] Ps 105:23
[940] This passage is not clear. St. Bernard seems to impose a reflexive meaning on the text to accommodate the point he wants to make about Christ.
[941] Is 45:15.
[942] Rom 6:6.
[943] 2 Cor 5:6.
[944] Is 59:2.

host of sins to that which my nature inherits, and by them I set the Bridegroom at too great a distance from me, so that if I am to speak the truth I must confess that to me he stands not behind a wall but behind walls.

4. Let me say it more plainly. Through the immediacy of his divine majesty and the greatness of his power the Bridegroom is present, equally and without distinction, in every place.[945] But with regard to rational creatures, angels and men, he is said to be near to some and far from others by holding out or withholding grace. For "salvation is far from the wicked."[946] And yet the holy man says: "why do you stand so far off, Lord?"[947] Indeed he sometimes, by a loving arrangement, withdraws far from his saints for a time, not entirely but in part. From sinners, however, he is always very far removed, and that in anger, not in mercy. Of them it is said: "Their pride rises up continually;"[948] and again: "his ways are filthy at all times."[949] Hence the holy man prays to the Lord and says: "Turn not away in anger from your servant,"[950] knowing that he can also turn away in mercy. And so the Lord is close to his saints and chosen ones even when he seems far away, though not at an equal distance from all, but farther from some, less far from others according to their varying merits. Although the Lord is near to all who call upon him in truth,[951] and though he is near to the brokenhearted,[952] he is not perhaps so close to all that they can say he stands behind the wall. Yet how close he is to the bride who is separated by one wall only! On this account she longs that the dividing wall be broken down, that she may die and be with him who,[953] she trusts, is behind the wall.

[945]Eph 1:19.
[946]Ps 118:155.
[947]Ps 9:22.

[948]Ps 73:23.
[949]Ps 9:26.
[950]Ps 26:9.

[951]Ps 144:18.
[952]Ps 33:19.
[953]Phil 1:23.

5. But I, because I am a sinful man,[954] have no wish to be dissolved. Instead I am afraid, knowing that the death of the wicked is very evil.[955] How can death not be very evil where Life brings no help? I am afraid to go forth. I tremble at the very entrance of the haven, because I have no assurance that he is standing by to receive me at my exit. And why? Do I go forth securely if the Lord does not guard my going forth?[956] Alas! Unless he who redeems and saves is standing by I shall be the laughingstock of the devils who intercept me.[957] Nothing like this troubled the soul of Paul, whom one wall only separated from the vision and embrace of his beloved, that is, the law of sin that he discovered in his members.[958] This is that sensuality of the body that he could not possibly avoid while living on earth.[959] But despite the obtrusion of this wall he did not wander far from the Lord. Therefore he cried out longingly: "who will deliver me from this body of death?"[960] He knew that by the short passage of death he would at once attain life. So Paul averred that he was in bonds to this one law, sensual desire, which he unwillingly endured because it was rooted in his flesh. As for the rest he could say: "I am not aware of anything against myself."[961]

III. 6. But is there anyone like Paul, anyone who does not consent at times to this sensual desire and so submits to sin?[962] Let him who yields to sin take note that he has raised another wall against himself by that wicked and unlawful consent. A man of this kind cannot boast that for him the Bridegroom stands behind the wall, because not one wall but walls now intervene. Much less still if the consent has

---

[954]Lk 5:8.
[955]Ps 33:22.
[956]Ps 120:8.
[957]Ps 7:3.
[958]Rom 7:23.

[959]1 Jn 2:16.
[960]Rom 7:24.
[961]1 Cor 4:4.
[962]Rom 6:16.

passed into action, for then a third wall, the sinful act itself, wards off and bars the Bridegroom's approach. But what if the repetition of sins becomes a habit, or the habit induces contempt, as Scripture says: "When wickedness comes, contempt comes also"?[963] If you die like this, will you not be devoured a thousand times by those that roar as they await their food,[964] before you can reach the Bridegroom now shut off from you not merely by one, but by a succession of walls? The first is sensual desire; the second, consent; the third, the action; the fourth, habit; the fifth, contempt. Take care then to resist with all your strength the first movements of sensual desire lest they lure you to consent, and then the whole fabric of wickedness will vanish. Then there will be but the wall of the body to hinder the Bridegroom's approach to you, so that you may proclaim with gladness: "behold, there he stands behind our wall."[965]

7. But there is one thing you must attend to with total vigilance: that you always open the windows and lattices of your confessions. Through them his kindly gaze may penetrate to your inward life, because his discerning is your learning. They say that lattices[966] are narrow windows, similar to what writers of books provide for themselves to direct light onto the page. I think this is why those whose work is the drawing up of official documents are called chancellors.[967] Since therefore there are two kinds of compunction—the one in sorrow for our deviations, the other in rejoicing for God's gifts—as often as I make that confession of my sins which is always accompanied by anguish of heart,[968] I seem to open for myself a lattice or narrow window. Nor

[963]Prv 18:3.
[964]Sir 51:4.
[965]Sg 2:9.
[966]cancelli.

[967]cancellarii.
[968]2 Cor 2:4.

do I doubt that the devoted examiner who stands behind the wall looks through it with pleasure, because God will not despise a humble and contrite heart.[969] One is even exhorted to do this: confess your iniquities that you may be made righteous.[970] But if at times, when the heart expands in love at the thought of God's graciousness and mercy, it is all right to surrender our mind, to let it go in songs of praise and gratitude, I feel that I have opened up to the Bridegroom who stands behind the wall not a narrow lattice but a wide-open window. Through it, unless I am mistaken, he will look in with greater pleasure the more he is honored by the sacrifice of praise.[971] I can easily show from Scripture that he approves of both these confessions; but I am speaking to those who are aware of this,[972] and I must not burden with superfluities men whose time scarce suffices to pursue the essentials: the great mysteries of this love song and the praises it proclaims to the Church and her Bridegroom, Jesus Christ our Lord, who is God over all, blessed forever.[973] Amen.

SERMON 64

I. The Different Kinds of Foxes, That Is, of Subtle Temptations, of Which There Are Four. II. Why We Are Ordered to Capture, Rather Than Kill or Drive Away The Foxes and Why They Are Called Little. III. The Foxes Are Heretics. How the Bridegroom Has Told Us to Capture Them.

I. 1. I stand by my promise: "Catch us the little foxes that spoil the vines, for our vines are in flower."[974] These foxes

---

[969] Ps 50:19.
[970] Is 43:26.
[971] Ps 49:23.

[972] Rom 7:1.
[973] Rom 9:5.
[974] Sg 2:15.

represent temptations. Now it is necessary that temptations come,[975] for who shall receive a crown of victory unless he has contended according to the rules?[976] And how shall they contend if there is no one to oppose them? When you come to serve God, then, stand in awe and prepare your soul for temptation,[977] certain that all who wish to live a godly life in Christ must suffer persecution.[978] Now there are different kinds of temptation, corresponding to different times [in our lives]. At the beginning of our course, when we are like tender flowers on young plants, a sharp frost attacks us openly, as I described in my last sermon,[979] and I have warned beginners to beware of this bane. Yet the powerful enemies of good do not dare openly to oppose the proficient, who have made some progress in sanctity, but they lie in wait for them in secret, like cunning little foxes, wearing the likeness of virtues, whereas they are really vices. How many, for instance, have I known who, at the beginning of life's journey,[980] started out all right on the paths of righteousness[981] and were making serene progress towards goodness when, for shame! they suffer the humiliation of being tripped up by these little foxes, and too late they grieve for the fruits of virtue which have been choked in them.

2. I have seen a man running his course well,[982] and then this thought occurs to him—is it not a little fox?—"If I were at home," he says, "I could share with so many of my brothers, kinsfolk, and acquaintances the good I here enjoy alone.[983] They love me, and would readily agree with me when I appeal to them. To what purpose is this waste?[984]

---

[975]Mt 18:7.
[976]2 Tm 2:5.
[977]Sir 2:1.
[978]2 Tm 3:12.
[979]Sermon 63:6–7; Ps 15:11.

[980]Ps 15:11.
[981]Prv 2:8.
[982]Gal 5:7.
[983]Lk 16:28.
[984]Mt 26:8.

I will go to them, and by saving many of them I shall save myself also. There is nothing to fear in a change of environment. As long as I am doing good, it does not matter where I am, although, of course, it is no doubt better to be where I may live a more useful life." Need I say more? He goes, poor wretch, not so much an exile returning home as a dog returning to his vomit,[985] and he is destroyed. Unhappy man, he loses his own soul without saving anyone else's. Surely this is a little fox—the vain hope of winning the souls of others? You can find one instance after another like this for yourselves from your own experience if you take the trouble.

3. Do you want me to show you yet another? I will, and I will describe a third and a fourth as well if I find you watchful[986] and eager to catch those, of whatever kind, which you may notice in your own vineyard. It sometimes happens that a man who is making good progress feels himself bedewed with heavenly grace to an extraordinary degree, and is possessed by a desire to preach, not indeed to his relatives and friends—you remember the saying "Immediately I conferred not with flesh and blood"[987]—but to all and sundry, as though that were a purer, more fruitful and more powerful procedure. He is acting with great caution. No doubt he is afraid of incurring the prophet's curse if he holds back from the people the grain which he received in secret,[988] and is afraid of acting contrary to the Gospel if he does not proclaim from the housetop what he hears whispered.[989] This too is a fox, even more dangerous than the last, because its coming is less obvious; but I will catch it for you. First, Moses says "You shall not plough with the firstborn or your bull."[990] This Paul interprets as: "Not a new convert, lest

[985] 2 Pt 2:22.
[986] Lk 12:37.
[987] Gal 1:16.

[988] Prv 11:26.
[989] Mt 10:27.
[990] Dt 15:19.

being lifted up with pride he fall into the condemnation of the devil,"[991] and again, "A man does not take this honor upon himself, but is called by God, as was Aaron,"[992] and yet again: "How can men preach unless they are sent?"[993] Now we know that the duty of a monk is not to teach but to weep.[994] Of these and like considerations I weave my net and catch the fox so that it may not spoil the vine. They make it quite clear that it is not expedient for a monk to preach in public, nor is it seemly for a novice, nor proper for anyone unless he is expressly sent. What devastation of the conscience to fly in the face of all these three! Therefore if any suggestion of this kind presents itself to you, whether it arises from your own mind or is suggested by an evil spirit,[995] you must recognize it as a cunning fox, evil disguised as good.

4. Look at another example. How many fervent souls have been drawn from their monasteries by the attraction of the solitary life,[996] and have then become lukewarm and have been spewed forth,[997] or if they have remained, have become slack and dissolute, violating the law of the hermit? A little fox has plainly been at work when such havoc has been caused in the vineyard! It is the destruction of a man's life and integrity. He supposed that the solitary life would produce the fruits of the Spirit in much greater abundance than the common life, where he had experienced, so he thought, only ordinary grace. The idea seemed to him a good one, but the outcome showed that it was more like a destructive fox.

---

[991] 1 Tm 3:6.
[992] Heb 5:4.
[993] Rom 10:15.
[994] St. Jerome, *Contra Vigilantium* 15; *Patres Latini* 23:367A.

[995] Ps 77:49.
[996] Rom 12:11.
[997] Rv 3:16.

5. Now I must mention a matter which frequently causes us serious trouble: the excessive and superstitious abstinence of some among us, which makes them a burden to themselves and everyone else. How can such discord do other than cause the destruction of the consciences of those concerned, and, as far as is in their power, the devastation of this great vine which the right hand of the Lord has planted, by destroying the unity of all of you?[998] "Woe to the man by whom the offense comes![999] Whoever causes one of these little ones to stumble"[1000]—what follows is hard, but how much harder a fate does the man deserve who causes so great and holy a multitude to stumble! Whoever he is,[1001] he will bear his judgment, and it will be very severe. But of this [I will speak] another time.

II. 6. Now let us consider what the Bridegroom said about these cunning little animals that spoil the vines. They are little, I would say, not because they have little malice, but because of their subtlety. This kind of creature is indeed cunning by nature, and exceedingly quick to do damage in secret, and it may, I think, be most appropriate to consider them as representing certain subtle vices cloaked in the likeness of virtues. I have already given a brief description of their nature and cited a few examples. They can do no damage at all except by falsely representing themselves as virtues, because of their very likeness to virtues. For they are either the vain thoughts of men or the promptings of Satan's evil angels,[1002] who disguise themselves as angels of light, making ready their arrows in the quiver[1003]—that is in secret—to shoot in the dark at the upright in heart.[1004] That,

[998]Ps 79:16.
[999]Mt 18:7.
[1000]Mt 18:6.
[1001]Gal 5:10.

[1002]Ps 93:11; Ps 77:49.
[1003]2 Cor 11:14; Ps 10:2.
[1004]Ps 10:3.

I think, is why they are called little, for while other vices show themselves as it were in bodily form, this kind are not easily recognized because of their subtlety. They cannot easily be avoided except by the perfect and the experienced, and by such as have the eyes of their souls enlightened for the discernment of good and evil, and particularly for the discernment of spirits,[1005] so that they can say with the Apostle Paul: "We are not ignorant of the designs of Satan"[1006] or of his thoughts. Perhaps it is for this reason that the Bridegroom has given orders that they are not to be exterminated or driven away or killed, but caught. Cunning little beasts of this kind must obviously be watched with the utmost vigilance and caution, and so trapped, that is caught in the toils of their own subtlety.[1007] Then, when their deception is made known and their falsity uncovered, it can truly be said that the little fox that destroys the vine has been caught. Thus we say that a man is trapped in his speech, as you find in the Gospel: "The Pharisees came together to trap Jesus in his speech."[1008]

7. This is why the Bridegroom gives orders that the little foxes who spoil the vines are to be caught, that is trapped, overcome, and brought out into the open. This kind of pest is the only one with the peculiarity that once recognized it can do no harm; if it is recognized it is conquered. Who but a madman would knowingly and consciously put his foot into a trap if he knew it was there. It is enough, then, for this kind to be caught, that is, discovered and brought into the light of day, since for them to be seen is to perish. It is not so with other vices, for they attack openly, and their damage is done openly. They ensnare even those who are aware of

---

[1005] Eph 1:18; 1 Cor 12:10.
[1006] 2 Cor 2:11.

[1007] Jb 5:13.
[1008] Mt 22:15.

them and overcome even those who resist them, and that by force, not by guile. When we are dealing with beasts of this kind who rage openly, we have not to flush them out, but to bring them under control. It is only these little foxes, these great deceivers, whom it suffices to bring into the light of day and catch in the toils of their cunning.[1009] Once they are recognized they can do no harm—but they do have holes. This is why we are commanded to catch these foxes, and why they are described as little. Or perhaps they are so called because it is by careful observation in the early stages, while they are still small, that you may catch vices in time and prevent them from growing larger and doing greater damage, besides becoming more difficult to catch.

III. 8. If we continue the allegory, taking vines to represent Christian congregations, and foxes heresies, or rather heretics themselves, the interpretation is simple: heretics are to be caught rather than driven away. They are to be caught, I repeat, not by force of arms but by arguments by which their errors may be refuted. They themselves, if it can be done, are to be reconciled with the Catholic [Church] and brought back to the true faith. This is His will,[1010] that all men should be saved and brought to the knowledge of the truth.[1011] This is what he shows us when he says not simply "Catch the foxes," but "Catch us the foxes." It is for himself and his bride, that is the Catholic [Church], that he orders these foxes to be apprehended when he says "Catch us the foxes." So if an experienced and well-instructed churchman undertakes to debate with a heretic, he should direct his intention to convincing him of the error of his ways in such a way as to convert him, bearing in mind the saying of the

---

[1009] Mt 8:20.
[1010] Jn 6:39–40.

[1011] Tm 2:4.

Apostle James, that anyone who causes a sinner to be converted from the error of his ways will save his soul from
death and cover a multitude of sins.[1012] But if he will not be
converted or convinced even after a first and second admo-
nition, then, according to the apostle, he is to be shunned as
one who is completely perverted.[1013] Consequently I think it
better that he should be driven away or even bound rather
than be allowed to spoil the vines.

9. Let it not be supposed, however, that it is a small and
unimportant thing for a man to vanquish a heretic and
refute his heresies, making a clear and open distinction
between shadows and reality and exposing the fallacies of
false teaching by plain and irrefutable reasoning in such a
way as to bring into captivity a depraved mind which had set
itself up against the knowledge revealed by God.[1014] The
man who has done this has in fact caught the fox, though not
to his salvation, and he has caught it for the Bride and Bridegroom, though in a different way. For even though the
heretic was not raised up from the error of his ways, the
Church has been strengthened in faith,[1015] and without
doubt the Bridegroom rejoices in the progress of the Bride.
"The joy of the Lord is our strength."[1016] He who has
deigned to unite himself with us does not look upon our
advantage as something foreign to himself, for he orders the
foxes to be caught, not for himself, but for us along with
him. Notice that he says "for us." What gracious condescension! Do you not think that he is speaking as the father
of a family, in that he keeps nothing for himself, but has
everything in common with his wife and children and

[1012]Jas 5:20.
[1013]Ti 3:10.
[1014]2 Cor 10:5.

[1015]Col 2:7.
[1016]Neh 8:10.

household? He who speaks is indeed God, yet it is not as God that he speaks, but as a Bridegroom.

10. "Catch us the foxes." You see how he speaks, as though to equals—he who has no equal. He could have said "me," but he preferred to say "us," for he delights in companionship. What sweetness! What grace! What mighty love! Can it be that the Highest of all is made one with all? Who has brought this about? Love has brought this about, without regard for its own dignity, strong in affection and efficacious in persuasion. What could be more violent? Love prevails even with God. What could be so nonviolent? It is love. What force is there, I ask, which advances so violently toward victory, yet is so unresisting to violence? For he emptied himself, so that you might know that it was the fullness of love which was outpoured,[1017] that his loftiness was laid low and that his unique nature made to be your fellow. With whom, O wonderful Bridegroom, have you such familiar friendship? "Catch them for us," he says. For whom, besides you? For the Church of the Gentiles? She is made up of mortals and sinners. What she is, we know; but who are you,[1018] so devoted to the Ethiopian woman,[1019] so eager a lover? Assuredly not a second Moses, but a greater than Moses. Are you not he who is the fairest of the children of men?[1020] I have said too little. You are the brightness of eternal life, the splendor and image of the being of God, God over all, blessed forever.[1021] Amen.

[1017]Phil 2:7.
[1018]Jn 1:19.
[1019]Nm 12:1.
[1020]Ps 44:3, Ws 7:26.
[1021]Heb 1:3; Rom 9:5.

SERMON 69

I. What Soul May Rightly Say "My Beloved is Mine" etc., and with What Justification. II. Of the Coming of the Father and the Son to the Soul, and How the Wrath and Anger of the Father Overthrows All Presumption in the Soul. III. Of the Burning Charity in which the Father and Son Come, and of Their Indwelling; and by What Means the Soul Becomes Aware of It.

I. 1. "My beloved is mine, and I am his."[1022] In my last sermon I attributed this saying to the Church Universal, because of the promises made to her by God in this present life as well as in the life to come.[1023] The question was raised whether it was possible for an individual soul to claim for itself what the whole Church might claim without presumption, or whether indeed it could appropriate the promise to itself in any way at all. If this may not be done, we must apply it to the Church in such a way that it may not refer to any individual—and not only this saying, but others like it which express great truths,[1024] like "I waited for the Lord and he inclined to me,"[1025] and others which were mentioned in the last sermon. If you think that they apply to the individual, I would not contradict you. But this is a matter of some importance, for it cannot apply to everyone indiscriminately. Certainly there are within the Church of God spiritual persons who serve him faithfully and with confidence,[1026] speaking with him as a man speaks with his friend,[1027] and whose consciences bear witness to his glory.[1028] But who these are is known only to God,[1029] and if

[1022] Sg 2:16.
[1023] 1 Tm 4:8.
[1024] Dn 7:20.
[1025] Ps 39:2.
[1026] Jn 14:23.
[1027] Ex 33:11.
[1028] Rom 9:1.
[1029] Phil 1:21.

you desire to be among them, then hear what sort of people you should be. I say this, not as one who knows it by experience, but as one who desires to do so. Show me a soul which loves nothing but God and what is to be loved for God's sake, to whom to live is Christ,[1030] and of whom this has been true for a long time now; who in work and leisure alike endeavors to keep God before his eyes, and walks humbly with the Lord his God;[1031] who desires that his will may be one with the will of God, and who has been given the grace to do these things. Show me a soul like this, and I will not deny that she is worthy of the Bridegroom's care, of the regard of God's majesty, of his sovereign favor, and of the attention of his governance. And if she is minded to boast, she will not be a fool,[1032] so long as she who boasts boasts in the Lord.[1033] Thus what many dare to boast of,[1034] one may also dare, though for a different reason.

2. These considerations do indeed give confidence to the many faithful, but there are two which apply to the faithful soul. First, the essential simplicity of the Godhead is able to see many persons as if they were one, and one as if he were many, without division of attention between many or restriction to one, with no diminishment on the one hand or intensification on the other, being neither disturbed by anxieties nor troubled by cares; thus he may occupy himself with one without preoccupation, and with many without distraction. Next, a thing very sweet to experience, as it is very rare; such is the courtesy of the Word, such the tenderness of the Father toward the well-disposed, well-ordered soul—itself the gift of the Father and the work of the Son—that they honor with their own presence the one whom they

[1030] Ps 15:8.
[1031] Mi 6:8.
[1032] 2 Cor 12:6.

[1033] 1 Cor 1:31.
[1034] 2 Cor 11:21.

have foreordained and prepared for themselves, and not only do they come to him, but they make their dwelling place with him.[1035] For it is not enough that their presence is revealed; they must also give of their fullness.

II. What does it mean for the Word to come into a soul? It means that he will instruct it in wisdom.[1036] What does it mean for the Father to come? It means that he will draw it to the love of wisdom, so that it may say, "I was a lover of her beauty."[1037] It is the Father's nature to love, and therefore the coming of the Father is marked by an infusion of love. What would happen to learning apart from love? It would be puffed up.[1038] What would happen to love apart from learning? It would go astray, as they went astray of whom it was said, "I grant that they have a zeal for God but it is not according to knowledge."[1039] It is not fitting that the Bride of the Word should be ignorant; moreover the Bridegroom does not allow the Bride to be uplifted with pride; for the Father loves the Son[1040] and never hesitates to cast down and to destroy[1041] whatever sets itself up against the knowledge of the Word, tempering zeal through judgment or increasing it through mercy. May he cast down in me all pride: destroy it, reduce it to nothingness, not by his blazing anger but by his welling love. May I learn not to be proud, but by the tutelage of anointing rather than of avenging. Lord, rebuke me not in your indignation,[1042] as you did the angel who exalted himself, neither chasten me in your wrath,[1043] as you did man in paradise. Both were resolved on wickedness,[1044] aspiring to exalt themselves, the one through power, the other through knowledge. For the woman foolishly

---

[1035] 1 Cor 8:1.
[1036] Ps 89:12.
[1037] Ws 8:2.
[1038] 1 Cor 8:1.
[1039] Rom 10:2.
[1040] Jn 5:20.
[1041] 2 Cor 10:5.
[1042] Ps 72:20.
[1043] Ps 6:1.
[1044] Ps 35:5.

believed the deceiver's promise: "You shall be gods, when you know good and evil."[1045] He had already deceived himself when he persuaded himself that he would be like the Most High.[1046] For he who thinks himself to be something when he is nothing deceives himself.[1047]

3. But they who exalted themselves were both cast down, yet the man more gently, for his judge was the one who orders all things by weight and measure.[1048] The angel was punished, even damned, in fury, but the man only suffered displeasure, not fury. "For though he was angry, he remembered his mercy."[1049] For this reason his seed are called the children of wrath,[1050] not of fury, until this day.[1051] If I were not born a child of wrath, I should not have needed to be reborn in baptism;[1052] if I were a child of fury, either I could not have attained to it, or it would not have benefited me. Would you wish to see a child of fury? If you have seen Satan falling as lightning from heaven,[1053] cast down by the force of God's fury, you know what the fury of God is. He did not remember his mercy[1054] then, whereas when he is angry he will remember it.[1055] It is not so when his fury is kindled.[1056] Woe to the children of disobedience, to those descended from Adam, who were born of wrath,[1057] but turned it into fury against themselves by their fiendish obstinacy, turning as it were a switch into a rod—or rather into a hammer! "For they store up wrath for themselves in the day of wrath."[1058] But what is stored-up wrath but fury? They have committed the devil's sin, and incur the same

[1045]Gn 3:5.
[1046]Ps 14:14.
[1047]Gal 6:3.
[1048]Ws 11:21.
[1049]Hb 3:2.
[1050]Eph 2:3.
[1051]1 Sm 5:5.

[1052]Cf. Jn 3:7.
[1053]Lk 10:18.
[1054]Cf. Ps 97:3, 108:6.
[1055]Hb 3:2.
[1056]Cf. Jdt 5:2.
[1057]Eph 5:6, 2:3.
[1058]Rom 2:5.

punishment as the devil. Woe too, though less terrible, to those children of wrath who, being born in wrath, have not looked forward to being reborn in grace. For they have died as they were born, and shall remain children of wrath. I say of wrath, not of fury, because piety and compassion lead us to believe that those who are infected by sin from outside themselves incur the mildest of punishments.

4. Therefore the devil is judged in fury, because his wickedness incurred hatred,[1059] while that of men incurred wrath, and so is chastised in wrath.[1060] Thus all pride is destroyed, both that which exalts a man and that which casts him down, for the Father is exceedingly zealous for his Son. And in both instances the Son is dishonored: in the first because power is usurped in opposition to the might of God, which is himself, and in the second because knowledge is presumed not in accordance with the wisdom of God,[1061] which is also he. Lord, who is like you?[1062] Who but your own image, the splendor and likeness of your being.[1063] He alone is in your form, he alone did not think it robbery to be equal with you,[1064] he, the most high Son of the Most High.[1065] How can he be other than equal with you? For you and he are one.[1066] His seat is at your right hand, not under your feet.[1067] How can anyone presume to usurp the position of your only begotten Son? Let such a one be cast down. Is he to take his seat on high?[1068] Let the chair of pestilence be overturned. Who shall teach man wisdom?[1069] Is it not you, O Key of David. Who open and shut to whomever you wish?[1070]

[1059] Ps 35:3.
[1060] Cf. Ps 6:2, 37:2.
[1061] Cf. 1 Cor 1:24.
[1062] Ps 88:9.
[1063] Col 1:15, Heb 1:3.
[1064] Phil 2:6.
[1065] Lk 1:32.
[1066] Jn 17:22.
[1067] Ps 109:1.
[1068] Ps 67:8.
[1069] Ps 93:10.
[1070] Rv 3:7.

How can the doors of the treasure of wisdom and knowledge be opened without a key?[1071] How could an entry be forced? He who does not enter by the door is a thief and a robber.[1072] Peter, of course, will enter, for he received the keys.[1073] But he will not be alone, for he will admit me also, if he sees fit, and shut out someone else if he sees fit, through the knowledge and the power conferred on him from above.[1074]

5. And what are these keys? They are the power of opening and closing[1075] and of discerning who should be let in and who should be kept out. They are not in the possession of the serpent,[1076] but of Christ. Therefore the serpent could not give knowledge which he did not possess but he who possessed it gave it. Nor could he have power which he had not received; it was he who received it, who had it. Christ it was who gave it, Peter who received it. He was not puffed up at his knowledge;[1077] nor did he deserve to be cast down because of his power. Why was this? It was because he did not exalt himself against the knowledge of God,[1078] nor did he lay claim to any of those things beyond the knowledge of God, as did he who acted deceitfully in the sight of God, whose wickedness became hateful.[1079] How indeed could Peter have claimed anything beyond the knowledge of God when he described himself as an apostle of Jesus Christ, according to the foreknowledge of God the Father?[1080] And these things were said with reference to the zeal of God which he directed against those who transgressed— whether angel or man, for he found wickedness in

[1071] Col 2:3.
[1072] Jn 10:1.
[1073] Mt 16:19.
[1074] Jn 19:11.
[1075] Rv 11:6.
[1076] Cf. Col 2:3.
[1077] 1 Cor 8:1.
[1078] 2 Cor 10:5.
[1079] Ps 35:3.
[1080] 1 Pt 1:1–2.

both[1081]—just as he destroyed in his furious anger all pride which sets itself up against the knowledge of God.[1082]

III. 6. We must now turn to the zeal of pity—not the zeal directed against us, but that which is extended toward us. For the zeal directed against us, as we have seen, is the zeal of judgment, and has inspired us with sufficient fear from the examples already quoted of those who have received so terrible a punishment. Therefore I will flee from the sight of the anger of the Lord[1083] and go to a place of refuge, to that zeal of mercy which burns sweetly and wholly purifies. Does not charity make amends? Truly it does powerfully. I have read that it covers a multitude of sins.[1084] But I would ask this: is it not right and sufficient to cast down and humble all pride of eyes and heart?[1085] Yes indeed, for love does not vaunt itself and is not puffed up.[1086] Therefore if Our Lord Jesus condescends to come to me, or rather enter into me, not in the zeal of anger or even in wrath, but in love and in a spirit of gentleness,[1087] striving with me with the striving of God[1088]—for what greater attribute of God is there than charity?[1089] Then he is indeed God. If he comes in such a spirit, then I know that he is not alone but that the Father is with him.[1090] What could be more like a father? Therefore he is not only called the Father of the Word, but the Father of mercies,[1091] because it is his nature always to have mercy and to pardon. If I feel that my eyes are opened to understand the Scriptures,[1092] so that I am enlightened from above to preach the word of wisdom from the heart[1093] or reveal the mysteries of God, or if riches from on high are showered

[1081] Jb 4:18.
[1082] 2 Cor 10:5.
[1083] Jer 4:26.
[1084] 1 Pt 4:8.
[1085] Sir 23:5.
[1086] 1 Cor 13:4.
[1087] 1 Cor 4:21.
[1088] 2 Cor 11:2.
[1089] 1 Jn 4:16.
[1090] Jn 16:32.
[1091] 2 Cor 1:3.
[1092] Lk 24:45.
[1093] 1 Cor 12:8.

upon me so that in my soul fruits of meditation are produced, I have no doubt that the Bridegroom is with me. For these are gifts of the Word, and it is of his fullness that we have received these gifts.[1094] Again if I am filled with a feeling of humility rich with devotion whereby love of the truth I have received produces in me so urgent a hatred and contempt for vanity that I cannot be inflamed with pride by reason of knowledge,[1095] nor elated by the frequency of heavenly visitations[1096] then truly I am aware of fatherly activity and do not doubt the Father's presence. But if I continue as far as I can to respond to this condescension in worthy disposition and action, and the grace of God in me has not been fruitless,[1097] then the Father will make his abode with me to nourish me, as the Son will teach me.[1098]

SERMON 74

I. How this passage applies to the soul and to the Word, and how the coming and returning of the Word works for the soul's salvation. II. How it behaves at the coming of the Word, and how this is perceived.
III. Of the grace and truth depicted by the roe and the young fawn, and how grace is bestowed by its own nature.

I. 1. "Return," she says.[1099] Clearly he whom she calls back is not there, yet he has been, not long before, for she seems to be calling him back at the moment of his going. So importunate a recall shows great love on the part of the one and great loveliness on the part of the other. Who are these who are so

---

[1094] Jn 1:16.
[1095] 1 Cor 8:1.
[1096] 2 Cor 12:7.
[1097] 1 Cor 15:10.
[1098] Jn 14:23.
[1099] Sg 2:17.

taken up with charity, these unwearying lovers, whose passion drives them on and gives them no rest? It is my task to fulfill my promise and apply this passage to the Word and to the soul,[1100] but to do this at all worthily I admit I need the help of the Word himself. Certainly this topic would more fitly be discussed by one with more experience and awareness of this holy and hidden love; but I cannot shirk my duty or disregard your requests. I am aware of the danger, but I will not refuse to meet it, for you force me to it.[1101] Indeed, you force me to walk in great matters and mysteries which are beyond me.[1102] Alas! how afraid I am to hear the words, "Why do you speak of my delights and put my mystery into words?"[1103] Hear me then as a man who is afraid to speak but cannot remain silent. My very trepidation will perhaps justify my presumption; even more, if it increases, your edification. Perhaps too God will have regard to my tears. "Return," she says. Good. He departed, he is called back. Who will disclose to me the mystery of this change? Who will adequately explain to me the going and returning of the Word? Surely the Bridegroom will not stoop to inconstancy? Where can he come from? Where can he return to, he who fills heaven and earth?[1104] How can he who is spirit[1105] move from place to place? How can any movement of any kind be attributed to him who is God? For he is immutable.

2. Yet let him receive this who can.[1106] But let us, as we proceed with caution and singleness of purpose in our exposition of this sacred and mystical utterance,[1107] follow the example of Scripture, which speaks of the wisdom hidden in

---

[1100] Sc 73:10.
[1101] 2 Cor 12:22.
[1102] Ps 130:1.
[1103] Cf. Ps 49:16.

[1104] Jer 23:24.
[1105] Jn 4:24.
[1106] Mt 19:12; Eph 5:15; Prv 11:20.
[1107] Is 3:3.

the mystery,[1108] but does so in words familiar to us, and which, even as it enlightens our human minds, roots our affections on God, and imparts to us the incomprehensible and invisible things of God by means of figures drawn from the likeness of things familiar to us, like precious draughts in vessels of cheap earthenware.[1109]

Let us then follow this discourse of pure love,[1110] and say that the Word of God, God himself, the Bridegroom of the soul, comes to the soul and leaves it again as he wishes,[1111] but we must realize that this happens as a result of the soul's sensitivity, and is not due to any movement of the Word. Indeed, when the soul is aware of the influence of grace she acknowledges the presence of the Word; but when she is not, she mourns his absence, and again seeks his presence, saying with the prophet, "My face has sought you; your face, Lord, I will seek."[1112] How could she do otherwise? For when so sweet a bridegroom withdraws from her, she cannot desire any other, nor even think of another. It must be that when he is absent she seeks him ardently, and when he goes away she calls him back. Thus the Word is recalled—recalled by the longing of the soul who has once enjoyed his sweetness.[1113] Is longing not a voice? It is indeed, and a very powerful one. Then the psalmist says, "The Lord has heard the longing of the poor."[1114] When the Word departs therefore, the one unceasing cry of the soul, its one unceasing desire, is "return"—until he comes.[1115]

3. Now show me a soul which the bridegroom, the Word, is accustomed to visit often, whom friendship has made bold, who hungers for what it has once tasted, whom

[1108] 1 Cor 2:7.
[1109] Rom 1:20; cf. 2 Cor 4:7.
[1110] Ps 11:7.
[1111] 1 Cor 12:11.
[1112] Ps 26:8.
[1113] Is 26:8.
[1114] Ps 9:38.
[1115] 1 Cor 11:26.

contempt of all things has given leisure, and without hesitation I will assign it the voice and name of the Bride, and will consider the passage we are studying applicable to it. So indeed is the speaker portrayed. For when she calls him back she proves that she deserves his presence, even if not in its fullness. Otherwise she would have called to him to come, not to return. But the word "return" signifies a recalling. Perhaps it was for this very reason that he withdrew, that the more eagerly she recalls him, the more closely she will cleave to him. For he once pretended that he was going further, not because that was his intention, but because he wanted to hear the words, "Stay with us, for evening is coming on."[1116] And another time, when the apostles were in a boat pulling on the oars, he walked on the sea,[1117] making as though he would pass them by, not because he intended to, but to try their faith and draw out their prayers. Then, so the evangelist says, they were troubled and cried out, thinking that he was a ghost.[1118] This kind of pious pretense, this saving gift, dispensed by the Word when in the body does not lose its effect when the Word in spirit employs it in his own spiritual manner in dealing with a soul devoted to him. He makes to go past, desiring to be held back, and seems to go away, wishing to be recalled; for he, the Word, is not irrevocable; he comes and goes according to his own good pleasure, visiting the soul at daybreak[1119] and then suddenly putting it to the test. His going is part of his own purpose, and his return is always part of his own will; both are within his infinite wisdom. His reasons he alone knows.

4. Now it is clear that his comings and goings are the fluctuations in the soul of which he speaks when he says, "I go

---

[1116]Lk 24:28–29.
[1117]Mk 6:48.
[1118]Mk 6:49.
[1119]Jb 7:18.

away, and come again to you,"[1120] and, "a little while and you shall not see me, and again a little while and you shall see me."[1121] Oh little while, little while! How long a little while! Dear Lord, you say it is for a little while that we do not see you. The word of my Lord may not be doubted, but it is a long while, far too long. Yet both are true: it is a little while compared to what we deserve, but a long while to what we desire. You have each meaning expressed by the prophet Habakkuk: "If he delays, wait for him, for he will come, and will not delay."[1122] How is it that he will not delay if he does delay, unless it is that he comes sooner than we deserve but not as soon as we desire? For the loving soul is carried away by her prayers and drawn on by her longing; she forgets her deserts, closes her eyes to the majesty of the Bridegroom but opens them to the pleasure he brings, looking only at his saving grace,[1123] and in that putting her confidence. Then without fear or dread she calls back the Word, and confidently asks again for his delights, calling him, with accustomed familiarity, not "Lord" but "beloved": "Return, my beloved."[1124] And she adds "Be like a fawn or a doe on the mountains of Bethel." But more of this later.

II. 5. Now bear with my foolishness for a little.[1125] I want to tell you of my own experience, as I promised. Not that it is of any importance.[1126] But I make this disclosure only to help you, and if you derive any profit from it I shall be consoled for my foolishness; if not, my foolishness will be revealed. I admit that the Word has also come to me—I speak as a fool[1127]—and has come many times. But although he has come to me, I have never been conscious of the moment of his coming. I perceived

[1120] Jn 14:28.
[1121] Jn 16:17.
[1122] Hb 2:3.
[1123] Ps 11:6.
[1124] Sg 2:17.
[1125] 2 Cor 11:1.
[1126] 2 Cor 12:1.
[1127] 2 Cor 11:17.

his presence, I remembered afterward that he had been with me; sometimes I had a presentiment that he would come, but I was never conscious of his coming or his going.[1128] And where he comes from when he visits my soul, and where he goes, and by what means he enters and goes out, I admit that I do not know even now; as John says, "You do not know where he comes from or where he goes."[1129] There is nothing strange in this, for of him was it said, "Your footsteps will not be known."[1130] The coming of the Word was not perceptible to my eyes, for he has no color; nor to my ears, for there was no sound; nor yet to my nostrils, for he mingles with the mind, not the air; he has not acted upon the air, but created it. His coming was not tasted by the mouth, for there was no eating or drinking, nor could he be known by the sense of touch, for he is not tangible. How then did he enter? Perhaps he did not enter because he does not come from outside? He is not one of the things which exist outside us.[1131] Yet he does not come from within me, for he is good,[1132] and I know that there is no good in me. I have ascended to the highest in me, and look! the word is towering above that. In my curiosity I have descended to explore my lowest depths, yet I found him even deeper. If I looked outside myself, I saw him stretching beyond the furthest I could see; and if I looked within, he was yet further within. Then I knew the truth of what I had read, "In him we live and move and have our being."[1133] And blessed is the man in whom he has his being, who lives for him and is moved by him.

6. You ask then how I knew he was present, when his ways can in no way be traced?[1134] He is life and power,[1135] and as soon as he enters in, he awakens my slumbering soul;

<hr>

[1128] Ps 120:8.
[1129] Jn 3:8.
[1130] Ps 76:20.
[1131] 1 Cor 5:12.

[1132] Ps 51:11.
[1133] Acts 17:28.
[1134] Rom 11:33.
[1135] Heb 4:12.

he stirs and soothes and pierces my heart,[1136] for before it was hard as stone,[1137] and diseased. So he has begun to pluck out and destroy, to build up and to plant, to water dry places and illuminate dark ones;[1138] to open what was closed and to warm what was cold; to make the crooked straight and the rough places smooth,[1139] so that my soul may bless the Lord, and all that is within me may praise his holy name.[1140] So when the Bridegroom, the Word, came to me, he never made known his coming by any signs, not by sight, not by sound, not by touch. It was not by any movement of his that I recognized his coming; it was not by any of my senses that I perceived he had penetrated to the depths of my being. Only by the movement of my heart, as I have told you, did I perceive his presence; and I knew the power of his might[1141] because my faults were put to flight and my human yearnings brought into subjection. I have marveled at the depth of his wisdom[1142] when my secret faults[1143] have been revealed and made visible; at the very slightest amendment of my way of life I have experienced his goodness and mercy; in the renewal and remaking of the spirit of my mind,[1144] that is of my inmost being, I have perceived the excellence of his glorious beauty,[1145] and when I contemplate all these things I am filled with awe and wonder at his manifold greatness.[1146]

7. But when the Word has left me, all these spiritual powers become weak and faint and begin to grow cold, as though you had removed the fire from under a boiling pot,

---

[1136]Sg 4:9.
[1137]Sir 3:27; Ez 11:19, 36:26.
[1138]Cf. Jer 1:10.
[1139]Is 40:4.
[1140]Ps 102:1.
[1141]Eph 1:13.

[1142]Eccl 7:25.
[1143]Ps 18:13.
[1144]Eph 4:23.
[1145]Ps 49:2.
[1146]Ps 150:2.

and this is the sign of his going. Then my soul must needs be sorrowful[1147] until he returns, and my heart again kindles within me[1148]—the sign of his returning. When I have had such experience of the Word, is it any wonder that I take to myself the words of the Bride, calling him back when he has withdrawn? For although my fervor is not as strong as hers, yet I am transported by a desire like hers. As long as I live the word "return," the word of recall for the recall of Word, will be on my lips.

As often as he slips away from me, so often shall I call him back. From the burning desire of my heart I will not cease to call him, begging him to return,[1149] as if after someone who is departing,[1150] and I will implore him to give back to me the joy of his salvation,[1151] and restore himself to me.

III. I assure you, my sons, I find joy in nothing else if he is not here, who alone gives me joy. And I implore him not to come empty-handed but full of grace and truth, as is his nature—as he did yesterday and the day before.[1152] Herein is shown his likeness to a roe or a fawn,[1153] for his truth has the sharp eyes of a roe, and his grace the gladness of a fawn.

8. I need both of these: I need truth that I may not be able to hide from him, and grace that I may not wish to hide. Indeed, without both of these his visitation would not be complete, for the stark reality of truth would be intolerable without grace, and the gladness of grace might appear intolerable without truth. Truth is bitter unless seasoned with grace, and devotion without the restraining power of truth can be capricious and uncontrolled and even arrogant. How many have received grace without profit because they have

[1147] Mt 26:38, Ps 41:6, 12.
[1148] Ps 42:5, Ps 108:22.
[1149] Ps 20:3.
[1150] Jas 18:23.
[1151] Ps 50:14.
[1152] Is 55:11; Jn 1:14; Gn 31:5.
[1153] Sg 2:17.

not also accepted a tempering measure of truth? In consequence they have luxuriated in it too much,[1154] without reverence or regard for truth; they have not considered the ripe maturity of the roe, but have given themselves over to the caprices and gladness of the fawn. Thus it has come about that they have been deprived of the grace which they wished to enjoy by itself. To them it could be said, though too late, "Go then, and learn what it means to serve the Lord in fear, and rejoice in him with awe."[1155] The holy soul which had said in her abundance "I shall never be moved,"[1156] and then feels that the Word has turned his face away finds herself not only moved but much troubled; thus she learns in sorrow that with the gift of devotion she needed also the steadying power of truth. The fullness of grace, then, does not consist of grace alone. What use is it to know what you ought to do, if you are not given the will to do it? But what is the use of having the will if you have not the power? How many have I known who are the sadder for knowing the truth because they could not plead ignorance as an excuse when they knew the demands of truth but did not fulfill them?

9. Neither then is sufficient without the other. That is an understatement: neither has any value without the other. How do we know this? Scripture says, "If a man knows what is good, and does not do it, that for him is sin";[1157] and again, "If a servant knows the will of his master and does not perform it duly, he shall be severely beaten."[1158] This refers to truth. What is said of grace? It is written, "And after the sop Satan entered into him."[1159] It is speaking of Judas, who received the gift of grace, but because he did not walk in

[1154] Is 42:1.
[1155] Mt 9:13; Ps 2:11.
[1156] Ps 29:7–8.
[1157] Jas 4:17.
[1158] Lk 12:47.
[1159] Jn 13:27.

truth with the Lord of truth,[1160] with truth as his teacher, he gave place in himself to the devil.[1161] Hear again, "He fed them with the finest wheat, and with honey from the rock he satisfied them."[1162] Who are they? "The enemies of the Lord have lied to him."[1163] Those whom he has fed with honey and wheat have lied to him and become his enemies, because they did not add truth to grace. In another place it says of them, "The strange children have lied to me, the strange children have grown weak and are limping off their paths."[1164] How can they help limping when they are supported on the one foot of grace, and do not stand on truth? Their fate will last forever, like that of their prince,[1165] who himself did not stand on the truth, but was a liar from the beginning,[1166] and therefore heard the words "You have destroyed your wisdom through your own splendor."[1167] I do not desire a splendor which can rob me of wisdom.

10. Do you ask what this elegance is, so harmful and so dangerous? It is your own. Do you still not understand?[1168] I will speak more plainly. It is a splendor which is inward-looking and personal. It is not the gift we condemn, but the use made of it. For, if you notice, Satan is said to have lost his wisdom not because of splendor but because of his own elegance. Surely the splendor of an angel and the splendor of a soul are one and the same. What is an angel or a soul without wisdom but a rough, shapeless mass? But with wisdom there is a splendor not only of form but of beauty.[1169] But Satan lost this when he appropriated it as his own, so that to lose wisdom through his own elegance was to lose it through

---

[1160] 2 Jn 4.
[1161] Eph 4:27.
[1162] Ps 80:17.
[1163] Ps 80:16.
[1164] Ps 17:46.
[1165] Ps 80:16.
[1166] Jn 8:44.
[1167] Ez 28:17.
[1168] Mt 15:16.
[1169] Cf. Ws 10:1; *formatus . . . formosus.*

his own wisdom. Possessiveness brings about the loss. It was because he was wise in his own eyes, not giving God the glory, nor returning grace for grace, and not walking in grace following truth but distorting it for his own purposes, that he lost it.[1170] Indeed, to possess it is to lose it. If Abraham, as the apostle says, was justified by his works, he possessed something in which to glory, but not before God.[1171] "I am not safe," I would say. "Anything I do not possess before God I have lost." Nothing can be as lost as that which is outside the presence of God. What is death but the loss of life? Perdition is nothing but alienation from God. "Woe to you who are wise in your own eyes, and prudent in your own minds."[1172] It is said of you, "I will destroy the wisdom of the wise and frustrate the prudence of the prudent."[1173] They have lost wisdom, because their own wisdom has caused them to be lost. How can they not lose everything, who are themselves lost; and those whom God does not recognize are indeed lost.

11. Now the foolish virgins[1174]—whom I do not think to have been foolish in other respects than by believing themselves wise they became silly—they, I tell you, will hear God saying, "I do not know you."[1175] So those who have made use of grace to perform miracles to enhance their own reputation will likewise hear the same condemnation, "I do not know you."[1176] From this it is quite clear that grace brings no profit where there is no truth in one's intention, but rather brings harm. Both [grace and truth] are found in the Bridegroom's presence. "Grace and truth came by Jesus Christ," says John the Baptist.[1177] If then the Lord Jesus knocks at my

[1170] Prv 26:5; Jn 9:24, 1:16; 2 Jn 4.
[1171] Rom 4:2.
[1172] Is 5:21.
[1173] 1 Cor 1:19.
[1174] Mt 12:12.
[1175] Mt 25:2; Rom 1:22; Mt 25:12.
[1176] Mt 7:23.
[1177] Jn 1:17.

door,[1178] with one of these gifts and not the other—and he is
the word of God, the Bridegroom of the soul—he will enter
not as a bridegroom but as a judge. God forbid that this may
ever happen! "Enter not into judgment with your servant."[1179] May he enter as one who brings peace, joy, and
gladness; but may he also enter with the gravity of maturity,
to purify my joy and control my arrogance with the stern
gaze of truth. May he come as a leaping fawn and a sharp-
eyed roe, to pass over my offenses and look at them only
with pity and forgiveness. May he come down as from the
mountains of Bethel, full of joy and radiance, descending
from the Father, sweet and gentle, not scorning to become
and to be known as the Bridegroom of the soul who seeks
him, for he is God, blessed above all forever.[1180] Amen.

SERMON 75

*I. Of The Meaning of the Saying "I Sought Him on My Bed"
etc., and Why His Finding is Unnoticed. II. Three Reasons
Why Those Who Seek are Disappointed: Time, Lukewarm-
ness, and Place. III. How in this Passage the Reason for
Disappointment is Place. IV. The Meaning of "Whom My
Soul Loves," and What the Nights are Through Which the
Bride Sought the Bridegroom.*

I. 1. "In my bed night after night I sought him whom my
soul loves."[1181] The Bridegroom has not returned when the
Bride calls him back with cries and prayers. Why not? He

[1178] Rv 3:20.
[1179] Ps 142:2.
[1180] Jn 15:26; Ps 85:5; Lam 3:25; Rom 9:5.
[1181] Sg 5:1.

wishes to increase her desire, test her affection, and exercise her faculty of love. He is not displeased with her, he is concealing his love. But he has been sought for, and we must ask whether he may be found, for he did not come when he was called. Yet the Lord said, "Everyone who looks finds";[1182] and the words used to recall him were "Return, my beloved, like a roe or a fawn."[1183] When he did not return at this call, for the reasons I have given, then she who loved him became more eager and devoted herself eagerly and entirely to seeking him. First she sought him in her bed, but she found him not at all. Then she arose and wandered through the city, going to and for among the streets and squares, but she did not meet him or catch sight of him.[1184] She questions everyone she meets, but there is no news; nor is this search and this disappointment confined to one night or one street, for she says, "I sought him night after night."[1185] How great must be her longing and her ardor, that she does not blush to rise in the night and be seen running through the city, questioning everyone openly about her beloved, not to be deflected for any reason from her search for him, undaunted by any obstacle, undeterred by any desire for rest, or by a bride's modesty, or by terrors of the night![1186] Yet in all this she is still disappointed of her hope.[1187] Why? What is the reason for this long, unrelenting disappointment, which induces weariness, foments suspicion, inflames impatience, acts as a stepmother to love and a mother to despair? If he is still concealing his love, it is too painful.

2. Perhaps this concealment may have had some good purpose for a time, until everything was concentrated on calling

[1182]Mt 7:8.
[1183]Sg 2:17.
[1184]Sg 3:1–3.

[1185]Sg 3:1.
[1186]Ps 90:5.
[1187]Ps 77:30.

him, or recalling him. But now she is seeking him and calling for him; what then can be the purpose of any further concealment? If these are incidents in a human marriage, and the love spoken of is physical love, as a superficial reading might imply, then I must leave the matter to those it concerns;[1188] but if my task is to give an answer which will satisfy, as far as I can, the minds and affections of those who seek the Lord, then I must draw from Holy Scripture—in which they trust that life to be found—something of vital spiritual importance, that the poor may eat and be satisfied and their hearts may live.[1189] And wherein is the life of their hearts but in Jesus my Lord, of whom one who lived in him said, "When Christ our life shall appear, you also will appear with him in glory."?[1190] Let him come into our midst so that it may be truly said to us, "One stands among you whom you do not know."[1191]

I do not know how the Bridegroom, who is Spirit, can fail to be recognized by spiritual men, who have made sufficient progress in the spirit to say with the prophet, "The Lord's Anointed is the spirit of life to us," and with the apostle, "If we think of Christ in a worldly way, we do not know him."[1192] Is it not he whom the Bride was seeking? Truly he is the Bridegroom, both loving and lovable. Truly, I tell you, he is the Bridegroom, and his flesh is truly food and his blood truly drink; he is wholly and truly himself, since he is none other than truth itself.[1193]

3. Why then is this Bridegroom not found when he is sought, when he is looked for so anxiously and so untiringly, now in the bed of the Bride,[1194] now in the city, or even in the

[1188] Acts 18:15.
[1189] Jn 5:39; Ps 21:27.
[1190] Col 3:4.
[1191] Jn 1:26.
[1192] Jeremiah, Lam 4:20; 2 Cor 5:16.
[1193] Jn 6:56, 14:6.
[1194] Sg 3:1–2.

streets and squares? For he himself says, "Seek and you shall find," and, "He who seeks finds," and the prophet says, "How good you are, Lord, to the soul who seeks you," and again, holy Isaiah says "Seek the Lord while he may be found."[1195] How then shall the Scriptures be fulfilled?[1196] For she who is here said to seek him is not one of those to whom he said "You will seek me and you will not find me."[1197]

II. But notice three reasons which occur to me why those who seek are disappointed: perhaps they seek at the wrong time, or in the wrong way, or in the wrong place. For if any time were the right time to seek, why does the prophet say, as I have already mentioned, "Seek the Lord while he may be found"?[1198] There must be a time when he will not be found. Then he adds that he should be called upon while he is near,[1199] for there will be a time when he will not be near. Who will not seek him then? "To me," he says, "every knee shall bow."[1200] Yet he will not be found by the wicked; the avenging angels will restrain them and prevent them from seeing the glory of God.[1201] In vain will the foolish virgins cry,[1202] for the door is shut and he will certainly not go out to them. Let them apply to themselves the saying "You will seek me and you will not find me."[1203]

4. But now is the acceptable time, now is the day of salvation.[1204] It is clearly the time for seeking and for calling, for often his presence is sensed before he is called. Now hear his promise: "Before you call me," he says, "I will answer. See, I am here."[1205] The psalmist, too, plainly describes the

[1195] Mt 7:7–8; Lam 3:25; Is 55:6.
[1196] Mt 26:54.
[1197] Jn 7:34.
[1198] Is 55:6.
[1199] *Ibid.*
[1200] Is 45:24.
[1201] Cf. Jn 11:40.
[1202] Mt 25:10.
[1203] Jn 7:34.
[1204] 2 Cor 6:2.
[1205] Is 65:24.

generosity of the Bridegroom, and the urgency: "The Lord hears the crying of the poor; his ear hears the movement of their hearts."[1206] If God is to be sought through good works, then while we have time let us do good to all men, all the more because the Lord says clearly that the night is coming when no one can work.[1207] Will you find any other time in ages to come to seek for God, or to do good, except that time which God has ordained, when he will remember you?[1208] Thus today is the day of salvation, because God our king before all ages has been working salvation in the midst of the earth.[1209]

5. Go then, wait in the midst of hell for the salvation which has already been worked in the midst of the earth. What use to dream of obtaining pardon among the everlasting fires, when the time for mercy has already passed?[1210] No victim will be left to atone for your sins; you will be dead in your sins.[1211] The Son of God is not crucified again.[1212] He died once, he dies no more.[1213] His blood, which was poured out over the earth,[1214] does not go down to hell. All the sinners on earth will drink of it,[1215] but it is not for demons to claim for putting out their flames, nor for men who have allied themselves with demons. It was his soul, not his blood, which once descended there; and this was the portion of the spirits in prison.[1216] That was his one visit there, by which he was present in spirit, while his body hung lifeless on earth. His blood bedewed and watered the thirsty earth; his blood refreshed it; his blood brought peace to these in heaven and those on earth,[1217] but to those in hell he did not bring peace.

[1206] Ps 9:38.
[1207] Gal 6:10; Jn 9:4.
[1208] Heb 6:5; Eph 4:28; Jb 14:13.
[1209] 2 Cor 6:12; Ps 73:12.
[1210] Is 33:14; Ps 101:14.
[1211] Heb 10:26; Jn 8:24.

[1212] Heb 6:6.
[1213] Rom 6:10, 9.
[1214] Mt 23:35.
[1215] Ps 74:9.
[1216] 1 Pt 3:19.
[1217] Ps 64:10; Eph 1:10.

His soul did descend there that once as I said, and wrought redemption in part;[1218] not even at that moment would he cease his works of mercy, but beyond that he will add nothing. Now is the acceptable time, now is the right time to seek him, when he who seeks will find,[1219] if he seeks at the right time and in the right way. This is one reason which prevents the Bridegroom from being found by those who seek him, that they do not seek him at the right time.[1220] But this is not what hinders the Bride, for she calls upon him and seeks him at the right time. Nor is she lukewarm, negligent, or perfunctory in her search, but ardent and untiring, as she should be.

III. 6. There remains the third reason which we must consider, whether she is looking in the wrong place. "In my little bed night after night I sought him whom my soul loves."[1221] Perhaps he should not be sought in a little bed, but in a bed, since the whole world is too narrow for him? Still, I am not displeased at the "little bed," for I know that Our Lord became little; "He was born for us as a little child."[1222] Rejoice and sing praises, O dweller in Zion, for great is the Holy One of Israel among you.[1223] That same Lord who is great in Zion is little and weak among us,[1224] and needs to lie down, and to lie in a little bed. Was his tomb not a little bed? Was the manger not a little bed? Was the Virgin's womb not a little bed? It was not a little bed but a great bed, of which the Father spoke when he said to the Son, "Out of the womb of the morning have I begotten you."[1225] That womb cannot be thought of as a bed at all; it is a place from which to rule rather than in which to rest. For he abides in the Father and

---

[1218]Lk 1:68.
[1219]2 Cor 6:2; Mt 7:8.
[1220]Cf. Rom 10:20; Ps 31:6.
[1221]Sg 3:1.

[1222]Is 9:6.
[1223]Is 12:6.
[1224]Ps 98:2; cf. Is 53:10; 1 Cor 1:25.
[1225]Ps 109:3.

with the Father he rules all things; our sure belief is that he does not lie down but sits at the right hand of God the Father.[1226] He himself says that the heavens are his throne,[1227] not his bed; in his own place, that is in the heavens, he does not seek comfort in weakness, but holds the emblems of power.

7. Rightly then does the Bride say, "*my* little bed," for any weakness in God[1228] is clearly not part of his nature, but of ours. It was from us that he took all those things which he took upon himself for our sake: his birth, his being nursed, his death and burial. The mortality of the newborn babe is mine, the weakness of the child is mine, the death on the cross is mine, and the sleep in the tomb is mine. All these are the former things which have passed away, and behold, all things are made new.[1229] "In my little bed I sought him whom my soul loves."[1230] What? Were you seeking him in your bed, when he had already returned to his own? Did you not see the Son of Man ascending where he was before?[1231] He has now changed the stable and the tomb for heaven, and are you still looking for him in your little bed? He is not here, he is risen.[1232] Why do you seek the strong in a cot, the great in a bed, the glorified in a stable? He has entered into the Lord's powers, he has clothed himself in majesty and strength; and look, he who lay under the gravestone sits above the cherubim.[1233] He lies down no more, he is enthroned; and are you preparing comforts for him as though he were reclining? To speak with greater accuracy, he is either enthroned as judge or stands as advocate.

[1226]The Apostles' Creed.
[1227]Cf. Is 66:1.
[1228]1 Cor 1:25.
[1229]2 Cor 5:17; Rv 21:4–5.

[1230]Sg 3:1.
[1231]Jn 6:63.
[1232]Mk 16:6.
[1233]Ps 70:16, 92:1, 98:1.

8. For whom then do you keep watch, O holy women? For whom do you buy spices and prepare ointments?[1234] If you knew the greatness of this man whom you are going to anoint, how, though dead, he is free from the dead,[1235] I think you would beg instead to be anointed by him.[1236] Is it not he whom God has anointed with the oil of gladness above his fellows?[1237] How happy you will be if you can return in exultation and say, "of his fullness we have all received"?[1238] For it was like this.[1239] The women who had gone to anoint him returned themselves anointed. How could they not, when they were anointed with the joy of the news of his fragrant resurrection? "How beautiful are the feet of those who spread the good tidings of peace."[1240] Sent by the angel they did the work of an evangelist,[1241] and became the apostles of the apostles, and while they hastened in the early morning to give their news of the mercy of God,[1242] they said, "We will run in the fragrance of your perfumes."[1243] Since that day, then, the Bridegroom has been sought in vain in a little bed, for until then the Church had known him according to the flesh, according to the weakness of the flesh,[1244] but she knows it no more. True, Peter and John sought him later in the sepulchre,[1245] but they did not find him. Do you see how fitly and appropriately each of them could then say, "In my little bed I sought him whom my soul loves; I sought him but I did not find him"?[1246] For his flesh, which was not of the Father,[1247] rid itself of every infirmity by the glory of

---

[1234]Lk 23:56.
[1235]Ps 87:6.
[1236]Jn 4:10.
[1237]Ps 44:8.
[1238]Lk 6:22; Jn 1:16.
[1239]Gn 1:7.
[1240]Rom 10:15.

[1241]Mt 28:7.
[1242]Ps 91:3.
[1243]Sg 1:3.
[1244]2 Cor 5:16; Rom 6:19.
[1245]Jn 20:3.
[1246]Sg 3:1.
[1247]Jn 14:28.

resurrection before it went to the Father. It girded itself with strength, it put on light as a garment,[1248] that it might present itself to the Father in the splendor and beauty which was its own.

IV. 9. How beautifully then does the bride speak when she says not "him whom I love," but "him whom my soul loves." For the love by which one loves spiritually, whether its object is God, or an angel, or another soul, is truly and properly an attribute of the soul alone. Of this kind also is the love of justice,[1249] truth, goodness, wisdom, and the other virtues. But when a soul loves—or rather yearns for—anything of a material nature[1250] be it food, clothing, property, or anything else of a physical or earthly nature, that love is said to pertain to the flesh rather than to the soul. So when the Bride says that her soul loves her Bridegroom, she uses an unusual expression, but one which is none the less appropriate, for it shows that the Bridegroom is a spirit, and that he is loved with a spiritual, not a physical, love. She is right, too, when she says that she sought him night after night. For if, as Paul says, "Those who sleep sleep at night, and those who are drunk are drunk at night,"[1251] I think that it is not absurd to say that those who are ignorant are ignorant at night, and likewise those who seek, seek at night. For who would seek what he obviously possesses?[1252] Now the day shows openly what the night concealed, so that in the daytime you may find what you sought by night. It is night, then, while the Bridegroom is being sought, for if it were day, he would be seen among us,[1253] and would not be sought at all. Enough about that subject, except that, as the Bride

[1248] Ps 64:7; Ps 103:2.
[1249] Ps 44:8.
[1250] Rom 8:5.

[1251] 1 Thes 5:7.
[1252] Rom 10:20.
[1253] 2 Thes 2:7.

said, not "by night" but "night after night," some questions may arise about the significance of there being more than one night.

10. If you have no better explanation, I suggest this as a possibility. This world has its nights—not few in number. I say the world has its nights, but it is almost all night, and always plunged in complete darkness. The faithlessness of the Jews, the ignorance of pagans, the perversity of heretics, even the shameless and degraded behavior[1254] of Catholics—these are all nights. For surely it is night when the things which belong to the Spirit of God are not perceived?[1255] There are as many nights as there are sects among heretics and schismatics. In those nights you will look in vain for the sun of justice and the light of truth, that is, the Bridegroom, because light has nothing to do with darkness.[1256] "But," you say, "the Bride would not be so blind or so foolish as to look for light in darkness,[1257] or to search for the beloved among those who do not know him or love him." But she does not say that she is seeking him now night after night, and cannot find him. No, what she says is, "Night after night I sought him whom my soul loves." Her meaning is that when she was a child she understood like a child and thought like a child,[1258] looking for truth where it was not,[1259] wandering but not finding it,[1260] as it says in the psalm, "I have strayed like a 'lost sheep.'"[1261] Indeed she mentions that she was still in a little bed, being as it were tender in age and young in sensitivity.

11. If, when you read "In my little bed I sought him whom my soul loves," you understand that she was reclining, then

[1254] *carnalis animalisque conversatio.*
[1255] 1 Cor 2:14.
[1256] 2 Cor 6:14.
[1257] Jn 1:5.
[1258] 1 Cor 13:11.
[1259] Dan 7:16.
[1260] Mt 18:12; Lk 11:24.
[1261] Ps 118:176.

the meaning is not "I sought him in my little bed," but "when I was in my little bed I sought him"; that is to say, when I was young and weak, and quite unfit to follow the Bridegroom wherever he went,[1262] to the steep and lofty heights of his glory, I encountered many who, knowing my desire, said to me, "Look, here is Christ; look, there he is."[1263] But he was not here nor was he there. Yet by encountering these men I became wiser,[1264] for the nearer I came to them and the more carefully I questioned them, the sooner I saw that the truth was not in them,[1265] and the surer I became of it. I sought him and did not find him, and I perceived that what was masquerading as day was in fact night.

12. And I said, "I will arise and go about the city; through the streets and squares will I seek him whom my soul loves."[1266] Notice now that when she says "I will arise" she is lying down. Quite rightly. How could she not arise when she heard of the resurrection of her beloved? Yet, O blessed one, if you are risen with Christ, set your heart on the things which are above, not on those below; you must seek Christ above, where he sits on the right hand of the Father.[1267] But you say, "I will go about the city."[1268] For what purpose? "The wicked prowl on every side."[1269] Leave that to the Jews, of whom the prophet rightly prophesied: "They shall suffer hunger like dogs, and go about the city."[1270] And another prophet says, "If you enter the city, behold those who are sick with hunger," which would not be so if the bread of life were to be found there.[1271] He has arisen from the heart of the earth, but did not remain on earth. He has ascended to where he was before. He

---

[1262] Rom 5:6; Rv 14:4.
[1263] Mk 13:21.
[1264] Ps 21:3.
[1265] Jn 8:32.
[1266] Sg 3:2.

[1267] Col 3:1–2.
[1268] Sg 3:2.
[1269] Ps 11:9.
[1270] Ps 58:7.
[1271] Jer 13:18; Jn 6:35; Mt 12:40.

who came down is indeed he who has ascended,[1272] the living bread which came down from heaven,[1273] he who is the Bridegroom of the Church, Jesus Christ Our Lord, who is God above all, blessed forever.[1274] Amen.

SERMON 84

I. How Great a Good it is to Seek God, and How the Soul is Awakened and the Will Inspired to Do This. II. Of the Soul Who is Able to Search for God, and What it Means to be Sought by God; That This is Necessary for the Soul, but Not for the Word.

I. 1. "Nightlong in my little bed I sought him whom my soul loves."[1275] It is a great good to seek God; in my opinion the soul knows no greater blessing. It is the first of its gifts and the final stage in its progress. It is inferior to none, and it yields place to none. What could be superior to it, when nothing has a higher place? What could claim a higher place, when it is the consummation of all things? What virtue can be attributed to anyone who does not seek God? What boundary can be set for anyone who does seek him? The psalmist says: "Seek his face always."[1276] Nor, I think, will a soul cease to seek him even when it has found him. It is not with steps of the feet that God is sought but with the heart's desire; and when the soul happily finds him its desire is not quenched but kindled. Does the consummation of joy bring about the consuming of desire? Rather it is oil poured upon the flames. So it is. Joy will be fulfilled,[1277] but there

---

[1272]Eph 4:10.
[1273]Jn 6:41.
[1274]Rom 9:5.

[1275]Sg 3:1.
[1276]Ps 104:4.
[1277]Ps 15:11.

will be no end to desire, and therefore no end to the search. Think, if you can, of this eagerness to see God as not caused by his absence, for he is always present; and think of the desire for God as without fear of failure, for grace is abundantly present.

2. Now see why I have begun in this way. Surely so that every soul among you who is seeking God may know that she has been forestalled, and that she was found before she was sought. This will avoid distorting her greatest good into a great evil; for this is what we do when we receive favors from God and treat his gifts as though they were ours by right, and do not give glory to God.[1278] Thus those who appear great because of the favors they have received are accounted as little before God because they have not given him thanks. But I am understating the case.[1279] The words I have used, "great" and "little," are inadequate to express my meaning, and confuse the issue. I will make myself clear. I should have said "good" and "evil." For if a man who is very good takes the credit for his goodness he becomes correspondingly evil. For this is a very evil thing. If anyone says "Far be it from me! I know that it is by the grace of God I am what I am,"[1280] and then is careful to take a little of the glory for the favor he has received, is he not a thief and a robber?[1281] Such a man will hear these words: "Out of your own mouth I judge you, wicked servant."[1282] What is more wicked than for a servant to usurp the glory due his master?

3. "In my little bed nightlong I sought him whom my soul loves."[1283] The soul seeks the Word, but has been first sought by the Word. Otherwise when she had gone away from the

[1278] Lk 17:18.
[1279] 1 Cor 7:28.
[1280] 1 Cor 15:10.

[1281] Jn 10:1.
[1282] Lk 19:22.
[1283] Sg 3:1.

Word, or been cast out, she would not turn back to look upon the good[1284] she had left unless she were sought by the Word. For if a soul is left to herself she is like a wandering spirit which does not return.[1285] Listen to someone who was a fugitive and a wanderer: "I have gone astray as a sheep that was lost. O seek your servant."[1286] O man, do you want to return? But if it is a matter of will, why do you ask for help? Why do you beg elsewhere for what you have within yourself in abundance? Clearly because one wills it, but cannot do it, and this is a spirit which wanders and does not return. He who has not the will is yet further away; if a soul desires to return and asks to be sought, I would not say that it was entirely dishonored and abandoned. Whence does it obtain this desire? If I am not mistaken, it is the result of the soul being already sought and visited, and that seeking has not been fruitless, because it has activated the will, without which there could be no return. But the soul is so feeble, and the return so difficult, that it is not enough to be sought only once. The soul may have the will, but the will cannot act unless it has some supporting power. Paul says, "The will is in me, but I have no power to perform it."[1287] We quoted the psalmist; what does he go on to ask? Simply to be sought. He would not ask this if he had not already been sought. He also prays, "O seek your servant";[1288] that is asking that the God who had given him the will might also give him the power to perform it, at his good will.[1289]

4. I do not think, however, that this passage can refer to such a soul, which has not yet received the next grace; it desires to approach him "whom her soul loves,"[1290] but is

[1284]Jb 7:7.
[1285]Ps 77:39.
[1286]Ps 118:176.
[1287]Rom 7:18.

[1288]Ps 118:176.
[1289]Phil 2:13.
[1290]Sg 3:1.

powerless to do so. How can you apply to it the words which follow?—that is, that she rises and goes about the city, and seeks her beloved through the streets and squares[1291]—if she herself needs to be sought? Let her seek him as she can, provided she remembers that she was first sought, as she was first loved; and it is because of this that she herself both seeks and loves. Let us also pray, beloved, that his mercies may speedily go before us,[1292] for our need is great. I do not say this of all,[1293] for I know that many of you walk in the love with which Christ has loved us, and seek him in simplicity of heart.[1294] But there are some, I am sad to say, who have not yet shown any sign of this saving and prevenient grace, and therefore no sign of salvation, men who love themselves, not the Lord, and are concerned with their own interests, not his.[1295]

5. "I sought him whom my soul loves"[1296]—this is what you are urged to do by the goodness of him who anticipates you, who sought him, and loved you before you loved him.[1297] You would not seek him or love him unless you had first been sought and loved. Not only in one blessing[1298] have you been forestalled but in two, being loved as well as being sought. For the love is the reason for the search, and the search is the fruit of the love, and its certain proof. You are loved so that you may not suppose you are sought to be punished. You are sought so that you may not complain you are loved in vain. Both these loving and manifest favors give you courage, and drive away your diffidence, persuading you to return, and stirring your affections.[1299] From this comes the zeal and ardor to seek him whom your soul loves,[1300] because

[1291]Sg 3:2.
[1292]Ps 78:8.
[1293]Jn 13:18.
[1294]Eph 5:2; Ws 1:1.
[1295]2 Tm 3:2; 1 Cor 13:5.

[1296]Sg 3:1.
[1297]1 Jn 4:10.
[1298]Gn 27:28.
[1299]*affectus.*
[1300]Sg 3:1.

you cannot seek unless you are sought, and when you are sought you cannot but seek.

6. Do not forget whence you came. Now, that I may take the words to myself[1301]—which is the safest course—is it not you, my soul, who left your first husband,[1302] with whom it went well with you, and cast aside your loyalty by going after lovers?[1303] And now that you have chosen to commit fornication with them and have been cast aside by them, do you have the effrontery, the insolence, to return to him whom you spurned in your arrogance? Do you seek the light when you are only fit to be hidden, and run to the Bridegroom when you are more deserving of blows than of embraces? It will be a wonder if you do not meet the judge rather than the bridegroom. Happy the person who hears his soul replying to these reproaches, "I do not fear, because I love; and I could not love at all if I were not loved; therefore this is love." One who is loved has nothing to fear. Let those fear who do not love; they must always live in fear of retribution. Since I love, I cannot doubt that I am loved, any more than I can doubt that I love. Nor can I fear to look on his face, since I have sensed his tenderness.[1304] In what have I known it? In this—not only has he sought me as I am, but he has shown me tenderness,[1305] and caused me to seek him with confidence. How can I not respond to him when he seeks me, since I respond to him in tenderness?[1306] How can he be angry with me for seeking him, when he overlooked the contempt I showed for him? He will not drive away someone who seeks him, when he sought someone who spurned him. The spirit of the Word is gentle,[1307] and brings

[1301] 1 Cor 4:6.
[1302] Sir 23:32.
[1303] 1 Tm 5:12; Hos 2:5, 13.
[1304] *sensui affectum.*
[1305] *affecit.*
[1306] *in affectu.*
[1307] Ws 1:6.

me gentle greetings, speaking to me persuasively of the zeal and desire of the Word, which cannot be hidden from him.[1308] He searches the deep things of God,[1309] and knows his thoughts—thoughts of peace and not of vengeance.[1310] How can I fail to be inspired to seek him, when I have experienced his mercy and been assured of his peace?

7. Brothers, to realize this is to be taught by the Word; to be convinced of it is to be found. But not everyone can receive this word.[1311] What shall we do for our little ones, those among us who are beginners—not foolish, since they have the beginning of wisdom and are subject to one another in the fear of Christ?[1312] How can we make them believe that it is the Bridegroom who deals thus with them, when they themselves cannot yet perceive what is happening to them? But I send them to one whom they should not disbelieve. Let them read in the book what they do not see in the heart of another, and therefore do not believe. It is written in the prophets, "If a man puts away his wife and she goes away and takes another husband, will he return to her? Will that woman not be dishonored and disgraced? But you have committed fornication with many lovers; yet return to me, says the Lord, and I will take you back.[1313] These are the words of the Lord; you cannot refuse to believe them. What they do not know from experience, let them believe, so that one day, by virtue of their faith, they may reap the harvest of experience.

I think enough has been explained of what is meant by being sought by the Word, and that this is necessary, not for

---

[1308] Mt 5:14.
[1309] 1 Cor 2:10.
[1310] Jer 29:11.
[1311] Mt 19:11.
[1312] *incipientes non-insipientes;* Ps 110:10; Eph 5:21.
[1313] Jer 3:1.

the Word but for the soul. We must however add that the soul which knows this by experience has fuller and more blessed knowledge. It remains for me to show in my next sermon how thirsty souls seek him by whom they are sought; or rather we should learn it from the one who is mentioned in this passage as seeking him whom her soul loves,[1314] the Bridegroom of the soul, Jesus Christ our Lord, who is God above all, blessed forever. Amen.[1315]

SERMON 85

I. Seven Reasons Why the Soul Seeks the Word; First, Concerning Correction and Recognition. II. That the Soul Suffers a Threefold Attack, and How Man Must Guard against This; of the Nature of Virtue, and How He Who Trusts in Christ Is All-Powerful, for It Is Christ Who Must Be Relied Upon in Pursuit of Virtue. III. How We Are Conformed Afresh to Virtue by the Word, and the Difference Between Wisdom and Virtue. IV. What It Means to Be Conformed to the Word in Beauty; of the Fruitfulness of Marriage, and Its Enjoyment, as Far as Possible, in This Life.

I. 1. "In my little bed I sought him whom my soul loves."[1316] For what? I have already spoken of that, and it is redundant to repeat it. But for the sake of some who were not present when it was discussed, I will give a short account, and perhaps those who were present will not object to listening; for it could not be treated fully on that occasion. The soul seeks the Word, and consents to receive correction, by which she

[1314]Sg 3:3.
[1315]Rom 9:5.
[1316]Sg 3:1.

may be enlightened to recognize him, strengthened to attain virtue, molded to wisdom, conformed to his likeness, made fruitful by him, and enjoy him in bliss. These are the reasons why the soul seeks the Word. No doubt there are countless others, but these occur to me at the moment. If anyone has a mind to do so, he can easily find many others in himself; for we experience many vicissitudes, many deep spiritual needs, and unnumbered anxieties.[1317] But the Word is so fully, so richly endowed with goodness that his Wisdom overcomes our malice, vanquishing evil with good.[1318] Now I will give you the reasoning behind my statement. See first how the soul consents to receive correction. We read in the Gospel how the Word says, "Agree with your adversary quickly, while you are in the way with him, so that he does not hand you over to the judge, and the judge to the executioner."[1319] What better counsel could there be? It is the counsel of the Word, who is himself the adversary of our carnal desires,[1320] when he says, "These people always err in their hearts."[1321] If you who are listening to me have conceived a wish to flee from the wrath to come,[1322] you will, I think, be anxious to know how you are to agree with this adversary who seems to threaten you so terribly.[1323] This will be impossible unless you disagree with yourself and become your own adversary, and fight against yourself without respite in a continual and hard struggle, and renounce your inveterate habits and inborn inclinations. But this is a hard thing. If you attempt it in your own strength, it will be as though you were trying to stop the raging of a torrent, or to make the Jordan run backward.[1324] What can you do then? You must seek the Word,

---

[1317] Ps 39:13.
[1318] Ws 7:30; Rom 12:21.
[1319] Cf. Mt 5:25.
[1320] 1 Pt 2:11.

[1321] Ps 94:10.
[1322] Lk 3:7.
[1323] Mt 5:25.
[1324] Ps 113:3.

to agree with him, by his operation. Flee to him who is your adversary, that through him you may no longer be his adversary, but that he who threatens you may caress you and may transform you by his outpoured grace more effectually than by his outraged anger.

2. This, I think, is the first and most urgent compulsion which drives the soul to seek the Word. But if you do not know what he wills with whom you have reached agreement of will, shall he not say of you that you have a zeal for God, but it is not knowledgeable?[1325] And if you think this unimportant, remember that it is written, "he who does not know will not be known."[1326] Do you want to know what advice I would give in this difficulty? First of all, my advice is that you go now to the Word, and he will teach you his ways,[1327] so that you will not go astray in your journey and, desiring the good but not recognizing it, wander in a pathless place[1328] instead of along the highway. The Word is the light.[1329] "The unfolding of your words gives light and imparts understanding to children."[1330] Happy are you if you too can say, "Your word is a lamp for my feet and a lantern for my path."[1331] Your soul has received great profit if your will is unswerving and your reason enlightened, willing and recognizing the good. By the first it receives life and by the second vision; for it was dead when it desired evil, and blind when it did not recognize the good.

3. But now it lives and sees, and stands firm in the good— but by the operation and with the help of the Word. Raised by the hand of the Word it stands, as it were, on the two feet of devotion and knowledge. It stands, I say; but let it take to

[1325]Rom 10:2.
[1326]1 Cor 14:38.
[1327]Ps 24:9.
[1328]Ps 106:40.

[1329]Jn 1:9.
[1330]Ps 118:130.
[1331]Ps 118:105.

itself the saying, "Let him who thinks he stands take heed lest he fall."[1332] Do you imagine he can stand in his own strength, when he could not rise in his own strength? How could he? "The heavens were established by the Word of the Lord"[1333]—can the earth stand without the Word? If it were able to stand in its own strength, why did a man, also of the earth, pray, "Strengthen me according to your word"?[1334] Surely he spoke from experience. It was his voice which said, "I was attacked and thrown down and would have fallen, but the Lord sustained me."[1335]

II. Who was it who attacked him? It was not only one. The devil attacked him, the world attacked him, a man attacked him. What man? Every man is his own attacker. Every man throws himself down—indeed you need not fear any attack from outside, if you can keep your hands from yourself. "For who can harm you," says the apostle, "if you follow what is good?"[1336] By your hand I mean the consent of your will. If the devil suggests you should do wrong, or the pressure of the world prompts you, and you withhold your consent and do not allow your limbs to be instruments of iniquity nor permit sin to control your mortal body,[1337] you have proved that you follow what is good, and the malice of the attack has done you no harm, but has instead benefitted you. For it is written, "Do good, and you shall receive praise for it."[1338] Those who tried to attack your soul have been routed, and you can sing, "If they have no dominion over me, then shall I be blameless."[1339] You have shown clearly that you follow what is good,[1340] if, following the wise

---

[1332] I Cor 10:12.
[1333] Ps 32:6.
[1334] Ps 118:28.
[1335] Ps 117:13.
[1336] I Pt 3:13.

[1337] Rom 6:13, 12.
[1338] Rom 13:3.
[1339] Ps 39:15.
[1340] Ps 18:14.

man's advice, you love your own soul,[1341] guard your heart with all vigilance,[1342] and keep yourself pure,[1343] as the apostle enjoins. If you do not, even if you gain the whole world, but let your soul go to ruin[1344] we cannot consider you as following what is good; for the Savior himself will not do so.

4. There are three agents, then, who always constitute a threat: the devil, who attacks with envy and malice; the world, with the blasting wind of vanity; and man, by the burden of his own corruption. The devil attacks, but he does not overthrow you if you refuse to help him or to give your consent. You know the saying, "Resist the devil, and he will flee from you."[1345] For it was he who in envy attacked the denizens of paradise and overthrew them, but they gave their consent and put up no resistance. It was he who fell from heaven in his pride; no one attacked him. You can see how much more danger there is that a man will precipitate his own fall, since he is weighed down by his own material being.

Then there is the attack from the world, which is rooted in wickedness.[1346] The world attacks everyone, but it only overthrows those who are its friends and acquiesce with it. I have no wish to be a friend to the world and court the danger of falling. "He who desires to be a friend of this world makes himself the enemy of God,"[1347] and there can be no worse fall than that. So it is quite clear that man is his own greatest threat, for he can fall by his own momentum without any impulse from anyone else, but not without an impulse of his own. Which of these needs to be resisted most? The last, for it is nearest to us, and therefore more

---

[1341]Sir 30:24.
[1342]Prv 4:23.
[1343]1 Tm 5:22.
[1344]Mt 16:26.

[1345]Jas 4:7.
[1346]1 Jn 5:19.
[1347]Jas 4:4.

troublesome, being enough in itself to cast us down, whereas without it no one else can harm us.[1348] It is not without reason that the wise man accounted the man who has command of his spirit greater than he who storms a city.[1349] This is very important for you: you have need of strength, and not simply strength, but strength drawn from above.[1350] For this strength if it is perfect, will easily give the mind control of itself,[1351] and so it will be unconquered before all its adversaries. It is a strength of mind which, in protecting reason, does not know how to retreat. Or, if you like, it is the strength of a mind standing steadfast with reason and for reason. Or again, it is a strength of mind which gathers up and directs everything toward reason.

5. "Who shall ascend the hill of the Lord?"[1352] If anyone aspires to climb to the summit of that mountain,[1353] that is to the perfection of virtue, he will know how hard the climb is, and how the attempt is doomed to failure without the help of the Word. Happy the soul which causes the angels to look at her with joy and wonder and hears them saying, "Who is this coming up from the wilderness, rich in grace and beauty, leaning upon her beloved?"[1354] Otherwise, unless it leans on him, its struggle is in vain. But it will gain force by struggling with itself and, becoming stronger, will impel all things toward reason: anger, fear, covetousness, and joy; like a good charioteer, it will control the chariot of the mind, bringing every carnal affect into captivity,[1355] and every sense under the control of reason in accordance with virtue. Surely all things are possible to someone who leans upon him who can do all things? What confidence there is in the

[1348]Jn 15:5.
[1349]Prv 16:32.
[1350]Lk 24:49.
[1351]*animus,* throughout.
[1352]Ps 23:3.
[1353]Ex 24:17.
[1354]Sg 8:5.
[1355]2 Cor 10:5.

cry, "I can do all things in him who strengthens me!"[1356] Nothing shows more clearly the almighty power of the Word than that he makes all-powerful all those who put their hope in him. For "all things are possible to one who believes."[1357] If all things are possible to him he must be all-powerful.[1358] Thus if the mind does not rely upon itself, but is strengthened by the Word, it can gain such command over itself that no unrighteousness will have power over it.[1359] So, I say, neither power, nor treachery, nor lure, can overthrow or hold in subjection the mind which rests upon the Word and is clothed with strength from above.[1360]

6. Do you wish to be free from fear of attack? Let the foot of pride not come near you, then the hand of an attacker shall not move you.[1361] "There lie those who work wickedness."[1362] There fell the devil and his angels, who were not attacked from without, yet could not stand and were driven out. So he who did not rest on the Word but relied on his own strength did not stand in the truth.[1363] Perhaps that is why he wished to sit, because he had not the strength to stand; for he said, "I will sit on the mountain of assembly."[1364] But the judgment of God was otherwise: he neither stood nor sat, but fell, as the Lord said, "I beheld Satan fallen like lightning from heaven."[1365] Therefore anyone who stands and does not wish to fall[1366] should not place his trust in himself, but lean on the Word. The Word says, "without me you can do nothing."[1367] And so it is. We can neither rise to the good nor stand in the good without the Word.

[1356] Phil 4:13.
[1357] Mk 9:22.
[1358] Mt 19:26.
[1359] Ps 118:133.
[1360] Lk 24:49.
[1361] Ps 35:12.
[1362] Ps 35:13.
[1363] Jn 8:44; Ps 48:7.
[1364] Is 14:13.
[1365] Lk 10:18.
[1366] 1 Cor 10:12.
[1367] Jn 15:5.

Therefore, you who stand, give glory to the Word[1368] and say, "He set my feet upon a rock, and directed my path aright."[1369] You must be held by the strength of him by whose hand you were raised.[1370] This is to explain what I meant when I said that we had need of the Word on whom to lean in our pursuit of virtue.

III. 7. Now we must consider my other words, that we are conformed to wisdom by the Word. The Word is strength and he is wisdom.[1371] Let the soul therefore draw strength from his strength and wisdom from his wisdom; let it ascribe both gifts to the Word alone. For if she ascribes either to another source, or claims the credit for herself, she might as well say that the river does not come from the spring, nor the wine from the grape, nor light from light. "If anyone has need of wisdom, let him ask it from God, who gives to all freely and utters no reproach, and he will give it to him."[1372] A faithful saying.[1373] I think the same applies to virtue, for virtue is the sister of wisdom.[1374] Virtue is God's gift and must be counted among his best gifts, coming down from the Father of the Word.[1375] If anyone thinks that wisdom is the same in all respects,[1376] I do not dissent, but this holds good in the Word, not in the soul. For the attributes which are in the Word, because of the singular simplicity of the divine nature, do not have a single action on the soul, but are applied to its various different needs as though they were different and could be divided. It follows this reasoning that to be moved by virtue[1377] is one thing and to be ruled by wisdom another; it is one thing to be controlled in virtue, and

---

[1368]Cf. Jn 9:24.
[1369]Ps 39:3.
[1370]Acts 9:41.
[1371]1 Cor 1:24.
[1372]Jas 1:5.

[1373]1 Tm 1:25.
[1374]*cognata sapientiae.*
[1375]Jas 1:17, 3:15.
[1376]Gal 6:3.
[1377]Ps 65:7.

another to be delighted by sweetness. For although wisdom is powerful and virtue sweet, if we are to give words their proper significance, virtue is characterized by strength of mind, and wisdom by peace of mind and spiritual sweetness.[1378] This I think was what the apostle meant when, after a long exhortation to virtue, he mentions what wisdom there is in sweetness, in the Holy Spirit.[1379] It is an honor, therefore, to stand firm, to resist, to meet force with force—these are considered works of virtue—but it is hard work. For defending your honor with toil is not the same as possessing it in peace. Nor is being moved by virtue the same as enjoying virtue. What virtue wins by toil, wisdom enjoys; and what is ordained, counseled, and guided by wisdom is accomplished by virtue.

8. "The wisdom of a scribe comes by leisure," says Solomon.[1380] Therefore the leisure of wisdom is exertion,[1381] and the more leisure wisdom has, the harder it works in its own fashion. But the more virtue is exercised in its own sphere, the more illustrious it is, and the more ready it is to serve, the more approval it wins. If anyone defines wisdom as the love of virtue, I think you are not far from the truth. For where there is love, there is no toil, but a taste. Perhaps *sapientia,* that is wisdom, is derived from *sapor,* that is taste, because, when it is added to virtue, like some seasoning, it adds taste to something which by itself is tasteless and bitter. I think it would be permissible to define wisdom as a taste for goodness. We lost this taste almost from the creation of our human race. When the old serpent's poison infected the palate of our heart, because the fleshly sense prevailed, the soul began to lose its taste for goodness, and a depraved taste

---

[1378] Cf. *Sir, Prol.*
[1379] 2 Cor 6:6.

[1380] Sir 38:25.
[1381] *sapientiae otia negotia sunt.*

crept in. "A man's imagination and thoughts are evil from his youth,"[1382] that is, as a result of the folly of the first woman. So it was folly which drove the taste for good from the woman, because the serpent's malice outwitted the woman's folly. But the reason which caused the malice to appear for a time victorious is the same reason why it suffers eternal defeat. For see! It is again the heart and body of a woman which wisdom fills and makes fruitful so that, as by a woman we were deformed into folly, so by a woman we may be reformed to wisdom. Now wisdom always prevails over malice in the minds[1383] which it has entered, and drives out the taste for evil which the other has brought to it, by introducing something better. When wisdom enters, it makes the carnal sense taste flat, it purifies the understanding, cleanses and heals the palate of the heart. Thus, when the palate is clean, it tastes the good, it tastes wisdom itself, and there is nothing better.

9. How many good actions are performed without the doers having any taste for them, because they are compelled to do them by their way of life or by some circumstance or necessity? And on the contrary many who do evil with no taste for it are led by fear or desire for something, rather than because they relish evil. But those who act in accordance with the affection of their hearts[1384] are either wise, and delight in goodness because they have a taste for it, or else they are wicked, and take pleasure in wrongdoing, even if they are not moved by any hope of gain. For what is malice but a taste for evil? Happy is the mind which is protected by a taste for good and a hatred of evil, for this is what it means to be reformed to wisdom, and to know by experience and to

[1382] Gn 18:21.
[1383] Ws 7:30; *mentes.*
[1384] Ps 72:7.

rejoice in the victory of wisdom. For in nothing is the victory of wisdom over malice[1385] more evident than when the taste for evil—which is what malice is—is purged away, and the mind's inmost task senses that it is deeply filled with sweetness. It looks to virtue to sustain tribulations with fortitude, and to wisdom to rejoice in those tribulations.[1386] To strengthen your heart and to wait upon the Lord—that is virtue;[1387] to taste and see that the Lord is good—that is wisdom.[1388] Now both goods are best seen as arising from their appropriate nature. Thus modesty of mind[1389] marks the man who is wise, and constancy the man of virtue. It is right to put wisdom after virtue, for virtue is, as it were, the sure foundation[1390] above which wisdom builds her home. But the knowledge of good should come before these, because there is no fellowship between the light of wisdom and the shadows of ignorance.[1391] Goodwill, too, should come before them, because wisdom will not enter a soul disposed to ill.[1392]

IV. 10. Now the soul has recovered its life by changing its will, its health by instruction, its stability by virtue, and its maturity by wisdom. It remains for us to find how to obtain the beauty without which it cannot please him who is lovelier than all the sons of men.[1393] For it hears that "the king shall desire your beauty."[1394] What great spiritual goods we have mentioned: gifts from the Word, goodwill, knowledge, virtue, wisdom! Yet we read that none of them is desired by the king, who is the Word, but it only says, "the king shall desire your beauty."[1395] The prophet says, "The Lord is king, he is clothed in beauty." How can he but desire a like garment for his Bride, who is also his likeness? And the

[1385] Ws 7:30.
[1386] 2 Cor 7:4.
[1387] Ps 26:14.
[1388] Ps 33:9.

[1389] *animus.*
[1390] Prv 9:1.
[1391] 2 Cor 6:14.
[1392] Ws 1:4.

[1393] Ps 44:3.
[1394] Ps 44:12.
[1395] Ps 92:1.

closer the likeness, the dearer she will be to him. What is this spiritual beauty? Does it consist of what we call honor? Let us take it as such for the moment, until we find something better. But honor concerns outward behavior—not that honor issues from it, but is perceived through it. Its root and its dwelling are in the conscience; and the evidence of a good conscience is its clarity. There is nothing clearer than this transparent goodness, which is the light of truth shining in the mind; there is nothing more glorious than the mind which sees itself in the truth. But what is this mind like? It is modest, reverent, filled with holy fear, watchful, guarding against anything which might dim the glory of its conscience,[1396] aware of nothing which might make it ashamed in the presence of the truth or cause it to avert its gaze from the light of God in confusion and terror. This is the glory which delights the eyes of God above all qualities of the soul,[1397] and this is what we mean by honor.

11. But when this beauty and brightness has filled the inmost part of the heart, it must become outwardly visible, and not be like a lamp hidden under a bushel,[1398] but be a light shining in darkness,[1399] which cannot be hidden. It shines out, and by the brightness of its rays it makes the body a mirror of the mind, spreading through the limbs and senses so that every action, every word, look, movement, and even laugh (if there should be laughter) radiates gravity and honor. So when the movements of the limbs and senses, its gestures and habits, are seen to be resolute, pure, restrained, free from all presumption and license, with no sign of triviality and idleness, but given to just dealing, zealous in piety, then the beauty of the soul will be seen

---

[1396] Cf. 2 Cor 3:7.
[1397] Cf. Mt 24:47.
[1398] Mt 5:15.
[1399] Jn 1:5.

openly—that is, if there is no guilt in the spirit,[1400] for these qualities can be counterfeited, and not spring from the heart's abundance.[1401] Now let us elucidate what we mean by honor, and wherein it may be found; so that the soul's beauty may shine forth even more. It is integrity of mind, which is concerned to keep the innocent reputation with a good conscience,[1402] and not only, as the apostle says, to provide things good in the sight of God,[1403] but in the sight of men also. Happy the mind which has clothed itself in the beauty of holiness and the brightness of innocence, by which it manifests its glorious likeness, not to the world but to the Word, of whom we read that he is the brightness of eternal life, the splendor and image of the being of God.[1404]

12. The soul which has attained this degree now ventures to think of marriage. Why should she not, when she sees that she is like him and therefore ready for marriage? His loftiness has no terrors for her, because her likeness to him associates her with him, and her declaration of love is a betrothal. This is the form of that declaration: "I have sworn and I purpose to keep your righteous judgments."[1405] The apostles followed this when they said, "See, we have left everything to follow you."[1406] There is a similar saying which pointing to the spiritual marriage between Christ and the Church, refers to physical marriage: "For this shall a man leave his father and mother and be joined to his wife, and they two shall be one flesh";[1407] and the prophet says of the Bride's glory: "It is good to me to cling to good, and to put my hope in the Lord."[1408] When you see a soul leaving

---

[1400]Ps 31:2.
[1401]Mt 12:34.
[1402]1 Tm 1:5.
[1403]2 Cor 8:21.
[1404]Ws 7:26; Heb 1:3.

[1405]Ps 118:106.
[1406]Mt 19:27.
[1407]Eph 5:31.
[1408]Ps 72:28.

everything[1409] and clinging to the Word with all her will and desire, living for the Word, ruling her life by the Word, conceiving by the Word what it will bring forth by him, so that she can say, "For me to live is Christ, and to die is gain,"[1410] you know that the soul is the spouse and bride of the Word. The heart of the Bridegroom has faith in her, knowing her to be faithful, for she has rejected all things as dross to gain him.[1411] He knows her to be like him of whom it was said, "He is a chosen vessel for me."[1412] Paul's soul indeed was like a tender mother and a faithful wife when he said, "My little children, with whom I travail in birth again, until Christ shall be formed in you."[1413]

13. But notice that in spiritual marriage there are two kinds of birth, and thus two kinds of offspring, though not opposite. For spiritual persons, like holy mothers, may bring souls to birth by preaching, or may give birth to spiritual insights by meditation. In this latter kind of birth the soul leaves even its bodily senses and is separated from them, so that in her awareness of the Word she is not aware of herself. This happens when the mind[1414] is enraptured by the unutterable sweetness of the Word, so that it withdraws, or rather is transported, and escapes from itself to enjoy the Word. The soul is affected in one way when it is made fruitful by the Word, in another when it enjoys the Word: in the one it is considering the needs of its neighbor; in the other it is allured by the sweetness of the Word. A mother is happy in her child; a bride is even happier in her bridegroom's embrace. The children are dear, they are pledge of his love, but his kisses give her greater pleasure. It is good to save

[1409] Lk 5:11.
[1410] Phil 1:21.
[1411] Prv 31:11; Phil 3:8.
[1412] Acts 9:15.
[1413] Gal 4:11.
[1414] *mens.*

many souls, but there is far more pleasure in going aside to be with the Word.[1415] But when does this happen, and for how long? It is sweet intercourse, but lasts a short time and is experienced rarely! This is what I spoke of before, when I said that the final reason for the soul to seek the Word was to enjoy him in bliss.

14. There may be someone who will go on to ask me, "What does it mean to enjoy the Word?" I would answer that he must find someone who has experience of it, and ask him. Do you suppose, if I were granted that experience, that I could describe to you what is beyond description? Listen to one who has known it: "If we are beside ourselves, it is for God; if we are in our right mind, it is for you."[1416] That is to say, it is one thing for me to be with God, and of that, God alone is the judge. It is another for me to be with you. I may have been granted this experience, but I do not speak of it. I have made allowance in what I have said, so that you could understand me. Oh, whoever is curious to know what it means to enjoy the Word, make ready your mind, not your ear! The tongue does not teach this, grace does. It is hidden from the wise and prudent, and revealed to children.[1417] Humility, my brothers, is a great virtue, great and sublime. It can attain to what it cannot learn; it is counted worthy to possess what it has not the power to possess; it is worthy to conceive by the Word and from the Word what it cannot itself explain in words. Why is this? Not because it deserves to do so, but because it pleases the Father of the Word,[1418] the Bridegroom of the soul, Jesus Christ our Lord, who is God above all, blessed forever. Amen.[1419]

[1415] 2 Cor 5:13.
[1416] 2 Cor 5:13.
[1417] Lk 10:21.

[1418] Cf. 1 Jn 3:22.
[1419] Rom 9:5.

SERMON 86

I. In Praise of the Modesty of the Bride, and How This is Fitting for the Young. II. Of the Place and Time Suitable for Prayer, and What Can Be Rightly Understood by the Bed and the Night.

I. 1. There is no reason to ask me further why the soul should seek the Word; I have said more than enough. Let us now continue our consideration of the rest of this passage, insofar as it refers to conduct of life. First then observe the modesty of the Bride; surely nothing in human conduct can be counted lovelier. This is what I should like above all to take in my hands and pluck, like a beautiful flower, to present to all our young people—not that it should not be held with the greatest care by everyone who is older, for the grace of modesty is an adornment to persons of all ages, but because, being tender, it shines out with greater brightness and beauty in those of tender age. What is more endearing in a young man than modesty? How lovely it is, and what a bright jewel in the life and bearing of a young man! What a true and sure indication of hope it is, the mark of a good disposition! It is the rod of discipline,[1420] chastening the affections and controlling the thoughtless actions and impulses of an age which lacks stability, and checking its arrogance. What is so far removed from evil-speaking or any kind of bad behavior? It is the sister of self-control. There is no clearer indication of dovelike simplicity,[1421] and thus it is the mark of innocence. It is the lamp which lights the unassuming mind,[1422] so that nothing dishonorable or unbecoming may attempt to dwell in it without being instantly

[1420]Prv 22:15.
[1421]Mt 10:16.
[1422]*mens.*

discovered. Thus it is the destroyer of evils and the protector of its inborn purity, the particular glory of the conscience, the guardian of its reputation, the adornment of its life, the seat of virtue and its firstfruits, the boast of nature and the mark of all honor. Even the blush which modesty brings to the cheeks gives grace and beauty to the countenance.

2. Modesty is a quality so natural to the mind[1423] that even those who do not fear to do wrong are reluctant to let it be seen. The Lord said, "Every man who does evil hates the light,"[1424] and also, "those who sleep sleep at night, and those who are drunk are drunk at night";[1425] the works of darkness which should be hidden conceal themselves in darkness. There is a difference, however, between the modesty of those who do not hesitate to commit deeds of wickedness, but are reluctant to reveal them, and that of the Bride who has no dealings with them, but rejects them and drives them away. Therefore Solomon says, "There is a shame which brings sin, and there is a shame which is glory and grace."[1426] The Bride seeks the Word with modesty, in her bed, at night; but this modesty brings glory, not sin. She seeks him to purify her conscience, she seeks him to obtain a testimony, so that she can say, "This is my glory, the testimony of my conscience.[1427] In my little bed nightlong I sought him whom my soul loves."[1428] Her modesty, you observe, is indicated both by the place and the time. What is more welcome to a modest mind than privacy? Night and her bed insures her privacy. Now when we wish to pray, we are bidden to enter our room,[1429] for the sake of privacy. This is a precaution, for if we pray when others are present, their approbation may rob our prayer of its fruit and nullify its effect. But

[1423]*animus.*
[1424]Jn 3:20.
[1425]1 Thes 5:7.
[1426]Sir 4:25.
[1427]2 Cor 1:12.
[1428]Sg 3:1.
[1429]Mt 6:6.

from this injunction you may also learn modesty. What is more appropriate to modesty than the avoidance of praise or ostentation? It is clear that the Son, our teacher, has enjoined us to seek privacy when we pray, in order to promote modesty. What is so unseemly, particularly in a young man, as showing off holiness? It is at this age that the elements of religious obedience can be best learned. Jeremiah said, "It is good for a man to bear the yoke in his youth."[1430] It is to be recommended that when you go to pray you first mention your modesty and say, "I am small and of no importance; yet I do not forget your precepts."[1431]

3. Anyone who wishes to pray must choose not only the right place but also the right time. A time of leisure is best and most convenient, the deep silence when others are asleep is particularly suitable, for prayer will then be freer and purer. "Arise at the first watch of the night, and pour out your heart like water before the face of the Lord, your God."[1432] How secretly prayer goes up in the night, witnessed only by God and the holy angel who received it to present it at the heavenly altar! How pleasing, how unclouded it is, colored with the blush of modesty! How serene, how calm, free from noise and interruption! How pure it is, how sincere, unsullied by the dust of earthly care, untouched by ostentation or human flattery! Therefore the Bride, as modest as she is cautious, when she desired to pray, that is, to seek the Word—for they are the same— sought the privacy of her bed at night. You will not pray aright, if in your prayers you seek anything but the Word, or seek him for the sake of anything but the Word; for in him are all things.[1433] In him is healing for your wounds, help in

---

[1430]Lam 3:27.
[1431]Ps 118:141.

[1432]Lam 2:19.
[1433]Col 1:17.

your need, restoration for your faults, resources for your further growth; in him is all that men should ask or desire, all they need, all that will profit them. There is no reason therefore to ask anything else of the Word, for he is all. Even if we seem sometimes to ask for material things, providing that we do so for the sake of the Word, as we should, it is not the things themselves that we are asking for, but him for whose sake we ask them. Those who habitually use all things to find the Word know this.

4. It will repay us to examine further the privacy of the bed and the time, to see if there is any hidden spiritual meaning which it will be to our advantage to reveal. If we take the bed to mean human weakness, and the darkness of night human ignorance, it follows logically that the Bride is seeking the Word, the power of God and the wisdom of God,[1434] to overcome these two ills: power to strengthen her weakness and wisdom to enlighten her ignorance. Nothing could be more fitting. But if any lingering doubt about this interpretation remains in the hearts of the simple, let them hear what the holy prophet says on this matter: "The Lord strengthens him on his bed of sickness; it is you who make his bed in his weakness."[1435] This is enough about the bed. Now as regards the night of ignorance, what could be clearer than what is said in another psalm: "They have not known, they have not understood, they walk in darkness."[1436] Does this not express perfectly the ignorance in which the whole human race was born? This is the ignorance, I think, which the blessed apostle admits he was born in, and gives thanks that he was rescued from, when he says, "He has snatched us from the power of darkness."[1437] Again,

[1434] 1 Cor 1:24.
[1435] Ps 40:4.
[1436] Ps 81:5.
[1437] Col 1:13.

he says to all the elect, "We are not children of the night or of darkness; walk as children of the light."[1438]

Bernard of Clairvaux died in 1153, without completing his sermon commentaries on the Song of Songs. The work was taken up by John, abbot of Ford, and then by Gilbert of Hoyland, abbot of Swineshead Abbey in England, who had perhaps been a monk at Clairvaux while Bernard was abbot.

[1438] 1 Thes 5:5; Eph 5:8.

On Conversion:
A Sermon to Clerics

**I. No one can be converted to the Lord unless
he is anticipated by the will of the Lord and unless
his voice cries out interiorly.**

1. To hear the word of God, I believe you have come.[1439] Nor
do I see any other reason for you to have flocked here so
eagerly. I entirely approve this desire and I congratulate you
on your zeal. Blessed are they who hear the Word of God,
but only if they observe it.[1440] Blessed are they who are mindful of his commandments, but only if they do them.[1441] For
he has the words of eternal life, and the hour is coming (if
only it were already here!) when the dead shall hear his
voice, and those who hear him shall live, for life is in his
will.[1442] And if you want to know, his will is our conversion.
Listen to him then:[1443] "Is it my will that the wicked shall
die," says the Lord, "and not instead that he should be converted and live?"[1444] From these words we realize that there
is no true life except in conversion and that there is no other
means of entering into life, as the Lord likewise says:
"Unless you are converted and become as little children, you
shall not enter the kingdom of heaven."[1445] It is quite right
that only little children should enter, for it is a little child
who leads them. For this, he was born and given to us.[1446] I

[1439]Acts 13:44, 19:10.
[1440]Lk 11:28.
[1441]Ps 103:18.
[1442]Jn 6:69, 5:25; Ps 30:5.

[1443]Mt 11:14.
[1444]Ez 18:23.
[1445]1 Tm 6:19; Mt 18:3.
[1446]Is 9:6.

seek then the voice which the dead are to hear,[1447] and by which, having once heard, they shall live. Perhaps the dead must have the good news preached to them as well.[1448] In the meanwhile, there occurs the short but pithy word spoken by the Lord's own mouth, as the prophet testified: "You have said"—obviously addressing the Lord his God—"be converted, sons of men."[1449] Nor is it at all out of place to view conversion as required of a son of man, for it is utterly necessary to sinners. The heavenly spirits are commanded rather to praise, as becomes the righteous, as the same prophet sings, "Praise your God, O Sion."[1450]

2. Moreover, the fact that he said, "you have said"[1451] should not, in my opinion, be passed over lightly or simply heard in passing. For who would dare to compare human discourse to what God is said to have spoken? Indeed, the word of God is living and active and his voice is powerful and majestic.[1452] For he spoke and they were created.[1453] He said "let there be light" and there was light.[1454] He said "be converted" and the children of men were converted.[1455] Clearly, then, the conversion of souls is the working of the divine, not the human, voice. Simon, the son of John, was called and appointed a fisher of men by the Lord, and yet even he toiled all night in vain and took nothing until, letting down his nets at the Lord's Word, he was able to enclose a great shoal.[1456] If only I too might at this Word let down the nets of the Word today and experience what has been written: "lo, he sends forth his voice, his mighty voice.[1457] If I lie,

[1447] Jn 5:25.
[1448] 1 Pt 4:6.
[1449] Is 1:20.
[1450] Ps 33:1; Ps 147:12.
[1451] Ps 90:3.
[1452] Heb 4:12; Ps 29:4.

[1453] Ps 148:5.
[1454] Gn 1:3.
[1455] Ps 90:3.
[1456] Jn 21:15; Mt 4:19; Lk 5:5–6.
[1457] Cf. *Vita prima* I. 13.61; Ps 68:33.

then clearly I shall be speaking from myself.[1458] And if I look after my own interests rather than those of Jesus Christ,[1459] then you may judge my word as coming from me and not from the Lord. What is more, even if we speak of God's justice and seek God's glory,[1460] it is from him alone that we must hope for results. We must ask him for it, so that our own voice may be in harmony with the voice of majesty. May I suggest then that you prick up the ears of your heart in order to hear this inner voice and that you make an effort to hear God speaking within rather than the man speaking without. For that is his voice, powerful and full of majesty, which shakes the wilderness,[1461] pierces all secret things and drives away the sluggishness of souls.

II. The voice of the Lord offers and presents itself to all men, proposing itself even to the unwilling soul.

3. Nor do we have much difficulty in hearing this voice; the difficulty is rather in stopping our ears from hearing it.[1462] For that voice offers itself, presents itself, and never ceases to knock at the door of each one of us.[1463] Indeed, it says, "For forty years I was close to this generation and said 'They are people who err in their heart.'"[1464] He is still close to us, he is still speaking and it is not by chance that someone hears him. He is still saying, "They are people who err in their heart"; wisdom is still crying aloud in the streets, "Turn back, transgressors, to your heart."[1465] For this is the Lord's first Word,[1466] and we notice that it is this Word which seems to have led the way for all those who convert to their hearts,[1467]

[1458] Jn 8:44.
[1459] Ph: 12:24.
[1460] Ps 58:1; Jn 8:50.
[1461] Cf. Ps 29:4, 8.

[1462] Is 33:15.
[1463] Rv 3:20.
[1464] Ps 95:10.
[1465] Pr 1:20–21; Is 46:8.

[1466] Hos 1:2.
[1467] Ps 85:8.

not only calling them back, but leading them back and laying the charge before their very face.[1468] For this voice is not only a mighty voice,[1469] but it is also a beam of light, both informing men of their transgressions and bringing to light things hidden in darkness.[1470] Nor is there any difference between this inward voice and this light, as the one same Son of God is both the Word of the Father and the brightness of his glory.[1471] Yet the substance of the soul, spiritual and simple in its nature, seems also devoid of any distinction in its senses, yet is whole—if we may speak of wholeness—both seeing and hearing. What other effect does that beam or that word have than to bring the soul to self knowledge? It opens the book of the conscience, passes in review the wretched sequence of life, unfolds the sad events of its history, enlightens the reason and, the memory having leafed is set, as it were, before its own eyes. What is more, these two [memory and reason] are not so much faculties of the soul as the soul itself, so that it is both observer and observed: it appears resolved against itself[1472] and is dragged by these heavy-handed officers before its own assizes to be judged by its own thoughts. Who can support this judgment without distress? "My soul is troubled within me,"[1473] says the Lord's prophet. Why be astonished then that you cannot stand before your own face without squirming, without feeling either distress or shame?

III. This enables the reason to read as in a book and to grasp the evil of its soul, and then to censure, condemn, and reprove.

4. Do not hope to hear from me what it is within your memory that your reason detects, censures, judges, and sentences.

[1468] Ps 50:21.
[1469] Ps 68:33.
[1470] Is 58:1; 1 Cor 4:5.
[1471] Heb 1:3.
[1472] Ps 50:21.
[1473] Ps 42:6.

Apply your hearing within, roll back the eyes of your heart, and you will learn by your own experience what is going on. For no one knows what is in a man, except the spirit of the man which is in him.[1474] If pride, envy, avarice, ambition, or any other like pest is hidden there, it will scarcely be able to escape this scrutiny.[1475] If it should be guilty of any fornication, theft,[1476] cruelty, any fraud or other fault whatever, the defendant will not remain hidden from this inner judge, nor can he be whitewashed in its presence. Even though all the itching of evil pleasure quickly passes and any charm of sensual satisfaction is short-lived, still it stamps on the memory certain bitter marks, it leaves filthy traces. Into that reservoir, as into a sewer, all these disgusting and dirty thoughts drizzle and run off. Weighty is the book wherein have been inscribed all these acts with the pen of truth.[1477] The stomach now endures bitterness,[1478] yet the wretched palate seemed to have been tickled for a fleeting instant by some frivolous sweetness. Wretched man! my stomach aches, my stomach aches![1479] How could the stomach of my memory not ache, when it is crammed with so much muck? Which of us, brothers, suddenly noticing that the outer garment he wears is stained with filthy spittings and soiled with all sorts of dirty stains, does not shudder from head to foot and, hastily tearing it off, throw it aside in disgust? Therefore, anyone who discovers that it is not his clothing, but his own inner self under his clothing, that is in such a state should ache all the more and be disturbed in mind because he is putting up with what makes him shudder. The contaminated soul cannot doff itself as easily as it doffs its garments.[1480] Who

[1474] 1 Cor 2:11.
[1475] Jb 2:8.
[1476] Mt 15:19.
[1477] Jb 19:23.

[1478] Rv 10:9–10.
[1479] Jer 4:19.
[1480] Sg 5:3.

among us, moreover, is so strong and so patient that if he should happen to see his flesh suddenly becoming white as if sick with leprosy—as Miriam the sister of Moses saw[1481]—could remain calm and give thanks to his Maker? For what is this flesh if not some sort of corruptible garment with which we are clothed? Or, what is this physical leprosy as the eyes of the elect see it, if not the rod of paternal reproof and a cleansing of the heart?[1482] There, there will be violent suffering and a very just cause for grief, when someone, awakening out of the sleep of lamentable passion,[1483] begins to perceive the inner leprosy which he worked so hard to contract. It is true that no one hates his own flesh; but how much less then shall a soul hate itself?[1484]

IV. If a person loves evil he proves that he hates not only his soul but even his flesh.

5. Perhaps one of you has been struck by this verse of the psalm: "The man who loves evil hates his soul."[1485] I would go on to say: he hates his flesh as well. Does a man not hate his soul when by his hard and impenitent heart he stores up wrath for himself on the day of wrath,[1486] trafficking today in hell's stocks? Moreover, it is not so much in the dispositions as in results that this hatred of body and soul is discovered.[1487] There is no doubt that a madman hates his body when he inflicts injury on himself in a frenzied delusion of mind. But is there any greater madness than that of the unrepentant heart and the obstinately sinful will? For now it is not the flesh which his hand attacks but the very mind

[1481]Nm 12:10.
[1482]Prv 29:15.
[1483]Jn 11:11.
[1484]Eph 5:29; Jn 12:25.

[1485]Ps 11:6.
[1486]Rom 2:5.
[1487]*non in affectu sed in effectu.*

which it tears and gnaws to pieces.[1488] If you have ever seen a man scratching at his hand and rubbing it until it bleeds, then you have a clear and distinct picture of a sinful soul.[1489] For craving gives way to suffering and mental itching yields to torment. And all the while he was scratching he was well aware that this would happen, but he pretended it would not. We tear our wretched souls to pieces the same way and make them sore with our own hands; only this is all the more serious in that our spiritual being is more precious and more difficult to heal. We act not so much out of a kind of obstinate enmity, as under a kind of numbness brought on by inner insensitivity. The mind[1490] sloshed out of itself does not feel the inward condemnation, for it is not at home,[1491] but probably in the belly, or still lower. Some minds dwell on stewpans, others on purses. The Lord says, "Where your treasure is, there will your heart be also."[1492] Is it any wonder that the soul[1493] should feel her own wounds so little when she has forgotten who she is and is inwardly estranged from herself, having taken her journey into a far country?[1494] Yet there will be a time when, coming to herself,[1495] she will realize how cruelly she has mutilated herself just to get a miserable piece of game. But she was not able to feel that as long as she was burning to lay hands on some vile prey of flies, like a spider spinning its web out of its own viscera.

[1488] Jb 13:14.
[1489] Rom 8:3.
[1490] *animus.*
[1491] Jn 11:12.

[1492] Mt 6:21.
[1493] *anima.*
[1494] Lk 15:13.
[1495] Lk 15:17.

THE PAIN OF BOTH BODY AND SOUL
WHICH WILL FOLLOW AFTER DEATH,
AND USELESS PENANCE.

6. She will come home to herself, of that there is no doubt, but after death has closed all those physical doors[1496] by which she used to go out after the figure of this world which passes away[1497] and wander about outside, busying herself with useless occupations. When that time comes she will be obliged to remain within herself, having no longer any means of going outside. But it will be a very sorry homecoming indeed; it will be eternal misery, for though she repents she will not be able to do penance. Where there is no body, there can be no activity.[1498] And, obviously, where there is no action, there can be no satisfaction either. So she will repent yet suffer, for penance is the balm of suffering. The person who has no hands can no longer lift up his heart to heaven with his hands.[1499] The person who does not come to himself before his physical death will be obliged to remain within himself for all eternity. What kind of self will that be? What a man has made for himself in this life, he will find when he leaves this life, except perhaps it may be still worse, certainly never better. This very body which he now lays aside he will take up again, not in order to do penance, but to suffer his penalty. The state of his body will be somehow in keeping with the state of his sin: just as his crime will be eternally punished and yet never purged, so also his body will be in constant torment without being consumed by the torments. Nothing is more fitting than that this vengeance should rage forever, for the guilt can never be effaced; nor shall the substance of the flesh vanish, lest someone even think that

[1496] Dn 13:17.
[1497] 1 Cor 7:31.
[1498] Mt 24:28.
[1499] Lam 3:41.

affliction of the flesh may come to an end.[1500] My brothers, anyone who dreads this, should be wary. Anyone who is careless, stumbles.

V. The worms of the conscience are to be discerned and destroyed in this life, not nursed along and nurtured for immortality.

7. But to get back to the Word where we started: really, it is best for us to return to our hearts,[1501] for this is where he who calls transgressors back with such anxious solicitude shows us his salvation.[1502] In the meantime it must not vex us to feel the worm devouring us within; we must not try to appease it out of delicacy of spirit and a dangerous irresolution, as though we hoped to cover up our present affliction. It is better to feel the worm now when we can still stifle it. Let it eat away now so it will decay, being gradually eaten up by its own overeating. Let it gnaw away at our corruption, and by its gnawing let it be itself consumed rather than nursed along to immortality. Scripture says: "Their worm shall not die, their fire shall not be quenched."[1503] Who can abide their gnawing?[1504] There is now many a consolation to relieve the torment of a guilty conscience. God is kind and does not let us be tempted beyond our strength;[1505] he will not let this worm harm us beyond repair. Especially at the beginning of a conversion, he anoints our wounds with the oil of mercy so that the acute nature of our sickness and the difficulty of the cure is perceived only to the extent that is expedient. On us seems to smile a sort of easiness, which

---

[1500] Eccl 12:12.
[1501] Is 46:8.
[1502] Ps 50:23.

[1503] Is 66:24.
[1504] Ps 147:17.
[1505] 1 Cor 10:13.

later disappears when the senses have been trained by practice to fight,[1506] so that one may overcome and come to learn that wisdom is more powerful than anything.[1507] Meanwhile, anyone who has heard the voice of the Lord saying, "Return, transgressors, to the heart,"[1508] and has discovered such foul things in his inmost chamber will set out like some assiduous detective to investigate them; he will examine each thing and search for the opening by which it filtered in. He will easily discover not just one but many holes. This will cause him no little sorrow, for he will realize that it is through his own windows that this death has entered.[1509] He realizes that the wantonness of his eyes has let many in, the itching of his ears, many,[1510] and the urge for gratifying touch and taste and smell yet many more. Because he is still carnal, he has great difficulty discerning the spiritual vices of which we spoke earlier.[1511] So it happens that though they are more serious, he is less conscious of them, perhaps altogether unconscious. He will be less afflicted by his pride and jealousy than by the memory of the more notorious and wicked deeds he has done.

VI. It is easily seen by some that the human will complies with the divine voice.

8. And listen, again the voice from the cloud says, "You have sinned, refrain." This is to say, "The drain is overflowing and is making the whole house stink intolerably. It is vain for you to attempt to empty it while the filth is still seeping in,[1512] vain to repent when you have not stopped sinning."

[1506]Heb 5:14.
[1507]Ws 10:12.
[1508]Is 46:8.
[1509]Jer 9:21.
[1510]2 Tm 4:3.
[1511]1 Cor 2:14.
[1512]Ps 127:2.

Now who can approve the fastings of those who fast only to quarrel and fight and strike out with disrespectful fist,[1513] those who hold to have their own will and gratifications?[1514] "It is not such a fast that I choose," says the Lord.[1515] Close the windows, lock the doors, block up the openings carefully and then, when fresh filth has ceased to flow, you can clean out the old.[1516] As long as a man is without experience in the spiritual combat, he thinks that what is asked of him is easy. He says, "Who can stop me from controlling my members?" So he prescribes fasting for his palate and proscribes drunkenness; he stops his ears from hearing about bloodshed,[1517] he turns away his eyes from looking at vanities,[1518] he withholds his hands from gain and instead holds them out to give alms,[1519] and he may even set them to work, forbidding them robbery, as it is written, "Let the thief no longer steal, but rather let him labor with his hands, that he may be able to give to those in need."[1520]

9. But while he is laying down laws and decrees in this way to his members, even while he is still issuing orders, they suddenly interrupt, screaming in a concerted onslaught, "May we know what this new teaching is?[1521] It is easy for you to give orders to suit your pleasure. But there is someone who is going to resist these new decrees and contest these new laws." "And who may that be?" he asks. And they say, "None other, of course, than the paralytic lying at home in terrible distress;[1522] that's the woman in whose service you first engaged us—in case you have forgotten—so that we might obey her desires."[1523] At these words the poor man has gone all pale and been struck dumb with confusion. His

[1513] Is 58:4.
[1514] Is 58:3.
[1515] Is 58:6.
[1516] 1 Cor 5:7.
[1517] Is 33:15.
[1518] Ps 119:37.
[1519] Ps 119:36.
[1520] Eph 4:28.
[1521] Acts 17:19.
[1522] Mt 8:6.
[1523] Rom 6:12.

spirit is vexed within him.[1524] Whereupon his members scuttle off to their wretched mistress to rouse her cruelly against the master and to clamor for more savage power. The palate complains of being invited to cheap fare and denied the pleasure of getting drunk. The eyes moan that they are condemned to weeping and forbidden all titillation. Provoked and violently enraged by these and other similar hostile critics, the will says, "Is this a dream or some tale you are spinning?"[1525] Then the tongue, finding the moment ripe for complaint, says "It is just as you have heard tell. I too have been ordered to restrain myself from storytelling and lies,[1526] and from now on I may say nothing but serious things and, worse yet, nothing but necessary things."

MAN'S WILL RESISTS THE DIVINE VOICE BY GLUTTONY, CURIOSITY, PRIDE, AND ALL THE BODILY SENSES.

10. Then the crazy old hag leaps up and, completely forgetting her ailments, storms out with her hair standing on end, her clothes torn, her breast bare; she picks at her sores, grinds her teeth, goes rigid, and infects even the air with her poisonous breath.[1527] Anyone still keeping his reason would be disconcerted at such insult and assault by the wretched will. "Is this all the faith you keep with your partner?" she says. "Is this the way you show compassion for someone who puts up with so much? Is this the way you devise for afflicting still more my grievous wounds?[1528] Maybe you intend to snatch away what you think is an excessive dowry; but if you take this away, what will be left? This is all you offered this feeble wretch, and you realize how all her services have been

[1524] Ps 143:4.
[1525] Gn 37:9.
[1526] 1 Tm 1:4.

[1527] Ps 35:16; Mk 9:17.
[1528] Ps 69:26.

rendered up till now. But now, even if you had been able to cut out the triple tumor of the terrible illness which lays me low, I cannot. I am passionate, inquisitive, ambitious; because of this triple festering sore, there is no soundness in me from the soles of my feet up to the top of my head![1529] And so the palate and the privy parts of this body have been handed over to passionate pleasure—I insist yet again because it seems I must. My roaming foot and roving eyes are enslaved to curiosity. My ear and tongue are the servants of vanity; the one causes the oil of the wicked to anoint my head,[1530] and the other leads me to heap praises on myself when others apparently forget to do so. I have great pleasure both in being praised by others and, when I conveniently can, in boasting in the presence of others. I am always anxious to be vaunted by my own mouth or by that of other people. Even you yourself are powerfully inclined to heap coals on this evil state of affairs. Even my hands, free to move about all over the place, are no longer set to a single occupation, but they busy themselves fiddling about with curiosity or with passionate pleasure. But even though these members have been appointed to such service, never have they succeeded in giving me satisfaction on even a single point. The eye is not satisfied with seeing, nor is the ear sated with hearing.[1531] Yet, I long for the whole body to become an eye for seeing,[1532] or all my members so many gullets for feasting. Are you going to rob me then of this small consolation which I beg you to give me?" With those words she retreats in fury and indignation, screaming, "I have you in my clutches and will keep hold of you for a long time to come."

[1529]Is 2:6.
[1530]Ps 141:5.
[1531]Eccl 1:8.
[1532]Cor 12:17.

THE REASONING POWER OF THE SOUL, HAVING BEEN SO LONG DISTRESSED, IS NOW DOWNCAST AT THE DIFFICULTY OF A TASK IT HAD THOUGHT EASY.

11. In the long run, however, this distress comes to enlighten the reason and makes it realize something of the difficulty of the undertaking which it had presumed would be an easy job. It sees the memory clogged with dirty things; it sees more and more bilge still flowing in; it sees itself incapable of closing the windows thrown wide open to death,[1533] and the will, though ailing, still in supreme command and spreading the suppuration of her festering wounds all over the place. Finally, the soul sees that it is itself contaminated and that the source of this contamination springs not from outside, but from its own body, and not from elsewhere but from itself. It is something in the soul: as the memory, which is tainted, as the very will which injects it. For, in fact, the soul itself is nothing but reason, memory, and will. Now, however, the reason, greatly reduced and, as it were, blind (for so far it has failed to see this state of affairs) is acutely sick; it has come to recognize its malady but finds no remedy; it discovers that the memory is both foul and fetid, and that the will is sick and festering with terrible sores.[1534] And so that his whole humanity should be taken, the body itself rebels: the members become like so many windows by which death enters into the soul and confusion springs up like weeds.[1535]

[1533] Jer 9:21.
[1534] 2 Mc 9:9.
[1535] Jer 9:21.

VII. The gentle breeze of consolation which comes from hearing of the blessedness of the promised kingdom of heaven.

12. Let the soul which is in this state harken to the divine voice, and to its own amazement and wonder it will hear it say, "Blessed are the poor in spirit, for theirs is the kingdom of heaven."[1536] Who is poorer in spirit than the man whose spirit finds no rest and who has nowhere to lay his head?[1537] This also is a counsel of devotion, that the man who is displeasing to himself is pleasing to God,[1538] and he who hates his own house, that is to say a house full of filth and wretchedness, is invited to the house of glory, a house not made with hands, eternal in the heavens.[1539] It is no wonder if he trembles with awe at the greatness of this honor, and finds it hard to believe what he has heard,[1540] if he starts in astonishment and says, "Is it possible for such wretchedness to make a man happy?" Whoever you are, if you are in this frame of mind, do not despair: it is mercy, not misery, that makes a man happy, but mercy's natural home is misery. Indeed it happens that misery becomes the source of man's happiness when humiliation turns into humility and necessity becomes a virtue. As it is written, "Rain in abundance, O God, you shed abroad; you restored your heritage as it languished."[1541] Sickness has real utility when it leads us to the doctor's hands, and he whom God restores to health gains by having been ill.

[1536] Mt 5:3.
[1537] Lk 11:24; Mt 8:20.
[1538] 1 Cor 7:32.
[1539] 2 Cor 5:1.
[1540] Rom 10:16.
[1541] Ps 68:9

THE PERSON WHO STILL HAS SIN RULING
HIS FLESH CANNOT HOPE FOR THIS KINGDOM
AND IS OBLIGED TO THINK ABOUT WHAT FOLLOWS:
BLESSED ARE THE MEEK, AND SO ON.

But since there is no way to the kingdom of God without the first fruits of the kingdom, and since the man who does not yet rule his own members cannot hope for the heavenly kingdom, the voice goes on to say, "Blessed are the meek, for they shall inherit the earth."[1542] Put more clearly, this means, "Tame the savage movements of your will and take pains to tame this cruel beast. You are all tied up; endeavor to untie what you cannot break outright. [Your will] is your Eve. Never will you be able to do her violence or overcome her."

VIII. The hungering gullet and the hankering caprice and their end; the vanity of curiosity and the love of money and their outcome.

13. Then, when the man hears these words, he breathes more easily and, thinking that his task will not be so hard, comes forward, though not without some shame, and sets about charming this fiery viper. He rebukes his fleshly lures and reproves the consolations of this flighty world as being trifling and unworthy of him, and also the shallowest and most fleeting of all his lovers.

"I condemn you," he says, "out of the very mouth of your worthless and wicked servant.[1543] You cannot deny that in spite of all his obsequious services he has never been able to give you the slightest satisfaction." The gullet whose pleasures he rates so highly nowadays is scarcely wider than

[1542]Mt 5:5.
[1543]Lk 19:22; Mt 25:30.

two fingers, and yet you go to no end of pains to procure the slightest delight for such a tiny member, and in return it only causes discomfort. The hips and shoulders broaden grotesquely, the belly swells up as though pregnant, not alas with healthy fruit but burdened with corruption, and this engenders all sorts of maladies because the skeleton cannot support the weight of the flesh. It is the same with the enticing whirlpool of lust: it calls for great expenditures in energy and money; it endangers reputation, honor, and even life itself, and its only effect is to fan with the fumes of burning brimstone our already flaming senses. And, like the honeybee, it leaves its sting firmly planted in the heart in which it once distilled its fey sweetness.[1544] Lust's appetites are anxiety and silliness; its actions an abomination and disgrace; its outcome remorse and shame.

14. I ask you, then, what good do all these frivolous images do the body, what use are they to the soul? Then again, you'll find that a curious man is an empty man. All curiosity brings is frivolous, vain, fleeting consolation. I cannot think what harsher curse I could call down upon a man than that he should always get what he asks for when he tears away from sweet repose out of a curiosity which revels in restlessness. The proof that these pleasures are unsatisfying lies in the very transitoriness which is so diverting. As for the vanity of vanities,[1545] it is nothing, as its very name demonstrates. It is vain labor indeed,[1546] to search after vanity. As a wise man once said, "O praise! O praise among thousands of mortals thou art nought but vain flatulence in the ear!"[1547] You cannot imagine how much unhappiness this brings forth; it is

[1544]Cf. Boethius, *Consol. Phil.* III, metr. 7 (CCh 94:47).
[1545]Eccl 1:2.
[1546]Ps 127:1.
[1547]Boethius, *Consol Phil.* III, pr. 6. Cf. Euripides, *Andromache* 319–20.

not so much blissful vanity as vain bliss. From it comes hardness of heart,[1548] as we find it written, "O my people, they who call you blessed mislead you."[1549] From it comes the stubborn fury of enmity, the anxious laborings of suspicion, the cruel torment of spite, the torture—more pitiable than pitiful—of burning jealousy. So an insatiable love of riches, far from refreshing the soul by its exercise, racks it with desire. Acquisition is fraught with toil, possession with terror, and loss with remorse. Finally, "When goods increase, they increase who devour them."[1550] The exercise of wealth goes to others; all that the rich man reaps from his possessions is excise and anxiety. And for so little, or rather, not even for so little but for nothing at all, he despises the glory which eye has not seen, nor ear heard, nor the heart of man conceived, which God has prepared for those who love him.[1551] This seems not so much foolishness as faithlessness.

THE BASENESS OF SERVITUDE TO VICE, THE UNCERTAINTY OF THE HOUR OF DEATH, AND THE MISFORTUNE OF AMASSED FORTUNES.

15. Surely it is not extraordinary that the world, set in wickedness,[1552] deludes with vain promises souls forgetful of their own condition and noble birth, unashamed at being reduced to slopping swine and sharing their cravings but without being satisfied on their wretched fodder.[1553] How did such faintheartedness and such miserable abjection come to be in so excellent a creature as man? He is capable of eternal blessedness and the glory of our great God.[1554] By

[1548]Mk 3:5.
[1549]Is 3:12.
[1550]Eccl 5:10.
[1551]1 Cor 2:9.

[1552]1 Jn 5:19.
[1553]Lk 15:15–16.
[1554]Ti 2:13.

his breath he was created, with his likeness he has been stamped, and by his blood he has been redeemed: he has been endowed with faith, adopted in the Spirit; how is it then that he does not blush to live in abject servitude beneath this corruption of bodily senses? It is not surprising that, having left such a spouse, this creature pursues such lovers without being able to overtake them.[1555] It is only right that he should hunger for husks without getting any,[1556] for he chose to feed swine rather than feast at his father's banquet.[1557] It is crazy labor indeed to feed a barren and fruitless lover while refusing to support a widow, to neglect the care of the heart and yet care for the flesh, gratifying its desires,[1558] to fatten and feed a rotten carcass,[1559] which one knows full well will soon become food for worms. Who does not know that to serve mammon,[1560] to worship avarice, which is to serve idols,[1561] or to pursue the search for vanity is the sign of a degenerate soul?

TEMPORAL WORKS ARE AS SEEDS OF AN ETERNAL REWARD.

16. After all, there are certain great and respectable things which the world seems to bestow for a time upon her lovers. But we all know how fickle they are. That they are short-lived is certain; uncertain is the term of their short life. They desert the living; yet never, not even once, do they follow the dying.[1562] And yet, among all human happenings, what is more certain than death, what more uncertain than the hour of death? It has no pity for poverty, no reverence for riches.

[1555]Hos 2:7.
[1556]Lk 15:16.
[1557]Cf. Lk 15:15–24.
[1558]Rom 13:14.
[1559]Is 14:19.
[1560]Mt 6:24.
[1561]Eph 5:5.
[1562]Cicero, *De sef nectute* 20.74.

It spares neither birth nor breeding nor even age; the only difference is that the old find it on the doorstep and the young fall into its snares. Unhappy is the man, who, trusting in the slippery ways and darkness of this life, takes up some perishable work, never realizing that he is a mist appearing for a little time, a vanity of vanities.[1563] Have you finally obtained, braggard, the dignity you have so long coveted? Hang on to what you have. Is your safe filled with riches, moneybags? Take care or you will lose it. Has your field produced copious fruit? Pull down your barns to build larger ones.[1564] Turn everything upside down; say to your soul, "You have ample goods laid up for many years." But you will hear someone say, "Fool! This night your soul is required of you; and the things you have prepared, whose will they be?"[1565]

17. How I wish it were only your savings which will perish and not the saver, who will perish worse. It would be far more tolerable to sweat in labors to be lost than to be snatched away. But the wages of sin is now death,[1566] and he who sows in his own flesh will from his own flesh reap corruption.[1567] Our works do not pass away, as they seem to do; rather they are scattered like temporal seeds of eternity. The fool will be astonished when he sees a great harvest shooting up from a little seed—good or bad harvest according to the differing quality of the sowing. A man who thinks about all this will never consider any sin little, for he does not value so much the sowing as the future harvest. Humans sow without even knowing it. They sow when they conceal the mystery of lawlessness, or hide the counsel of vanity, going about the business of darkness in the dark.[1568]

[1563] Jas 4:15; Qoh 1:2.
[1564] Lk 12:16.
[1565] Lk 12:19–20.

[1566] Rom 6:23.
[1567] Gal 6:8.
[1568] 2 Thes 2:7; Ps 26:4, 91:6.

IX. It is impossible for the sinner to lie hidden.

18. A man may say to himself, "The walls hide me, who sees me?"[1569] Maybe no one sees you, but even so something does. The wicked angel sees you, the good angel sees you, and he who is greater than either the wicked or the good angels, God sees you, your accuser sees you, a host of witnesses sees you, the Judge himself sees you, he before whose judgment seat you must stand[1570] and under whose eye it is just as foolish to sin as it is fearful to fall into the hands of the living God.[1571] Do not think yourself safe: there is many a lurking snare which you cannot escape. Yes, I tell you, there are lurking snares from which you cannot escape and which yet escape you. Surely, he who plants the ear hears all, and he who forms the eye sees all.[1572] A mere heap of stones cannot obstruct the rays of the Sun who made them; nor can the walls of the body block the gaze of truth. It is as though they did not exist before his eyes, which are sharper than a two-edged sword. Not only do they pierce, they also perceive the ways of our thoughts and the marrow of our intentions.[1573] Moreover, were it not true that He sees the deepest abyss of the human heart and all that lies in it and round about it, the person unaware of anything against himself would not have been in such fear of the Lord's judgment. "It is a very small thing that I should be judged by you or by any human court," it says. "I do not even judge myself. I am not aware of anything against myself, but I am not thereby acquitted. It is the Lord who judges me."[1574]

19. If you flatter yourself that you can frustrate human judgment by throwing up a wall or by making excuses, be

[1569] Sir 23:25.
[1570] Rom 14:10.
[1571] Heb 10:31.

[1572] Ps 94:9.
[1573] Heb 4:12.
[1574] 1 Cor 4:3–4.

sure that you cannot cover up the real crimes you commit or hide them from him who is accustomed falsely to accuse you. If you are so afraid of your neighbor's opinion—who probably cares not a hoot about yours—how much less ought you to despise those witnesses who have a much greater hatred of evil and horror of corruption. If you do not fear God, and dread only the gaze of men,[1575] remember that Christ who became man cannot ignore the deeds of men; then you will never dare to do in his sight what you would hesitate to do in mine. If the Lord were looking on, you would be horrified even to think of doing deeds you would never carry out in the presence of a fellow servant. Moreover, if you fear the eye of the flesh more than the sword which is able to devour the flesh,[1576] what you fear most will come upon you and what you dread will befall you.[1577] Nothing is covered up that will not be revealed, or hidden that will not be known.[1578] The works of darkness, once come to light,[1579] will be confounded by the light; not only the secret abominations of lewdness, but also the wicked negotiations of those who traffic in sacraments, the deceitful whisperings of those who plot wrongdoing, and the judgments of those who subvert everything, will he who knows everything make known to everyone on the day when the searcher of hearts and reins begins to search Jerusalem with lamps.[1580]

[1575]Lk 18:4.
[1576]Dt 32:42.
[1577]Jb 3:25.

[1578]Lk 12:2.
[1579]Rom 13:12; Jn 3:20.
[1580]Jn 3:20; Ps 7:9; Zep 1:2.

X. The fate of evildoers and whether
those who neglect to do good will perish.

20. What are those who have committed crimes going to do, or rather what will they endure, when those who have not done good works shall hear it said to them, "Depart into the eternal fire?"[1581] How can a man who failed to gird up his loins to give up doing evil,[1582] or failed to hold his lamp to do good, be admitted to the marriage feast when neither the integrity of virginity, nor the brightness of the lamp can make up for a shortage of oil?[1583] Surely they must expect untold anguish, they who, not content merely to do harm during their life, perpetrated heinous crimes,[1584] if those who received good things here must there be in such anguish that in the midst of the flames they shall not have even the tiniest drop of water to cool their parched tongues.[1585] Let us steer clear of evil works then; let us not, confident of being in the net,[1586] willingly be derelict within the Church. We know that not everything gathered in by the net will be put in the fishermen's baskets, for when they come ashore they sort the good into baskets and throw away the bad.[1587] Nor must we be content merely to gird our loins;[1588] we must also light our lamps and do good purposefully,[1589] thinking over the fact that every tree which does not bear good fruit—not just the one which bears bad fruit—will be cut down and thrown into the fire, the "eternal fire prepared for the devil and his angels."[1590]

21. Again, let us so turn away from evil and do good as to seek peace rather than pursue glory.[1591] That belongs to

[1581] Mt 25:41.
[1582] Lk 12:35.
[1583] Cf. Mt 25:1–13.
[1584] Eccl 8:11.
[1585] Lk 16:24–25.
[1586] Mt 13:47.

[1587] Mt 13:48.
[1588] Lk 12:35.
[1589] Mt 5:15; Ga 1 6:10.
[1590] Mt 3:10, 25:41.
[1591] Ps 34:14.

God, and he will not give it to another. He has said, "My
glory I give to no other."[1592] And a man after God's heart has
said, "Not to us, O Lord, not to us, but to your name give
glory."[1593] We remember too what Scripture says: "Even if
you offer rightly but do not rightly divide the offering, you
sin."[1594] Ours is the right division, brothers; let no one depre-
ciate it. However, if anyone should find it not to his liking,
let him know that it is not our invention but comes from the
angels. Did not the angels first sing, "Glory to God in the
highest, and peace on earth to men of goodwill"?[1595] Let us
therefore keep oil in our lamps, lest—God forbid—knocking in vain at the already closed door of the marriage feast,
we receive from the bridegroom the bitter answer "I do not
know you."[1596] Death has taken up its post close to wickedness, barrenness, and vainglory; it follows on the heels of
pleasure. So we need fortitude against the temptings of sin
in order to resist the roaring lion, firm in the faith and manfully fending off his fiery darts with this shield.[1597] We need
justice to do good works.[1598] We need prudence lest we be
rejected with the foolish virgins. Finally, we need temperance lest we indulge in pleasures and someday hear said to
us what that wretched fellow heard when his feastings and
fine clothes had come to an end and he begged for mercy:
"Son, remember that you in your lifetime received good
things, and Lazarus in like manner bad things, but now he is
comforted here, and you are in anguish."[1599] Surely God is
terrible in his determinations upon the sons of men![1600] But
if he is terrible, he is also found merciful, for he does not
hide from us the plan of the judgment to come. "The soul

[1592]Is 42:8.
[1593]Ps 115:1.
[1594]Gn 4:7.

[1595]Lk 2:14.
[1596]Mt 25:4, 12.
[1597]1 Pt 5:8–9.

[1598]Gal 6:10.
[1599]Lk 16:25.
[1600]Ps 66:5.

that sins shall die";[1601] the branch that bears no fruit shall be cut away;[1602] the virgin who has no oil shall be excluded from the marriage feast,[1603] and he who receives good things in this life shall suffer anguish in the life to come.[1604] If these four should happen to be found in one and the same person, clearly he has reached the depths of despair.

XI. The spirit is corrected by the fear of God and the flesh resists doing good.

22. The reason suggests inwardly to the will all these and similar things, more insistently as it is perfectly instructed by the light of the spirit. Happy indeed in the person whose will gives way and follows reason's advice, so that, conceiving in fear she may bear heavenly promise and give birth to the spirit of salvation. But it may happen that the will is rebellious and recalcitrant. After all these warnings she is not only impatient in the face of these threats but, worse still, callous. And after basking in blandishments, she is still sour. Far from being moved by the suggestions made by reason, she may be stirred up to even greater fury and retort, "How long am I to bear with you?[1605] Your words find no place in me.[1606] I know you are shrewd, but your shrewdness finds no place in me." She may even summon each of her members and order them to be more obsequious than usual in obeying her lusts and in serving her villainy. Daily experience teaches us that those who are bent upon conversion find themselves goaded more sharply by the lust of the flesh,[1607]

[1601] Ez 18:20.
[1602] Jn 15:2.
[1603] Mt 25:12.
[1604] Lk 16:25.

[1605] Mt 17:16.
[1606] Jn 8:37.
[1607] 1 Jn 2:16.

and those who have come out of Egypt, determined to flee from Pharaoh, are driven to work harder at making mortar and brick.[1608]

WHILE WE STRUGGLE WE WEEP; AFTER THE
STRUGGLE WE HAVE COMFORT,
FOR BLESSED ARE THEY WHO WEEP . . .

23. Would to God, however, that the man who has turned away from evil in this manner might also be on his guard against that terrible depth of which we read, "The wicked man, when he has come into the depth of sin, sneers."[1609] He can, of course, be cured, but only by the most drastic remedy, and he will easily run risks unless he takes great pains to follow the doctor's instructions and do very carefully what he says. The temptation is violent, near to hopelessness,[1610] unless he pulls himself together and takes pity on his soul, which he sees to be in so pitiful and pitiable a state that he turns his natural affection [to God] and listens to his voice say:[1611] "Blessed are those who mourn for they shall be comforted."[1612] He must mourn greatly for the time of mourning has arrived and to swallow down an ever-flowing stream of tears only these suffice. He must mourn, but with deeply felt piety and ensuing comfort. Let him consider that within himself he will find no rest for himself,[1613] because he is full of misery and desolation. Let him consider that there is no good in his flesh[1614] and that the present evil age[1615] contains nothing but vanity and affliction of spirit.[1616] Let him

---

[1608] Ex 2:15, 1:14.
[1609] Prv 18:3.
[1610] Heb 6:8.
[1611] Rv 10:4.
[1612] Mt 5:5.

[1613] Lk 11:24.
[1614] Ps 38:3.
[1615] Gal 1:4.
[1616] Eccl 1:14.

consider, I repeat, that he will find no comfort—not within nor under nor around himself, until he at last learns to seek it from above and to hope that it will come down from above.[1617] Meanwhile let him mourn and lament his sorrow, let his eyes well with tears and his eyelids find no slumber.[1618] Tears will wash the darkness from his eyes,[1619] his sight will become keen so he will be able to turn his gaze toward the brightness of glistering light.[1620]

XII. After mourning and comfort,
the kindling desire for heavenly contemplation.

24. All this will enable him to peer through the keyhole,[1621] to look through the lattices and in sweet regard to follow the trail of that guiding ray, seeking light by the light, like some eager imitator of the wise men.[1622] He shall then discover the place of the wonderful tabernacle, where man shall eat the bread of angels;[1623] he shall discover the paradise of pleasure planted by the Lord;[1624] he shall discover a flowering and thoroughly lovely garden; he shall discover a place of refreshment and he shall exclaim: "Oh! if only this wretched will of mine would heed my voice, that she might come here and visit this place.[1625] Here surely she would find great rest, and she would be less troublesome to me, being herself less troubled." He did not lie who said: "Take my yoke upon you, and you will find rest for your souls."[1626] Buoyed up by trust in this promise, let him speak more soothingly to his angered will and, putting on a smile, let him approach her in a spirit

[1617]Col 3:1.
[1618]Jb 10:20; Ps 119:136; Prv 6:4.
[1619]Jb 16:17.
[1620]Acts 22:11.
[1621]Sg 5:4.
[1622]Sg 2:9; Mt 2:1ff.
[1623]Ps 42:4, 78:25.
[1624]Gn 2:8.
[1625]Jn 10:17; Gn 28:17.
[1626]Mt 11:29.

of gentleness, and say: "Turn away your indignation."[1627] I will do you no harm; I could not. This body is yours, I myself am yours; have no fear, there is nothing to be afraid of." He must not be astonished if she should retort even more bitterly, and say "much thinking is driving you mad."[1628] Let him for now endure all this calmly, carefully dissimulating what he intends to do and then, while they are chatting, let him seize a suitable opportunity to put in another word and say: "Today I have found a very beautiful garden, a really lovely place. It would be good for us to be there;[1629] it is not good for you to lie on this sickbed, tossing about on this mattress in pain and eating your heart out in grief in your room."[1630] The Lord is near to those who seek him, near the soul that hopes in him.[1631] He is near you who call upon him and he lends efficacy to your words. The will's desire shall be stirred not only to see the place,[1632] but even to go in a little way. And she will long to make her home there.[1633]

XIII. In this contemplation lies rest, and in savoring him lie sweetness and instruction.

25. You must not suppose this paradise of inner pleasure is some material place:[1634] you enter this garden not on foot, but by deeply felt affections. You will be enchanted not by a copse of earthly trees, but by gracious and seemly beds of spiritual virtues.[1635] A garden enclosed, where the sealed fountain flows out into four streams,[1636] and from this single vein of wisdom flows fourfold virtue. There, too, the most

---

[1627] 1 Cor 4:21; Gn 27:45.
[1628] Acts 26:24.
[1629] Mt 17:4.
[1630] Ps 4:3, 5.
[1631] Lam 3:25.

[1632] Mt 28:6.
[1633] Jn 14:23.
[1634] Gn 2:8.
[1635] Ps 147:1.
[1636] Is 17:10; Gn 2:10.

splendid lilies bloom, and as these flowers appear, the voice of the turtledove is also heard.[1637] There the bride's nard breathes forth its utterly fragrant perfume and other aromatic oils flow when the south wind blows, and the north wind hies away.[1638] In the midst of the garden is the tree of life,[1639] the apple tree mentioned in the Song, more precious than all the trees of the woods, whose shadow refreshed the bride and whose fruit was sweet to her taste.[1640] There the radiance of continence and the beholding of unblemished truth, enlighten the eyes of the heart;[1641] and the sweet voice of the inner comforter gives joy and gladness to the hearing as well.[1642] There the nostrils inhale the exquisite scent of hope, of a rich field which the Lord has blessed.[1643] There eagerly we have a foretaste of the incomparable delights of charity, and, once all the thorns and briars which earlier pricked the soul have been burned,[1644] the spirit is pervaded with the balm of mercy and rests happily in good conscience.[1645] But these are not yet the rewards of eternal life, but only the wages paid for military service;[1646] they have nothing to do with the future promise made to the Church, but concern rather her present due. This is the hundred-fold[1647] tendered already in this world to those who scorn the world. Do not hope to hear me sing the praises of all that. That is revealed through the Spirit alone:[1648] you will consult books to no avail; you must try to experience it instead. That is wisdom, and man does not know its price. It is drawn from things hidden, and this delight is not to be found in the land of those who live delightfully.[1649] Yes, it is the Lord's own

[1637] Sg 2:12.
[1638] Sg 1:11, 2, 4:16.
[1639] Gn 2:9.
[1640] Sg 2:3.
[1641] Eph 1:18.
[1642] Sg 2:14; Ps 50:10.
[1643] Gn 27:29.
[1644] Is 10:17.
[1645] Acts 23:1.
[1646] 1 Cor 9:7.
[1647] Mt 19:29.
[1648] 1 Cor 2:10.
[1649] Jb 28:12–13.

delight and unless you taste it, you shall not see it. Has it not been said: "Taste and see that the Lord is delightful"?[1650] This is hidden manna, it is the new name which no one knows except him who receives it.[1651] Not learning but anointing teaches it;[1652] not science but conscience grasps it. He is holy, they are pearls,[1653] and he will not do what he forbade us to do when he began to do and teach.[1654] No longer does he treat like dogs or swine those who have renounced their crimes and evil deeds. He even consoles them with the words of the apostle: "And such were some of you. But you were washed, you have been made holy."[1655] Take care that the dog does not turn back to its own vomit, or the scrubbed sow wallow again in the mire.[1656]

XIV. Those who have had this taste know they are refreshed, for blessed are those who hunger and thirst for righteousness. . . .

26. At the gate of paradise a voice is heard[1657] whispering an utterly sacred and secret plan which is hidden from the wise and prudent and revealed to little ones.[1658] The sound of this voice reason now not only grasps, but happily transmits to the will. Blessed are those who hunger and thirst for righteousness, for they shall be satisfied.[1659] Deep indeed is this plan and unfathomable the mystery. This word is sure and worthy of full acceptance.[1660] It came to us from heaven, from the royal throne.[1661] A great famine has struck the earth, and not only have we all begun to be in want,[1662] but we have

[1650] Ps 34:8.
[1651] Rv 2:17.
[1652] 1 Jn 2:27.
[1653] Mt 7:6.
[1654] Acts 1:1.
[1655] 1 Cor 6:11.
[1656] 2 Pt 2:22.
[1657] Gn 3:24; Sg 2:12.
[1658] Mt 11:25.
[1659] Mt 5:6.
[1660] 1 Tm 1:15.
[1661] Ws 18:15.
[1662] Lk 15:14.

come to extreme destitution. We have even been compared to senseless beasts and have become like them.[1663] We even hunger greedily after the swine's husks.[1664] Anyone who loves money is dissatisfied; anyone who loves luxury is dissatisfied; anyone who loves glory is dissatisfied; in short, anyone who loves this world is always dissatisfied. I have myself known men sated with this world and sick at the very thought of it. I have known men sated with money, sated with honors, sated with the pleasures and curiosities of this world, sated not just a little, but to the point of repugnance. Yet, one can have satisfaction only through the grace of God. Satisfaction is born not of repletion, but of scorn. So, foolish sons of Adam, when you devour the husks of swine, you are feeding not your famished souls, but their very famine. Yes, this fodder fosters your starvation, this unnatural food does no more than sustain famine. And to put it more clearly, let me give just one example taken from among the many things which human vanity covets: the human body will be sated with air before the heart of man is sated with gold. The miser need not take offense. This is true for the ambitious man, the self-indulgent man, and the vicious man. If any of you does not perhaps believe me, let him believe experience, either his own or that of many others.

27. Is there someone among you, brothers, who desires to be satisfied and would like this desire to be fulfilled? Then let him begin to be hungry for righteousness,[1665] and he cannot fail to be satisfied. Let him yearn for those loaves which abound in his father's house, and he will immediately find he is disgusted with the husks of swine. Let him endeavor, however little, to experience the taste of righteousness that

[1663] Ps 49:12.
[1664] Lk 15:16.
[1665] Lk 15:16.

he may desire it more and thus merit more; as it has been written: "He who eats me will hunger for more and he who drinks me will thirst for more."[1666] This desire is more akin to the spirit, and because it is natural to it, the heart is more eagerly preoccupied with this and manfully shoves out all other desires. In this way a strong man fully armed is overcome by one stronger than he;[1667] in this way one nail is driven out by another.[1668] "Blessed are they who hunger and thirst for righteousness." Then, "for they will be satisfied."[1669] Not yet by that one thing by which man is never sated, the one thing by which he lives, but by everything else, all those things for which he previously longed insatiably, so that thereafter the will ceases delivering up the body to obey its former passions,[1670] and delivers it over to reason, urging it to serve righteousness for holiness's sake[1671] with no less zeal than it formerly showed in serving evil for iniquity's.

XV. Once our sins have been punished and forgiven, they no longer harm us if they are not repeated, but they work together for our good.

28. Once the will has been turned and the body subdued to service,[1672] as if the fountain were dry and the breach filled up, a third and very serious thing remains still to be done: the memory must be purified and the bilgewater drawn off. But how am I going to cut my life out of my memory? The dark ink has drenched my cheap, flimsy parchment: by

---

[1666] Sir 24:29.
[1667] Lk 11:21–22.
[1668] Cf. Cicero, *Tusculan Disputations* 4:35:75; Aristotle, *Politics* 1314â5.

[1669] Mt 5:6.
[1670] Rom 6:12.
[1671] Rom 6:19.
[1672] 1 Cor 9:27.

what technique can I blot it out? It has not only stained the surface, it has soaked into the whole thing. It is useless for me to attempt to rub it out: the skin will be torn before the wretched characters have been effaced. Forgetfulness might perhaps efface the memory if, for example, I were touched in the head and did not remember what I had done. But to leave my memory intact and yet wash away its blotches, what penknife can I use? Only that living and effective word sharper than a two-edged sword:[1673] "Your sins are forgiven you."[1674] Let the Pharisee mutter and say: "Who can forgive sins but God alone?"[1675] To me it is God himself who speaks, and no other can be compared to him. He it was who devised the whole way of discipline and gave it to Jacob his servant and to Israel whom he loved, and afterward appeared on earth and lived among men.[1676] His forbearance wipes away sin, not by cutting it out of the memory, but by leaving in the memory what was there causing discoloration, and blanching it thoroughly. We then remember many sins, which we know to have been committed either by ourselves or by others, but only our own stain us; those of others do us no harm. How is this? Surely it is because we blush only for our own sins, and it is only for these that we fear reproach. Take away damnation, take away fear, take away confusion; full remission takes all of these away, and our sins no longer harm us, but even work together for our good,[1677] enabling us to offer devout thanks to him who has remitted them.

[1673]Heb 4:12.
[1674]Mk 2:5.
[1675]Mk 2:7.

[1676]Bar 3:36–38.
[1677]Rom 8:28.

XVI. The mercy which has been promised to those who repent and are merciful, as has been said: blessed are the merciful . . .

29. Anyone who asks for pardon is fittingly answered with these words: "Blessed are the merciful, for they shall obtain mercy."[1678] If you want God to be merciful to you, then, you must yourself be merciful toward your soul. Flood your bed every night with your tears, remember to drench your couch with your weeping.[1679] If you have compassion on yourself, if you struggle on in groanings of penance—for this is mercy's first step—then you will arrive at mercy. And if you are perhaps a great and frequent sinner and seek great mercy and frequent forgiveness,[1680] you must also work at increasing your mercy. You are reconciled to yourself whereas you had become a burden to yourself,[1681] because you had set yourself up against God. Once peace has been restored this way in your own house, the first thing to do is to extend it to your neighbors so that God may come at last to kiss you with the very kiss of his mouth.[1682] In this way being reconciled to God, as it has been written, you may have peace.[1683] Forgive those who have sinned against you, and you will be forgiven your sins when you pray to the Father with an easy conscience and say: Forgive us our trespasses, as we forgive those who trespass against us.[1684] If you have defrauded someone, restore the exact amount: what is left over you must distribute to the poor,[1685] and because you have been merciful you will obtain mercy. "Though your sins are like scarlet, they shall be white as snow; though they

---

[1678]Mt 5:7.
[1679]Ps 6:6.
[1680]Ps 51:1.
[1681]Jb 7:20.

[1682]Sg 1:1.
[1683]Rom 5:10, 1.
[1684]Mt 6:12.
[1685]Lk 19:8, 18:22.

are red like crimson, they shall become like wool."[1686] Give alms so you are not put to shame by all the chicaneries by which you have gone astray and for which you are now ashamed.[1687] If you are not able to do this from your earthly substance,[1688] do it out of goodwill, and everything will be wiped clean.[1689] Not only is the reason enlightened and the will straightened, but the memory too is cleansed so that you may now call upon the Lord and hear his voice say:

XVII. The heart must be purified in order to see God, for blessed are the pure in heart . . .

30. "Blessed are the pure in heart, for they shall see God."[1690] A great promise, my brothers, and one to be responded to with our whole desire.[1691] This vision is also our assurance, as John the apostle said: "We are now God's children. It does not yet appear what we shall be, but we know that when he appears we shall be like him, for we shall see him as he is."[1692] This vision is eternal life,[1693] as Truth himself said in the Gospel: "This is life eternal, to know you the one true God, and Jesus Christ whom you have sent."[1694] It is a hateful blotch which deprives us of this vision, and a damnable negligence which makes us meanwhile neglect to cleanse our eye. Just as our bodily sight is blurred by some inner fluid or some outer speck of dust, so spiritual insight is impeded either by the lust of our own flesh or by worldly curiosity and ambition. This we learn as much from our own experience as from Holy Scripture, where we find it written: "A perishable body weighs down the soul, and this earthly tent burdens the

---

[1686]Is 1:18.
[1687]Zep 3:11; Rom 6:21.
[1688]Tb 4:7.
[1689]Lk 11:41.
[1690]Mt 5:8.
[1691]*affectanda*.
[1692]1 Jn 3:2.
[1693]Jn 12:50.
[1694]Jn 17:3.

thoughtful mind."[1695] In both instances, however, it is sin that dims and blurs the eye, and that alone screens the light from the eye, and God from man. Yet while we are in this body, we wander apart from the Lord,[1696] and the fault lies not in our body itself, but in the fact that our flesh is still a body of death, or rather a sinful body, in which there is no good, but only the law of sin.[1697] It sometimes happens too that the physical eye seems to remain dim[1698] for a little while even after the speck has been taken out or blown away. And it is the same with the inner eye, as the man who walks in the Spirit[1699] has often experienced. Even when you have taken out shrapnel, a wound does not immediately begin to heal, but you must then first apply fomentations and nurse it. Let no one imagine he is cleaned up right away, once he has emptied out the bilgewater. Washing with water is not sufficient; you must also be purified and refined with fire,[1700] so you may say: "We have gone through fire and water; and you have brought us forth into a place of refreshment."[1701] "Blessed are the pure in heart, then, for they shall see God."[1702] Now we see in a mirror dimly, but in the future we shall see face-to-face,[1703] once our face shall have been cleansed of all smut and he shall present it to himself resplendent, without spot or wrinkle.[1704]

XVIII. The pacified, the pacifying, and the peacemaker: blessed are the peacemakers . . .

31. This leads us immediately to add: "Blessed are the peacemakers, for they shall be called sons of God."[1705] It is a

[1695] Ws 9:15.
[1696] 2 Cor 5:6.
[1697] Rom 7:24, 6:6, 7:23.
[1698] Gn 27:1.
[1699] Gal 5:16.
[1700] Ps 12:6.
[1701] Ps 66:12.
[1702] Mt 5:8.
[1703] 1 Cor 13:12.
[1704] Eph 5:27.
[1705] Mt 5:9.

pacified man who repays good for good, as far as in him lies, and wishes harm to no one. Someone else may be patient and repay no one evil for evil,[1706] being even able to bear with the man who hurts him. There is also the peacemaker: he is always ready to repay good for evil and to help the man who hurts him. The first is one of those little ones who is easily scandalized;[1707] for him it will not be easy to win salvation in this present evil age so full of stumbling blocks.[1708] The second possesses his soul in patience, as has been written.[1709] As for the third, he not only possesses his own soul, but wins many more.[1710] The first, as far as he is able, is in peace. The second keeps peace. The third makes peace. Appropriately therefore is he blessed with the name son, for he accomplishes the duty incumbent on the son: that once he has himself been acceptably reconciled, he in turn reconciles others to his Father.[1711] Now someone who serves well gains good standing for himself,[1712] and what better standing could there be in the father's house than that of the son? For, "if sons, then heirs, heirs of God and fellow heirs with Christ."[1713] And so it is, as he himself has said, that where he is, there shall his servant be also.[1714]

But I am tiring you by this rambling sermon, and I have already detained you longer than I should. So I will come to the end of my chatter, not because I am shamed into it, but because I see that time is getting short. But remember that the apostle once went on preaching until midnight.[1715] I wish then—to use his own words—that you would bear with me in a little foolishness, for I feel a divine jealousy for you.[1716]

[1706]Rom 12:17.
[1707]Mk 9:41.
[1708]Gal 1:4.
[1709]Lk 21:19.

[1710]1 Cor 9:19.
[1711]2 Cor 5:18.
[1712]1 Tm 3:13.
[1713]Rom 8:17.

[1714]Jn 12:26.
[1715]Acts 20:7.
[1716]2 Cor 11:2.

XIX. A rebuke to the ambitious who presume to make peace between God and others when they themselves are not yet pure in heart.

32. Little children, "who warned you to flee from the wrath to come?"[1717] No one deserves greater wrath than the enemy who pretends to be a friend. "Judas, you betray the Son of man with a kiss."[1718] You, a familiar friend, who used to hold sweet converse with him, who have dipped your hand in the same dish![1719] You have no share in that prayer which he prayed to the Father when he said: "Father, forgive them, for they do not know what they do."[1720] Woe to you who have taken away the key not only of knowledge but also of authority, for you did not enter yourselves, and you have hindered variously those whom you ought to have led in.[1721] Yes, you have taken, you have not received, the keys. Of such people the Lord said by his prophet: "They made kings, but not through me; they set up princes, but without my knowledge."[1722] Where does this great zeal for the prelacy come from? Whence this ambitious impudence? Whence this lunacy of human presumption? Would someone who did not uphold any of our territorial laws but actually hindered them, dare to busy himself in their service, snatch at their benefits or regulate their business? Do not suppose that God approves all this, who in his great home endures the vessels of wrath fit for destruction.[1723] Many come, but consider who is called. Notice the conditions laid down in the Lord's own statement: "Blessed are the pure in heart," he said, "for they shall see God";[1724] and then: "Blessed are the

[1717] Mt 3:7.
[1718] Lk 22:48.
[1719] Ps 55:13–14; Mt 26:23.
[1720] Lk 23:34.

[1721] Lk 11:52.
[1722] Hos 8:4.
[1723] Rom 9:22.
[1724] Mt 5:8.

peacemakers, for they shall be called sons of God."[1725] The heavenly Father[1726] calls pure of heart those who do not look to their own interests but those of Jesus Christ,[1727] those who do not seek their own advantage, but that of many.[1728] "Peter" he asked, "do you love me?" "Lord, you know I love you." And he said, "Feed my sheep."[1729] Would anyone confide beloved sheep like this to a man who did not love them? No wonder what is required of stewards is that they be found trustworthy.[1730] Woe to those untrustworthy servants who busy themselves like justices of the peace with reconciling others when they themselves have not been reconciled. Woe to the children of wrath[1731] who set themselves up as ministers of grace! Woe to the children of wrath who are not ashamed to usurp the rank and title of the peacemakers! Woe to the children of wrath who pretend to mediate peace in order to feed upon people's sins. Woe to those who walk in the flesh; they cannot please God[1732] and yet they aspire presumptuously to reconcile others.

ASTONISHMENT THAT CERTAIN MEN USURP
THE SUPREME DIGNITY OF PEACEMAKERS
WHEN THEY HAVE NOT REACHED
EVEN THE LOWEST RANK.

33. We should not be bemused, brothers, when we bemoan the present state of the Church, we should not be bemused at seeing a petty prince growing up from the serpent's root.[1733] We should not be bemused at seeing how anyone who passes

[1725]Mt 5:9.
[1726]Mt 5:48.
[1727]Phil 2:21.
[1728]1 Cor 10:33.
[1729]Jn 21:16–17.
[1730]1 Cor 4:2.
[1731]Eph 2:3.
[1732]Rom 8:8.
[1733]Is 14:29.

along the path[1734] set out by the Lord can gather grapes in the Lord's vineyard. Impudently a man arrogates the rank of peacemaker and the standing of the Son of God, a man who has not yet heard the Lord's voice first calling him back to his heart or who, if he did begin to hear it, at once hopped back to hide himself behind the bushes.[1735] This is why he has not yet given up sinning and still trails a long tether. He has not yet come to be a man who sees his own poverty,[1736] but he says "I am rich and need nothing," whereas in fact he is poor, naked, wretched, and pitiable.[1737] There is in him nothing of the spirit of gentleness[1738] which would enable him to edify those given up to sin and yet to look out for himself, lest he too be tempted.[1739] Unacquainted with tears of compunction, he rejoices more in doing evil and delights in utterly perverse things.[1740] No wonder that it was to one of these that the Lord said: "Woe to you who laugh now, for you shall mourn and weep."[1741] It is money, not justice, he is looking for; his eyes look at everything high up.[1742] Insatiably he hungers for honors, he thirsts for human glory. He is far removed from tender mercy,[1743] taking his pleasure in venting his wrath and strutting about like a tyrant and imagining that godliness is a means of gain.[1744] What shall I say about purity of heart? How I wish that it were not forgotten, as if dead at heart. How I wish it were not a dove led astray yet having no heart.[1745] How I wish what is outside were clean, and what is physical were not found to be a soiled garment, so that purity of heart could say, "You have been purified, you who bear the Lord's vessels."[1746]

[1734]Ps 79:13; Is 5:7.
[1735]Gn 3:9–10.
[1736]Lam 3:1.
[1737]Rv 3:17.
[1738]1 Cor 4:21.

[1739]Gal 6:1.
[1740]Prov 2:14.
[1741]Lk 6:25.
[1742]Jb 41:25.
[1743]Lk 1:78.

[1744]1 Tm 6:5.
[1745]Hos 7:11.
[1746]Is 52:11.

XX. It is to be regretted that the impure are not ashamed impudently to defile sacred orders.

34. I do not accuse everyone, but I cannot excuse everyone either. God has kept many thousands for himself.[1747] Otherwise—were their justice not there to excuse us, had the Lord of Sabaoth not left us a holy seed[1748]—we should already have been overthrown like Sodom of old; we should have perished like Gomorrah.[1749] The Church has increased, and the clerks in sacred orders have multiplied beyond number.[1750] Truly, Lord, even though you have multiplied the nation, you have not magnified its joy,[1751] for its merit seems to have decreased as its numbers increased. People rush into holy orders all over the place, and, without awe, without stopping to think, men appropriate for themselves the ministry which awes angelic spirits. They are not even afraid to grab the sign of the kingdom of heaven or to wear the imperial crown; then avarice reigns over, ambition commands, pride dominates, iniquity sits in, luxury lords over, and perhaps, were we to dig under the wall as the prophet Ezekiel suggests,[1752] within these very walls we should see vile abominations, horrors in the house of God. Beyond fornication, adultery,[1753] and incest, there are even some who have given themselves up to dishonorable passions and shameless acts.[1754] Would that they not commit those acts which are unbefitting the apostle to put into writing or me into words. Would that when someone hints that human spirits are given to such abominable passion he could be called a liar.

[1747]Rom 11:4.
[1748]Rom 9:29.
[1749]Jer 50:40.
[1750]Ps 40:5.

[1751]Is 9:3.
[1752]Ez 8:8–10.
[1753]1 Cor 6:9.
[1754]Rom 1:26.

35. Were not in times past those cities which nurtured such foul deeds condemned by divine judgment and destroyed by flames?[1755] Did not the flames of hell, not brooking delay, lick that detestable nation whose crimes were so flagrant as to advance the judgment? Did not coals of fire, brimstone, and scorching wind devour that land which was accomplice to so much confusion?[1756] Was not the whole lot reduced to a single horrible quagmire? The five heads of Hydra have been cut off, but alas! they sprout again without number. Who rebuilt these sordid cities? Who widened the walls of wickedness? Who spread abroad the deadly virus? Woe! Woe! The enemy of mankind has scattered the wretched remains of that fiery brimstone all over the place. He has strewn the body of the Church[1757] with those damnable ashes, and even spattered some of her ministers with that stinking, putrid discharge! Alas! "Chosen race, royal priesthood, holy nation, God's own people";[1758] who could believe that such things should have come to pass in you when he thinks of your godly origin and the beginnings of the Christian religion and the spiritual gifts which accompanied it?

36. Stained like this, they go into the tabernacle of the living God.[1759] They dwell in the temple with these stains, profaning the Lord's holy place,[1760] calling down upon themselves manifold judgment because no matter how weighed down they are with an overburdened conscience, they push themselves into the sanctuary of God.[1761] Not only do such men fail to please God, they irritate him far more, for in their hearts they say, "He will never see it."[1762] Of course, they irritate him, they enrage him against themselves, I am afraid,

---

[1755] Gn 19:1–29.
[1756] Ps 11:6.
[1757] Col 1:18.
[1758] 1 Pt 2:9.
[1759] Ex 28:43; Dt 5:26.
[1760] Lv 19:8.
[1761] Ps 73:17.
[1762] Ps 10:13.

through the very things by which they ought to placate him. If only they would sit down to count the cost of the tower they have begun, in case they have not the means to finish it.[1763] If only those who are incapable of remaining continent would fear to profess perfection rashly and to assume the title of celibacy. This is a costly tower, a great precept which not everyone can accept.[1764] It would without doubt have been better to marry than to burn,[1765] to be saved in the humble ranks of the faithful than to live less worthily in the lofty ranks of the clergy and be more severely judged. Many, not everyone but certainly many, such a crowd that they cannot pass unnoticed—and they are so unabashed they do not even try to do so—many use the freedom to which they have been called as an opportunity for the flesh.[1766] They abstain from the remedy afforded by marriage and give themselves up to all forms of vice.

XXI. An exhortation to penance: as they taste first of lowly things, so may they then worthily move up to loftier.

37. Spare your souls, brothers, I beg you, spare, spare the blood which has been poured out for you.[1767] Beware of the terrifying danger, turn away from the fire which has been made ready.[1768] Let your profession of perfection not be found later to be a mockery and let its power now appear in the form of godliness.[1769] Let it not be an empty appearance of the celibate life, and void of truth. Can chastity remain unscathed amid delights, or humility among riches, or piety in business, or truth amid much talking, or charity in this

---

[1763] Lk 14:28.
[1764] Mt 19:11.
[1765] 1 Cor 7:9.
[1766] Gal 5:13.
[1767] Mt 26:28.
[1768] Mt 25:41.
[1769] 2 Tm 3:5.

present evil age?[1770] Flee from the midst of Babylon.[1771] Flee and save your souls![1772] Flock to the city of refuge,[1773] where you can do penance for the past, obtain grace in the present, and confidently wait for future glory. Do not let the consciousness of your sins hold you back, for where they abound, grace always superabounds.[1774] Do not let the austerity of penance deter you: the sufferings of this present time are not worth comparing[1775] with the forgiveness to be granted to our past sins, with the present grace of consolation which is now given to us, or with the future glory which has been promised us. For nothing is so bitter that the flour of the prophet cannot sweeten it and wisdom, the tree of life, cannot make it savory.[1776]

38. If you do not believe my words, believe the works;[1777] acknowledge the examples of many. Sinners flock from everywhere to do penance, and even though they are delicate by nature or training, they do not mind roughing it outwardly if only they can soothe their rasping conscience. Nothing is impossible to believers, nothing difficult to lovers, nothing hard to the meek, nothing arduous to the humble; to them grace lends its aid, and devotion gentles a command to the obedient person. Why occupy yourselves with things too great and marvelous for you?[1778] Indeed it is a great and marvelous thing to be the servant of Christ and a steward of the mysteries of God.[1779] The rank of peacemakers is far above you, unless perhaps, skipping the aforementioned steps, you prefer to leap rather than to climb up. If only someone, if it were possible, were to get in in such a way and

---

[1770]Gal 1:4.
[1771]Jer 51:6.
[1772]Jer 48:6.
[1773]Jo 21:36.
[1774]Rom 5:20.

[1775]Rom 8:18.
[1776]2 Sam 4:41; Prv 3:18.
[1777]Jn 10:38.
[1778]Ps 131:1.
[1779]1 Cor 4:1.

minister as faithfully as confidently he intruded! But it is a difficult, probably even an impossible, thing for the sweet fruit of charity to burn on the bitter root of ambition. If you are willing to listen, I will tell you, or rather not I but the Lord: "When you are invited to a marriage feast, go and sit in the lowest place, for everyone who exalts himself will be humbled, and he who humbles himself will be exalted."[1780]

XXII. The persecution which we must suffer according to the last beatitude: blessed are those who are persecuted . . . blessed will you be . . .

39. "Blessed are the peacemakers," he has said, "for they shall be called sons of God."[1781] Consider attentively that it is not the peace-preachers, but the peacemakers, who are praised. For there are some who preach but do not practice it.[1782] Just as it is not the hearers of the law who are righteous, but the doers,[1783] so it is not those who proclaim peace who are blessed, but those who practice it. If only those among us who today seem to be Pharisees—and perhaps they are—could at least preach what they ought, even if they do not practice it. If only those who are not willing to set forth the Gospel free of charge,[1784] might at least offer something for the charge! If only they would preach the Gospel to earn their bread. "The hireling," he said, "sees the wolf coming and flees."[1785] If only those today who are not shepherds would at least show themselves hirelings and not wolves. If only they would not devour [the sheep], if only they would not flee when no one is chasing them. If only

[1780]Lk 14:8–10, 14:11.
[1781]Mt 5:9.
[1782]Mt 23:3.
[1783]Rom 2:13.
[1784]1 Cor 9:18.
[1785]Jn 10:12.

they would not leave the flock unprotected until they see the wolf coming. Perhaps, after all, it would be better to support them, especially in times of peace, when they are found receiving their reward,[1786] and in return for their wages, working at keeping the flock, as long as they do not trouble the flock and lead it astray from the pastures of righteousness and truth. For any persecution will soon separate and distinguish the hirelings from the shepherds.[1787] How will the man who pursues temporal gain be able to support passing pain? How will the man who prefers an earthly reward to righteousness be able to endure persecution for the sake of righteousness? "Blessed are those who are persecuted for righteousness' sake," he said, "for theirs is the kingdom of heaven."[1788] This is the beatitude of shepherds, not hirelings, still less of robbers and wolves. Never yet having been persecuted for righteousness' sake, they choose to put up with persecution rather than justice. This is opposed to their efforts[1789] and it is even hard for them to hear tell of it.

40. Yet for the sake of their greed, for the sake of ambition, you will see them ready to support all sorts of dangers, to cause scandal, to endure hatred, to mask shameful doings, to ignore curses. In the end, such ill will is no less harmful than the cowardice of hirelings. The Shepherd, the Good Shepherd who did not spare his life for his sheep says therefore to real shepherds: "Blessed are you when men hate you, and when they exclude you and revile you, and cast out your name as evil, on account of the Son of man! Rejoice in that day, and leap for joy, for great is your reward in heaven."[1790] Indeed, why should people fear thieves while they are laying

---

[1786] Mt 6:2.
[1787] Mt 25:32.
[1788] Mt 5:10.

[1789] Ws 2:12.
[1790] Lk 6:22.

up treasure in heaven?[1791] They are not disturbed by increasing tribulations while they anticipate an increased reward. In fact, they are even more pleased—as is only right—because the recompense increases more than the suffering. They leap and dance for joy because they suffer many things for Christ's sake and lay up for themselves thereby an even greater reward close to him. "Why are you afraid, O ye of little faith?"[1792] A sure statement of undeniable truth has it that adversity will not harm a person on whom no evil has a grip. But it is not enough to say "it does no harm," for it brings great and ever-increasing benefit, as long as we have justice in our intention and Christ in our cause, with whom the "hope of the poor shall not perish forever."[1793] To him be the glory, both now and in the day of eternity.[1794]

[1791]Mt 6:19.
[1792]Mt 8:26.
[1793]Ps 9:18.
[1794]Pt 3:18.

From *Sermons on the Nativity*

FOURTH SERMON FOR ADVENT

*On true and false Virtue and that our Virtues must be
modeled on the Virtues of Christ*

> Length of days is in (His) right hand, and in (His) left
> hand riches and glory. PROV 3:16

It is fitting, my brethren, that we should celebrate this season
of Advent with all possible devotion, rejoicing in so great a
consolation, marveling at so great a condescension, inflamed
with love by so great a manifestation of charity. But let us
not think of that advent only whereby the Son of man has
"come to seek and to save that which was lost," but also
of that other by which He will come again and will take
us to Himself. Would to God you kept these two advents
constantly in your thoughts, revolving them in assiduous
meditation, pondering in your hearts how much we have
received by the first, how much we are promised at the second! Would to God you were able thus to "sleep among the
midst of lots"![1795] For these two comings of the Lord are the
two arms of the Bridegroom, between which the Bride was
sleeping when she said, "His Left Hand is under my head,

[1795]"If you sleep among the midst of lots, you shall be as the wings of a dove,
covered with silver, and the hinder parts of her back with the paleness of
gold" (Ps 67: 14). This is one of the most difficult verses in the whole Psalter.
According to most commentators, to "sleep among the midst of lots" signifies
to rest in the truth of the Old and New Testaments, or to devote oneself alter-
nately to the exercises of the active and contemplative life, or to die between
the hope of heavenly happiness and the contempt of worldly enjoyments. Cf.
Bellarmine's Commentary (Transl.).

and His Right shall embrace me"; because, as we read elsewhere, "Length of days is in (His) Right Hand, and in (His)
Left Hand riches and glory." "In His Left Hand riches and
glory," so speaks the inspired author of the book of Proverbs.
Attend to this, you sons of Adam, slaves to avarice and
ambition. What concern have you with earthly riches and
temporal glory, which are neither solid nor subject to your
dominion? Silver and gold! What are these but clay of the
earth, colored white and yellow, which the error of men
alone makes, or rather reputes, of value? I say they are not
subject to your dominion, for if they are, why, then, not take
them away with you? But it is written of man, "When he
shall die he shall take nothing away; nor shall his glory
descend with him."

Consequently, my brethren, true riches do not consist in
the external goods of fortune, but in the virtues of the soul,
which accompany the conscience to judgment and render us
everlastingly wealthy. And with regard to glory, the apostle
writes, "Our glory is this, the testimony of our conscience."
This indeed is true glory which comes from the Spirit of
truth: "For the Spirit Himself gives testimony to our spirit
that we are the sons of God." But the glory which is given
and received among men, who "seek not the glory which is
from God alone," that is only vainglory, because the sons of
men are vain. What a fool you are who consigns your money
to a sack full of holes, who puts your treasure in the mouths
of men![1796] Do you not know that this coffer is never closed
and has no lock to secure it? How much wiser they who
guard their treasure themselves and refuse to entrust it to

[1796]"The glory of men is in their own consciences, not in the mouths of
others," Thomas à Kempis, *Imitation of Christ,* bk. 2, chap. 6.

others! But shall they keep it always concealed? Shall it be hidden forever? No, surely not. The time will come when the hidden things of the heart shall be made manifest, and when that which was boastfully exhibited shall no longer appear. Hence it is that at the coming of the Bridegroom the lamps of the foolish virgins go out; hence too they who receive their reward from men are ignored by Christ. Wherefore I say to you, my dearest brethren, it is much more profitable to hide whatever good we may seem to possess than to make a public display of it. Thus, when beggars solicit alms, it is their custom to show, not splendid garments, but half-naked bodies, and sores or ulcers if they have them, in order that the heart of the beholder may more quickly be moved to mercy. This practice was observed much better by the publican of the Gospel than by the Pharisee, and therefore it was that "he went down to his house justified rather than the other."

My brethren, "the time is that judgment should begin at the house of God." What shall be the end of them that obey not the Gospel? They that rise not in this judgment, what judgment shall they receive? Let me tell you: all who are unwilling to be judged by this judgment which now is and in which "the prince of this world is cast out," must await or rather must fear the coming of the eternal Judge by Whom they shall themselves be cast out together with their prince. But as for us, let us now judge ourselves strictly, and then securely may "we look for the Savior, Our Lord Jesus Christ, Who will reform the body of our lowness, made like to the Body of His glory." "Then shall the just shine," those who possessed little learning in this life being now as resplendent in glory as they that had greater; for they "shall shine as the sun in the kingdom of their Father." But "the light of (that) sun shall be sevenfold, as the light of seven days."

The Savior, when He comes, "will reform the body of our lowness, made like to the Body of His glory," only on condition, however, that He finds our hearts already reformed and made like to the humility of His own Heart. Therefore has He said, "Learn of Me, because I am meek and humble of Heart." In connection herewith, I would have you take notice, my brethren, that there are two kinds of humility, the one appertaining to knowledge (or to the understanding), the other belonging to the affections (or to the will). It is this latter which Christ calls humility of the heart. By humility of the understanding we know that we are nothing; and we learn this humility from ourselves and from the experience of our own infirmity. Humility of the will, or of the heart, enables us to trample underfoot the glory of the world; but it is only to be learned from Him Who "emptied Himself, taking the form of a servant," Who fled when the people desired to make Him King, and Who freely offered Himself when they wished to make Him suffer all kinds of ignominy and the shameful death of the cross. Therefore, if we desire to "sleep among the midst of lots," that is to say, if we would rest in security between the two comings of Christ, let our "wings be covered with silver," that is, let us express in our lives that form of the virtues which Christ, when present in the flesh, commended to us both by word and example. For silver may be taken not unreasonably as symbolic of His Human Nature, just as gold is understood to represent His Divinity.

Accordingly, in as far as every virtue of ours falls short of the pattern given us by Christ, insofar does it fall short of true virtue: no wing that we possess is of any worth to bear us aloft unless it be covered with silver. A powerful wing is evangelical poverty, which enables us to fly speedily to the kingdom of heaven. Observe that the other virtues which follow in the Beatitudes obtain only a promise of this kingdom, to be fulfilled at a future time; but to poverty it is not so much promised as actually given. Hence the reason of the blessedness belonging to the poor is assigned in the present time, "For theirs *is* the kingdom of heaven"; whereas the future is employed in all the other instances, thus, "Blessed are the meek for they *shall* possess the land," "Blessed are they that mourn for they *shall* be comforted," and so on. But some even of the voluntary poor whom we meet with have not the true poverty beatified by Christ; because if they had they would not appear so downcast and disconsolate, as being truly kings, yes, kings of heaven. Such are those who desire indeed to be poor, yet on condition that they shall never want for anything; and they love poverty in such a manner that they will submit to no privation. There are others again who appear to be meek enough so long as there is nothing said or done except what is according to their liking; but on the slightest occasion, they will show how far they are from true meekness. How can such counterfeit meekness hope to inherit the land, since it does not survive to receive the inheritance? There are some also who I see mourning; but if the tears which flow from their eyes came really from their heart, they would not so easily and so speedily give place to laughter. As it is, however, while idle and jocose words issue forth in greater abundance than did the tears upon which they quickly follow, I cannot believe that it is to such tears the divine consolation has been promised, since unworthy consolation is so soon admitted. There are others still who manifest such ardent zeal against their neighbor's shortcomings that they might be supposed to "hunger and thirst after justice," if only they appeared to judge their own failings with the same rigorous severity. But, as a matter of fact, they do not weigh others in the same balance as themselves, and "diverse weights are an abomination before the Lord." For while with equal impudence and futility they are pouring out their anger upon their brother, they are also just as foolishly and just as idly commending themselves.

Some, too, there are who can be very merciful in regard to things with which they have no concern, who are scandalized if all are not abundantly provided for, yet so that they themselves are made to suffer no inconvenience, even the smallest. Now if such persons would be truly merciful, they ought to exercise mercy at their own expense. And if they cannot show mercy by giving alms out of their earthly substance, they should at any rate grant pardon with a good will to all who may seem to have offended them. They should give the pleasant look and the kind word—which is better than any gift—in order to soften the hearts of their enemies and to bring them to repentance. Moreover, they should give the alms of their compassion and their prayer not only to such as injure them, but likewise to all whom they know to be in a state of sin; otherwise, their mercifulness is a mere pretense, and shall not avail to obtain mercy. We may also meet with some who confess their sins in such a way as to lead one to think that they are influenced solely by the desire of purifying their hearts, for confession is a laver in which all things are made clean. And yet the fact that they cannot bear to be accused by others of the very faults of which they voluntarily accuse themselves shows that such is not the case. Were they really as anxious as they seem to be cleansed of their stains, instead of feeling irritated, they would rather feel thankful to those who point out to them their failings. And finally there are people who, when they see another scandalized even in the least particular, are filled with anxiety, studying how they can restore him to peace; and so they appear to be peacemakers. Yet when something is said or done which seems to give offense to them, it takes more time and trouble to calm their own agitation than that of anybody else.[1797] But evidently, if they had a true love of peace, they would seek it for themselves as much as for their neighbors.

Therefore, my brethren, let us silver our wings in the life of Christ, just as the holy martyrs "have washed their robes" in the Blood of His passion. Let us imitate, as best we can, Him Who loved poverty to such a degree that, although "in His Hand are all the ends of the earth," He yet "had not where to lay His Head," so that the disciples who followed Him (so we read), as they went through the cornfields, compelled by hunger, "plucked the ears and did eat, rubbing them in their hands." Let us imitate the meekness of Him Who was "led as a sheep to the slaughter" and was "dumb as a lamb before His shearer and opened not His Mouth." Let us imitate Him Who wept over Lazarus and over Jerusalem, and Who passed whole nights "in the prayer of God," but Who is nowhere said to have laughed or jested.[1798] Let us imitate Him Who so hungered and thirsted after justice that, although He had no sins of His own, He nevertheless exacted

[1797]"You can also give good advice and encourage others with your words; but when any unexpected trouble comes to knock at your door, then your counsel and your courage fail you," *Imitation of Christ,* bk. 3, chap. 57.

[1798]Similarly St. John Chrysostom (Homily 14 on 1 Tm); "You laugh and give yourself up to mirth: you, who are a monk by profession, who are crucified, who ought rather to weep, you laugh! Tell me, pray, when did Christ ever act thus? You have never heard of it, but you have often read of His being sad. He wept on beholding Jerusalem, He was troubled at the thought of Judas's treachery, He shed tears when about to call Lazarus from the tomb: and do you give way to laughter?" St. Bernard probably owed his strict views on jesting to the teaching of his master, St. Benedict, who says in chapter 6 of his Rule, "But as to jests (*scurrilitates* = buffoonery) or idle and jocose words, we utterly condemn them, and forbid the brethren to utter a single word of this kind, under any circumstances." Yet the Mellifluous Doctor could appreciate innocent pleasantries. Replying to a facetious epistle sent him by Peter the

from Himself so terrible a satisfaction for ours, and on the cross thirsted for nothing else but justice. Let us imitate Him Who refused not to die for His enemies, Who prayed for His executioners, Who, though "He did no sin," listened with patience when falsely accused, and Who endured such torments in order to reconcile sinners to Himself.

SIXTH SERMON FOR ADVENT
On the Glorification of the Body, and how it must be merited

> We look for a Savior, Our Lord Jesus Christ, Who
> will reform the body of our lowness, made like to the
> body of His glory. [PHIL 3: 20–21]

Brethren, I would not have you to be in ignorance of the time of your visitation, or of the special object which the Divinity has in view in coming to you now. For the present is the time appointed for attending to the interests, not of the body, but of the soul; since the soul, being far nobler than the body, has in virtue of this natural superiority the first claim on our solicitude. Besides, that which was the first to fall should also be the first to be raised up. Now it was the soul that, having first brought corruption on herself by sin,

---

Venerable, Abbot of Cluny, he says (Ep. ccxxviii.): "And so you are pleased to be jocular. You are indeed very condescending and sociable. . . . Your letter was most welcome. I read it with avidity, I read it a second time with renewed pleasure, I read it over and over again and always with fresh delight. The humor (*jocus*), I confess, pleased me very much. It charms by its gracefulness, without offending against decorum. I know not how, with all your jesting, you can still 'dispose your words in judgment,' so that your humor detracts nothing from your dignity, and your dignity is no obstacle to the sprightliness of your wit" [Trans.].

brought corruption on the body also as a punishment. Furthermore, if we desire to be found true members of Christ, it is manifest that we must imitate our Head. Hence our first attention must be devoted to the purification of our souls, for the sake of which He has come to us and whose corruption He has first endeavored to heal. But as for our bodies, let us postpone all concern for these to that time and to that occasion when He shall come again for the purpose of reforming them, as the apostle assures us, where he says, "We look for the Savior, Our Lord Jesus Christ, Who will reform the body of our lowness, made like to the Body of His glory." Hence, at the time of the first coming, St. John Baptist, who seemed to be, and in truth was, the herald of the Savior, cried aloud, "Behold the Lamb of God, behold Him Who takes away the sin of the world." Notice how he does not say "Who takes away the diseases of the body," or "the afflictions of the flesh," but, "Who takes away sin," which is a malady of the soul and a corruption of the mind. "Behold Him Who takes away the sin of the world." From where, do you ask? From the hand, from the eye, from the neck, even from the flesh itself, in which it is deeply rooted.

He takes away sin from our hands, by cleansing us from the crimes we have committed; from our eyes, by purifying the mind's intention; from our necks, by removing the galling yoke of spiritual tyranny, according to what is written, "The yoke of their burden and the scepter of their oppressor You have overcome, as in the day of Madian," and again, "The yoke shall putrefy at the presence of the oil." And with regard to the flesh, the apostle, writing to the Romans, says, "Let not sin, therefore, reign in your mortal bodies," and in another place, "I know that there dwells not in me, that is to say, in my flesh, that which is good," and also, "Unhappy man that I am, who shall deliver me from the body of this death?" For he knew well that he could not be without that most baneful root which is implanted in our flesh, that law of sin which is in our members, until his soul was separated from his body. Therefore he desired "to be dissolved and to be with Christ," knowing that sin, which "makes a division between God and us," cannot be completely taken away so long as we are imprisoned in the flesh. You have read of one who the Lord delivered from the power of the devil, how the demon went out of him at the divine command, casting him down and "greatly tearing him." I say to you, that this kind of sin—I mean carnal appetites and evil desires which so often assail us—can indeed and ought to be kept down by the grace of God, so far as this, that it shall not reign in us, and that we shall not yield our members unto it "as instruments of iniquity"— and so there shall be "no condemnation to them that are in Christ Jesus"; but that it cannot be cast out except by death, when we shall be so "greatly torn" that our souls shall be parted from our bodies.

I have now explained to you, my brethren, the purpose of Christ's coming, and I have told you what should be the great object of the Christian's solicitude. Wherefore, do not, O body, do not, I pray you, anticipate your time. For although you have the power to hinder the salvation of the soul, you can do absolutely nothing to secure your own. "All things have their season," as the wise man says. Permit the soul now to work for her own interests, or rather cooperate with her, because if you suffer with her, you shall also reign with her. On the other hand, by impeding her restoration you would be impeding your own in the same proportion. For you cannot be perfected until the Creator beholds His image restored in her. O mortal flesh, noble is the guest who you are entertaining, yes, very noble, and on her welfare your own entirely depends. Honor your guest so distinguished. You are residing here in your native country, but the soul, which has taken lodging with you, is a pilgrim and an exile on the earth. Where, I ask you, is the peasant who, if some powerful nobleman wished to spend the night under his roof, would not gladly (as is only proper) place his best bed at the service of his guest even though he should himself have to sleep in some corner of the house, under the stairs, or on the very hearthstone? Therefore, "go and do the same." Do not consider the sufferings and inconveniences you may have to endure, provided your guest can be honorably lodged with you. Esteem it as your greatest honor to be stripped of all honor in this life for the sake of the soul.

And lest you should perhaps feel tempted to despise or to undervalue this guest of yours, because she seems to you a stranger and a pilgrim, consider diligently the many precious advantages which you owe to her presence. For it is she that gives sight to your eyes and hearing to your ears; it is from her your tongue borrows its power of speech, your palate its discernment of taste, and all your members their various motions. Whatever of life, whatever of sense or feeling, whatever of beauty you possess in yourself, know that it is all the benefit of your guest. It is only her departure from you that will show how much you owe to her presence. For as soon as the soul withdraws, the tongue shall be silent, the eyes shall become blind, the ears shall lose their hearing, pallor shall overspread the countenance, the whole body shall grow rigid, and after a brief interval shall be changed into a sink of corruption, all its beauty being converted to rottenness. And will you, then, O body, wound and grieve this guest for the sake of any temporal delight whatever, which you could not even enjoy except through her? Besides, if even now, in the time of her banishment, when exiled for her sins from the presence of her Maker; she bestows on you such a multitude of benefits, what shall she not do for you, after she has been restored to favor? Be careful, then, oh, be careful not to hinder that reconciliation, since from it you shall yourself derive a generous endowment of glory. Expose yourself with patience, no, with gladness, to all kinds of sufferings and privations. Refuse no sacrifice which may seem to conduce to so happy a restoration. Speak to your guest in the words of Joseph to his fellow captive, "The Lord will remember you and will restore you to your former place. Only remember me when it shall be well with you."

Yes, she will undoubtedly be mindful to render you good, if meanwhile you faithfully serve her. And when she comes into the presence of her Lord, she will speak to Him of you. Out of gratitude for your hospitality, she will plead your cause with Him, saying, "When your servant was an exile, in punishment for her sin, a poor fellow servant with whom I lodged treated me with great kindness, and I pray that my Lord may be pleased to make him a return in my behalf. For, in the first place, he sacrificed all he possessed in my service, and then his very self, not sparing anything of his own, in order to further my interests, 'in labor and painfulness, in much watchings, in hunger and thirst, in fastings often, in cold and nakedness.'" What, then, will the Lord do? Surely, the Scripture does not lie when it says, "He will do the will of them that fear Him and He will hear their prayer." Oh, if you could only taste this sweetness, if only you could conceive this glory of which I am about to speak! For what I shall say is in very truth strange and astonishing, yet nonetheless certain and indubitable to faithful souls. He Himself, the Lord God of Sabaoth, the Lord of Hosts and the King of Glory, He will Himself come down to reform our bodies and to make them like the Body of His brightness! Oh, how great shall be that glory, how unspeakable that exultation, when the Creator of the universe, Who before came hidden and humble for the purpose of justifying souls, comes now visible and sublime to glorify you, O flesh, so poor at present and so miserable; comes not in weakness as of old, but in all the splendor of His Majesty! "Who shall be able to think of the day of (this) coming" of the Lord, when He will descend in the fullness of His glory, preceded by the angels, who with the sound of the trumpet shall "raise up the needy (body) from the dust," "taking it up together with them into the clouds to meet Christ, into the air."

Shall we therefore continue to allow this flesh of ours, this miserable, foolish, blind, and senseless flesh, this utterly infatuated flesh, to seek after earthly and transitory consolations, or rather desolations, with the risk of being rejected and judged unworthy of that glory, and of being condemned besides to suffer inexpressible torments for all eternity? Let it not be so, I beseech you, brethren, let it not be so. Rather let our spirits find their delight in holy meditations, and let our flesh rest in hope, while "we look for the Savior, Our Lord Jesus Christ, Who will reform the body of our lowness, made like the Body of His glory." For so the psalmist sings, "For you my soul has thirsted, for you my flesh, oh, how many ways!" Thus did the soul of the royal prophet yearn for the first advent, whereby she knew that she was to be redeemed; and with much greater eagerness did his flesh look forward to the final coming, at which shall be accomplished its glorification. For then all our desires shall be satisfied, and the whole earth shall be filled with the Majesty of the Lord. To this glory, to this happiness, to this "peace which surpasseth all understanding," may He bring us by His mercy and not "confound us in our expectation," the

Savior Whom we look for, Jesus Christ Our Lord, Who is over all things, God blessed forever. Amen.

SEVENTH SERMON FOR ADVENT
On our threefold need of Christ

If God be for us, who is against us?   [Rom 8: 31]

My brethren, if we celebrate with devotion the advent of the Lord, we are doing nothing more than our duty, because not only has He come to us, but He has come also for our sakes, He Who "has no need of our goods." Yes, rather it was our need of Him that induced Him to visit us, and the greatness of that need is clearly indicated by the greatness of His condescension. And just as the gravity of the disease may be inferred from the costliness of the medicine employed for its cure, so too may we ascertain the number of our ailments from the multitude of the remedies provided for us. For wherefore the "divisions of graces," unless they correspond to a variety of necessities? It would be a difficult undertaking to attempt to discuss in one sermon all the spiritual wants which we experience; but there are three which now occur to my mind, which are common to all, and which may be regarded as the principal. For there is not a soul among us that does not sometimes feel the need of counsel, of help, and of protection. It is indubitable that the whole human race labors under a threefold misery, a triple burden, which painfully oppresses every man so long as he lives in this region of the shadow of death, subject to the infirmities of the flesh and the assaults of temptation. For we are easily led astray; we soon weary of labor; we quickly yield to violence. We are deceived when we try to discern between good and evil; we faint and give up as often as we undertake a good work; if we endeavor to resist evil, we are promptly cast down and overcome.

Very necessary, therefore, is the advent of the Savior; very necessary is the presence of Christ to men so encompassed with dangers. God grant that He may not only come to us, but that He may also in His infinite mercy dwell in us by faith to illumine our blindness, remain with us by His grace to assist our utter impotence, and stand by us with His power to protect and defend our fragility! For if He dwells in us, who shall seduce us? If He remains with us, surely we "can do all things in Him Who strengthens" us. If He "be for us who is against us"? He is a faithful Counselor, Who never can deceive us or be deceived; He is a strong Helper, Whom labor never wearies; He is a mighty Protector, Who will speedily enable us to trample underfoot the power of Satan and will bring to naught all his cunning machinations. For He is the Wisdom of God, Who is ever ready to instruct the ignorant; and He is the Power of God, to Whom it is easy to strengthen the fainting and to rescue the perishing. Therefore, my brethren, in all doubts and perplexities, let us have recourse to so wise a Master; in all our undertakings, let us invoke the assistance of so powerful a Helper; in our every combat let us commit our souls to the keeping of so faithful a Protector, Who for this purpose has come into the world, that, living here in men, with men, and for men, He may illuminate their darkness, lighten their labors, and guard them from all danger. Amen.

FIFTH SERMON FOR CHRISTMAS EVE

On the Manner in which we must prepare and sanctify ourselves for the Vision of God

Sanctify yourselves today and be prepared, for tomorrow you shall see in you the Majesty of God.

—FROM THE RESPONSORY OF THE OFFICE OF
VIGILS FOR CHRISTMAS EVE

Today, my brethren, on the eve of the Lord's nativity, the Church wisely admonishes us to prepare ourselves in all holiness for the celebration of so unspeakable a mystery. For the Holy of Holies is at hand: He is at hand Who has said, "Be holy, because I the Lord your God am holy." How can that which is holy be given to dogs, or how can pearls be offered to swine, unless the dogs are first converted from their wickedness and the swine cleansed from their foulness, and unless they are resolved for the future to shun with all solicitude, the former the vomit, the latter the slough? Of old, when the carnal Israelites were about to receive the commandments of God, they sanctified themselves with the justifications of the flesh, with various ablutions, with gifts and sacrifices, none of which had the power of purifying the conscience of him who performed them. But now all these rites and ceremonies have passed away, because they were only given to be observed until the time of interior justification by the grace of redemption, which time, as you know, has already come. Rightly therefore has perfect holiness been from that moment expected and demanded of us, rightly has purification of the conscience been enjoined and spiritual cleanliness exacted. For the Lord Himself has said, "Blessed are the clean of heart, for they shall see God." For this we live, my brethren, for this we have been born, for this we have been called, for this it has been granted us to see the sun today. It was night in times past when no man was able to do these things. It was night all over the world before the dawn of the true Light, before the birth of the Savior. It was also night for each one of us before his conversion to God and his spiritual regeneration.

Shall it be questioned that a most profound night and densest darkness covered the whole face of the earth, when our fathers of old worshipped gods made with hands, and with a sacrilegious madness fell down in adoration before stocks and stones? And with regard to each of ourselves, was it not gloomy night while we were "living without God in this world," while we were "going after our lusts," while we were consenting to our carnal inclinations, while we were obeying "worldly desires," while we were yielding our "members as instruments of iniquity unto sin," while we were "serving uncleanness and iniquity unto iniquity," "of which we are now ashamed" as of the works of darkness? Hence the apostle says, "They that sleep, sleep in the night, and they that are drunk are drunk in the night." Such have we been, my brethren; but we have been awakened and sanctified, if yet we be the sons of light and day rather than of night and of darkness. For he is the herald of day who cries out to us "Be sober and watch." And to the Jews the same apostle (St. Peter) said on the feast of Pentecost, speaking of his fellow disciples, "These are not drunk as you suppose, seeing that it is but the third hour of the day." This is also the burden of his brother apostle, St. Paul, where he says, "The night is past and the day is at hand. Let us therefore cast off the works of darkness and put on the armor of light." "Let us cast off the works of darkness," such as drowsiness and drunkenness—since, as you have just heard, "they that sleep, sleep in the night; and they that are drunk are drunk in the night"—and, as being now in the day, let us not slumber but "walk," and let us "walk honestly," not with the staggering steps of the wine-bibber. Do you see a man whose "soul slumbers through heaviness" with regard to every good work? Such a one "is in darkness even until now." Do you see a man "inebriated with wormwood," "more wise than it behooves to be wise," and not "wise unto sobriety," whose "eye is not filled with seeing, neither is his ear filled with hearing," who, loving money or something similar, longs for it with a desire as insatiable as the thirst of a dropsical patient? He is the son of night and darkness. These two evils of sloth and inordinate desire are not easy to separate. Hence it is said in Holy Scripture that "the idle man is full of desires";[1799] that is to say every sluggard is given to intemperance. Let us therefore sanctify ourselves today, and let us be prepared. Let us prepare ourselves today by shaking off the drowsiness which belongs to the night; and let us sanctify ourselves as in the day, and cleanse ourselves from nocturnal excesses, restraining the impetuosity of wicked desires. In other words, let us avoid evil and do good, because "on these two commandments depend the whole law and the prophets."

But it is only for today we shall be thus employed. Tomorrow we shall spend neither in sanctifying ourselves, nor in preparing ourselves, but in contemplating the Divine Majesty. For so sings the Church in her office, "Tomorrow you shall see in you the Majesty of God." This is the same as what the patriarch Jacob said of old, "My justice shall answer for me tomorrow." Today we cultivate justice, tomorrow it will respond to our labors. It is exercised today, it will bear

---

[1799]The text most nearly resembling this in the Vulgate is Proverbs 21:25: "Desires kill the slothful man" (Trans.).

fruit tomorrow. For no man shall reap what he has not sown. So he who now neglects internal holiness shall not be admitted hereafter to the contemplation of Majesty; the Sun of glory shall never shine on him on whom the Sun of justice has not risen; nor shall he see the dawn of tomorrow who has not lived in the light of today. For, as the apostle teaches, the same Christ, "Who of God is made unto us Justice" today, shall appear as our Life tomorrow, when we "also shall appear with Him in glory." Today He is born for us as a Little One, "that man may no more presume to magnify himself upon earth," but that we may rather "be converted and become as little children." But tomorrow He will show Himself to us as the "great Lord and greatly to be praised," so that we also shall be magnified in glory when "every man shall have praise from God." For those whom He justifies today, He will magnify tomorrow, and to the consummation of holiness shall succeed the vision of Majesty. Neither is that an unprofitable vision which constitutes a resemblance to the Godhead. For "we shall be like to Him, *because* we shall see Him as He is." Hence in our text also it is not said simply, "you shall see the Majesty of God," but, "you shall see *in you* the Majesty of God." That is: today, when He appears in our human nature, we see ourselves in Him as in a mirror; but tomorrow we shall see Him in ourselves, when He will clothe us with His own Divinity, when He will unveil to us His Countenance, when He will take us to Himself. This is the promise He has made to those who watch for His coming, "that He will gird Himself and make them sit down to meat and passing will minister to them." Meantime, we all receive of His fullness, not yet indeed glory for glory, but only "grace for grace." But it is written, "The Lord will give grace and glory." Despise not, therefore, the foregoing gifts if you wish to obtain the following. Do not disdain the food which is first served if you would partake of that which comes after. Even for the sake of the dish which contains it, refuse not the meat that is offered. For our Divine Peacemaker has fashioned for Himself an incorruptible dish, "fitting" to Himself an incorruptible Body, and in this most precious dish He ministers to us the food of salvation. "You will not let Your Holy One," sings the psalmist, "see corruption." And it is of the same the angel Gabriel says to Mary, "The Holy one Which shall be born of you shall be called the Son of God."

Therefore, let us be sanctified today by this Holy One, in order that we may see His Majesty in us when that future day shall dawn. For the day of sanctification has already shone upon us, and the day of salvation, but not yet the day of glory and of bliss. It is only proper that so long as the passion of the Holy One (Who suffered on the Parasceve, that is, on the day of preparation) is still announced, it should be said to all, "Sanctify yourselves today and be prepared. Sanctify yourselves more and more, by advancing from virtue to virtue, and prepare yourselves by perseverance in good." But in what things are we to be sanctified? I have read in the Scriptures of Moses how the Lord "sanctified him in his faith and meekness." For it is quite as impossible to please men without meekness as to please God without faith. Rightly, then, are we admonished to prepare ourselves in these virtues whereby we shall give satisfaction to God Whose Majesty we are destined to contemplate, and also to each other, so that we may behold that Majesty even in ourselves. For this is the reason why it behooves us to "provide good things not only in the sight of God, but also in the sight of all men," namely, in order that we may render ourselves agreeable to our fellow citizens and brothers-in-arms, as well as to our King.

In the first place, therefore, we must seek after faith, by

which, as St. Peter testifies, God purifies our hearts. For "blessed are the clean of heart because they shall see (the Majesty of) God." Abandon yourself, therefore, to God, commit yourself to Him, "cast your care upon the Lord and He shall sustain you." Then may you say with confidence, "The Lord is careful for me." But such confidence is unknown to men who love themselves, who are wise in their own conceit, who "seek the things that are their own," and "make provision for the flesh in its concupiscences," who are deaf to the voice which calls out to them, saying, "Cast all your care upon Him, for He has care of you." For to believe in one's self is not faith but perfidy, and it is rather diffidence than confidence to trust in one's self. He is truly faithful who neither believes in himself nor hopes in himself, but, like the prophet, becomes to himself "as a broken vessel," so losing his life in this world that he may preserve it eternally in the next. But it is only humility of heart that can induce the faithful soul not to rely on her own strength, but, abandoning herself, to rest upon the Lord, and thus to "ascend from the desert, flowing with delights, (because) leaning upon her Beloved."

But in order that our sanctification may be perfect, it is also clearly incumbent on us to learn from the Saint of saints the sweetness and kindliness which are necessary in human society. Hence He Himself has said, "Learn of Me, because I am meek and humble of heart." But of him, who has thus made perfect his sanctification; who "is sweet and mild and plenteous in mercy," like God Himself; who is "all things to all men," like the apostle; who, in a manner, anoints all his brethren with that ointment of gentleness and meekness with which he is himself so saturated, so full, so brimming over that he seems to diffuse it on every side—why should I not say of such a one that he is "flowing with delights"? Happy the man who by reason of this double preparation of faith and meekness is able to say with the psalmist, "My heart is ready, O Lord, my heart is ready." For he has today his "fruit unto sanctification" and tomorrow shall have "the end, life everlasting," because tomorrow he shall see the Majesty of God, in which everlasting life consists, according to the words of Truth Itself, "This is eternal life, that they may know You, the only true God, and Jesus Christ Whom You have sent." And "the Lord, the just Judge, will render to (him) in that day," to which no other shall succeed, the "crown of justice." "Then shall he see and abound, and his heart shall wonder and be enlarged." By how much shall his heart be enlarged? By so much as shall enable him to behold in himself the Majesty of God. But do not imagine, my brethren, that I can explain to you in words what that promise means.

"Sanctify yourselves today and be prepared." Tomorrow you shall see and shall rejoice, and "your joy shall be full." For what capacity is so great that the Majesty of God cannot fill it? Yes, you shall be filled up to overflowing when the "good measure, and pressed down, and shaken together, and running over, they shall give into your bosom." And so superabundant is this reward that it transcends "above measure exceedingly" not only our merits but even our desires. For God is able to accomplish what is beyond our hope and power of understanding. There are, my brethren, three ultimate objects of human desire, namely, the honorable, the useful, and the delectable. These are the goods which we all covet: we all covet all of them, but in varying degrees, for this has more attractions for one and that for another. Thus some men are so given up to pleasure that they have but little regard either for the honorable or the useful. Others, devoting themselves particularly to the pursuit of gain, viz., the useful, pay less attention to the honorable and the pleasurable. Others again make honor their chief or only object of endeavor, looking upon the useful and the delectable with comparative indifference. Now, we do nothing reprehensible in desiring these things, provided we seek them there where alone they can be truly found. But where they are truly found, they are one. For the one Sovereign Good is at once supremely useful, supremely delectable, and supremely honorable. And this is our hope—so far as we can conceive it in the present life—and the promised vision, whereby we shall see in us the Divine Majesty: that God shall be all in all to us, all our pleasure, all our profit, all our honor. Amen.

SECOND SERMON FOR CHRISTMAS DAY

*On the Three Principal Works of God and the
Special Virtue conspicuous in each*

The Lord has done great things for us.   —Ps 125:3

"Great are the works of the Lord," cries out the prophet
David. All God's works are great indeed, my brethren,
because He is Himself so great. But those which appear to be
the greatest among them have a special relation to ourselves.
Hence it is that the same prophet declares in one of the
psalms, "The Lord has done great things for us." And there
are three of His works particularly which proclaim aloud
how magnificently He has dealt with us. These are the work
of our first creation, the work of our present redemption,
and the work of our future glorification. But how many
great operations, O Lord, does not each of the three comprise! To You it belongs to "show forth to Your people the
power of Your works," but concerning the works themselves
we must not be silent. In each of the three works of creation,
redemption, and glorification, we have to consider a special
union or blending of opposite elements, truly worthy of the
divine power and efficacy. In the first work of our creation,
"God formed man of the slime of the earth, and breathed
into his face the breath of life." Oh, what an Artist, what a
Compounder of things diverse, at Whose command the
slime of the earth and the spirit of life are thus intimately
wedded together! The slime indeed had already received
existence, when "in the beginning God created heaven and
earth." But the spirit had a creation proper to itself. It was
not produced in common with other things. Neither was
it created in the bodily mass, but was infused into it in a
singular and excellent manner. Acknowledge, O man, your

dignity. Acknowledge the glory of your human nature. You have a body like other earthly creatures, since it is only fitting that, as you are set over all the material world, you should resemble it at least in part. But you are also possessed of something more sublime, something which lifts you entirely above the level of other visible beings. For in you are united and compacted together spirit and flesh, the former infused, the latter fashioned from the slime.

But for the sake of which element are they thus combined? Which of the two gains by their partnership? According to the wisdom of the children of this world, whenever there is an alliance between high and low, he that is stronger obtains the dominion and uses for his pleasure his weaker associate. The more powerful trample upon the less powerful, the learned laugh at the ignorant, the crafty deceive the simple, the mighty contemn the feeble. But it is not so in Your works, O Lord; it is not so in this union which You have made. It is not for the sole advantage of the superior partner You have associated the slime of the earth with the spirit of life, the lofty with the lowly, a noble and excellent creature with a mass of vile and worthless clay. For who does not know how much the soul benefits the body? What would the body be without the soul but a lifeless trunk? To the soul it owes its beauty, to the soul it owes its increase and development, to the soul it owes its clearness of vision and the sound of its voice: in fine, it owes to the soul all its various powers of sensation. This union speaks to me of charity. I thus find the record of charity in the very page which tells me of my own creation. For the Creator has not only announced to me the law of charity at the very commencement of my career, but with His own Hand He has lovingly inscribed it on my being and substance.

Truly great, my dearest brethren, was this alliance of spirit and flesh, if only it had continued firm. As a matter of fact, however, notwithstanding that it had been strengthened with the divine seal (for God made man to His own image and likeness) the seal was broken and the union, alas! destroyed. When as yet that seal was fresh and new, the infernal robber came and broke it. The divine image having been thus lost, miserable man is now "compared to senseless beasts and is become like to them." God made man righteous, and so stamped upon him His own likeness, the likeness of Him of whom the psalmist sings, "The Lord our God is righteous and there is no iniquity in Him." He also made him truthful and just, as He Himself is Truth and Justice. Nor could the union between flesh and spirit be dissolved while this seal of likeness remained unbroken. But there appeared an impostor, who, promising our unsuspecting first parents a better seal, alas! alas! destroyed that which had been impressed by the Hand of God. "You shall be as gods," whispered the serpent, "knowing good and evil." O malevolent one! O most wicked one! What advantage can it be to them to resemble their Creator by such knowledge? Let them by all means be as gods: let them be truthful as God is truthful, to Whom sin can never approach. For so long as the seal of such likeness endures, the original union of soul and body is safe. But we know now from experience to what we have been persuaded by the deceit of the devil's craft. For when the seal had been violated, there followed bitter dissension between the partners and lamentable divorce. Where now, O impious one, where now is thy promise, "You shall not die the death"? For behold we all die, so that the psalmist says, "Who is the man that shall live and not see death?"

But what will You do, O Lord our God? Is this work of Yours never to be repaired? Shall not he who has fallen be assisted to rise? But there is none that can help him except the Lord Who created him. Therefore, "By reason of the misery of the needy and the groans of the poor, now will I arise, says the Lord"; and "The enemy shall have no advantage over him, nor the son of iniquity have power to hurt him." "I will form another union," He seems to say, "which I will secure with a stronger and deeper Seal, with that, namely, Which is not something made to My Image, but is Itself My Image, the Figure of My Substance and the Splendor of My Glory, a Seal not made but begotten before the daystar." And lest you should have any fears that this new Seal may be broken like the other, listen to the prophet speaking thereof, "My strength," he says in one of the psalms, "is dried up, viz., hardened, like a potsherd." Yes, "like a potsherd," but such a potsherd as Satan, the mighty hammer of the whole earth, has no power to break. The first union was an alliance of two, the second is a conjunction of three, suggesting to us a resemblance to the mystery of the Most Holy Trinity. The Word Who "was in the beginning with God" and "was God"; the Soul which had been created out of nothing and before was not; and the Flesh which divine wisdom separated from the mass of corruption and preserved undefiled: these three elements have coalesced in the unity of a single Person, and are bound together with an indissoluble bond. In this union we find a threefold manifestation of power: that which was not has been created; that which had perished has been restored; that which was over all things has been "made a little less than the angels." These three ingredients, my brethren, are symbolized by the "three measures of meal," which, as the Gospel tells us, were leavened together, and made into the "Bread of angels" of which man eats, the Bread Which "strengthens man's heart." Happy that woman, and blessed among all women, in whose chaste bosom this heavenly Bread was baked, baked over the fire of the Holy Spirit. Blessed, I say, is that woman who hid the leaven of her faith in these three measures. For it was by faith she conceived and by faith she brought forth. To this St. Elizabeth bears witness when she says, "Blessed are you that has believed, because those things shall be accomplished that were spoken to you by the Lord." And do not be surprised to hear that it was by means of Mary's faith that the Word was united to flesh, because it was from Mary's flesh Christ's Flesh was taken. Nor is it any objection to this interpretation that, according to the Gospel, "the kingdom of heaven is like to leaven." For, as it seems to me, the faith of Mary may also be likened to the kingdom of heaven, since it was by her faith the kingdom of heaven has been restored.

Therefore no creature has power to break the bond of this second union, since even "the prince of this world has not anything" he can claim in Christ, and the Baptist is not worthy to loose the latchet of His shoe. What then? It is plainly needful that it be dissolved to some extent. Otherwise the first union, which has been destroyed, can never be restored. Bread that is unbroken, a treasure that is concealed, wisdom that is not manifest—what is the use of such things? With good reason did St. John weep, as he tells us in the Apocalypse, "because no man was found worthy to open the book and to loose the seals thereof." For while it remained closed none of us could gain access to the divine wisdom it contained. Open the book, O Lamb of God, O You Who are meekness itself. Present Your Hands and Your Feet to the Jew, to be pierced with nails, so that the treasure of salvation, the "plentiful redemption" concealed within, may at last pour itself out. "Break Your bread to the hungry," because You alone can break it Who alone are able to stand in order to repair Your broken creatures. For in the general breaking[1800] You alone

[1800] Allusion to Psalm 105–23.

possess the power to lay down Your life and to take it up again when You please. Therefore, in Your compassion for our need, let this Temple be dissolved in part, but not utterly destroyed. Let the Soul be separated from the Body, but let the Divinity guard the incorruption of the Flesh, and confer upon the Spirit full liberty, so that It alone may be "free among the dead" to lead forth from their prison-house those who are shut up and sitting in darkness and in the shadow of death. Let Your holy Soul lay aside Its immaculate Flesh, but only to take It up again on the third day, so that by dying You may destroy death, and by rising from the dead may restore life to man. So it has been, dearest brethren, and it is a cause of joy to us that it has so been. Death has been slain by His death, and we have been "regenerated unto the hope of life by the resurrection of Jesus Christ from the dead."

But as for the third union, who shall describe it? "Eye has not seen, nor ear heard, neither has it entered into the heart of man what things God has prepared for them that love Him." That will be the consummation, when Christ shall "deliver up the kingdom to God and the Father," and they, viz., Christ and His Bride, the Church, shall be two, not now in one flesh, but in one spirit. For if the Word by cleaving to the flesh was made flesh, much more shall she that cleaves to God become one spirit with Him. In the second union of the Word with flesh, humility is manifested, a humility exceedingly great. But in that for which we look, for which we sigh, there is laid up for us—if indeed for us—the perfection of heavenly glory. If you recall now what I said about the first of these unions, in which man is compacted of spirit and flesh, namely, that therein charity is commended to us, you will see with what reason humility is so conspicuous in the second, because it is only the virtue of humility that can repair the injury done to charity. The union of such a noble creature as the rational soul with a body fashioned from the slime of the earth must not be ascribed to humility. For it is not by its own deliberate choice that the spirit is mixed with matter, since it is infused by the very act which creates it and created by the very act which infuses it.[1801] But the same is not true of the Sovereign and Divine Spirit, Who being infinitely good, has united Himself by His own free will and pleasure to a Body pure and undefiled. Then the union of glory follows upon that of charity and humility: because without charity nothing is of any avail, and, according to the words of Christ, no one shall be exalted but he that humbles himself.

[1801]"Creando immittur, immitendo creatur." By these few words the saint excludes all the various false theories touching the origin of the human soul: the traducianism of Tertullian, according to which the infant's soul is derived by material generation from the bodies of the parents; the more spiritual but equally unintelligible traducianism to which St. Augustine inclined, and which Frohshammer and Klee resuscitated in Germany at the beginning of the last century, viz., that the soul of the offspring proceeds somehow from the souls of the parents; the theory of Origen who, influenced by Plato's philosophy, and misinterpreting Psalm 32:15, taught that all souls were created together at the beginning of time; and finally the strange doctrine of Rosmini, that the sentient soul, produced by generation, is in man transformed into a rational, spiritual soul "by the manifestation to it of the idea of being." The teaching of St. Bernard is the teaching of the Catholic Church: that the human soul does not exist before its union with the body, and that it is produced by creation out of nothing. Cf. Maher, *Psychology,* 572–74; Hickey, *Summula,* vol. 2, 456–59; also Bellarmine, *Comment* in Ps 32:15 [Trans.].

From *Homilies in Praise of the Blessed Virgin Mary*

HOMILY III

Whenever I see that the words of Holy Scripture suit my purpose I willingly make them my own so that what I have to say may charm my readers at least by the beauty of the vessels. That is why, for example, I now begin with this prophetic utterance, "Woe is me." Not because I have held my tongue as the prophet did, but because I dare to speak, "for I am a man of unclean lips."[1802] Alas! I cannot forget how many vain, lying, and dirty words I once vomited out of this foul mouth from which I now presume to speak about heavenly things. I am very much afraid that I shall hear said to me, "What right have you to recite my statutes or to take my covenant on your lips?"[1803] Oh, if only someone would bring down to me from the altar on high not just one burning coal[1804] but a huge fiery globe by which the ingrained and thick rust would be entirely burned out of my lewd mouth. Perhaps then I should be worthy to repeat in my own very ordinary language those gracious and chaste words of the angel to the Virgin and of the Virgin to him.

The evangelist says: "And the angel went into her—to Mary of course—and said, 'Hail, full of grace, the Lord is with you.'"[1805] "Went in" where? Into the private chamber of her modest room where, I suppose, having shut the door

[1802] Is 6:5.
[1803] Ps 50:16.
[1804] Is 6:6.
[1805] Lk 1:26.

she was praying to the Father in secret.[1806] Angels are accustomed to taking their stand beside those who pray, and they delight in those whom they see lifting pure hands in prayer.[1807] They are happy to be able to carry to God in the fragrance of its sweetness the sacrifices of holy devotion.[1808] By going into Mary and greeting her so reverently, the angel showed just how pleasing were her prayers to the Most High.[1809] It was not hard for the angel to enter the Virgin's private room through a closed door; it was natural to him, for so great was the subtleness of his nature that an iron gate could not have prevented him from going wherever his mission sent him.[1810] Angelic spirits are not hindered by walls. All visible things give way to them and every bulky mass, however thick and solid, is penetrable and pervious to them. There is no reason to suspect that the angel found the Virgin's little door ajar. She clearly had it in mind to flee human company, to avoid conversation lest the silence of one given to prayer should be disturbed and the purity of one given to chastity be assailed. Surely then the most prudent virgin had at that time closed the door of her private room to men, but not to angels. Thus, even though the angel could go into her the way was barred to any human being.

2. "The Angel came in to her and said, 'Hail, full of grace, the Lord is with you.'"[1811] In the Acts of the apostles we read that Stephen was full of grace and that the apostles were filled with the Holy Spirit,[1812] but quite differently from Mary. The fullness of the godhead did not dwell bodily in Stephen as it did in Mary.[1813] The apostles did not conceive by

---

[1806]Mt 6:6.
[1807]1 Tm 2:8.
[1808]Eph 5:2.
[1809]Sir 35:8.

[1810]Ez 1:12.
[1811]Lk 1:28.
[1812]Acts 6:8, 2:4.
[1813]Col 2:9.

the Holy Spirit as she did. "Hail, full of grace, the Lord is with you," said the angel. What wonder is there that she would be full of grace when the Lord was with her? But what is more astonishing is that when the angel arrived he found the person by whom he had been sent was already with the Virgin. Could God have hastened down to earth more swiftly than his winging messenger in order to get to earth before him? I should not be surprised. While the King was on his couch, the Virgin's nard was sending forth its fragrance[1814] and a sweet-smelling smoke was rising up in the sight of his glory, and in this way she found grace in the Lord's eyes.[1815] Those who were gathered round him exclaimed, "who is this coming up from the wilderness, like a column of smoke, perfumed with myrrh and frankincense?"[1816] At once the King set out from his holy place.[1817] He rejoiced like a giant to run his course.[1818] And though he set out from the highest heaven, he was moved by so great a desire that he sped ahead of his messenger and came to the Virgin whom he loved, whom he had chosen for his own, whose beauty he ardently desired.[1819] It is this same lover whom the Church, looking from afar and seeing him coming,[1820] greets with joy and gladness exclaiming, "Behold, he comes leaping upon the mountains, bounding over the hills."[1821]

3. The King rightly desired the Virgin's beauty. She was doing what her father David long before had advised her to do when he said, "Harken, O daughter, consider and incline your ear, forget your people and your father's house and the King will desire your beauty."[1822] She had both heard and

---

[1814] Sg 1:11.
[1815] Lk 1:30.
[1816] Sg 3:6.

[1817] Is 26:21.
[1818] Ps 19:5.
[1819] Ps 45:11.

[1820] Jn 1:9.
[1821] Sg 2:8.
[1822] Ps 45:10.

seen, not like those who, hearing do not listen[1823] and seeing do not understand.[1824] When she heard she believed,[1825] when she saw, she understood. She inclined her ear, that is, to obedience and her heart to discipline. And she forgot her own people and her father's house. She was not anxious to increase her people by giving birth to a new generation, she did not seek to leave an heir to her father's house. Whatever honor she might have had from her father's house was all counted as refuse that she might gain Christ.[1826] Nor was she disappointed in any way. She was able to claim a son in Christ and yet not violate her vow of chastity. Truly may we say that she was full of grace: while retaining the grace of virginity she was blessed in addition with the honor of motherhood.

4. "Hail full of grace, the Lord is with you," he said. He did not say, "The Lord is in you" but "the Lord is with you." For God, simple by nature, is equally and entirely everywhere at once. But in his rational creatures he is present in a different way than in other creatures. Again, even among his rational creatures, he is not present with the same efficacy in the bad as in the good. Though he is present in irrational creatures, they cannot be said to grasp him. And though every rational creature can grasp him by some concept [of him], it is only the good who can grasp him by love as well. Only the good, because of the union of their will with his, deserve to have it said of them that he is with them. That they will what he wills does not demean God because they have bent their wills to his justice: there is no conflict and they are spiritually united to their God. But if this may be said of all the saints, it is especially true of Mary. Her will

[1823]Mk 4:12.
[1824]Cf. Ws 4:14.

[1825]Cf. Jn 5:24.
[1826]Phil 3:8.

was in such great harmony with God's that he joined not only her will, but even her flesh, to himself so completely that from his substance and the Virgin's He made one Christ, or rather He became one Christ. He was neither entirely from God nor entirely from the Virgin, yet he was fully God's son and also fully the Virgin's son. Nor were there two sons, but the one son of them both. Therefore the angel said "Hail full of grace, the Lord is with you." Not only the Lord, your son, is with you, whom you have clothed with your flesh, but also the Lord, the Holy Spirit by whom you conceived. The Father is with you, I say, he who makes his Son yours. The Son is with you, he who in order to bring about within you a marvelous mystery shut himself in a marvelous way in the retirement of your womb and preserved the seal of your virginity. The Holy Spirit is with you, he who being one with the Father and the Son, sanctifies your womb. Indeed "the Lord is with you"!

5. "Blessed are you among women."[1827] To these words of Elizabeth we must add those which she spoke immediately afterward: "And blessed is the fruit of your womb."[1828] It is not because you are blessed that the fruit is blessed as well, but you are blessed because he has come to you with the blessings of sweetness.[1829] The fruit of your womb is truly blessed, for in him all nations shall be blessed and of his fullness you also have received,[1830] as have we all, yet how differently. Therefore you are blessed, blessed among women, though he was not blessed among men or even among the angels. As the apostle says, he is "God above all, blessed forever."[1831] We are accustomed to speaking of a blessed man, blessed bread, a blessed woman, the blessed earth and to

[1827] Lk 1:28.
[1828] Lk 1:42.
[1829] Ps 21:3.

[1830] Gal 3:8; Jn 1:16.
[1831] Rom 9:5.

remark on any other creature which we know has received a blessing, but in quite a special way is the fruit of your womb blessed because he is God above all, blessed forever.

6. Blessed then is the fruit of your womb.[1832] Blessed in his fragrance, blessed in his savor, blessed in his comeliness. It was the fragrance of this sweet-smelling fruit that [Isaac] smelled when he said, "This is the fragrance of my son, similar to the smell of a field which the Lord has blessed."[1833] Ah! Is he not truly blessed whom the Lord has blessed? And someone else, having tasted the savor of this fruit, gave vent to his satisfaction saying, "Taste and see how sweet the Lord is."[1834] And in another place, "How great is the abundance of your sweetness, Lord, which you have laid up for those who fear you."[1835] And someone else said, "If only you could taste and see how sweet the Lord is."[1836] And the Fruit himself, inviting us to go to him, said of himself, "Those who eat me will hunger for more, and those who drink me will thirst for more."[1837] He was referring to the sweetness of his savor[1838] which, once it has been tasted, whets the appetite for more. This good fruit is both food and drink to the souls of those who hunger and thirst for righteousness.[1839]

You have heard of his fragrance; you have heard of his savor. Now listen about his comeliness. If it is true, as Scripture says,[1840] that the fruit of death was not only sweet to eat, but also beautiful to look at, how much greater must be the life-giving beauty of this living fruit upon which, according to another passage of Scripture, "even the angels longed to look"?[1841] He who said "Out of Sion comes the loveliness

[1832]Lk 1:42.
[1833]Gn 27:27.
[1834]Ps 34:8.
[1835]Ps 31:19.
[1836]1 Pt 2:3.
[1837]Sir 24:29.
[1838]Ws 16:20.
[1839]Mt 3:10, 7:19, 5:6.
[1840]Cn 3:3.
[1841]1 Pt 1:12.

of his beauty"[1842] was contemplating in his mind this come-liness and desired ardently to see it also in the flesh. And, in case you think he was praising some ordinary beauty, recall that you read in another psalm, "You are the comeliest of the sons of men: grace is poured upon your lips. Therefore God has blessed you forever."[1843]

7. Blessed, then, is the fruit of your womb,[1844] whom God has blessed forever.[1845] And in virtue of this blessing you too are blessed among women,[1846] for a bad tree cannot bear good fruit.[1847] Blessed, I say, among women, you are free not only from the general curse which decrees that "In pain you shall bring forth children,"[1848] but because you escape no less that other curse uttered long afterward: cursed be the childless woman in Israel.[1849] Yours was an exceptional blessing. You were not childless, yet you did not bring forth your child in pain. This is the hard burden and the heavy yoke laid on every daughter of Eve.[1850] If they bear children, they are in anguish; if they are childless, then they are cursed. The pain keeps them from having children and the curse from not having them. What will you do, virgin maid, you who have heard these words and read them? Will you give birth to a child and suffer agony or remain sterile and be cursed? Which will you choose, wise virgin?[1851] "On every side," she says, "I am hemmed in,[1852] yet I prefer to be cursed and to remain chaste than to conceive a child because of lust and then to bring him forth in pain deservedly. On one side I see a curse but no sin, and on the other, not only sin but anguish as well. Yet what is this curse but men's censure? There is no real reason why a childless woman should be cursed except

[1842]Ps 50:2.
[1843]Ps 45:3.
[1844]Lk 1:42.
[1845]Ps 45:3.

[1846]Lk 1:42.
[1847]Mt 7:18.
[1848]Gn 3:16.
[1849]Ex 23:26.

[1850]Sir 40:1.
[1851]Mt 25:2.
[1852]Dn 13:22.

because she is considered shameful and contemptible as if she were barren and worthless, and this is only so in Israel. But for me it is a very small thing that I should be displeasing to men when I can present myself a pure virgin to Christ."[1853] O wise virgin! O dedicated virgin! Whoever taught you that virginity is pleasing to God? What law, what justice, what page of the Old Testament either commands or counsels or urges you to live in the flesh yet not according to the flesh,[1854] to live on earth an angelic life? Where did you read, blessed Virgin, that "wisdom according to the flesh is death" and to "make no provision for the flesh never gratifying its desire"?[1855] Where did you read that virgins will sing a new song which no other person can sing?[1856] That they "follow the Lamb wherever he goes"?[1857] Where did you read that those who make themselves eunuchs for the sake of the kingdom of heaven are praised?[1858] Where did you read, though living in the flesh, we do not war with the flesh's weapons?[1859] Or: he who gives his virgin daughter in marriage does well, but that he who does not give her in marriage does better still?[1860] Where did you hear: "I wish that all were as I am myself," and, "It is good for a man if he follows my advice"?[1861] "Concerning virgins I have no command," he says, "but I give my advice"?[1862] In your case, however, I would say there is no other command, advice or example, but the anointing which taught you about everything, the living and active Word of God.[1863] He was your Master long before he became your son. He instructed your mind before he

[1853] 1 Cor 4:3; 2 Cor 11:2.
[1854] Cf. Rom 8:4.
[1855] Rom 8:6, 13:14.
[1856] Rv 14:3.
[1857] Rv 14:4.
[1858] Mt 19:12.
[1859] 2 Cor 10:3.
[1860] 1 Cor 7:38.
[1861] 1 Cor 7:7, 40.
[1862] 1 Cor 7:26.
[1863] 1 Jn 2:27; Heb 4:12.

clothed himself with your flesh. It was thus you resolved to present yourself to Christ as a virgin[1864] before you knew that you would also be presented to him as his mother. You chose to be despised in Israel. You preferred to risk being cursed for barrenness in order to be found pleasing to him who searched you out. Lo, this curse is changed into a blessing: your barrenness is rewarded with child bearing.

8. Virgin maid, open up your bosom, enlarge your womb, for he who is mighty is about to do great things for you.[1865] According to the Law in Israel you are cursed, but henceforth all generations will call you blessed.[1866] Do not distrust your own childbearing, wise Virgin, it will not stain your integrity. You shall conceive, but without sin. You will be heavy with child and yet not bowed down. You will give birth, but not in sadness.[1867] Though you know no man you will bear a son. What sort of son? You are to become the mother of a child whose father is God himself. A son of the brightness of the Father will be the crown of your love. The wisdom of the Father's heart shall become the fruit of your virginal womb. You are to give birth to God, you conceive by God. Take courage, pregnant Virgin, chaste maid with child, undefiled mother, for you will no longer be cursed in Israel or considered barren. And if Israel still curses you in fleshly terms, not because you are barren but because they are jealous of your childbearing, then remember that Christ also will bear the curse of the cross and it is he who blesses you, his mother, in heaven. But you are blessed on earth as well by the angel and by all generations after you. So "blessed are you among women, and blessed is the fruit of your womb."[1868]

[1864] 2 Cor 11:2.
[1865] Lk 1:49.
[1866] Lk 1:48.

[1867] Gn 3:6.
[1868] Lk 1:42.

9. "But when she heard this, she was troubled at the saying and pondered what sort of greeting this might be."[1869] It is usual for virgins—those who really are virgins—always to be timid and never to feel safe. They are so constantly on guard against danger that they easily take fright, because they know that they carry a precious treasure in an earthen vessel[1870] and that it is very difficult to live as an angel among men, to follow the ways of heaven on earth and to lead a heavenly life while still in the flesh. Any new or unexpected thing they suspect of being harmful and they think they see snares everywhere. That explains why Mary was troubled by what the angel said to her. She was troubled, but not distressed. It is written, "I am troubled and do not speak, but I consider the days of old, I remember the years long past."[1871] And so it was with Mary. She was troubled, she did not speak, but she pondered what sort of greeting this might be.[1872] That she should be troubled is only virginal reserve. Not to be distressed shows courage. That she was silent and pondered shows prudence. But she pondered what sort of greeting this might be. This wise Virgin knew only too well that Satan's angel often disguises himself as an angel of light[1873] and because she was all humility and simplicity she had never hoped to hear such words coming from a holy angel. That was why she pondered what sort of greeting this might be.

10. Then the angel, looking at the Virgin, immediately realized that she was turning over in her mind varied thoughts, and allayed her fears, cleared away her doubtfulness. He called her familiarly by her name, gently comforted her with soothing words saying, "Do not be afraid, Mary, you have found favor with God."[1874] It is as if he wanted to say, There is no ruse here, no trickery. You need not suspect any harm, or any trap. I am

---

[1869]Lk 1:29.
[1870]2 Cor 4:7.
[1871]Ps 77:4–5.
[1872]Lk 1:29.
[1873]2 Cor 11:14, 12:7.
[1874]Lk 1:30.

not a man, but a spirit, an angel of God not of Satan. Do not be afraid, Mary, you have found favor with God. Oh, if you only knew how pleasing your humility is to the Most High and what greatness has been prepared for you close to himself, you would not consider yourself too unworthy of this greeting and this homage. Why should you not find favor with angels when you have found favor with God? You have found what you were seeking,[1875] you have found what no one before you has ever been able to find, you have found favor with God. What is this favor? Peace between God and men, the destruction of death, the restoration of life. This is the favor you have found with God. And this will be a sign for you: "behold you will conceive and bear a son, and you shall call his name Jesus."[1876]

Wise Virgin, understand by the name of this promised son what great and special favor you have found with God. "And you shall call his name Jesus," said the angel. Another evangelist gives the reason for this name. He records the interpretation given by the angel: "he will save his people for their sins."[1877]

11. I have read of two Jesuses who prefigured the one we are dealing with here. Both were leaders of their nations. One of them led his people out of Babylon and the other took them into the promised land. Both defended the people against the enemy, but did they save them from their sins? Yet this Jesus, our Jesus, not only saves his people from their sins, he leads them into the land of the living.[1878] It is he who will save his people from their sins.[1879] Who is this who even forgives sins?[1880] Ah, if only the Lord Jesus would deign to count me, a sinner,[1881] among his people that he might save

---

[1875] Mt 7:7.
[1876] Lk 2:12, 1:31.
[1877] Mt 1:21.

[1878] Ps 116:9, 27:13.
[1879] Mt 1:21.

[1880] Lk 7:49.
[1881] Cf. Lk 18:13.

me from my sins. How blessed is the people whose God is the Lord Jesus,[1882] for he will save his people from their sins. I am afraid that a good many say they belong to his people whom he himself does not count as his people. I am afraid that to many of those who appear to be the most religious among his people he will one day say, "This people honors me with their lips, but their heart is far from me."[1883] The Lord Jesus knows his own. He knows them and he has chosen them from the beginning. Does he not say, "Why do you call me 'Lord, Lord,' and do not do what I tell you?"[1884] Do you want to know whether or not you belong to his people? Or rather, do you want to be among his people? Do what Jesus says, and he will count you among his people. Do what the Lord Jesus commands in the Gospel, what he commands in the law and the prophets;[1885] what he commands by his ministers who are in the Church.[1886] Be subject to his vicars, your leaders, not only to those who are modest and gentle, but also to the over-bearing,[1887] and learn from Jesus himself that he is meek and humble of heart,[1888] then you will be numbered among that blessed people of his whom he has chosen as his heritage,[1889] you will be one of the praiseworthy people whom the Lord blessed when he said, "You are the work of my hands, Israel my heritage."[1890] And for fear that you should strive to imitate the carnal Israel, he bears witness[1891] saying, "A people whom I have not known have served me, as soon as they heard of me they obeyed me."[1892]

12. Let us now hear what this same angel thinks about this child to whom, even before his conception, he has given so great a name. He says, "He will be great and will be called

[1882] Ps 33:12.
[1883] Mt 15:8.
[1884] Lk 6:46.
[1885] Lk 24:44.
[1886] 1 Cor 6:4.
[1887] 1 Pt 2:18.
[1888] Mt 11:29.
[1889] Ps 33:12.
[1890] Is 19:25.
[1891] Jn 1:15.
[1892] Ps 18:43–44.

the Son of the Most High."[1893] Is he not great when there is no end of his greatness?[1894] And he says, "Who is great like our God?"[1895] He is clearly great, he is as great as the Most High, for he is himself none other than the Most High. Nor, being the Son of the Most High, did he count it robbery to be equal to the Most High.[1896] The one who must be thought to have premeditated robbery is he who, having been called out of nothing into the form of an angel, likened himself to his Maker and snatched at what belongs to the Son of the Most High, to him who in the form of God was not made by God but begotten. The Most High Father, although he is almighty, could neither fashion a creature equal to himself nor beget a Son unequal to himself. He made the angel very great then, but not as great as himself, and therefore not most high. That the only-begotten Son whom he did not make but begot, the Almighty from the Almighty, the Most High from the Most High, coeternal with the eternal, claimed to be compared to him in every way, he thought neither robbery nor effrontery. How rightly then will he be called great: he is the Son of the Most High.

13. But why does the angel say "He will be" and not "he is" great? His greatness, forever unvarying, is not subject to growth. He will not be greater after his conception than before. Is it possible the angel meant to say that he who is a great God will become a great man? In that case he was right to say "He will be great," for he will be a great man, a great teacher, a great prophet. We do in fact read in the Gospel of him, "A great prophet has risen up among us."[1897] In the past there were lesser prophets who foretold the

---

[1893] Lk 1:32.
[1894] Ps 145:3.
[1895] Ps 113:5.

[1896] Phil 2:6.
[1897] Lk 7:16.

coming of this great prophet: "Behold, a great prophet shall come and he shall restore Jerusalem."[1898] You, however, virgin maid, will give birth to a little child, you will feed a little child and suckle a little one. But as you gaze at this little one, think how great he is. He will indeed be great, for God will magnify him in the sight of kings,[1899] and all kings will come to adore him, all nations shall serve him.[1900] So let your soul magnify the Lord,[1901] for he will be great and will be called the Son of the Most High. He will be great and he who is mighty will do great things in you, holy is his name.[1902] What holier name could he have than to be called the Son of the Most High? May this great Lord be magnified by us little ones as well; that he might make us great, he was made a little child. "Unto us a child is born," someone said, "For us a son is given."[1903] For us, I repeat, not for himself. He who was born of the Father before all ages was of more noble birth and had no need to be born in time from a mother. And he was not even born for the angels. They had him great among them and had no need of a little child. He was born for us, therefore, and given to us because we need him.

14. Now that he has been born and given to us, let us accomplish the purpose of this birth and this donation. He came for our good, let us use him to our good, let us work out our salvation from the Savior.[1904] Look, a little child is put in our midst.[1905] O little child so desired by your children! You are indeed a little child, but a child in evildoing,[1906] not a child in wisdom. Let us make every effort to become like this little child.[1907] Because he is meek and

[1898] Advent I Antiphon at None.
[1899] Sir 45:3.
[1900] Ps 72:11.
[1901] Lk 1:46.
[1902] Lk 1:49.
[1903] Is 9:6.
[1904] Phil 2:12.
[1905] Mt 18:2.
[1906] 1 Cor 14:20.
[1907] Mt 18:3.

humble in heart,[1908] let us learn from him, lest he who is great, even God, should have been made a little man for nothing, lest he should have died to no purpose,[1909] and have been crucified in vain. Let us learn his humility, imitate his gentleness, embrace his love, share his sufferings, be washed in his blood.[1910] Let us offer him the propitiation for our sins[1911] because for this he was born and given for us. Let us offer him up in the sight of the Father, offer him too to his own,[1912] for the Father did not spare his own Son but gave him up for us all.[1913] And the Son emptied himself, taking the form of a servant.[1914] He freely poured out his soul in death and was numbered with brigands and he bore the sins of many and interceded for transgressors that they might not perish.[1915] How can they perish whom the Son prayed might not perish, and for whose life the Father gave up his Son to death?[1916] We equally may hope therefore for forgiveness from them both for they are equally merciful in their steadfast love, united in a single powerful will, one in the substance of the Godhead, in which together with the Holy Spirit, they live and reign, one God forever and ever. Amen.

[1908] Mt 11:29.
[1909] Gal 2:21.
[1910] 1 Pt 4:13; Rv 1:5.
[1911] 1 Jn 2:2.
[1912] Jn 1:11.
[1913] Rom 8:31.
[1914] Phil 2:7.
[1915] Is 53:12.
[1916] Jn 10:10.

PART III

Selected Letters

TO BRUNO, [1917] ARCHBISHOP ELECT
OF COLOGNE
(A.D. 1131)

Bernard having been consulted by Bruno as to whether he ought to accept the See of Cologne, so replies as to hold him in suspense, and render him in awe of the burden of so great a charge. He advises him to seek counsel of God in prayer.

1. You seek counsel from me, most illustrious Bruno, as to whether you ought to accept the episcopate, to which it is desired to advance you. What mortal can presume to decide this for you? If God calls you, who can dare to dissuade you, but if He does not call you, who may counsel you to draw near? Whether the calling is of God or not who can know, except the Spirit, who searches even the deep things of God, or one to whom God Himself has revealed it? That which renders advice still more doubtful is the humble, but still terrible, confession in your letter, in which you accuse your own past life gravely, but, as I fully believe, in sincerity and truth. And it is undeniable that such a life is unworthy of a function so holy and exalted. On the other hand, you are very right to fear (and I fear the same with you) if, because of the unworthiness you feel, you fail to make profitable use of the talent of knowledge committed to you, unless you could, perhaps, find another way, less abundant, perhaps, but also less perilous, of making increase from it. I tremble, I confess it, for I ought to say to you as to myself what I feel: I tremble, I say, at the thought of the state whence, and that whither, you are called, especially since no period of penitence has intervened to prepare you for the perilous transition from

[1917]Bruno, son of Englebert, Count of Altena, was consecrated in 1132.

the one to the other. And, indeed, the right order requires that you should study to care for your own conscience before charging yourself with the care of those of others. That is the first step of piety, of which it is written, To pity your own soul is pleasing unto the Lord.[1918] It is from this first step that a well-ordered charity proceeds by a straight path to the love of one's neighbor, for the precept is to love him as ourselves. But if you are about to love the souls that would be confided to you as you have loved your own hitherto, I would prefer not to be confided rather than be so loved. But if you shall have first learned to love yourself then you will know, perhaps, how you should love me.

2. But what if God should quicken His grace and multiply His mercy upon you, and His clemency is able more quickly to replace the soul in a state of grace than daily penitence? Blessed, indeed, is he unto whom the Lord will not impute sin,[1919] for who shall bring accusation against the elect of God? If God justifies, who is he that condemns? This short road to salvation that holy thief attained, who in one and the same day both confessed his iniquities and entered into glory. He was content to pass by the cross as by a short bridge from the religion of death unto the land of the living, and from this foul mire into the paradise of joy.[1920] This sudden remedy of piety that sinful woman happily obtained, in whose soul grace of a sudden began to abound, where offenses had so abounded. Without much labor of penitence her sins were pardoned, because she loved much,[1921] and in a short time she merited to receive that amplitude of charity which, as it is written, covers the multitude of sins.[1922] This double benefit and most rapid goodness also

[1918] Eccl 30:23.
[1919] Ps 32:2.
[1920] Lk 23:43.
[1921] Lk 7:37–50.
[1922] 1 Pt 4:8.

that paralytic in the Gospel experienced, being cured first in the soul, then in the body.

3. But it is one thing to obtain the speedy forgiveness of sins, and another to be borne in a brief space from the sins themselves to the badges (fillets) of high dignities in the Church. Yet I see that Matthew from the receipt of custom was raised to the supreme honor of the apostolate. But this again troubles me, because he did not hear with the other apostles the charge, "Go into all the world and preach the Gospel to every creature,"[1923] until after he had done penitence, accompanying the Lord wherever He went, bearing long privation and remaining with Him in His temptations. I am not greatly reassured, though St. Ambrose was taken from the judge's tribunal to the priesthood, because he had from a boy led a pure and clean life, though in the world, and then he endeavored to avoid the episcopate even by flight and by hiding himself and many other means. Again, if Saul also was suddenly changed into Paul, a vessel of election, the Doctor of the Gentiles, and this be adduced as an example, it entirely destroys the similarity of the two cases to observe that he, therefore, obtained mercy because, as he himself says, he sinned ignorantly in unbelief. Besides, if such incidents, done for good and useful purposes, can be cited, it should be, not as examples, but as marvels, and it can be truly said of them, "This is the change of the right hand of the Highest."[1924]

4. In the meantime let these provisional replies to your queries suffice. If I do not express a decisive opinion, it is because I do not myself feel assured. This must needs be the case, for the gift of prophecy and of wisdom only could

[1923] Mk 16:15.
[1924] Ps 77:10.

resolve your doubt. For who could draw clear water out of a muddy pool? Yet there is one thing that I can do for a friend without danger, and with the assurance of a good result; that is to offer to God my petition that He will assist you in this matter. Leaving, therefore, to Him the secret things of His Providence, of which we are ignorant, I will beg Him, with humble prayer and earnest supplication, that He will work in you and with respect to you that which shall be for His glory, and at the same time for your good. And you have also the Lord Norbert,[1925] whom you may conveniently consult in person on all such subjects. For that good man is more fitted than I to explain the mysterious acts of Providence, as he is nearer to God by his holiness.

TO THE PRIOR AND MONKS OF
THE GRAND CHARTREUSE

He commends himself to their prayers.

To the very dear Lord and Reverend father Guigues, Prior of the Grande Chartreuse, and to the holy brethren who are with him, Brother Bernard of Clairvaux offers his humble service.

In the first place, when lately I approached your parts, I was prevented by unfavorable circumstances from coming to see you and to make your acquaintance; and although my excuse may perhaps be satisfactory to you, I am not able, I confess, to pardon myself for missing the opportunity. It is a

---

[1925]The founder of the Premonstratensian Order.

vexation to me that my occupations brought it about, not that I should neglect to come to see you, but that I was unable to do so. This I frequently have to endure, and therefore my anger is frequently excited. Would that I were worthy to receive the sympathy of all my kind friends. Otherwise I shall be doubly unhappy if my disappointment does not excite your pity. But I give you an opportunity, my brethren, of exercising brotherly compassion toward me, not that I merit it. Pity me not because I am worthy, but because I am poor and needy. Justice inquires into the merit of the suppliant, but mercy only looks to his unhappiness. True mercy does not judge, but feels; does not discuss the occasion which presents itself, but seizes it. When affection calls us, reason is silent. When Samuel wept over Saul it was by a feeling of pity, and not of approval.[1926] David shed tears over his parricidal son, and although they were profitless, yet they were pious. Therefore do you pity me (because I need it, not because I merit it), you who have obtained from God the grace to serve Him without fear, far from the tumults of the world from which you are freed. Happy those whom He has hidden in His tabernacle in the day of evil men; they shall trust in the shadow of His wings until the iniquity be overpast. As for me, poor, unhappy, and miserable, labor is my portion. I seem to be as a little unfledged bird almost constantly out of the shelter of its nest, exposed to wind and tempest. I am troubled, and I stagger like a drunken man, and my whole conscience is gnawed with care. Pity me, then; for although I do not merit pity I need it, as I have said.

[1926] 1 Sm 15:13.

TO THE SAME

(c. A.D. 1127)

He protests against the reputation for holiness which is attributed to him, and promises to communicate the treatises which he has written.

1. Even if I should give myself to you entirely that would be too little a thing still in my eyes, to have recompensed toward you even the half of the kindly feeling which you express toward my humility. I congratulate myself, indeed, on the honor which you have done me; but my joy, I confess, is tempered by the thought that it is not anything I have accomplished, but only an opinion of my merit which has brought me this favor. I should be greatly ashamed to permit myself in vain complacency when I feel assured that what is loved or respected in me is not, indeed, what I am, but what I am thought to be; for when I am thus loved it is not then I that am loved, but something in me, I know not what, and which is not me, is loved in my stead. I say that I know not, but, to speak more truly, I know very well that it is nothing. For whatever is thought to exist, and does not, is nothing. The love and he who feels it is real enough, but the object of the love does not exist. That such should be capable of inspiring love is wonderful, but still more it is regrettable. It is from that we are able to feel whence and whither we go, what we have lost, what we find. By remaining united to Him, who is the real Being, and who is always happy, we also shall attain a continued and happy existence. By remaining united to Him, I said; that is, not only by knowledge, but by love. For certain of the sons of Adam when they had known God, glorified Him not as God, nor were thankful, but became vain in their

imaginations."[1927] Rightly, then, were their foolish hearts darkened, because since they recognized the truth and despised it, they were justly punished for their fault by losing the power to recognize it. Alas! in thus adhering to the truth by the mind, but with the heart departing from it, and loving vanity in its place, man became himself a vain thing. And what is more vain than to love vanity, and what is more repugnant to justice than to despise the truth? What is more just than that the power to recognize the truth should be withdrawn from those who have despised it, and that those who did not glorify the truth when they recognized it should lose the power of boasting of the knowledge? Thus the love of vanity is the contempt of truth, and the contempt of truth the cause of our blindness. And because they did not like, he says, to retain God in their knowledge, He gave them over unto a reprobate mind."[1928]

2. From this blindness, then, it follows that we frequently love and approve that which is not for that which is; since while we are in this body we are wandering from Him who is the Fullness of Existence. And what is man, O God, except that You have taken knowledge of him? If the knowledge of God is the cause that man is anything, the want of this makes him nothing. But He who calls those things which are not as though they were, pitying those reduced in a manner to nothing, and not yet able to contemplate in its reality, and to embrace by love that hidden manna, concerning which the apostle says: "Your life is hidden with Christ in God."[1929] But in the meantime He has given us to taste it by faith and to

[1927] Rom 1:21.
[1928] Rom 1:28.
[1929] 1 Cor 3:3.

seek for by strong desire. By these two we are brought for the second time from not being, to begin to be that His (new) creature, which one day shall pass into a perfect man, into the measure of the stature of the fullness of Christ. That, without doubt, shall take place, when righteousness shall be turned into judgment, that is, faith into knowledge, the righteousness which is of faith into the righteousness of full knowledge, and also the hope of this state of exile shall be changed into the fullness of love. For if faith and love begin during the exile, knowledge and love render perfect those in the Presence of God. For as faith leads to full knowledge, so hope leads to perfect love, and, as it is said, "If you will not believe, you will not understand,"[1930] so it may equally be said with fitness, if you have not hoped, you will not perfectly love. Knowledge then is the fruit of faith, perfect charity of hope. In the meantime the just lives by faith,[1931] but he is not happy except by knowledge; and he aspires toward God as the hart desires the water-brooks; but the blessed drinks with joy from the fountain of the Savior, that is, he delights in the fullness of love.

3. Thus understanding and love, that is, the knowledge of and delight in the truth, are, perhaps, as it were, the two arms of the soul, with which it embraces and comprehends with all saints the length and breadth, the height and depth, that is the eternity, the love, the goodness, and the wisdom of God. And what are all these but Christ? He is eternity, because "this is life eternal to know You the true God and Jesus Christ whom You have sent."[1932] He is Love, because He is God, and God is Love.[1933] He is both the Goodness of God and the Wisdom of God,[1934] but when shall these things

[1930] Is 7:9, acc. to 70.
[1931] Hb 2:4.
[1932] Jn 17:3.

[1933] 1 Jn 4:16.
[1934] 1 Cor 1:24.

be? When shall we see Him as He is? For the expectation of the creature waits for the revelation of the sons of God. For the creature was subjected unto vanity, not willingly.[1935] It is that vanity diffused through all which makes us desire to be praised even when we are blamable, and not to be willing to praise those whom we know to be worthy of it. But this too is vain, that we, in our ignorance, frequently praise what is not, and are silent about what is. What shall we say to this, but that the children of men are vain, the children of men are deceitful upon the weights, so that they deceive each other by vanity.[1936] We praise falsely, and are foolishly pleased, so that they are vain who are praised, and they false who praise. Some flatter and are deceptive, others praise what they think deserving, and are deceived; others pride themselves in the commendations which are addressed to them, and are vain. The only wise man is he who says with the apostle: "I forbear, lest any man should think of me above that which he sees me to be or that he hears of me."[1937]

4. For the present I have noted down these things too hastily (because of this in not so finished a way), rather than dictated them for you, perhaps also at greater length than I should, but to the best of my poor ability. But that my letter may finish at the point whence it began, I beg you not to be too credulous of uncertain rumor about me, which, as you know well, is accustomed to be wrong both in giving praise and in attaching blame. Be so kind, if you please, as to weigh your praises, and examine with care how far your friendship for me and your favor are well founded, thus they will be the more acceptable from my friend as they are fitted to my humble merit. Thus when praise shall have proceeded from

[1935]Rom 8:19, 20.
[1936]Ps 61:9, 70.
[1937]2 Cor 12:6.

grave judgment, and not from the error of the vulgar, if it is more moderate it will be at the same time more easy to bear. I assure you that what attaches me (humble person as I am), to you is the zeal, industry, and sincerity with which you employ yourself, as they say, in the accomplishment of your charge in holy things. May it be always thus with you that this may be said of you always with truth. I send you the book which you desire to have in order to copy; as for the other treatises of mine which you wish that I should send, they are but few, and contain nothing which I should think worthy of your attention, yet because I should prefer that my want of intelligence should be blamed rather than my good-will, and I would rather endanger my inexperience than my obedience in your sight, be so good as to let me know by the present messenger which of my treatises you wish that I should send you, so that I may ask for them again from those persons to whom they have been lent, and send them wherever you shall direct. That you may know what you wish for, I may say that I have written a little book on Humility, four Homilies on the Praises of the Virgin Mother (for the little book has this title), upon that passage of St. Luke where it is said the angel Gabriel was sent.[1938] Also an Apology dedicated to a certain friend of mine, in which I have treated of some of our observances, that is to say, those of Citeaux, and those of Cluny. I have also written a few Letters to various persons, and finally, there are some of my discourses which the brethren who heard them have reproduced in their own words and keep them in their hands. Would that any of the simple productions of my humble powers might be of any service to you, but I do not dare to expect it.

[1938] Lk 1:26.

TO ALEXANDER, [1939] BISHOP OF LINCOLN
(C. A.D. 1129)

A certain canon named Philip, on his way to Jerusalem, happening to turn aside to Clairvaux, wished to remain there as a monk. He solicits the consent of Alexander, his bishop, to this, and begs him to sanction arrangements with the creditors of Philip. He finishes by exhorting Alexander not to trust too much in the glory of the world.

To the very honorable lord, Alexander, by the grace of god, Bishop of Lincoln, Bernard, Abbot of Clairvaux, wishes honor more in Christ than in the world.

1. Your Philip, wishing to go to Jerusalem, has found his journey shortened, and has quickly reached the end that he desired. He has crossed speedily this great and wide sea, and after a prosperous voyage has now reached the desired shore, and anchored at length in the harbor of salvation. His feet stand already in the Courts of Jerusalem, and Him whom he had heard of in Ephrata he has found in the broad woods, and willingly worships in the place where his feet have stayed. He has entered into the Holy City and has obtained a heritage with those of whom it is rightly said: "Now you are no longer strangers and foreigners, but fellow citizens with the saints and of the household of God."[1940] He goes in and out with the saints and is become as one of them, praising God and saying as they: "Our conversation is in heaven."[1941] He is become, therefore, not a curious spectator only, but a devoted inhabitant and an enrolled citizen of

---

[1939]This Alexander was bishop of Lincoln in England from 1123 to 1147.
[1940]Eph 2:19.
[1941]Phil 3:20.

Jerusalem; but not the Jerusalem of this world with which is joined Mount Sinai, in Arabia, which is in bondage with her children, but of her who is above, who is free, and the mother of us all.[1942]

2. And this, if you are willing to perceive it, is Clairvaux. This is Jerusalem, and is associated by a certain intuition of the spirit, by the entire devotion of the heart, and by conformity of daily life, with her which is in heaven. This shall be, as he promises himself, his rest forever. He has chosen her for his habitation, because with her is, although not yet the realization, at least the expectation, of true peace of which it is said: The peace of God which passes all understanding.[1943] But this is true happiness; although he has received it from above, he desires to embrace it with your good permission, or rather he trusts that he has done this according to your wish, knowing that you are not ignorant of that sentence of the wise man, that a wise son is the glory of his father.[1944] He makes request, therefore, of your paternity, and we also make request with him and for him, to be so kind as to allow the payments which he has assigned to his creditors from his prebend to remain unaltered, so that he may not be found (which God forbid) a defaulter and breaker of his covenant, and so that the offering of a contrite heart, which he makes daily, may not be rejected by God, inasmuch as any brother has a claim against him. And lastly, he entreats that the house which he has built for his mother upon church land, with the ground which he has assigned there, may be preserved to his mother during her life. Thus much with regard to Philip.

3. I have thought well to add these few words for yourself,

[1942]Gal 4:25–26.

[1943]Phil 4:17.

[1944]Prv 10:1. Bernard always quotes this passage thus. In the Vulgate, it is *Filius sapiens laetificat patrem.*

of my own accord, or rather at the inspiration of God, and venture to exhort you in all charity, not to look to the glory of the world which passes away, and to lose that which abides eternally; not to love your riches more than yourself, nor for yourself, lest you lose yourself and them also. Do not, while present prosperity smiles upon you, forget its certain end, lest adversity without end succeed it. Let not the joy of this present life hide from you the sorrow which it brings about, and brings about while it hides. Do not think death far off, so that it come upon you unprepared, and while in expectation of long life it suddenly leaves you when ill-prepared, as it is written: "When they say 'Peace and safety,' then sudden destruction comes upon them, as travail upon a woman with child, and they shall not escape."[1945] Farewell.

TO RAINALD, ABBOT OF FOIGNY

Bernard declares to him how little he loves praise; that the yoke of Christ is light; that he declines the name of father, and is content with that of brother.

1. In the first place, do not wonder if titles of honor affright me, when I feel myself so unworthy of the honors themselves; and if it is fitting that you should give them to me, it is not expedient for me to accept them. For if you think that you ought to observe that saying, "In honor preferring one another,"[1946] and, "Submit yourselves one to another in the fear of God,"[1947] yet the terms one another, one to another,

[1945] 1 Thes 5:3.
[1946] Rom 12:10.
[1947] Eph 5:21.

are not used at random, and concern me as well as you. Again, if you think that the declaration of the Rule is to be observed, "Let the younger honor their elders,"[1948] I remember what the Truth has ruled: "The last shall be first, and the first last,"[1949] and, "He that is the greater among you, let him be as the younger,"[1950] and "The greater You are, the more humble Yourself,"[1951] and "Not because we have dominion over your faith, but are helpers of your joy"[1952] and, "Have they made you the master? Be then among them as one of them,"[1953] and "Be not called Rabbi"; and "Call no man your father upon the earth."[1954] As much, then, as I am carried away by your compliments, so much am I restrained by the weight of these texts. Wherefore I rightly, I do not say sing, but mourn; While I suffer your terrors I am distracted, and "You have lifted me up and cast me down."[1955] But I should, perhaps, represent more truly what I feel if I say that he who exalts me really humiliates me; and he who humiliates me, exalts. You, therefore, rather depress me in heaping me with terms of honor and exalt me by humbling. But that you may not humble so as to crush me, these and similar testimonies of the Truth console me, which wonderfully raise up those whom they make humble, instruct while they humiliate. Thus this same Hand that casts me down raises me up again and makes me sing with joy. "It was good for me, O Lord, that I was afflicted, that I might learn Your statutes; the law of Your mouth is good unto me, above thousands of gold and silver."[1956] This marvel the word of God, living and efficacious, produces. This, that Word by which all things

[1948]Rule of St. Benedict, chap. 63.
[1949]Mt 20:16.
[1950]Lk 22:26.
[1951]Eccl 3:18.
[1952]2 Cor 1:24.
[1953]Eccl 32:1.
[1954]Mt 23:8, 9.
[1955]Ps 88:15; Ps 102:10.
[1956]Ps 119:71, 72.

are done, gently and powerfully brings to pass; this, in short, is the work of the easy yoke and light burden of Christ.[1957]

2. We cannot but wonder how light is the burden of Truth. Is not that truly light which does not burden, but relieves him who bears it? What lighter than that weight, which not only does not burden, but even bears everyone upon whom it is laid to bear? This weight was able to render fruitful the Virgin's womb, but not to burden it. This weight sustained the very arms of the aged Simeon, in which He was received. This caught up Paul, though with weighty and corruptible body, into the third heaven. I seek in all things to find if possible something like to this weight which bears them who bear it, and I find nothing but the wings of birds which in any degree resembles it, for these in a certain singular manner render the body of birds at once more weighty and more easily moved. Wonderful work of nature! that at the same time increases the material and lightens the burden, and while the mass is greater the burden is in the same degree less. Thus plainly in the wings is expressed the likeness of the burden of Christ, because they themselves bear that by which they are borne. What shall I say of a chariot? This, too, increases the load of the horse by which it is drawn, but at the same time renders capable of being drawn a load which without it could not be moved. Load is added to load, yet the whole is lighter. See also how the Chariot of the Gospel comes to the weighty load of the Law, and helps to carry it on to perfection, while decreasing the difficulty. His word, it is said, runs very swiftly.[1958] His word, before known only in Judea, and not able, because of its weightiness, to extend beyond, which burdened and

[1957] Mt 11:30.
[1958] Ps 147:15.

weighed down the hands of Moses himself, when lightened by Grace, and placed upon the wheels of the Gospel, ran swiftly over the whole earth, and reached in its rapid flight the confines of the world.

3. Do you, therefore, my very dear friend, cease from overwhelming me rather than raising with undeserved honors; otherwise you range yourself, though with a friendly intention, in the company of my enemies. These are they of whom I am in the habit of thus complaining to God alone in my prayers. Those who praised me were sworn against me.[1959] To this, my complaint, I hear God soon replying, and bearing witness to the truth of my words: Truly they who bless you lead you into error.[1960] Then I reply, "Let them be soon brought to shame who say unto me, There, There!"[1961] But I ought to explain in what manner I understand these words, that it may not be thought I launch maledictions or imprecations against any of my adversaries. I pray, then, that whosoever think of me above that which they see in me or hear respecting me may be turned back, that is, return from the excessive praises which they have given me without knowing me. In what way? When they shall know better him whom they praise without measure, and consequently shall blush for their error, and for the ill service that they have rendered to their friend. And in this way it is that I say, Turn back! and blush! to both kinds of my enemies; those who wish me evil and commend me in order to flatter, and those who innocently, and even kindly, but yet to my injury, praise me to excess. I would wish to appear to them so vile and abject that they would be ashamed to have praised such

---

[1959] Ps 102:8, Vulgate.
[1960] Is 9:16, cited from memory.
[1961] Ps 70:3.

a person, and should cease to bestow praises so indiscreetly. Therefore, against panegyrists of each kind I am accustomed to strengthen myself with those two verses: against the hostile with the former, Let them be turned back and soon brought to shame who wish me evil, but against the well-meaning, Let them be turned backward and made to blush who say over me, There, There!

4. But as (to return to you) I ought, according to the example of the apostle, to rejoice with you only, and not to have dominion over your piety, and according to the word of God we have one Father only who is in heaven, and all we are brethren, I find myself obliged to repel from me with a shield of truth the lofty name of Lord and Father with which you have intended, I know well, to honor me, not to burden; and in place of these I think it fitter that you should name me brother and fellow servant, both because we have the same heritage, and because we are in the same condition, lest perchance if I should usurp to myself a title which belongs to God, I shall hear from Him: "If I be a Father: where is my honor, and I be a Lord where is my fear?"[1962] It is very true, however, that if I do not wish to attribute to myself over you the authority of a father, I have all the feelings of one, nor is the love with which I embrace you less, I think, than that of a father or of a son. Sufficient, then, on the subject of the titles which you give me.

5. I wish to reply now to the rest of your letter. You complain that I do not come to see you. I could complain equally of you for the same reason, unless, indeed (which you yourself do not deny), the will of God must be preferred to our feelings and our needs. If it were otherwise, if it were not the work of Christ that was in question, would I suffer to be so

[1962]Mal 1:6.

far away from me a companion so dear and necessary to me, so obedient in labor, so persevering in studies, so useful in conference, so prompt in recollection? Blessed are we if we still remain thus until the end always and in everything, seeking not our own interests, but those of Jesus Christ.

TO THE SAME

He instructs Rainald, who was too anxious and distrustful, respecting the duty of superior which had been conferred upon him; and warns him that he must bestow help and solace upon his brethren rather than require it from them.

To his very dear son, Rainald, Abbot of Foigny, that God may give him the spirit of strength.

1. You complain, my very dear son, of your many tribulations, and by your pious complaints you excite me also to complain, for I am not able to feel that you are sorrowing without sharing your sorrow, nor can I be otherwise than troubled and anxious when I hear of your troubles and anxieties. But since I foresaw these very difficulties which you say have happened to you, and predicted them to you, if you remember; it seems to me that you ought to be better prepared to endure them, and to spare me vexation when you can. For am I not sufficiently tried, and more than sufficiently, to lose you, not to see you, nor to enjoy your society, which was so pleasant to me; so that I have almost regretted that I should have sent you away from me. And although charity obliged me to send you, yet not being able to see you where you have been sent, I mourn you as if lost to me. When, then, besides this, you who ought to be the staff of my

support, belabor me as it were with the rod of your faint-heartedness, you heap sorrow upon sorrow, and torment upon torment; and if it is a mark of your filial affection toward me that you do not hide any of your difficulties from me, yet it is hard to add fresh trouble to one already burdened. Why is it needful to occupy with fresh anxieties one already more than anxious enough, and to torture with sharper pains the bosom of a father, already wounded by the absence of his son? I have shared with you my weight of cares, as a son, as an intimate friend, as a trusty assistant; but how do you help to bear your father's burden, if, instead of relieving me, you burden me still more? You, indeed, are loaded, but I am not lightened of my load.

2. For this burden is that of sick and weak souls. Those who are in health do not need to be carried, and are not, therefore, a burden. Whomsoever, then, of your brethren you shall find sad, mean-spirited, discontented, remember well that it is of these and for their sakes you are father and abbot. In consoling, in exhorting, in reproving, you do your duty, you bear your burden; and those whom you bear in order to cure, you will cure by bearing. But if anyone is in such spiritual health that he rather helps you than is helped by you, recognize that to him you are not father and abbot, but equal and friend. Do not complain if you find more trials than consolations from those among whom you are. You were sent to sustain and console others, because you are spiritually stronger and better able to bear than they, and because with the grace of God you are able to aid and sustain all without needing yourself to be aided and sustained by any. Finally, if the burden is great, so also is the reward; but, on the other hand, the more assistance you receive, the more your own reward is diminished. Choose, therefore; if you prefer those who are for you a burden, your merit will be the

greater; but if, on the contrary, you prefer those who console you, you have no merit at all. The former are the source whence it arises for you; the second as the abyss in which it is swallowed up; for it is not doubtful that those who are partakers of the labor will be also sharers of the reward. Knowing, then, that you were sent to help, not to be helped, bear in mind that you are the vicar of Him who came not to be ministered unto, but to minister. I could have wished to write at greater length, in order to comfort you, but that it was not necessary; for what need is there of filling a dead leaf with superfluous words, while the living voice is speaking? I think that when you have seen our prior, these words will be sufficient for you, and your spirit will revive at his presence, so that you will not require the consolation of written words, in the delight and help which his discourse will give you. Do not doubt that I have communicated to him, as far as was possible, my inmost mind, which you begged in your letters might be sent to you. For you know well that he and I are of one mind and one will.

TO THE ABBOT OF ST. JOHN AT CHARTRES
(c. A.D. 1128)

Bernard dissuades him from resigning his charge and undertaking a pilgrimage to Jerusalem.

1. As regards the matters about which you were so good as to consult so humble a person as myself, I had at first determined not to reply. Not because I had any doubt what to say, but because it seemed to me unnecessary or even presumptuous to give counsel to a man of sense and wisdom. But considering that it usually happens that the greater number of persons of

sense, or I might say that all such trust the judgment of another person rather than their own in doubtful cases, and that those who have a clear judgment in the affairs of others, however obscure, frequently hesitate and are undecided about their own, I depart from my first resolution, not, I hope, without reason, and without prejudice to any wiser opinion explain to you simply how the matter appears to me. You have signified to me, if I do not mistake, by the pious Abbot Ursus of St. Denis, that you have it in contemplation to desert your country and the monastery over which, by the Providence of God, you are head, to undertake a pilgrimage to Jerusalem, to occupy yourself henceforth only with God and the salvation of your own soul. Perhaps, if you aspire unto perfection, it may be expedient for you to leave your country, when God says, "Go forth from Your country and from Your kindred."[1963] But I do not see at all on what ground you ought to risk, by your departure, the safety of the souls entrusted to you. For is it pleasant to enjoy liberty after having laid down your burden? But charity does not seek her own interests. Perhaps the wish for quiet and rest attracts you? But it is obtained at the price of the peace of others. Freely will I do without the enjoyment of any desire, even a spiritual one, which cannot be obtained except at the price of a scandal. For where there is scandal, there, without doubt, is loss of charity: and where there is loss of charity, surely no spiritual advantage can be hoped for. Finally, if it is permitted to anyone to prefer his own quiet to the common good, who is there that can say with truth: "For me to live is Christ, and to die is gain"?[1964] And where will that principle be which the apostle declares: "No one lives to himself, and no

[1963] Gn 12:1.
[1964] Phil 1:21.

one dies to himself"[1965] and, "Not seeking mine own profit, but the profit of many";[1966] and, "That he who lives should not any longer live unto himself, but unto Him who died for all"?[1967]

2. But you will say: Whence comes my great desire, if it is not from God? With your permission I will say what I think. Stolen waters are sweet;[1968] and for whosoever knows the devices of the devil, it is not doubtful that the angel of darkness is able to change himself into an angel of light, and to pour upon the thirsting soul those waters of which the sweetness is more bitter than wormwood. In truth, what other can be the suggester of scandals, the author of dissension, the troubler of unity and peace, except the devil, the adversary of truth, the envier of charity, the ancient foe of the human race, and the enemy of the Cross of Christ? If death entered into the world through his envy, even so now he is jealous of whatever good he sees you doing; and since he is a liar from the beginning, he falsely promises now better things which he does not see. For when did the Truth oppose that most faithful saying, "Art You bound unto a wife? Seek not to be loosed."[1969] Or when did charity urge to scandal, who at the scandals of all shows herself burning with regret? He, then, the most wicked one, opposed to charity by envy, and to truth by falsehood, mixing falsehood and gall with the true honey, promises doubtful things as certain, and gives out that true things are false, not that he may give you what you vainly hope for, but that he may take away what you are profitably holding now. He prowls around and seeks how he may take away from the flock the care of the pastor, to make a prey of it when there is none to

---

[1965] Rom 14:7.
[1966] 1 Cor 10:33.
[1967] 2 Cor 5:15.

[1968] Prv 9:17.
[1969] 1 Cor 7:27.

defend it from his attacks; and, besides this, to bring down upon the pastor that terrible rebuke, "Woe to him by whom scandal cometh."[1970] But I have full confidence in the wisdom given to you by God, that by no cunning devices of the wicked one you will be seduced or made to renounce certain good, and for the hope of uncertain advantage to incur certain evil.

TO THE SAME
(A.D. 1137)

He expresses his regret at his very long absence from his beloved Clairvaux and his desire to return to his dear sons. He tells them of the consolations that he feels nevertheless in his great labors for the Church.

1. My soul is sorrowful until I return, and it refuses to be comforted till it see you. For what is my consolation in the hour of evil, and in the place of my pilgrimage? Are not you in the Lord? Wherever I go, the sweet memory of you never leaves me; but the sweeter the memory the more I feel the absence. Ah, me! that the time of my sojourning here is not only prolonged, but its burden increased, and truly, as the prophet says, they who for a time separate me from you have added to the pain of my wounds.[1971] Life is an exile, and one that is dreary enough, for while we are in the body we are absent from the Lord. To this is added the special grief which almost makes me impatient, that I am forced to live without you. It is a protracted sickness, a wearisome waiting, to be so long subject to the vanity which possesses everything here, to

[1970]Mt 18:7.
[1971]Ps 69:26.

be imprisoned within the horrid dungeon of a noisome body, to be still bound with the chains of death, and the ropes of sin, and all this time to be away from Christ. But against all these things one solace was given me from above, instead of His glorious countenance which has not yet been revealed, and that is the sight of the holy temple of God, which is you. From this temple it used to seem to me an easy passage to that glorious temple, after which the prophet sighed when he said: "One thing have I desired of the Lord, which I will require, even that I may dwell in the house of the Lord all the days of my life, to behold the fair beauty of the Lord and to visit His temple."[1972]

2. What shall I say? How often has that solace been taken from me? Lo, this is now the third time, if I mistake not, that my children have been taken from me. The babes have been too early weaned, and I am not allowed to bring up those whom I begot through the Gospel. In short, I am forced to abandon my own children and look after those of others, and I hardly know which is the more distressing, to be taken from the former, or to have to do with the latter. O, good Jesu! is my whole life thus to waste away in grief, and my years in mourning? It is good for me, O Lord, rather to die than to live, only let it be among my brethren, those of my own household, those who are dearest to my heart. That, as all know, is sweeter and safer, and more natural. Nay, it would be a loving act to grant to me that I might be refreshed before I go away, and be no more seen. If it please my Lord that the eyes of a father, who is not worthy to be called a father, should be closed by the hands of his sons, that they may witness his last moments, soothe his end, and raise

[1972]Ps 26:4.

his spirit by their loving prayers to the blissful fellowship, if you think him worthy to have his body buried with the bodies of those who are blessed because poor, if I have found favor in Your sight, this I most earnestly ask that I may obtain by the prayers and merits of these my brethren. Nevertheless, not my will but Yours be done. Not for my own sake do I wish for either life or death.

3. But it is only right, that as you have heard of my grief, you should also know what consolation I have. The first solace for all the trouble and misfortune that I undergo is the thought that the cause I strive for is that of Him to whom all things live. Whether I will or no, I must live for Him who bought my life at the price of His own, and who is able, as a merciful and righteous judge, to recompense us in that day whatever we may suffer for Him. But if I have served as His soldier against my will, it will be only that a dispensation has been entrusted unto me, and I shall be an unprofitable servant; but if I serve willingly I shall have glory. In this consideration, then, I breathe again for a little. My second consolation is that often, without any merit of mine, grace from above has crowned me in my labors, and that grace in me was not in vain, as I have many times found, and as you have seen to some extent. But how necessary just now the presence of my feebleness is to the Church of God, I would say for your consolation were it not that it would sound like boasting. But as it is, it is better that you should learn it from others.

4. Moved by the pressing request of the emperor, by the apostolic command, as well as by the prayers of the Church and the princes, whether with my will or against my will, weak and ill, and, to say truth, carrying about with me the pallid image of the King of terrors, I am borne away into Apulia. Pray for the things which make for the Church's peace and our salvation, that I may again see you, live with

you, and die with you, and so live that ye may obtain. In my weakness and time of distress, with tears and groanings, I have dictated these words, as our dear brother Baldwin[1973] can testify, who has taken them down from my mouth, and who has been called by the Church to another office and elevated to a new dignity. Pray, too, for him, as my one comfort now, and in whom my spirit is greatly refreshed. Pray, too, for our lord the Pope, who regards me and all of you equally with the tenderest affection. Pray, too, for my lord the Chancellor, who is to me as a mother; and for those who are with him—my lord Luke, my lord Chrysogonus, and Master Ivo[1974]—who show themselves as brothers. They who are with me—Brother Bruno and Brother Gerard[1975]—salute you and ask for your prayers.

TO THOMAS, PRIOR OF BEVERLEY

This Thomas had taken the vows of the Cistercian Order at Clairvaux. As he showed hesitation, Bernard urges his tardy spirit to fulfill them. But the following letter will prove that it was a warning to deaf ears, where it relates the unhappy end of

---

[1973]Baldwin, first cardinal of the Cistercian Order, was created by Innocent, A.D. 1130, at a council held at Claremont. He was afterward made archbishop of Pisa; cf. *Life of St. Bernard* (lib. ii. n. 49): "In Pisa was Baldwin born, the glory of his native land, and a burning light to the Church." So great a man did not think it beneath him to act as Bernard's secretary, and his praises are sung in Ep. 245; cf. Ep. 201.

[1974]All these were cardinals. Luke, of the title of SS. John and Paul, was created A.D. 1132; Chrysogonus, of the title of St. Maria de Porticu, A.D. 1134; Ivo, a regular canon of St. Victor of Paris, A.D. 1130, of the title of St. Laurence in Damascus; to him Ep. 193 was written.

[1975]Bruno is called (Ep. 209) the father of many disciples in Sicily. Gerard seems to be Bernard's brother. For Bruno, see also Ep. 165n4.

Thomas. In this letter Bernard sketches with a master's hand the whole scheme of salvation.

Bernard to his beloved son Thomas, as being his son.

1. What is the good of words? An ardent spirit and a strong desire cannot express themselves simply by the tongue. We want your sympathy and your bodily presence to speak to us; for if you come you will know us better, and we shall better appreciate each other. We have long been held in a mutual bond as debtors one to another; for I owe you faithful care and you owe me submissive obedience. Let our actions and not our pens, if you please, prove each of us. I wish you would apply to yourself henceforth and carry out toward me those words of the Only Begotten: "The works which the Father has given Me to finish, the same works bear witness of Me."[1976] For, indeed, only thus does the spirit of the Only Son bear witness with our spirit that we also are the sons of God, when, quickening us from dead works, He causes us to bring forth the works of life. A good or bad tree is distinguished, not by its leaves or flowers, but by its fruit. So "By their fruits, He says, you shall know them."[1977] Works, then, and not words, make the difference between sons of God and sons of unbelief. By works, accordingly, do you display your sincere desire and make proof of mine.

2. I long for your presence; my heart has long wished for you, and expected the fulfillment of your promises. Why am I so pressing? Certainly not from any personal or earthly feeling. I desire either to be profited by you or to be of service to you. Noble birth, bodily strength and beauty, the glow

[1976] Jn 5:36.
[1977] Mt 7:16.

of youth, estates, palaces, and sumptuous furniture, external badges of dignity, and, I may also add, the world's wisdom—all these are of the world, and the world loves its own. But for how long will they endure? Forever? Assuredly not; for the world itself will not last forever; but these will not last even for long. In fact, the world will not be able long to keep these gifts for you, nor will you dwell long in the world to enjoy them, for the days of man are short. The world passes away with its lusts, but it dismisses you before it quite passes away itself. How can you take unlimited pleasure in a love that soon must end? But I ever love you, not your possessions; let them go whence they were derived. I only require of you one thing: that you would be mindful of your promise, and not deny us any longer the satisfaction of your presence among us, who love you sincerely, and will love you forever. In fact, if we love purely in our life, we shall also not be divided in death. For those gifts which I wish for in your case, or rather for you, belong not to the body or to time only; and so they fail not with the body, nor pass away with time; nay, when the body is laid aside they delight still more, and last when time is gone. They have nothing in common with the gifts above-mentioned, or such as they with which, I imagine, not the Father, but the world has endowed you. For which of these does not vanish before death, or at last fall a victim to it?

3. But, indeed, that is the best part, which shall not be taken away forever. What is that? "Eye has not seen it, nor ear heard, neither has it entered into the heart of man."[1978] He who is a man and walks simply according to man's nature only, he who, to speak more plainly, is still content with flesh and blood, is wholly ignorant what that is,

[1978] 1 Cor 2:9.

because flesh and blood will not reveal the things which God alone reveals through His Spirit. So the natural man is in no way admitted to the secret; in fact, he receives not the things of the Spirit of God.[1979] Blessed are they who hear His words. I have called you friends, for all things that I have heard of My Father I have made known to you.[1980] O, wicked world, which will not bless Your friends except You make them enemies of God, and consequently unworthy of the council of the blessed. For clearly he who is willing to be Your friend makes himself the enemy of God. And if the servant knows not what his Lord does, how much less the enemy? Moreover, the friend of the Bridegroom stands, and rejoices with joy because of the Bridegroom's voice; whence also it says, "My soul failed when [my beloved] spoke."[1981] And so the friend of the world is shut out from the council of the friends of God; who have received not the spirit of this world but the spirit which is of God, that they may know the things which are given to them of God. I thank You, O Father, because You have hid these things from the wise and prudent, and have revealed them unto babes; even so, Father, for so it seemed good in Your sight,[1982] not because they of themselves deserved it. For all have sinned, and come short of Your glory, that You may freely send the Spirit of Your Son, crying in the hearts of the sons of adoption: Abba, Father. For those who are led by this Spirit, they are sons, and cannot be kept from their Father's council. Indeed, they have the Spirit dwelling within them, who searches even the deep things of God. In short, of what can they be ignorant whom grace teaches everything?

4. Woe unto you, you sons of this world, because of your wisdom, which is foolishness! You know not the spirit of

[1979] 1 Cor 2:14.
[1980] Jn 15:15.
[1981] Sg 5:6.
[1982] Mt 11:25, 26.

salvation, nor have share in the counsel, which the Father alone discloses alone to the Son, and to him to whom the Son will reveal Him. For who has known the mind of the Lord? Or who has been His counselor?[1983] Not, indeed, no one; but only a few, only those who can truly say: The only begotten Son, which is in the bosom of the Father, He has declared Him. Woe to the world for its clamor! That same Only Begotten, like as the angel of a great revelation, proclaims among the people: He who has ears to hear let him hear. And since He finds not ears worthy to receive His words, and to whom He may commit the secret of the Father, He weaves parables for the crowd, that hearing they might not hear, and seeing they might not understand. But for His friends how different! With them He speaks apart: "To you it is given to know the mysteries of the kingdom of God";[1984] to whom also He says: "Fear not, little flock, for it is your Father's good pleasure to give you the kingdom."[1985] Who are these? These are they whom He foreknew and foreordained to be conformed to the image of His Son, that He might be the firstborn among many brethren. The Lord knows who are His. Here is His great secret and the counsel which He has made known unto men. But He judges no others worthy of a share in so great mystery, except those whom He has foreknown and foreordained as His own. For those whom He foreordained, them also He called. Who, except he be called, may approach God's counsel? Those whom He called, them also He justified. Over them a Sun arises, though not that sun which may daily be seen arising over good and bad alike, but He of whom the prophet speaks when addressing himself to those alone who have

---

[1983]Rom 11:34.
[1984]Lk 8:8–10.
[1985]Lk 12:32.

been called to the counsel, he says: "Unto you that fear My name shall the Sun of Righteousness arise."[1986] So while the sons of unbelief remain in darkness, the child of light leaves the power of darkness and comes into this new light, if once he can with faith say to God: I am a companion of all them that fear You.[1987] Do you see how faith precedes, in order that justification may follow? Perchance, then, we are called through fear and justified by love. Finally, the just shall live by faith,[1988] that faith, doubtless, which works by love.[1989]

5. So at his call let the sinner hear what he has to fear; and thus coming to the Sun of Righteousness, let him, now enlightened, see what he must love. For what is that saying: "The merciful goodness of the Lord endures from everlasting to everlasting upon them that fear Him."[1990] From everlasting, because of predestination, to everlasting, because of glorification. The one process is without beginning, the other knows no ending. Indeed, those whom He predestines from everlasting, He glorifies to everlasting, with an interval, at least, in the case of adults, of calling and justification between. So at the rising of the Sun of Righteousness, the mystery, hidden from eternity, concerning souls that have been predestined and are to be glorified, begins in some degree to emerge from the depths of eternity, as each soul, called by fear and justified by love, becomes assured that it, too, is of the number of the blessed, knowing well that whom

---

[1986]Mal 4:2. So all texts, except a few, in which the reading is: "Indeed, that Sun is promised to those who have been called," and so on. In the first edition, and many subsequent ones, it is: "For the Sun which arises is not that which is daily to be seen rising over good and bad, but one promised by the prophetic warning to such as fear God, to those only who have been called," and so on.
[1987]Ps 119:63.
[1988]Rom 1:17.
[1989]Gal 5:6.
[1990]Ps 103:17.

He justified, them also He glorified.[1991] What then? The soul hears that it is called when it is stricken with fear. It feels also that it is justified when it is surrounded with love. Can it do otherwise than be confident that it will be glorified? There is a beginning; there is continuation. Can it despair only of the consummation? Indeed, if the fear of the Lord, in which our calling is said to consist, is the beginning of wisdom, surely the love of God—that love, I mean, which springs from faith, and is the source of our justification—is progress in wisdom. And so what but the consummation of wisdom is that glorification which we hope for at the last from the vision of God that will make us like Him? And so one deep calls another because of the noise of the water-pipes,[1992] when, with terrible judgments, that unmeasured Eternity and Eternal Immensity, whose wisdom cannot be told, leads the corrupt and inscrutable heart of man by Its own power and goodness forth into Its own marvelous light.

6. For instance, let us suppose a man in the world, held fast as yet in the love of this world and of his flesh; and, inasmuch as he bears the image of the earthly man, occupied with earthly things, without a thought of things heavenly, can anyone fail to see that this man is surrounded with horrible darkness, unless he also is sitting in the same fatal gloom? For no sign of his salvation has yet shone upon him; no inner inspiration bears its witness in his heart as to whether an eternal predestination destines him to good. But, then, suppose the heavenly compassion vouchsafes sometime to have regard to him, and to shed upon him a spirit of compunction to make him bemoan himself and learn wisdom, change his life, subdue his flesh, love his

[1991] Rom 8:30.
[1992] Ps 62:9.

neighbor, cry to God, and resolve hereafter to live to God and not to the world; and suppose that from then on, by the gracious visitation of heavenly light and the sudden change accomplished by the Right Hand of the Most High, he sees clearly that he is no longer a child of wrath, but of grace, for he is now experiencing the fatherly love and divine goodness toward him—a love which hitherto had been concealed from him so completely as not only to leave him in ignorance whether he deserved love or hate, but also as to make his own life indicate hatred rather than love, for darkness was still on the face of the deep—would it not seem to you that such a one is lifted directly out of the profoundest and darkest deep of horrible ignorance into the pleasant and serene deep of eternal brightness?

7. And then at length God, as it were, divides the light from the darkness, when a sinner, enlightened by the first rays of the Sun of Righteousness; casts off the works of darkness and puts on the armor of light. His own conscience and the sins of his former life alike doom him as a true child of hell to eternal fires; but under the looks with which the Dayspring from on high deigns to visit him, he breathes again, and even begins to hope beyond hope that he shall enjoy the glory of the sons of God. For rejoicing at the near prospect with unveiled face, he sees it in the new light, and says: "Lord, lift up the light of Your countenance upon us; You have put gladness in my heart";[1993] "Lord, what is man that You have such respect for him, or the son of man that You so regard him?"[1994] Now, O good Father, vile worm and worthy of eternal hatred as he is, he yet trusts that he is loved, because he feels that he loves; no, because he has a

[1993] Ps 4:7.
[1994] Ps 144:3.

foretaste of Your love he does not blush to make return of love. Now in Your brightness it becomes clear, Oh! Light that no man can approach, what good things You have in store for so poor a thing as man, even though he is evil! He loves not undeservedly, because he was loved without his deserving it; and his love is for everlasting, because he knows that he has been loved from everlasting. He brings to light for the comfort of the sorrowful the great design which from eternity had lain in the bosom of eternity, namely, that God wills not the death of a sinner, but rather that he should be converted and live. As a witness of this secret, Oh! man, you have the justifying Spirit bearing witness with your spirit that you yourself also are the son of God. Acknowledge the counsel of God in your justification; confess it and say, "your testimonies are my delight and my counselors."[1995] For your present justification is the revelation of the Divine counsel, and a preparation for future glory. Or rather, perhaps, predestination itself is the preparation for it, and justification is more the gradual drawing near unto it. Indeed, it is said, "Repent, for the kingdom of heaven is at hand."[1996] And hear also of predestination that it is the preparation: "Come, inherit," He says, "the kingdom prepared for you from the foundation of the world."[1997]

8. Let none, therefore, doubt that he is loved who already loves. The love of God freely follows our love which it preceded. For how can He grow weary of returning their love to those whom He loved even while they yet loved Him not? He loved them, I say; yes, He loved. For as a pledge of His love you have the Spirit; you also have Jesus, the faithful witness, and Him crucified. Oh! double proof, and that most sure, of

[1995]Ps 119:24. [1997]Mt 25:34.
[1996]Mt 3:2.

God's love toward us. Christ dies, and deserves to be loved by us. The Spirit works, and makes Him to be loved. The One shows the reason why He is loved: the Other how He is to be loved. The One commends His own great love to us; the Other makes it ours. In the One we see the object of love; from the Other we draw the power to love. With the One, therefore, is the cause; with the Other the gift of charity. What shame to watch, with thankless eyes, the Son of God dying— and yet this may easily happen, if the Spirit is not with us. But now, since "The love of God is shed abroad in our hearts by the Holy Ghost which is given unto us,"[1998] having been loved we love; and as we love, we deserve to be loved yet more. For if, says the apostle, while we were yet enemies, we have been reconciled to God through the death of His Son; much more, being reconciled, shall we be saved through His life.[1999] For He that spared not His own Son, but delivered Him up for us all, how shall He not with Him also freely give us all things?

9. Since, then, the token of our salvation is twofold, namely, a twofold outpouring, of the Blood and of the Spirit, neither can profit without the other. For the Spirit is not given except to such as believe in the Crucified, and faith avails not unless it works by love. But love is the gift of the Spirit. If the second Adam (I speak of Christ) not only became a living soul, but also a quickening spirit, dying as being the one, and raising the dead as being the other, how can that which dies in Him profit me, apart from that which quickens? Indeed, He Himself says: "It is the spirit that quickens, the flesh profits nothing."[2000] Now, what does "quicken" mean except "justify"? For as sin is the death of the soul[2001] (The soul that sins shall die; Ez 18:4), without

[1998] Rom 5:5.
[1999] Rom 8:32.
[2000] Jn 6:63.
[2001] Ez 18:4.

doubt righteousness is its life; for "The just shall live by faith."[2002] Who, then, is righteous, except he who returns to God, who loves him, His meed of love? And this never happens unless the Spirit by faith reveals to the man the eternal purpose of God concerning his future salvation. Such a revelation is simply the infusion of spiritual grace, by which, with the mortification of the deeds of the flesh, man is made ready for the kingdom which flesh and blood cannot inherit. And he receives by one and the same Spirit both the reason for thinking that he is loved and the power of returning love, lest the love of God for us should be left without return.

10. This, then, is that holy and secret counsel which the Son has received from the Father by the Holy Spirit. This by the same Spirit He imparts to His own whom He knows, in their justification, and by the imparting He justifies. Thus in his justification each of the faithful receives the power to begin to know himself even as he is known: when, for instance, there is given to him some foretaste of his own future happiness, as he sees how it lay hid from eternity in God, who foreordains it, but will appear more fully in God, who is effecting it. But concerning the knowledge that he has now, for his part, attained, let a man glory at present in the hope, not in the secure possession of it. How must we pity those who possess as yet no token of their own calling to this glad assembly of the righteous. Lord, who has believed our report?[2003] Oh! that they would be wise and understand. But except they believe they shall not understand.

11. But you, too, you unhappy and heedless lovers of the world, have your purpose far from that of the just. Scale sticks close to scale, and there is no airhole between you.

[2002] Rom 1:17.
[2003] Is 53:1.

You, too, oh! sons of impiety, have your purpose communicated one to another, but openly against the Lord and against His Christ.[2004] For if, as the Scripture says, "The fear of God, that is piety,"[2005] of course anyone who loves the world more than God is convicted of impiety and idolatry, of worshipping and serving the creature rather than the Creator. But if, as has been said, the holy and impious have each their purpose kept for themselves, doubtless there is a great gulf fixed between the two. For as the just keeps himself aloof from the purpose and council of evil men,[2006] so the impious never rise in the judgment, nor sinners in the purpose for the just.[2007] For there is a purpose for the just, a gracious rain which God has set apart for His heritage. There is a purpose really secret, descending like rain into a fleece of wool—a sealed fount whereof no stranger may partake—a Sun of Righteousness rising only for such as fear God.

12. Moreover, the prophet, noting that the rest remain in their own dryness and darkness, being ignorant of the rain and of the light of the just, mocks and brands their unfruitful gloom and confused perversity. This is a nation, he says, that obeys not the voice of the Lord their God.[2008] You are not ready, oh! miserable men, to say with David, "I will hearken what the Lord God will say with regard to me,"[2009] for being exhausted abroad upon [the quest of] vanity and false folly, you seek not for the deepest and best hearing of the truth.

[2004]Ps 2:2.
[2005]Jb 28:28. The Septuagint has *Idou theosebeia esti Sophia.* The Vulgate reads *Ecce timor Domini iosa est sapientia,* with which the Authorized Version coincides. "Behold the fear of the Lord, that is wisdom." Does Bernard quote from memory?
[2006]Cf. Ps 1:6.
[2007]This must be the reading, not "congregation" (*concilio*), as in Psalm 1, for the sense demands "purpose" (*consilio*), and the MSS. so read.
[2008]Jer 7:28.
[2009]Ps 85:8.

Oh! you sons of men, how long will you blaspheme my honor, and have such pleasure in vanity and seek after leasing.[2010] You are deaf to the voice of truth, and you do not know the purpose of Him who thinks thoughts of peace, who also speaks peace to His people, and to His saints, and to such as are converted in heart. Now, he says, you are clean through the word which I have spoken to you.[2011] Therefore, they who do not hear this word are unclean.

13. But you, dearly beloved, if you are making ready your inward ear for this Voice of God that is sweeter than honey and the honeycomb, flee from outward cares, that with your inmost heart clear and free you also may say with Samuel, "Speak, Lord, for Your servant hears."[2012] This Voice sounds not in the marketplace, and is not heard in public. It is a secret purpose, and seeks to be heard in secret. It will of a surety give you joy and gladness in hearing it, if you listen with attentive ear. Once it ordered Abraham to get out of his country and from his kindred, that he might see and possess the land of the living.[2013] Jacob left his brother and his home, and passed over Jordan with his staff, and was received in Rachel's embrace.[2014] Joseph was lord in Egypt,[2015] having been torn by a fraudulent purchase from his father and his home. Thus the Church is bidden, in order that the King may have pleasure in her beauty, to forget her own people and her Father's house.[2016] The boy Jesus was sought by His parents among their kinsfolk and acquaintance, and was not found.[2017] Also flee from your brethren, if you wish to find the way of salvation. Flee, I say, from the midst of Babylon, flee from before the sword of the northwind. A bare

---

[2010] Ps 4:2.
[2011] Jn 15:3.
[2012] 1 Sm 3:9.
[2013] Gn 12:1.

[2014] Gn 32:10; 29:11.
[2015] Gn 37 and 41.
[2016] Ps 45:11, 12.
[2017] Lk 2:44, 5.

sustenance I am ready to offer for the help of everyone that
flees. You call me your abbot; I refuse not the title for obedience's sake—obedience, I say, not that I demand it, but that I
render it in service to others, even as "The Son of Man came
not to be ministered unto, but to minister and to give His life
a ransom for many."[2018] But if you deem me worthy, receive
as your fellow disciple him whom you choose for your master. For we both have one Master, Christ. And so let Him be
the end of this letter, who is the end of the law for righteousness to everyone that believes.[2019]

TO THOMAS OF ST. OMER, AFTER HE HAD BROKEN HIS PROMISE OF ADOPTING A CHANGE OF LIFE

*He urges him to leave his studies and enter religion and sets
before him the miserable end of Thomas of Beverley.*

To his dearly beloved son, Thomas, Brother Bernard,
called Abbot of Clairvaux, that he may walk in the fear
of the Lord.

1. You do well in acknowledging the debt of your promise,
and in not denying your guilt in deferring its performance.
But I beg you not to think simply of what you promised, but
to whom you promised it. For I do not claim for myself any
part of that promise which you made, in my presence,
indeed, but not to me. Do not fear that I am going to reprove
you on account of that deceptive delay: for I was summoned

[2018] Mt 20:28.
[2019] Rom 10:4.

as the witness, not as the lord of your vow.[2020] I saw it and rejoiced; and my prayer is that my joy may be full—which it will not be until your promise is fulfilled. You have fixed a time which you ought not to have transgressed. You have transgressed it. What is that to me? To your own lord you shall stand or fall. I have determined, because the danger is so imminent, to deal with you neither by reproofs nor threats, but only by advice—and that only so far as you take it kindly. If you shall hear me, well. If not, I judge no man; there is One who seeks and judges; for He who judges us is the Lord.[2021] And I think for this cause you ought to fear and grieve the more, inasmuch as you have not lied unto men, but unto God. And though, as you wish, I spare your shame before men, is that shamelessness to go unpunished before God? For what reason, pray, is there in feeling shame before the judgment of man and not fearing the face of God? For the face of the Lord is against them that do evil.[2022] Do you, then, fear reproaches more than torments; and do you, who tremble at the tongue of flesh, despise the sword which devours the flesh? Are these the fine moral principles with which, as you write, you are being stored in the acquisition of knowledge, the ardor and love for which so heats and excites you that you do not fear to slight your sacred vow?

2. But, I pray you, what proof of virtue is it, what instance of self-control, what advance in knowledge, or artistic skill, to tremble with fear where no fear is needful, and to lay aside even the fear of the Lord. How much more wholesome the knowledge of Jesus and Him crucified—a knowledge,

---

[2020]Bernard regards as a vow that kind of promise by which a man had determined in his presence to enter the religious state. See Letter 395 and Sermons on Canticles, 63n6, in which he mourns the lapse and fall of novices.
[2021]1 Cor. 4:4.
[2022]Ps 34:16.

of course, not easy to acquire except for Him who is crucified to the world. You are mistaken, my son, quite mistaken,
if you think that you can learn in the school of the teachers
of this world that knowledge which only the disciples of
Christ, that is, such as despise the world, attain; and that by
the gift of God. This knowledge is taught, not by the reading of books, but by grace; not by the letter, but by the spirit;
not by learning, but by the practice of the commandments of
God: Sow, says the prophet, to yourselves in righteousness,
reap the hope of life, kindle for yourselves the light of
knowledge.[2023] You see that the light of knowledge cannot
be duly attained, except the seed of righteousness [first] enter
the soul, so that from it may grow the grain of life, and not
the mere husk of vainglory. What then? You have not yet
sown to yourself in righteousness, and therefore you have
not yet reaped the sheaves of hope; and do you pretend that
you are acquiring the true knowledge? Perchance for the
true there is being substituted that which puffs up. You err
foolishly, spending your money for that which is not bread,
and your labor for that which satisfies not.[2024] I entreat you,
return to the former wish of your heart, and realize that this
year of delay which you have allowed to yourself has been a
wrong to God; is not a year pleasing to the Lord, but a seed
plot of discord, an incentive to wrath, a food of apostasy,
such as must quench the Spirit, shut off grace, and produce
that lukewarmness which is wont to provoke God to spew
men out of His mouth.[2025]

3. Alas! I think that, as you are called by the same name,
so you walk in the same spirit as that other Thomas, once, I

[2023]Cf. Hos 10:12.
[2024]Is 55:2.
[2025]Cf. Rv 3:16.

mean, provost of Beverley. For after devoting himself, like you, to our Order and House with all his heart, he began to beg for delay, and then by degrees to grow cold, until he openly ended by being a secular, an apostate, and, twofold more, a child of hell, and was cut off prematurely by a sudden and terrible death[2026]—a fate which, if it may be, let the pitiful and clement Lord avert. The letter which I wrote to him in vain still survives.[2027] I simply freed my own mind, by warning him, so far as I could, how it must soon end. How happy would he have been if he had taken my advice! He cloaked his sin. I am clean from his blood. But that is not enough for me. For though in so acting I am quite at ease on my own account, yet that charity which seeks not her own[2028] urges me to mourn for him who died not in safety, because he lived so carelessly. Oh! the great depth of the judgments of God! Oh! my God, terrible in Your counsels over the sons of men! He bestowed the Spirit, whom he was soon again to withdraw, so that a man sinned a sin beyond measure, and grace found entrance that sin might abound; though this was the fault, not of the Giver, but of him who added the transgression. For it was the act of the man's own free will (whereby, using badly his freedom, he had the power to grieve the free Spirit) to despise the grace instead of bringing to good effect the inspiration of God, so as to be able to say: "His grace which was bestowed on me was not in vain."[2029]

4. If you are wise, you will let his folly profit you as a warning; you will wash your hands in the blood of the sinner, and take care to release yourself at once from the snare of perdition, and me from horrible fear on your account. For, I confess, I

[2026]Mt 23:15.
[2027]No. 107.
[2028]1 Cor 13:5.
[2029]1 Cor 15:10.

feel your erring steps as the rending of my heart, because you have become very dear to me, and I feel a father's affection for you. Therefore, at every remembrance of you that sword of fear pierces through my heart the more sharply, as I consider that you have too little fear and uneasiness. I know where I have read of such: "For when they shall say peace and safety, then sudden destruction comes upon them, as travail upon a woman with child, and they shall not escape."[2030] Yea, I foresee that many fearful consequences threaten you if you still delay to be wise. For I have had much experience; and Oh! that you would share and profit by it. So believe one who has had experience; believe one who loves you. For if you know for the one reason that I am not deceived, for the other you know also that I am not capable of deceiving you.

TO GUIGUES, THE PRIOR, AND TO THE OTHER MONKS OF THE GRAND CHARTREUSE
(c. A.D. 1125)

He discourses much and piously of the law of true and sincere charity, of its signs, its degrees, its effects, and of its perfection which is reserved for Heaven (Patria).

Brother Bernard, of Clairvaux, wishes health eternal to the most reverend among fathers, and to the dearest among friends, Guigues, Prior of the Grande Chartreuse, and to the holy Monks who are with him.

1. I have received the letter of Your Holiness as joyfully as I had long and eagerly desired it. I have read it, and the letters

---

[2030] 1 Thes 5:3.

which I pronounced with my mouth, I felt, as it were, sparks of fire in my heart, which warmed my heart within me; as coming from that fire which the Lord has sent upon the earth.[2031] How great a fire must glow in those meditations from which such sparks fly forth! This, your inspired and inspiring salutation, was to me, I confess, not as if coming from man, but like words descending surely from Him who sent the salutation to Jacob. It is not for me, in fact, a simple salutation given in passing, according to the custom and usage of men, but it is plainly from the very bowels of charity, as I feel, that this benediction, so sweet and so unhoped for, has come forth. I pray God to bless you, who have had the goodness to prevent me with benedictions of such sweetness, that confidence is granted to me, your humble servant, to reply, since you have first written; for though I had meditated writing, I had hitherto not presumed to do so. For I feared to trouble, by my eager scribbling, the holy quiet which you have in the Lord, and the religious silence which isolates you from the world. I feared, also, to interrupt, even for a moment, those mysterious whispers from God, and to pour my words into ears always occupied with the secret praises of heaven. I feared to become as one who would trouble even Moses on the mountain, Elias in the desert, or Samuel watching in the temple, if I had tried to turn away ever so little, minds occupied with divine communion. Samuel cries out: "Speak, Lord, for Your servant hears."[2032] And should I presume to make myself heard? I feared, I say, lest presenting myself out of season before you, as it were to David engaged in flight, or abiding in solitude, you might not wish to listen, and might say, "Excuse me, I

[2031]Lk 12:49.
[2032]1 Sm 3:10.

cannot hear You now; I prefer rather to give ear to words sweeter than thine." I will hear what the Lord God will say unto me; for He shall speak peace unto His people, and to His saints, and to those who are converted at heart.[2033] Or, at least, this: "Depart from me, you evil-disposed, and I will study the commandments of my God."[2034] For could I be so rash as to dare to arouse the much-loved spouse sweetly resting in the arms of her bridegroom as long as she will? Should I not hear from her on the instant: "Do not be troublesome to me; I am for My Beloved, and My Beloved is for Me; He feeds among the lilies"?[2035]

2. But what I do not dare to do, charity dares, and with all confidence knocks at the door of a friend, thinking that she ought by no means to suffer repulse, who knows herself to be the mother of friendships; nor does she fear to interrupt for an instant your rest, though so pleasant, to speak to you of her own task. She, when she will, causes you to withdraw from being alone with God; she, also, when she willed, made you attentive to me; so that you did not regard it as unworthy of you, not merely to benignantly endure my speaking, but more, to urge me to break the silence. I esteem the kindness, I admire the worthiness, I praise and venerate the pure rejoicing with which you glory in the Lord, for the advances in virtue which, as you suppose, I have made. I am proud of so great a testimony, and esteem myself happy in a friendship so grateful to me as that of the servants of God toward me. This is now my glory, this is my joy and the rejoicing of my heart, that not in vain I have lifted up mine eyes unto the mountains whence there has now come to me help of no

---

[2033] Ps 84:9, Vulgate.
[2034] Ps 119:115.
[2035] Sg 2:16.

small value. These mountains have already distilled sweetness for me; and I continue to hope that they will do so until our valleys shall abound with fruit. That day shall be always for me a day of festival and perpetual memorial, in which I had the honor to see and to receive that worthy man, by whom it has come about that I should be received into your hearts. And, indeed, you had received me even before, if I may judge by your letter; but now with a more close and intimate friendship, since, as I find, he brought back to you too favorable reports concerning me which, doubtless, he believed, though without sufficient cause. For, as a faithful and pious man, God forbid that he should speak otherwise than he believed. And truly I experience in myself what the Savior says: "He who receives a righteous man in the name of a righteous man shall receive a righteous man's reward."[2036] I have said, the reward of a righteous man, because I am regarded as righteous, only through receiving one who is righteous. If he has reported of me something more than that, he has spoken not so much according to the truth of the case as according to the simplicity and goodness of his heart. You have heard, you have believed, you have rejoiced, and have written, thereby giving me no little joy, not only because I have been honored with a degree of praise and a high place in the estimation of Your Holiness, but also because all the sincerity of your souls has made itself known to me in no small measure. In few words, you have shown to me with what spirit you are animated.

3. I rejoice, therefore, and congratulate you on your sincerity and goodness as I congratulate myself on the edification which you have afforded to me. That is, indeed, true and sincere charity, and must be considered to proceed from a heart

[2036]Mt 10:41.

altogether pure and a good conscience and faith unfeigned, with which we love our neighbor as ourself. For he who loves only the good that himself has done, or, at least, loves it more than that of others, does not love good for its own sake, but on account of himself, and he who is such cannot do as the prophet says: "Give thanks unto the Lord, because He is good."[2037] He gives thanks, indeed, perhaps, because the Lord is good to him, not because He is good in Himself. Wherefore let him understand that this reproach from the same prophet is directed against him: "They will praise You when You do well unto Your own soul."[2038] One man praises the Lord because He is mighty; another because He is good unto him; and, again, another simply because He is good. The first is a slave, and fears for himself; the second mercenary, and desires somewhat for himself; but the third is a son, and gives praise to his Father. Therefore both he who fears and he who desires are each working for his own advantage; charity which is in him alone who is a son, seeks not her own. Wherefore I think that it was of charity that was spoken, "The law of the Lord is pure, converting the soul,"[2039] because it is that alone which can turn away the mind from the love of itself and of the world and direct it toward God. Neither fear nor selfish love converts the soul. They change sometimes the outward appearance or the actions, but never affect the heart. No doubt even the slave does sometimes the work of God, but because he does it not of his own free will he remains still in his hardness. The mercenary person does it also, but not out of kindness, only as drawn by his own particular advantage. Where there is distinction of persons, there are personal interests, and where there are personal

[2037]Ps 118:1.
[2038]Ps 49:18.
[2039]Ps 19:7.

interests there is a limit of willingness, and there, without doubt, a rusting meanness. Let the very fear by which he is constrained be a law to the slave, let the greedy desire, with which the mercenary is bound, be a law to him, since it is by it that he is drawn away and enticed. But of these neither is without fault or is able to convert the soul. But charity does convert souls when it fills them with disinterested zeal.

4. Now, I should say that this charity is faultless in him who has become accustomed to retain nothing for himself out of that which is his own. He who keeps nothing for himself gives to God quite certainly all that he has, and that which belongs to God cannot be unclean. Thus that pure law of the Lord is no other than charity, which seeks not what is advantageous to herself, but that which profits others. But law is said to be of the Lord, either because He Himself lives by it or because no one possesses it except by His gift. Nor let it seem absurd what I have said, that even God lives by law, since I declared that this law was no other than charity. For what but charity preserves in the supreme and blessed Trinity, that lofty and unspeakable unity which it has? It is law, then, and charity the law of the Lord, which maintains in a wonderful manner the Trinity in Unity and binds it in the bond of peace. Yet let no one think that I here take charity for a quality or a certain accident in God, or otherwise to say that in God (which God forbid) there is something which is not God; but I say that it is the very substance of God. I say nothing new or unheard of, for St. John says God is love.[2040]

It is then right to say that charity is God, and at the same time the gift of God. Therefore Charity gives charity, the substantial gives the accidental.[2041] Where the word signifies

---

[2040] 1 Jn 4:16.
[2041] Mabillon reads *substantiva,* but another reading is *substantia* [Ed.].

the Giver it is a name of the substance, and where the thing given, it is a name of the accident. This is the eternal law, Creator and Ruler of the Universe. Since all things have been made through it in weight and measure and number, and nothing is left without law, not even He who is the Law of all things, yet He is Himself none other than the law which rules Him, a law untreated as He.

5. But the slave and the mercenary have a law, not from God, but which they have made for themselves—the one by not loving God, the other by loving something else more than Him. They have, I say, a law which is their own and not of the Lord, to which, nevertheless, their own is subjected; nor are they able to withdraw themselves from the unchangeable order of the divine law, though each should make a law for himself. I would say, then, that a person makes a law for himself when he prefers his own will to the common and eternal law, perversely wishing to imitate his Creator; so that as He is a law unto Himself, and is under no authority but His Own, so the man also will be his own master, will make his own will a law to himself. Alas! what a heavy and insupportable yoke upon all the sons of Adam, which weighs upon and bows down our necks, so that our life is drawn near to the grave. Unhappy man that I am, who shall deliver me from the body of this death,[2042] with which I am so weighed down that unless the Lord had helped me, my soul would almost have dwelt in the grave?[2043] With this load was he burdened who groaned, saying: "Why have You set me as a mark against You, so that I am a burden to myself?"[2044] Where he says, "I am made a burden to myself," he showed that he was a law unto himself, and the law no

[2042]Rom 8:24.
[2043]Ps 94:17.
[2044]Jb 7:20.

other than he himself had made it. But when, speaking to God, he commenced by saying, "You have set me as a mark against You," he showed that he had not escaped from the Divine law. For this is the property of that eternal and just law of God, that he who would not be ruled with gentleness by God, should be ruled as a punishment by his own self; and that all those who have willingly thrown off the gentle yoke and light burden of charity should bear unwillingly the insupportable burden of their own will.

6. Thus the everlasting law does in a wonderful manner, to him who is a fugitive from its power, both make him an adversary and retain him as a subject; for while, on the one hand, he has not escaped from the law of justice, by which he is dealt with according to his merits, on the other he does not remain with God in His light, or peace, or glory. He is subjected to power, and excluded from happiness. O Lord, my God, why do You not take away my sin, and pardon my transgression?[2045] So that throwing down the heavy weight of my own will, I may breathe easily under the light burden of charity; that I may not be overborne any longer by servile fear, nor allured by selfish cupidity, but may be impelled by Your spirit, the spirit of liberty, which is that of Your children. Who is it, who witnesses to my spirit that I, too, am one of Your children, since Your law is mine, and as You are, so am I also, in this world? For it is quite certain that those who do this which the apostle says owe no one anything except to love one another are themselves as God is in this world,[2046] nor are they slaves or mercenaries, but sons. Therefore neither are sons without law, unless, perhaps, someone should think the contrary because of this which is

[2045]Jb 7:21.
[2046]Rom 13:8.

written, the law is not made for a righteous man.[2047] But it ought to be remembered that the law promulgated in fear by a spirit of slavery is one thing, and that given sweetly and gently by the spirit of liberty is another. Those who are sons are not obliged to submit to the first, but they are always under the rule of the second. Do you wish to hear why it is said that law is not made for the righteous? You have not received, he says, the spirit of slavery again in fear. Or why, nevertheless, they are always under the rule of the law of charity? But you have received the spirit of the adoption of sons.[2048] Listen, now, in what manner the righteous man confesses that at the same time he is and is not under the law. I became, he says, to those which were under the law as being under the law, although I myself was not under the law: but to those who were without law, I was as being without law, since I was not without the law of God but in the law of Christ.[2049] Whence it is not accurately said the righteous have no law, or the righteous are without law, but that the law was not made for the righteous; that is, it is not, as it were, imposed upon unwilling subjects, but given freely to willing hearts by Him to whose sweet inspiration it is due. Wherefore the Lord also beautifully says, "Take My yoke upon you."[2050] As if He would say, I do not impose it upon you against your will, take it if you are willing; otherwise you will find not rest, but labor, for your souls.

7. The law of charity, then, is good and sweet, it is not only light and sweet to bear, but it renders bearable and light the laws even of slaves and mercenaries. But it does not destroy

---

[2047] 1 Tm 1:9.
[2048] Rom 8:15.

[2049] 1 Cor 9:20, 21.
[2050] Mt 11:29.

these, but brings about their fulfillment, as the Lord says, "I am not come to destroy the law, but to fulfill."[2051] The one it moderates, the other it reduces to order, and each it lightens. Charity will never be without fear, but that fear is good; it will never be without any thought of interest, but that a restrained and moderated one. Charity, therefore, perfects the law of the slave when it inspires a generous devotion, and that of the mercenary when it gives a better direction to interested wishes. So, then, devotion mixed with fear does not annul those last, but purifies them, only it takes away the fear of punishment which servile fear is never exempt from; and this fear is clean and filial, enduring forever.[2052] For that which is written, perfect love takes away fear,[2053] is to be understood of the fear of punishment, which is never wanting, as we have said, to slavish fear. It is, in fact, a common mode of speech which consists in putting the cause for the effect. As for cupidity, it is then rightly directed by the charity which is joined with it, since ceasing altogether to desire things which are evil, it begins to prefer those which are better, nor does it desire good things except in order to reach those which are better; which when, by the grace of God, it has fully obtained, the body and all the good things which belong to the body will be loved only for the sake of the soul, the soul for the sake of God, and God alone for Himself.

8. However, as we are in fleshly bodies, and are born of the desire of the flesh, it is of necessity that our desire, or affection, should begin from the flesh; but if it is rightly directed, advancing step-by-step under the guidance of grace, it will at length be perfected by the Spirit, because that is not first

[2051] Mt 5:17.
[2052] Ps 19:9.
[2053] 1 Jn 4:18.

which is spiritual, but that which is natural, and afterward that which is spiritual; and it is needful that we should first bear the image of the earthly and afterward that of the heavenly.[2054] First, then, a man loves his own self for self's sake, since he is flesh, and he cannot have any taste except for things in relation with him; but when he sees that he is not able to subsist by himself, that God is, as it were, necessary to him, he begins to inquire and to love God by faith. Thus he loves God in the second place, but because of his own interest, and not for the sake of God Himself. But when, on account of his own necessity, he has begun to worship Him and to approach Him by meditation, by reading, by prayer, by obedience, he comes little by little to know God with a certain familiarity, and in consequence to find Him sweet and kind; and thus having tasted how sweet the Lord is, he passes to the third stage, and thus loves God no longer on account of his own interest, but for the sake of God Himself. Once arrived there, he remains stationary, and I know not if in this life man is truly able to rise to the fourth degree, which is no longer to love himself except for the sake of God. Those who have made trial of this (if there be any) may assert it to be attainable; to me, I confess, it appears impossible. It will be so without doubt when the good and faithful servant shall have been brought into the joy of his Lord, and inebriated with the fullness of the house of God. For being, as it were, exhilarate, he shall in a wonderful way be forgetful of himself, he shall lose the consciousness of what he is, and being absorbed altogether in God, shall attach himself unto Him with all his powers, shall thenceforth be one spirit with Him.

9. I consider that the prophet referred to this when he said: "I will enter into the powers of the Lord: O, Lord, I

[2054] I Cor 15:46, 49.

will make mention of Your righteousness only."[2055] He knew well that when he entered into the spiritual powers of God he would be freed from all the infirmities of the flesh, and would have no longer to think of them, but would be occupied only with the perfections of God. Then, for certain, each of the members of Christ would be able to say of himself, what Paul said of their Head: "If we have known Christ according to the flesh, yet now henceforth know we Him no more."[2056] There no one knows himself according to the flesh, because flesh and blood will not inherit the kingdom of God.[2057] Not that the substance of flesh will not be there, but that every fleshly necessity will be away; the love of the flesh is to be absorbed into the love of the spirit, and the weak human passions which exist at present will be absorbed into powers divine. Then the net of charity, which is now drawn through a great and vast sea, and does not cease to bring together from every kind of fish, at length drawn to the shore, shall retain only the good, rejecting the bad. And while in this life charity fills with all kinds of fishes the vast spaces of its net, suiting itself to all according to the time, making, in a sense, its own, and partaking of the good and evil fortunes of all, it is accustomed not only to rejoice with them that rejoice, but to weep with them that weep. But when it shall have reached the shore [of eternity], casting away as evil fish all that it bore with grief before, it will retain those only which are sources of pleasure and gladness. Then Paul will no longer be weak with the weak, or be scandalized with those who are scandalized, since scandal and weakness will be far away. We ought not to think that he will still let fall tears over those who have not repented here

[2055] Ps 71:16.
[2056] 2 Cor 5:16.
[2057] 1 Cor 15:50.

below; and as it is certain that there will no longer be sinners, so there will be no one to repent. Far be it from us to think that he will mourn and deplore those whose portion is everlasting fire with the devil and his angels when in that City of God which the streams of that river make glad,[2058] the gates of which the Lord loves more than all the dwellings of Jacob,[2059] because in those dwellings, although the joy of victory is sometimes tasted, yet the combat always continues, and sometimes the struggle is for life; but in that dear country there is no place for adversity or sorrow, as in that psalm we sing: "The abiding place of all those who rejoice is in You,"[2060] and again: "Everlasting joy shall be unto them."[2061] How, then, shall any remembrance be of mercy, where the justice of God shall be alone remembered? There can be no feeling of compassion called into exercise where there shall be no place for misery or occasion for pity.

10. I am impelled to prolong this already lengthy discourse, dearly beloved and much-longed-for brethren, by the very strong desire I have of conversing with you; but there are three things which show me that I ought to come to an end. First, that I fear to be burdensome to you; that I am ashamed to show myself so loquacious; third, that I am pressed with domestic cares. In conclusion, I beg you to have compassion for me, and if you have rejoiced for the good things you have heard of me, sympathize with me also, I pray, in my too real temptations and cares. He who related these things to you has, no doubt, seen some few little things, and has valued these little things as great, while your indulgence has easily believed what it willingly heard. I felicitate

---

[2058] Ps 46:4.
[2059] Ps 87:2.

[2060] Ps 87:7, Vulgate.
[2061] Is 61:7.

you, indeed, on that charity which believes all things.[2062] But I am confounded by the truth which knows all things. I beg you to believe me in what I say of myself rather than another who has only seen me from without. No man knows the things that are in a man save the spirit of man which is in him.[2063] I assure you that I do not speak of myself by conjecture, but out of full knowledge, and that I am not such as I am believed and said to be. I feel assured of this, and confess it frankly; that so I may obtain your special prayers, and thus may become such as your letter sets forth, than which there is nothing I desire more.

[2062] 1 Cor 13:7.
[2063] 1 Cor 2:11.

APPENDIX

DOCTOR MELLIFLUUS

ENCYCLICAL OF POPE PIUS XII ON ST. BERNARD
OF CLAIRVAUX, THE LAST OF THE FATHERS, TO
OUR VENERABLE BRETHREN, THE PATRIARCHS,
PRIMATES, ARCHBISHOPS, BISHOPS, AND OTHER
LOCAL ORDINARIES IN PEACE AND COMMUNION
WITH THE APOSTOLIC SEE

Health and Apostolic Benediction.

The "Doctor Mellifluus," "the last of the Fathers, but certainly not inferior to the earlier ones,"[2064] was remarkable for such qualities of nature and of mind, and so enriched by God with heavenly gifts, that in the changing and often stormy times in which he lived, he seemed to dominate by his holiness, wisdom, and most prudent counsel. Wherefore, he has been highly praised, not only by the sovereign pontiffs and writers of the Catholic Church, but also, and not infrequently, by heretics. Thus, when in the midst of universal jubilation, our predecessor, Alexander III, of happy memory, inscribed him among the canonized saints, he paid reverent tribute when he wrote: "We have passed in review the holy and venerable life of this same blessed man, not only in himself a shining example of holiness and religion, but also shone forth in the whole Church of God because of his faith and of his fruitful influence in the house of God by word and example; since he taught the precepts of our holy religion even to foreign and barbarian nations, and so recalled a countless multitude of sinners . . . to the right path of the spiritual

[2064]Mabillon, *Bernardi Opera, Praef. generalis,* n. 23; Migne, *Patrologia Latina,* |hereafter *P.L.*| 182:26.

life"[2065] "He was," as Cardinal Baronius writes, "a truly apostolic man, nay, a genuine apostle sent by God, mighty in work and word, everywhere and in all things adding luster to his apostolate through the signs that followed, so that he was in nothing inferior to the great apostles . . . and should be called . . . at one and the same time an adornment and a mainstay of the Catholic Church."[2066]

2. To these encomiums of highest praise, to which almost countless others could be added, we turn our thoughts at the end of this eighth century when the restorer and promoter of the holy Cistercian Order piously left this mortal life, which he had adorned with such great brilliance of doctrine and splendor of holiness. It is a source of gratification to think of his merits and to set them forth in writing, so that not only the members of his own Order, but also all those who delight principally in whatever is true, beautiful, or holy may feel themselves moved to imitate the shining example of his virtues.

3. His teaching was drawn, almost exclusively, from the pages of sacred Scripture and from the Fathers, which he had at hand day and night in his profound meditations: and not from the subtle reasonings of dialecticians and philosophers, which, on more than one occasion, he clearly held in low esteem.[2067] It should be remarked that he does not reject that human philosophy which is genuine philosophy, namely, that which leads to God, to right living, and to Christian wisdom. Rather does he repudiate that philosophy which, by recourse to empty wordiness and clever quibbling, is overweening enough to climb to divine heights and to delve into all the

---

[2065]Litt. Apost. *Contigit olim,* 15 Kal. Feb., 1174, Anagniae d.

[2066]*Annal.,* t. 12, *An.* 1153, p. 385, D–E; Rome, *ex Tipografia Vaticana,* 1907.

[2067]Cf. Sermon in *Festo SS. Apost. Petri et Pauli,* n. 3; Migne, P. L., 183:407, and Sermon 3, in *Festo Pentec.,* n. 5; Migne, P. L., 183:332-b.

secrets of God, with the result that, as often happened in those days, it did harm to the integrity of faith and, sad to say, fell into heresy.

4. "Do you see . . ." he wrote, "how St. Paul the Apostle[2068] makes the fruit and the utility of knowledge consist in the way we know? What is meant by 'the way we know'? Is it not simply this, that you should recognize in what order, with what application, for what purpose and what things you should know? In what order—that you may first learn what is more conducive to salvation; with what zeal—that you may learn with deeper conviction what moves you to more ardent love; for what purpose—that you may not learn for vainglory, curiosity, or anything of the kind, but only for your own edification and that of your neighbor. For there are some who want knowledge for the sole purpose of knowing, and this is unseemly curiosity. And there are some who seek knowledge in order to be known themselves; and this is unseemly vanity . . . and there are also those who seek knowledge in order to sell their knowledge, for example, for money or for honors; and this is unseemly quest for gain. But there are also those who seek knowledge in order to edify, and this is charity. And there are those who seek knowledge in order to be edified, and this is prudence."[2069]

5. In the following words, he describes most appropriately the doctrine, or rather the wisdom, which he follows and ardently loves: "It is the spirit of wisdom and understanding which, like a bee bearing both wax and honey is able to kindle the light of knowledge and to pour in the savor of grace. Hence, let nobody think he has received a kiss, neither he who understands the truth but does not love it, nor he who

[2068] Cf. 1 Cor, 8:2.
[2069] *In Cantica,* Sermon 36, 3; Migne, P. L., 183:968c, d.

loves the truth but does not understand it."[2070] "What would be the good of learning without love? It would puff up. And love without learning? It would go astray."[2071] "Merely to shine is futile; merely to burn is not enough; to burn and to shine is perfect."[2072] Then he explains the source of true and genuine doctrine, and how it must be united with charity: "God is Wisdom, and wants to be loved not only affectionately, but also wisely . . . Otherwise, if you neglect knowledge, the spirit of error will most easily lay snares for your zeal; nor has the wily enemy a more efficacious means of driving love from the heart, than if he can make a man walk carelessly and imprudently in the path of love."[2073]

6. From these words it is clear that in his study and his contemplation, under the influence of love rather than through the subtlety of human reasoning, Bernard's sole aim was to focus on the supreme Truth all the ways of truth which he had gathered from many different sources. From them he drew light for the mind, the fire of charity for the soul, and right standards of conduct. This is indeed true wisdom, which rides over all things human, and brings everything back to its source, that is, to God, in order to lead men to Him. The "Doctor Mellifluus" makes his way with care deliberately through the uncertain and unsafe winding paths of reasoning, not trusting in the keenness of his own mind nor depending upon the tedious and artful syllogisms which many of the dialecticians of his time often abused. No! Like an eagle, longing to fix his eyes on the sun, he presses on in swift flight to the summit of truth.

[2070]Ibid., Sermon 8, n. 6; Migne, P. L., 183:813-a, b.
[2071]Ibid., Sermon 69, n. 2; Migne, P. L., 183:1113-a.
[2072]In *Nat. S. Joan. Bapt.,* Sermon 3; Migne, P. L., 183:399-b.
[2073]*In Cantica,* Sermon 19, n. 7; Migne, P. L., 183:866-d.

7. The charity which moves him, knows no barriers and, so to speak, gives wings to the mind. For him, learning is not the final goal, but rather a path leading to God; it is not something cold upon which the mind dwells aimlessly, as though amusing itself under the spell of shifting, brilliant light. Rather, it is moved, impelled, and governed by love. Wherefore, carried upward by this wisdom and in meditation, contemplation, and love, Bernard climbs the peak of the mystical life and is joined to God Himself, so that at times he enjoyed almost infinite happiness even in this mortal life.

8. His style, which is lively, rich, easy flowing, and marked by striking expressions, has such pleasing function that it attracts, delights, and recalls the mind of the reader to heavenly things. It incites to, nourishes, and strengthens piety; it draws the soul to the pursuit of those good things which are not fleeting, but true, certain, and everlasting. For this reason, his writings were always held in high honor. So from them the Church herself has inserted into the Sacred Liturgy not a few pages fragrant with heavenly things and aglow with piety.[2074] They seem to have been nourished with the breath of the Divine Spirit, and to shine with a light so bright that the course of the centuries cannot quench it; for it shines forth from the soul of a writer thirsting after truth and love, and yearning to nourish others and to make them like to himself.[2075]

9. It is a pleasure, venerable brethren, for the edification of us all, to quote from his books some beautiful extracts from this mystical teaching: "We have taught that every soul, even though weighed down with sins, ensnared in vice,

---

[2074]Cf. *Brev. Rom. in festo SS. Nom. Jesu; die III infra octavam Concept. immac. B.M.V.; in octava Assumpt. B.M.V.; in festo septem Dolor. B.M.V.; in festo sacrat. Rosarii B.M.V.; in festo S. Josephi Sp. B.M.V.; in festo S. Gabrielis Arch.*
[2075]Cf. Fénelon, *Panégyrique de St. Bernard.*

caught in the allurements of the passions, held captive in
exile, and imprisoned in the body . . . even, I say, though it
be thus damned and in despair, can find within itself not
only reasons for yearning for the hope of pardon and the
hope of mercy, but also for making bold to aspire to the nup-
tials of the Word, not hesitating to establish a covenant of
union with God, and not being ashamed to carry the sweet
yoke of love along with the King of the angels. What will
the soul not dare with Him whose marvelous image it sees
within itself, and whose striking likeness it recognizes in
itself?"[2076] "By this likeness of charity . . . the soul is wedded
to the Word, when, namely, loving even as she is loved, she
shows herself, in her will, likened to Him to Whom she is
already likened in her nature. Therefore, if she loves Him
perfectly, she has become His bride. What can be more
sweet than such a likeness? What can be more desirable
than this love, whereby you are enabled of yourself to draw
nigh with confidence to the Word, to cleave to Him steadfastly, to question Him familiarly, and to consult Him in all
thy doubts, as daring in your desires as you are receptive in
your understanding? This is in truth the alliance of holy and
spiritual wedlock. No, it is saying too little to call it an
alliance: it is rather an embrace. Surely we have then a spiritual embrace when the same likes and the same dislikes
make of two one spirit. Nor is there any occasion to fear lest
the inequality of the persons should cause some defect in the
harmony of wills, since love knows nothing of reverence.
Love means an exercise of affection, not a showing of
honor . . . Love is all sufficient for itself. Whithersoever love
comes, it keeps under and holds captive to itself all the other

[2076] *In Cantica,* Sermon, 83, n. 1; Migne, P. L., 183:1181-c, d.

affections. Consequently, the soul that loves, simply loves and knows nothing else except to love."[2077]

10. After pointing out that God wants to be loved by men rather than feared and honored, he adds this wise and penetrating observation: "Love is sufficient of itself; it pleases of itself, and for the sake of loving. A great thing is love, if yet it returns to its Principle, if it is restored to its Origin, if it finds its way back again to its fountainhead, so that it may thus be enabled to flow on unfailingly. Amid all the emotions, sentiments, and feelings of the soul, love is outstanding in this respect, namely, that it alone among created things, has the power to correspond with, and to make return to the creator in kind, though not in equality."[2078]

11. Since in his prayer, and his contemplation he had frequently experienced this divine love, whereby we can be intimately united with God, there broke forth from his soul these inspired words: "Happy is the soul to whom it has been given to experience an embrace of such surpassing delight! This spiritual embrace is nothing else than a chaste and holy love, a love sweet and pleasant, a love perfectly serene and perfectly pure, a love that is mutual, intimate, and strong, a love that joins two, not in one flesh, but in one spirit, that makes two to be no longer two but one undivided spirit, as witness St. Paul,[2079] where he says, 'He who cleaves to the Lord is one spirit with Him.' "[2080]

12. In our day this sublime teaching of the Doctor of Clairvaux on the mystical life, which surpasses and can satisfy all human desires, seems to be sometimes neglected and relegated to a secondary place, or forgotten by many who,

[2077]Ibid., n. 3; Migne, P. L., 183:1182-c, d.
[2078]Ibid., n. 4; Migne, P. L., 183:1183-b.
[2079]Cf. 1 Cor 6:17.
[2080]*In Cantica,* Sermon 83, n. 6; Migne, P. L., 183:1184-c.

completely taken up with the worries and business of daily life, seek and desire only what is useful and profitable for this mortal life, scarcely ever lift their eyes and minds to heaven, or aspire after heavenly things and the goods that are everlasting.

13. Yet, although not all can reach the summit of that exalted contemplation of which Bernard speaks so eloquently, and although not all can bind themselves so closely to God as to feel linked in a mysterious manner with the Supreme Good through the bonds of heavenly marriage; nevertheless, all can and must, from time to time, lift their hearts from earthly things to those of heaven, and most earnestly love the Supreme Dispenser of all gifts.

14. Wherefore, since love for God is gradually growing cold today in the hearts of many, or is even completely quenched, we feel that these writings of the "Doctor Mellifluus" should be carefully pondered, because from their content, which in fact is taken from the Gospels, a new and heavenly strength can flow both into individual and on into social life, to give moral guidance, bring it into line with Christian precepts, and thus be able to provide timely remedies for the many grave ills which afflict mankind. For, when men do not have the proper love for their Creator, from Whom comes everything they have when they do not love one another, then, as often happens, they are separated from one another by hatred and deceit, and so quarrel bitterly among themselves. Now God is the most loving Father of us all, and we are all brethren in Christ, we whom He redeemed by shedding His precious Blood. Hence, as often as we fail to return God's love or to recognize His divine fatherhood with all due reverence, the bonds of brotherly love are unfortunately shattered and—as, alas, is so often evident—discord, strife, and enmity unhappily are the

result, so much so as to undermine and destroy the very foundations of human society.

15. Hence, that divine love with which the Doctor of Clairvaux was so ardently aflame must be re-enkindled in the hearts of all men, if we desire the restoration of Christian morality, if the Catholic religion is to carry out its mission successfully, and if, through the calming of dissension and the restoration of order, justice, and equity, serene peace is to shine forth on mankind so weary and bewildered.

16. May those who have embraced the Order of the "Doctor Mellifluus," and all the members of the clergy, whose special task it is to exhort and urge others to a greater love of God, be aglow with that love with which we must always be most passionately united with God. In our own day, more than at any other time—as we have said—men are in need of this divine love. Family life needs it, mankind needs it. Where it burns and leads souls to God, Who is the supreme goal of all mortals, all other virtues wax strong. When, on the other hand, it is absent or has died out, then quiet, peace, joy, and all other truly good things gradually disappear or are completely destroyed, since they flow from Him who is love itself.[2081]

17. Of this divine charity, possibly nobody has spoken more excellently, more profoundly, or more earnestly than Bernard: "The reason for loving God," as he says, "is God; the measure of this love is to love without measure."[2082] "Where there is love, there is no toil, but delight."[2083] He admits having experienced this love himself when he writes: "O holy and chaste love! O sweet and soothing affection! . . . It is the more soothing and more sweet, the more the whole

[2081] 1 Jn 4:8.
[2082] *De Diligendo Deo,* c. 50, Migne, P. L., 182:974-a.
[2083] *In Cantica,* Sermon 85, n. 8; Migne, P. L., 183:1191-d.

of that which is experienced is divine. To have such love means being made like God."[2084] And elsewhere: "It is good for me, O Lord, to embrace You all the more in tribulation, to have You with me in the furnace of trial rather than to be without You even in heaven."[2085] But when he touches upon that supreme and perfect love whereby he is united with God Himself in intimate wedlock, then he enjoys a happiness and a peace, than which none other can be greater; "O place of true rest . . . For we do not here behold God either, as it were, excited with anger, or as though distracted with care; but His will is proved to be 'good and acceptable and perfect.' This vision soothes. It does not frighten. It lulls to rest, instead of awakening our unquiet curiosity. It calms the mind instead of tiring it. Here is found perfect rest. God's quiet quietens all about Him. To think of His rest is to give rest to the soul."[2086]

18. However, this perfect quiet is not the death of the mind but its true life. "Instead of bringing darkness and lethargy, the sleep of the Spouse is wakeful and life-giving; it enlightens the mind, expels the death of sin, and bestows immortality. Nevertheless, it is indeed a sleep, which transports rather than stupefies the faculties. It is a true death. This I affirm without the least hesitation, since the apostle says, in commendation of some who were still living in the flesh, 'You are dead, and your life is hid with Christ in God.'"[2087]

19. This perfect quiet of the mind, in which we enjoy the loving God by returning His love, and by which we turn and direct ourselves and all we have to Him, does not make us lazy and slothful. Rather it is a constant, effective, and

[2084]*De Diligendo Deo,* c. 10, n. 28; Migne, P. L., 183:991-a.

[2085]In Ps. 90, Sermon 17, n. 4; Migne, P. L., 183:252-c.

[2086]*In Cantica,* Sermon 13, n. 16; Migne, P. L., 183:893-a, b.

[2087]Col 3:3; *In Cantica,* Sermon 52, n. 3; Migne, P. L., 183:1031-a.

active zeal that spurs us on to look to our own salvation, and, with the help of God, to that of others also. For this lofty contemplation and meditation, which is brought about by divine love, "regulates the affections, directs the actions, cuts away all excesses, forms the character, orders and ennobles the life, and lastly . . . endows the understanding with a knowledge of things divine and human. It . . . undoes what is tangled, unites what is divided, gathers what is scattered, uncovers what is hidden, searches out what is false and deceptive. It . . . lays down beforehand what we have to do, and passes in review what has been accomplished, so that nothing disordered may remain in the mind, nothing uncorrected. Finally . . . it makes provision for trouble, and thus endures misfortune, so to say, without feeling it, of which the former is the part of prudence, and the latter the function of fortitude."[2088]

20. In fact, although he longs to remain fixed in this most exalted and sweet contemplation and meditation, nourished by the Spirit of God, the Doctor of Clairvaux does not remain enclosed within the walls of his cell that "waxes sweet by being dwelled in,"[2089] but is at hand with counsel, word, and action wherever the interests of God and Church are at stake. For he was wont to observe that "no one ought to live for himself alone, but all for all."[2090] And moreover, he wrote about himself and his followers: "In like manner, the laws of brotherliness and of human society give our brethren, among whom we live, a claim upon us for counsel and help."[2091] When, with sorrowing mind, he beheld the holy faith endangered or troubled, he spared neither toil,

---

[2088] *De Consid.,* 1, c. 7; Migne, P. L., 182:737-a, b.
[2089] *De Imit. Christi,* 1, 20, 5.
[2090] *In Cantica,* Sermon 41, n. 6; Migne, P. L., 183:987-b.
[2091] *De adventu D.,* Sermon 3, n. 5; Migne, P. L., 183:45-d.

nor journeyings, nor any manner of pains to come stoutly to its defense, or to bring it whatever assistance he could. "I do not regard any of the affairs of God," he said, "as things with which I have no concern."[2092] And to St. Louis of France he penned these spirited words: "We sons of the Church cannot on any account overlook the injuries done to our mother, and the way in which she is despised and trodden underfoot . . . We will certainly make a stand and fight even to death, if need be, for our mother, with the weapons allowed us; not with shield and sword, but with prayers and lamentations to God."[2093]

21. To Abbot Peter of Cluny he wrote: "And I glory in tribulations if I have been counted worthy to endure any for the sake of the Church. This, truly, is my glory and the lifting up of my head: the triumph of the Church. For if we have been sharers of her troubles, we shall be also of her consolation. We must work and suffer with our mother."[2094]

22. When the mystical body of Christ was torn by so grave a schism, that even good men on both sides became heated in dispute, he bent all his efforts to settling disagreements and happily restoring unity of mind. When princes, led by desire of earthly dominion, were divided by fearful quarrels, and the welfare of nations was thereby seriously threatened, he was ever the peacemaker and the architect of agreement. When, finally, the holy places of Palestine, hallowed by the blood of our Divine Savior, were threatened with gravest danger, and were hard pressed by foreign armies, at the command of the Supreme Pontiff, with loud voice and a still wider appeal of love, he roused Christian princes and peoples to undertake a new crusade; and if indeed it was not

[2092]*Epist.* 20 *(ad Card. Haimericum);* Migne, P. L., 182:123-b.

[2093]*Epist.* 221, 3; Migne, P. L., 182:386-d, 387-a.

[2094]*Epist.* 147, 1; Migne, P. L., 182:304-c, 305-a.

brought to a successful conclusion, the fault was surely not his.

23. And above all, when the integrity of Catholic faith and morals—the sacred heritage handed down by our forefathers—was jeopardized, especially by the activities of Abelard, Arnold of Brescia, and Gilbert de la Porée, strong in the grace of God he spared no pains in writing works full of penetrating wisdom and making tiring journeys, so that errors might be dispelled and condemned, and the victims of error might as far as possible be recalled to the straight path and to virtuous living.

24. Yet, since he was well aware that in matters of this kind the authority of the Roman Pontiff prevails over the opinions of learned men, he took care to call attention to that authority which he recognized as supreme and infallible in settling such questions. To his former disciple, our predecessor of blessed memory Eugene III, he wrote these words which reflect at once his exceeding great love and reverence and that familiarity which becomes the saints: "Parental love knows nothing of lordship, it recognizes not a master but a child even in him who wears the tiara . . . Therefore shall I admonish you now, not as a master, but as a mother, yes, as a most loving mother."[2095]

25. Then he addresses to him these powerful words: "Who are you? You are the High Priest and the Sovereign Pontiff. You are the prince of pastors and the heir of the apostles . . . by your jurisdiction, a Peter; and by your unction, a Christ. You are he to whom the keys have been delivered and the sheep entrusted. There are indeed other gatekeepers of heaven, and there are other shepherds of the flock; but you are in both respects more glorious than they in

[2095]*De Consid.,* Prologue, Migne, P. L., 182:727-a, 728-a, b.

proportion as you have inherited a more excellent name. They have assigned to them particular portions of the flock, his own to each; whereas you are given charge of all the sheep, as the one Chief Shepherd of the whole flock. Yes, not only of the sheep, but of the other pastors also are you the sole supreme Shepherd."[2096] And again: "He who wishes to discover something which does not belong to your charge, will have to go outside the world."[2097]

26. In clear and simple fashion he acknowledges the infallible magisterium of the Roman Pontiff in questions of faith and morals. For, recognizing the errors of Abelard, who when he "speaks of the Trinity savors of Arius; when of grace, of Pelagius; when of the person of Christ, of Nestorius,"[2098] "who . . . predicated degrees in the Trinity, measure in majesty, numbers in eternity";[2099] and in whom "human reason usurps for itself everything, leaving nothing for faith";[2100] he not only shatters, weakens, and refutes his subtle, specious, and fallacious tricks and sophisms, but also, on this subject, writes to our predecessor of immortal memory, Innocent II, these words of utmost importance: "Your See should be informed of all dangers that may arise, especially those that touch faith. For I consider it meet that damage to the faith be repaired in the particular place where faith is perfectly whole. These indeed are the prerogatives of this See . . . It is time, most loving Father, that you recognized your preeminence. Then do you really take the place of Peter, whose See you hold, when by your admonitions you strengthen hearts weak in faith; when, by your authority, you break those who corrupt the faith."

[2096]Ibid., 2, c. 8; Migne, P. L., 182:751-c, d.
[2097]Ibid., 3, c. L; Migne, P. L., 182:757-b.
[2098]Epist. 192; Migne, P. L., 182:358-d, 359-a.
[2099]De error. Abaelardi, 1, 2; Migne, P. L., 182:1056-a.
[2100]Epist. 188; Migne, P. L., 182:353-a, b.

27. How it was that this humble monk, with hardly any human means at his disposal, was able to draw the strength to overcome difficulties so thorny, to settle questions so intricate, and to solve the most troublesome cases, can only be understood when one considers the great holiness of life which distinguished him, and his great zeal for truth. For, as we have said, he was, above all, on fire with a most burning love of God and his neighbor (which as you know, venerable brethren, is the chief and, as it were, all embracing commandment of the Gospel), so that he was not only united to the heavenly Father by an unfailing mystical bond, but he desired nothing more than to win men to Christ, to uphold the most sacred rights of the Church, and to defend as best he could the integrity of the Catholic faith.

28. Although he was held in great favor and esteem by popes, princes, and peoples, he was not puffed up, he did not grasp at the slippery and empty glory of men, but ever shone with that Christian humility which "acquires other virtues . . . having acquired them, keeps them . . . keeping them, perfects them"; so that "without it the others do not even seem to be virtues."[2101] Wherefore "proffered honor did not even seem to be virtues."[2102] Wherefore "proffered honor did not tempt his soul, nor did he set his foot on the downward path of world glory; and the tiara and ring delighted him no more than the lecture platform and garden hoe."[2103] And while he undertook so often such great labors for the glory of God and the benefit of the Christian name, he was wont to call himself "the useless servant of the servants of God," "a vile worm," "a barren tree," "a sinner,

---

[2101] *De error. Abaelardi, Praef.*; Migne, P. L., 182:1053, 1054-d. *De moribus et off. Episc., seu Epist.* 42, 5, 17; Migne, P. L., 182:821-a.
[2102] Ibid.
[2103] *Vita Prima,* II, 25; Migne, P. L., 185:283-b.

ashes . . ."[2104] This Christian humility, together with the other virtues, he nourished by diligent contemplation of heavenly things, and by fervent prayer to God, by which he called down grace from on high on the labors undertaken by himself and his followers.

29. So burning was his love, particularly of Jesus Christ our Divine Savior, that, loved thereby, he penned the beautiful and lofty pages which still arouse the admiration and enkindle the devotion of all readers. "What can so enrich the soul that reflects upon it (the holy name of Jesus)? What can . . . strengthen the virtues, beget good and honorable dispositions, foster holy affections? Dry is every kind of spiritual food which this oil does not moisten. Tasteless, whatever this salt does not season. If you write, your composition has no charms for me, unless I read there the name of Jesus. If you debate or converse, I find no pleasure in your words, unless I hear there the name of Jesus. Jesus is honey on the lips, melody in the ear, joy in the heart. Yet not alone is that name light and food. It is also a remedy. Is anyone among you sad? Let the name of Jesus enter his heart; let it leap then to his mouth; and lo! the light shining from that name shall scatter every cloud and restore peace. Has someone perpetrated a crime, and then misled, moved despairingly toward the snare of death? Let him but invoke this life-giving name, and straightaway he shall find courage once more . . . Whoever, all atremble in the presence of danger, has not immediately felt his spirits revive and his fears depart as soon as he called upon this name of power? There is nothing so powerful as the name of Jesus to check anger,

[2104]*Epist.* 37; Migne, P. L., 182:143-b; *Epist.* 215; Migne, P. L., 182:379-b; *Vita prima,* V, 12; Migne, P. L., 185:358-d; *In Cantica,* Sermon 71, n. 5: Migne, P. L., 183:1123-d.

reduce the swelling of pride, heal the smarting wound of envy . . ."[2105]

30. To this warm love of Jesus Christ was joined a most sweet and tender devotion toward His glorious Mother, whose motherly love he repaid with the affection of a child, and whom he jealously honored. So great was his confidence in her most powerful intercession that he did not hesitate to write: "It is the will of God that we should have nothing which has not passed through the hands of Mary."[2106] Likewise: "Such is the will of God, Who would have us obtain everything through the hands of Mary."[2107]

31. And here it is well, venerable brethren, to bid you all consider a page in praise of Mary than which there is perhaps none more beautiful, more moving, more apt to excite love for her, more useful to stir devotion and to inspire imitation of her virtuous example: "Mary . . . is interpreted to mean 'Star of the Sea.' This admirably befits the Virgin Mother. There is indeed a wonderful appropriateness in this comparison of her with a star, because as a star sends out its rays without harm to itself, so did the Virgin bring forth her Child without injury to her integrity. And as the ray does not diminish the brightness of the star, so neither did the Child born of her tarnish the beauty of Mary's virginity. She is therefore that glorious star, which, as the prophet said, arose out of Jacob, whose ray enlightens the whole earth, whose splendor shines out for all to see in heaven and reaches even unto hell . . . She, I say, is that shining and brilliant star, so much needed, set in place above life's great and spacious sea, glittering with merits, all aglow with examples for our imitation. Oh, whoever you are who perceive yourself during

---

[2105]*In Cantica,* Sermon 15, n. 6; Migne, P. L., 183:846-d, 847-a, b.
[2106]*In vigil. Nat. Domini,* Sermon 3, n. 10; Migne, P. L., 183:100-a.
[2107]*Serm. in Nat. Mariae,* 7; Migne, P. L., 183:441-b.

this mortal existence to be rather drifting in treacherous waters, at the mercy of the winds and the waves, than walking on firm ground, turn not away your eyes from the splendor of this guiding star, unless you wish to be submerged by the storm! When the storms to temptation burst upon you, when you see yourself driven upon the rocks of tribulation, look at the star, call upon Mary. When buffeted by the billows of pride, or ambition, or hatred, or jealousy, look at the star, call upon Mary. Should anger, or avarice, or fleshly desire violently assail the frail vessel of your soul, look at the star, call upon Mary. If troubled on account of the heinousness of your sins, distressed at the filthy state of your conscience, and terrified at the thought of the awful judgment to come, you are beginning to sink into the bottomless gulf of sadness and to be swallowed in the abyss of despair, then think of Mary. In dangers, in doubts, in difficulties, think of Mary, call upon Mary. Let not her name leave your lips, never suffer it to leave your heart. And that you may more surely obtain the assistance of her prayer, see that you walk in her footsteps. With her for a guide, you shall never go astray; while invoking her, you shall never lose heart; so long as she is in your mind, you shall not be deceived; while she holds your hand, you cannot fall; under her protection, you have nothing to fear; if she walks before you, you shall not grow weary; if she shows you favor, you shall reach the goal."[2108]

32. We can think of no better way to conclude this encyclical letter than in the words of the "Doctor Mellifluus" to invite all to be more and more devout to the loving Mother of God, and each in his respective state in life to strive to imitate her exalted virtues. If at the beginning of the

---

[2108] *Hom. 2 super "Missus est,"* 17; Migne, P. L., 183:70-b, c, d, 71-a.

twelfth century grave dangers threatened the Church and human society, the perils besetting our own age are hardly less formidable. The Catholic faith, supreme solace of mankind, often languishes in souls, and in many regions and countries is even subjected to the bitterest public attacks. With the Christian religion either neglected or cruelly destroyed, morals, both public and private, clearly stray from the straight way, and, following the tortuous path of error, end miserably in vice.

33. Charity, which is the bond of perfection, concord, and peace, is replaced by hatred, enmities, and discords.

34. A certain restlessness, anxiety, and fear have invaded the minds of men. It is indeed to be greatly feared that if the light of the Gospel gradually fades and wanes in the minds of many, or if—what is even worse—they utterly reject it, the very foundations of civil and domestic society will collapse, and more evil times will unhappily result.

35. Therefore, as the Doctor of Clairvaux sought and obtained from the Virgin Mother Mary help for the troubles of his times, let us all through the same great devotion and prayer so strive to move our divine Mother, that she will obtain from God timely relief from these grave evils which are either already upon us or may yet befall, and that she who is at once kind and most powerful, will, by the help of God, grant that the true, lasting, and fruitful peace of the Church may at last dawn on all nations and peoples.

36. Such, we hope, through the intercession of Bernard, may be the rich and wholesome effects of the centenary celebration of his most holy death. Do you, all, join us in prayer for this intention, and as you study and ponder on the example of the "Doctor Mellifluus," strive earnestly and eagerly to follow his footsteps.

Now as a pledge of these benefits, we bestow with heart-felt affection upon you, venerable brothers, upon the flocks entrusted to you, and particularly on those who have embraced the Institute of St. Bernard, the apostolic blessing.

Given at Rome, St. Peter's, on the 24th of May, on the feast of Pentecost, 1953, in the 15th year of our pontificate.

PIUS XII

SUGGESTIONS FOR FURTHER READING

WORKS OF BERNARD OF CLAIRVAUX

1. Cistercian Publications of Kalamazoo, Michigan, provides the bulk of modern English-language translations of the works of St. Bernard. An incomplete list follows:

Cistercians and Cluniacs: St. Bernard's Apologia to Abbot William. Translated by Michael Casey, OCSO. Introduced by Jean Leclercq, OSB.

Five Books on Consideration: Advice to a Pope. Translated by John Anderson and Elizabeth T. Kennan.

Homilies in Praise of the Blessed Virgin Mary. Translated by Marie-Bernard Said, OSB. Introduced by Chrysogonus Waddell, OCSO.

The Letters of St. Bernard of Clairvaux. Translated by Bruno Scott James. Introduced by Beverly Mayne Kienzle.

Magnificat: Sermons in Praise of the Blessed Virgin Mary. Translated by Marie-Bernard Saïd and Grace Perigo. Introduced by Chrysogonus Waddell, OSCO.

In Praise of the New Knighthood. Translated by Conrad Greenia, OCSO. Introduced by R. J. Zwi Werblowsly.

On Grace and Free Choice. Translated by Daniel O'Donovan, OCSO. Introduced by Bernard McGinn.

On Loving God. Translated and introduced by Robert Walton, OSB.

On the Song of Songs. Four vols. Vol. 1, translated Kilian Walsh, OSCO; introduced by M. Corneille Halflants, OSCO. Vol. 2, translated by Kilian Walsh, OCSO; introduced by Jean Leclercq, OSB. Vol. 3, translated by Kilian Walsh, OCSO, and Irene M. Edmonds; introduced by Emero Stiegman; Vol. 4, translated by Irene Edmonds; introduced by Jean Leclercq.

Sermons for Advent and the Christmas Season. Translated by Irene Edmonds, Wendy Beckett, and Conrad Greenia. Edited by Rozanne Elder.

Sermons for the Summer Season. Translated by Beverly Mayne Kienzle with James Jarzembowski.

Sermons on Conversion. Translated and introduced by Marie-Bernard Saïd, OSB.

Steps of Humility and Pride. Introduced by M. Basil Pennington, OCSO.

The Life and Death of Saint Malachy the Irishman. Translated by Robert T. Meyer.

The Parables and Sentences. Translated by Michael Casey, OCSO, and Francis R. Swietek. Introduced by Michael Casey and John R. Sommerfeldt.

Letters of Saint Bernard of Clairvaux. Translated by Bruno Scott James. Introduced by Beverly Mayne Kienzle.

2. Other English translations of St. Bernard:

St. Bernard's Sermons on the Nativity. Translated by "A Priest of Mount Melleray." Devon, England: Mount Melleray Trust, 1985.

SECONDARY WORKS ABOUT BERNARD OF CLAIRVAUX

Bredero, Adriaan H. *Bernard of Clairvaux; Between Cult and History.* Grand Rapids, Mich.: William B. Eerdmans, 1993.

Casey, Michael. *Athirst for God: Spiritual Desire in Bernard of Clairvaux's Sermons on the Song of Songs.* Kalamazoo, Mich.: Cistercian Publications, 1987.

Daniel-Rops, Henri. *Bernard of Clairvaux.* Foreword by Thomas Merton. Translated by Elisabeth Abbott. New York: Hawthorne Books, 1964.

Evans, G. R. *Bernard of Clairvaux.* Great Medieval Thinkers series. Edited by Brian Davies. New York: Oxford University Press, 2000.

Gilson, Etienne. *The Mystical Theology of Saint Bernard of Clairvaux.* New York: Sheed and Ward, 1940.

Kirk, K. E. *The Vision of God.* New York: HarperTorchbooks, 1966.

Lackner, Bede K. *The Eleventh-Century Background of Citeaux.* Washington, D.C.: Cistercian Publications, Consortium Press, 1972.

Lawrence, C. H. *Medieval Monasticism.* 2nd ed. New York: Longman, 1989.

Leclercq, Jean. *Bernard of Clairvaux and the Cistercian Spirit.* Kalamazoo, Mich.: Cistercian Publications, 1976.

————. *The Love of Learning and the Desire for God: A Study of Monastic Culture.* Translated by Catharine Misrahi. New York: Fordham University Press, 1982.

————, François Vandenbroucke, and Louis Bouyer. *The Spirituality of the Middle Ages.* A History of Christian Spirituality. Vol. 2. New York: Desclee, 1968.

Lubac, Henri de. *Medieval Exegesis.* Vol. 2, *The Four Senses of Scripture.* Translated by E. M. Macierowski. Grand Rapids, Mich.: William B. Eerdmans, 2000.

McGinn, Bernard, John Meyendorff, and Jean Leclercq, eds. *Christian Spirituality: Origins to the Twelfth Century.* New York: Crossroad, 1985.

————. *The Doctors of the Church.* New York: Crossroad, 1999.

————. *The Growth of Mysticism: Gregory the Great Through the Twelfth Century.* New York: Crossroad, 1994.

McGinn, Bernard, and Patricia Ferris McGinn. *Early Christian Mystics.* New York: Crossroad, 2003.

Merton, Thomas. *The Last of the Fathers.* New York: Harvest Book, 1982; first published by Harcourt Brace, 1954.

————. *Thomas Merton on St. Bernard.* Kalamazoo, Mich.: Cistercian Publications, 1980.

Mullins, Edwin. *In Search of Cluny: God's Lost Empire.* Oxford, England: Signal Books, 2006.

Posset, Franz. *Pater Bernhardus: Martin Luther and Bernard of Clairvaux.* Foreword by Michael Casey. Preface by Bernhard Lohse. Kalamazoo, Mich.: Cistercian Publications, 1999.

Squire, Aelred. *Asking the Fathers.* London: S.P.C.K., 1975.

Tamburello, Dennis E., OFM. *Bernard of Clairvaux: Essential Writings.* New York: Crossroad, 2000.

William of St. Thierry, Arnold of Bonnevaux, Geoffrey and Philip of Clairvaux, and Odo of Deuil. *St. Bernard of Clairvaux.* Translated by Geoffrey Webb and Adrian Walker. Westminster, Md.: Newman Press, 1960.

WEB SITE

http://www.ccel.org/b/bernard/ The Christian Classics Ethereal Library also offers a wide array of public-domain texts for downloading.

TAILPIECE

Among the hymn texts attributed to St. Bernard are "O Sacred Head, Now Wounded" and "Jesus, the Very Thought of You." Tradition holds that he is also the author of the prayer to Mary known by its original Latin opening as the Memorare:

Remember, O most gracious Virgin Mary,
That never was it known
That anyone who fled to your protection,
Implored your help or sought your intercession,
Was left unaided.
Inspired by this confidence, I fly unto you,
O Virgin of virgins, my Mother.
To you do I come, before you I stand,
Sinful and sorrowful;
O Mother of the Word Incarnate,
Despise not my petitions, but in your mercy
Hear and answer me. Amen.

THOMAS MERTON (1915–68) was a priest and monk who spent most of his adult life in the Trappist Abbey of Our Lady of Gethsemani in Kentucky. He was born in Prades, France, raised by his widower father, a painter, and after boarding school in England, studied at Cambridge University before completing his undergraduate education at Columbia University in 1939. It was in New York City at Corpus Christi Church near Columbia that he converted to Catholicism, a decision that soon grew into a vocation to the religious life when he entered the monastery in 1941. At the urging of his abbot, he wrote his famous memoir of conversion, *The Seven Storey Mountain* (1948). It was the best-known work of his highly prolific literary output over the two decades that followed—books, journals, essays, letters, poems, commentaries, translations, and other unpublished materials poured forth. Indeed, so much was left behind at his death that new works have continuously been added to his bibliography to this day. In December 1968 Thomas Merton followed his interest in Eastern monasticism to a conference in Bangkok, Thailand, where he died in an accidental electrocution.

On the occasion of the issuing of the encyclical letter conferring on St. Bernard of Clairvaux the title *Doctor Mellifluus* by Pius XII in 1953, Merton, in the following year, published a small book, *The Last of the Fathers,* from which the preface to this collection of St. Bernard's writings is taken.

JOHN F. THORNTON is a literary agent, former publishing executive, and the coeditor, with Katharine Washburn, of *Dumbing Down* (1996) and *Tongues of Angels, Tongues of Men: A Book of Sermons* (1999). He is chairman of the Friends of Liturgical Music at Corpus Christi Church in Manhattan, and he is currently at work on a biography of the American publishers Alfred and Blanche Knopf.

SUSAN B. VARENNE is a New York City teacher with a strong avocational interest in and wide experience of spiritual literature. She holds an M.A. from the University of Chicago Divinity School and a Ph.D. from Columbia University.

Printed in the United States
by Baker & Taylor Publisher Services